T0399256

Jihadism in Europe

RELIGION AND GLOBAL POLITICS

Series Editor

John L. Esposito
University Professor and Director
Prince Alwaleed Bin Talal Center for Muslim-Christian Understanding
Georgetown University

Islamic Leviathan
Islam and the Making of State Power
Seyyed Vali Reza Nasr

Rachid Ghannouchi
A Democrat within Islamism
Azzam S. Tamimi

Balkan Idols
Religion and Nationalism in Yugoslav States
Vjekoslav Perica

Islamic Political Identity in Turkey
M. Hakan Yavuz

Religion and Politics in Post-Communist Romania
Lavinia Stan and Lucian Turcescu

Piety and Politics
Islamism in Contemporary Malaysia
Joseph Chinyong Liow

Terror in the Land of the Holy Spirit
Guatemala under General Efrain Rios Montt, 1982–1983
Virginia Garrard-Burnett

In the House of War
Dutch Islam Observed
Sam Cherribi

Being Young and Muslim
New Cultural Politics in the Global South and North
Asef Bayat and Linda Herrera

Church, State, and Democracy in Expanding Europe
Lavinia Stan and Lucian Turcescu

The Headscarf Controversy
Secularism and Freedom of Religion
Hilal Elver

The House of Service
The Gülen Movement and Islam's Third Way
David Tittensor

Answering the Call
Popular Islamic Activism in Sadat's Egypt
Abdullah Al-Arian

Mapping the Legal Boundaries of Belonging
Religion and Multiculturalism from Israel to Canada
Edited by René Provost

Religious Secularity
A Theological Challenge to the Islamic State
Naser Ghobadzadeh

The Middle Path of Moderation in Islam
The Qur'ānic Principle of Wasaṭiyyah
Mohammad Hashim Kamali

One Islam, Many Muslim Worlds
Spirituality, Identity, and Resistance across Islamic Lands
Raymond William Baker

Containing Balkan Nationalism
Imperial Russia and Ottoman Christians (1856–1914)
Denis Vovchenko

Inside the Muslim Brotherhood
Religion, Identity, and Politics
Khalil al-Anani

Politicizing Islam
The Islamic Revival in France and India
Z. Fareen Parvez

Soviet and Muslim
The Institutionalization of Islam in Central Asia
Eren Tasar

Islam in Malaysia
An Entwined History
Khairudin Aljunied

Salafism goes Global
From the Gulf to the French Banlieues
Mohamed-Ali Adraoui

Jihadism in Europe
European Youth and the New Caliphate
Farhad Khosrokhavar

Jihadism in Europe

European Youth and the New Caliphate

FARHAD KHOSROKHAVAR

OXFORD UNIVERSITY PRESS

Oxford University Press is a department of the University of Oxford. It furthers the University's objective of excellence in research, scholarship, and education by publishing worldwide. Oxford is a registered trade mark of Oxford University Press in the UK and certain other countries.

Published in the United States of America by Oxford University Press
198 Madison Avenue, New York, NY 10016, United States of America.

Library of Congress Cataloging-in-Publication Data
Names: Khosrokhavar, Farhad, author.
Title: Jihadism in Europe: European Youth and the New Caliphate /
Farhad Khosrokhavar.
Description: New York : Oxford University Press, 2021. |
Series: Religion and global politics series |
Includes bibliographical references and index.
Identifiers: LCCN 2021003262 (print) | LCCN 2021003263 (ebook) |
ISBN 9780197564967 (hardcover) | ISBN 9780197602522 (paperback) |
ISBN 9780197564981 (epub) | ISBN 9780197564974 | ISBN 9780197564998
Subjects: LCSH: Jihad. | Muslims—Europe—Attitudes. | Islamic fundamentalism—Europe. |
Muslims—Cultural assimilation—Europe. | IS (Organization) | Ethnic conflict—Europe.
Classification: LCC BP182 .K5228 2021 (print) | LCC BP182 (ebook) | DDC 305.6/97094—dc23
LC record available at https://lccn.loc.gov/2021003262
LC ebook record available at https://lccn.loc.gov/2021003263

DOI: 10.1093/oso/9780197564967.001.0001

Hardback printed by Bridgeport National Bindery, Inc., United States of America

To my wife Noussy, and my parents

Contents

Preface

Two types of works are used in this book. On one hand, academic research; on the other, journalistic reports, biographies, and essays, Journalists' descriptions are not "thick"; they are usually created on an ad hoc basis, but they can provide precious, although not always reliable, information.

As for the statistics on the different European countries, they are not always homogeneous from one country to another, neither for the size of the samples nor for the dates. They can nevertheless be compared by taking the necessary precautions.

A major source for the analysis of jihadism in this book is my work on prisons and poor districts in France. I participated in two major projects on French prisons, in 2001–2003 and 2011–2013, respectively.

In the first period, the major sites for my study of Islam and Islamic extremism were the prison Fresnes in Ile-de-France, close to Paris; Fleury-Mérogis, the largest European prison, also in Ile-de-France; and Loos, close to the city of Lilles. I conducted extensive interviews in those prisons that became the ingredients for three books.[1]

The second project was on radicalization in prison between 2011 and 2013, and it was financed by the Ministry of Justice in France. I was able to interview prisoners, guards, prison authorities, and medical services personnel. A major part of the interviews in this book was made in this period in four French prisons: Fresnes, Fleury-Mérogis, Lilles-Séquedin (in Lilles), and Saint-Maur high security prison, close to the town of Châteauroux in central France. I was not allowed to record the interviews. I took notes, sometimes alone and sometimes with my assistant Ouisa Kies, and I put them together in a book as well.[2]

I also took part in three specific projects financed by the Social Housing Organizations in France between 2011 and 2018 on Cité des Indes in 2012 (in Sartrouville, within the Yvelines in the Ile-de-France department), Toulouse in Southern France in 2017 (two poor districts, La Reynerie and Bellefontaine in Le Mirail), and the third one, close to the town of Gien in the department of Le Loiret, the poor district Le quartier des Champs in 2018.

A project on youth in the poor districts of the town of Maubeuge was ongoing from January to August 2020 while I was putting the finishing touches on this book.

In another project, financed by the Association Française des Victimes du Terrorisme (French Association of the Victims of Terrorism) in 2014 on French Muslim Middle classes, I supervised lengthy interviews with some sixty middle-class Frenchmen of North African and, occasionally, Turkish origin in Paris, Seine-Saint-Denis (a poor district close to Paris), and Bondy (in Ile-de-France).

Besides the cases already mentioned, in the research on this book I was able to choose 105 jihadis from the public data available to me (the media, academic publications, my own interviews with around twenty jihadis over a decade, and between 2000 and 2013 in French prisons).

Many of the people interviewed were not jihadi but were more or less sympathetic to them, and most jihadis came from their social milieu, largely among young people from the poor districts, of immigrant origin and multiple repeat offenders (some were condemned for having taken part in terrorist activities). Their interviews shed light on the mental universe of jihadis.

One should bear in mind that the dual source (biographies and interviews) has its pros and cons, and the link between them is not established automatically but depends on the researcher's viewpoint. I believe that they shed light on jihadism, the back-and-forth between them enriching our anthropological knowledge of this complex phenomenon.

I should also mention that many prison inmates and young Muslims in the poor neighborhoods unveiled their views to me in part because they knew I wasn't all French: I have a dual identity, Iranian by birth and French by acquisition, sharing in part their duality as Arab (Algerian, Moroccan, Tunisian) and French, and because I am a Muslim by birth. Still, they usually ignored that I was a Shiite, which in their eyes was an adulterated Islam. They did not hide from me their antagonistic feelings toward the "Whites" (non-Muslim Frenchmen of European background), in part because they believed I was not entirely "White," which was true. Some of them characterized themselves as "Greys" ("Gris," the disaffected youth of North African origin), being neither White nor Black, but closer to the Blacks due to their stigmas.

The interviews produced in this book are not verbatim what the interviewees said; they are condensed to spare the space. I only took notes (recording was not authorized in prison, and elsewhere I preferred spontaneous talk without a recorder). During the interviews I summarized on the spot what the interviewees said in order to keep up with their pace. Transcripts were synthesized later. That means that the definitive transcripts bear in part the mark of my viewpoint (I had to choose quickly what was meaningful from what my interlocutors said during our verbal exchanges). But I never willfully changed their statements in my transcriptions.

I have chosen many examples of jihadis in the media. The interpretations I offer on this subject are, of course, mine. But they are inspired by the interviews I conducted with different types of more or less radicalized people in prisons and in poor, ethnic neighborhoods. The cases that had been reported in the press and interpreted by me are, as I said, in dialogue with my interviews and my observations in the fieldwork. The relatively high number of jihadis that I analyze from the press and field research is not simply an accumulation of cases. It is, each time, illustrative of their complex motivations from a phenomenological perspective—that is, by trying to understand their subjectivity and their intentions, in short, their way of capturing the world and the meaning they attached to it. This is why the high number of concrete cases is not without interest. They give me the opportunity to test the theories I put forward and make them more complex in order to explain diverse forms of radicalization among different people. I try to tie biographical data to a phenomenological analysis, back and forth, one informing the other. I shed light on what is stated descriptively in the available biographies of Jihadis from my interviews and field experience and vice versa. Biographies are thus more than illustrative, they are part of the "proof," their reading substantiating or, more rarely, contradicting my conclusions (I call them in that case "counter-intuitive," or "exceptional"). To make it short, the biographies of known jihadis are complementary to the interviews I made with people who were mostly from the social backgrounds of the jihadis. The interplay between the two is one of the specific features of this book. That is why the examples provided in the sections entitled "Examples of . . ." are not only illustrative but also essential to our understanding of the "intentionality" of jihadis or wannabe jihadis. They also provide a kind of small encyclopedic dimension to this book. Of course, the reader in a hurry can skip them.

This book draws heavily on my fieldwork in France over the last two decades (Khosrokhavar, 1997, 2004, 2009, 2012, 2014, 2016, 2018, 2020), but it owes also a large debt to the work of many scholars quoted or listed in the bibliography.

Concepts Developed in This Book

A few concepts have been developed in this book in order to explain the social and anthropological dimensions of the new jihadi landscape in Europe.

Arab

In France, besides meaning the citizen of Arab countries, "Arab" means those people of North African origin, sons of migrants, who usually have acquired French citizenship but are still considered by many people as not being totally "French" in their mores, still preserving Arab features that disqualify them as genuinely French citizens. Its vernacular mutation is "Beur" or "Rebeux."

White, White Man

In some European countries, the word "White" in the mouths of young people of migrant origin means those who belong to the mainstream society, are of European origin and, in general, are contemptuous or condescending toward the descendants of immigrants. They are often accused of racism or Islamophobia by "non-Whites."

Jihadism

By "jihadism" I mean an interpretation of Islam that combines ideological extremism and direct use of violence in order to promote its radical version of Allah's religion. Jihadism is marked by the violent rupture with non-Muslims and non-jihadi Muslims. It is based on an ideology that denounces dialogue as a perversion and tolerance as a heresy. The legitimate way of solving problems related to Islam in a world dominated by the atheist West is violent jihad.

Jihadogenic Urban Structures

By "jihadogenic urban structure" I mean those urban settings that have been the places with higher numbers of jihadi agents than other districts.

In many European countries, stigmatized, disadvantaged districts with a high proportion of ethnic migrants from the Muslim world are hotbeds for radicalization. Economic problems (unemployment, stigmatization, imprisonment, radicalization) coupled with identity crisis are the hallmarks of this type of urban setting. Next to this kind of neighborhood, there are some districts in the middle-class areas that had a history of radicalization due to the arrival and stay of jihadis in the 1990s.

Mainstream Society

Mainstream society, from the viewpoint of European Muslims, stigmatizes them. Middle-class Muslims suffer from it but also cope with it in a manner that is distinct from the disaffected Muslim youth, who are also economically excluded. They find its values opposed to theirs, their relationship being antagonistic, and judicial institutions and police being regarded by them as repressive. They don't call the police by that name, they refer to law enforcement personnel as "they" in an anonymous manner, or "Whites." This view is in part grounded in the imagination of young Muslims, whose feelings of stigmas are also partly real.

Islamistan

In many European countries, a new type of urban structure has emerged that I call "Islamistan." It is a district that has become "almost exclusively Islamic" in a rigid, fundamentalist way (e.g., Salafism, Deobandi Islam among the Pakistanis). Islamistan can be of two types. The first is marked by the combination of poverty, ghettoization, cultural withdrawal, de-schooling of children, unemployment, delinquency, rejection of mainstream society (mainly through "hatred") and lack of self-respect (deep feelings of indignity) as well as lack of hope ("no future"). Social exclusion and the adoption of a religiosity more and more inflexible (for instance, the expansion of the "total veil" among other signs of introversion) engender incommunicability between the district and the mainstream society. A deficient multicultural identity, marked by the absence of a shared culture with the mainstream society, sets in motion.

The second type of Islamistan is a mostly middle-class urban quarter that combines introverted, fundamentalist Islamic culture to the exclusion of the secular or non-Islamic ways of life. It is a means of preserving the mores of the Muslim community, over and above their ethnicity (the different Muslim countries from which they come). Middle-class or lower-middle-class Muslims build up this type of district in which Muslims live together, non-Muslims leaving gradually, non-Islamic businesses disappearing, exclusive *halal* food replacing a more diversified offering, and women without veils almost vanishing from the public space. This type of urban structure gives birth to a fundamentalist "enclaved identity" that evolves, in minority cases, into jihadism, in reaction to which extreme-right movements set in.

Salafism as a Counter-Secular Religiosity

European societies are distinguished by a dominant trend toward secularization. Secularism as a "civil religion" has had its heyday in France (la laïcité), Denmark, and some other European countries (Spain before the Franco regime). The simultaneous weakening of religion and secular utopias (socialism, communism, fascism, republicanism in France) has ushered in a type of religious sentiment marked by an anti-secular tendency in order to assert a new identity, mostly among those who are at the bottom of the social ladder or feel hopeless about the future (the "no future" generation in the lower-middle classes). In Europe, Islamic religiosity among the migrants' sons is particularly close to this counter-secular attitude, in part because of stigmas. The anti-secular stance is a sign of a provocative identity: the more they are culturally stigmatized, the more they become counter-secular by assuming a "negative" identity. Salafism, Tabligh, and jihadism wield a counter-secular dimension in distinct ways.

Headless Patriarchal Family, Neo-Traditional Family

Some migrant families in Western Europe develop a feature due to their anthropological crisis: the father who assumed the role of a norm-setter has either gone away (due to divorce or to a return to his country after retirement) or has almost abdicated his authority because of his subaltern position in society and in the family (he does not understand the twists and turns of modern European society, his language is deficient, etc.). This type of migrant family has not undergone the evolution of its European counterparts that have become more egalitarian, the role of women being revalued and the father becoming less central, not only in fact but also in symbolic terms, the mother sharing authority with him in a conflicted manner. In the families of migrant origin, even though the role of the father has been weakened by the involvement of the mother, the patriarchal mindset hovers over the family, even though the father is absent or marginalized. This situation pushes older brothers to vie for the paternal role. Since they do not have his moral authority, they usually resort to violence. The crisis of authority exacerbates relations among the family members, real and symbolic violence becoming prominent in the management of family relationships. This type of family is found most prevalently in societies where secularism is enshrined in the political culture of the mainstream society, such as France, marked by "laïcité." Other types of migrant families express the crisis otherwise, in particular in what I call the "neo-traditional family." What characterizes this type of family is the fixed role of the father. Unlike the family in the country of origin (Pakistan, Algeria, Turkey) which is evolving, this type of family casts the father beyond time, giving him an intangible, hyper-patriarchal status, to protect him from the onslaught of a European society marked by the questioning of patriarchy. It has an anti-secular dimension as well, the father becoming a sacred pole against the desecration that is taking place in society.

The Negative Hero

Many male European Muslims who went to Syria (the so-called Foreign Fighters) or staged attacks in Europe (homegrown jihadis) aspired to a kind of heroism at odds with the dominant values of European societies. They intended to achieve an exceptional status and attain worldwide stardom, not for having achieved good deeds but for perpetrating "bad" ones according to the mainstream Western culture. For them, the yardstick for goodness was the opposite of those of the "Infidel" societies in which they lived. This "negative heroism" enhanced them in their self-esteem in proportion to their dismissal by their own society. Before they joined jihadism, they had feelings of self-depreciation, stemming from their stigmas. The new self-esteem, based on the turndown by others, pushed them toward violence in reaction to their having been humiliated. Negative heroes inverted the vector of humiliation: they felt demeaned by others and treated as inferior. In return, they debased their society to which they no longer wished to belong, the new caliphate giving them the golden opportunity as a pole of reference (without it, their task would have been harder, their numbers having been marginal before and after the Islamic State, or Daesh). Negative heroes made "conspicuous violence" in the name of religion one of the major ingredients of their identity: they used social media, Western TV, and interviews with journalists to exhibit in an ostentatious manner their violence against the values of mainstream European culture, among them tolerance and non-violence.

Neo-Ummah

"Neo-Ummah" is an imaginary construction of an organic, effervescent community in vivid contrast to the "cold" and "soulless" societies in which young Europeans live, where freedom is often synonymous with loneliness and confusion, and ties between the citizens is loosened to a large extent, creating the need for "close-knit" groups and "sects." Neo-Ummah was the image of the Muslims living in Syria, provided by the Islamic State to the young Europeans, through its propaganda machine (mainly through the internet), in quest of meaningful communities in which they would not feel alone. It was an imagined community where a patriarchal family would be solid (in contrast to its fragility in the secular European world) and women would become mothers rather than competitors to men. Neo-Ummah satisfies the need for certainty, the attachment to a model of family and community in which sacred values become paramount: the more repressive they are, the more reassuring they become.

Slum Culture

The slum culture in Europe is mainly that which grows in neighborhoods with succeeding generations of poor Muslim immigrants. These neighborhoods are marked by new forms of ethnicity: the derogatory expressions "Arabs," "Bougnoules," or "Picots" in France, which refers to those who have Algerian, Moroccan, or Tunisian parents; and "Pakis," which includes young people of Pakistani origin and, by extension, those of South Asian origin; as well as racism against British African-Caribbean people that includes Blacks from different African countries, called "Perker" in Denmark to characterize Muslim migrants' sons.

The major hallmark of slum culture is an identity that protests mostly in a self-destructive manner against social domination and the biased attitude of the mainstream society toward the sons of migrants, but also submits to it in more or less hidden forms. This culture is marked by its deficiency (people belonging to it do not master the cultural codes of the mainstream society) and by the anger and outrage against this predicament (aggressiveness, a specific language, a body language different from that of the global society). It is usually embedded in a parallel economy in which small groups find ways of overcoming poverty through illegal means, but others are condemned to it because of the bad reputation that deviance causes for the neighborhood. To be from these poor ethnic districts results in being rejected by employers for whom these young people bear the mark of the slum culture and are deemed unfit for serious work. In general, the overall image of the districts where slum culture prevails is degraded through the media, but also in these neighborhoods by those who live there and feel deeply stigmatized.

Jihadi Fratriarchy

By "fratriarchy" I mean primarily the brothers, but also the cousins or the young members of a family, and often an elderly brother as a substitute for the authority of the father who has been dethroned by the undermining influence of the Western societies after immigration to Europe, primordially within headless patriarchal families. Since the father has abdicated, usually the older brother (sometimes, another brother) assumes his role and pushes toward violent action, being devoid of his moral authority. Jihad becomes the cement among the young family members. (I chose "fratriarchy" instead of "fraternity" or "brotherhood" because of their extensive meaning in common usage.)

Jihadophile Family

This type of family is characterized by the fact that a large part of the household has accepted (or even encouraged the others) to join IS or other jihadi organizations. The family, in particular the father and the mother (sometimes the uncles and aunts), have aligned themselves with their son (or sons) who usually took the initiative of moving to the holy land of jihad, or the family has put their resources at the disposal of their male offspring in order to provide the sons with the means to achieve their ends. The difference with jihadi fratriarchy lies in the fact that in "jihadophile families," the generation of parents adheres to the vision of the sons, which is not the case in jihadi fratriarchies.

I

The European Societies and Jihadism

Societies do not usually realize the extent of the alienation experienced among particular segments of their population. This is particularly the case for young Muslims of immigrant origin, whose deep frustration and humiliation are not understood by much of Europe. This book attempts to penetrate the subjectivity of this youth to reveal the depth of their distress. Desperate before the creation of the new caliphate, they found hope through it. The new state, called the Islamic State, gave them the illusion of a new world where they would finally find the legitimate place they had been denied in Europe, mainly through violence. But it is not only this population that has been spellbound by the new caliphate. A section of European middle-class youth, marked by a loss of meaning in life and a lack of hope in the future, also joined the new caliphate, mainly as converts. This work attempts to understand what motivated them and how they accepted to play a repressive role in killing and maiming thousands of people, and dying themselves at the service of an apocalyptic theocracy.

The revival of European jihadism in the years 2013–2016 had a major external cause: the creation of the so-called Islamic State, which provided a utopia and a territorial base that enabled young Europeans to identify with it, to seek to join it, and to put themselves at its service. But alongside this external cause there were internal causes—namely, young people's aspiration to a utopia, their frustration with everyday life in Europe, and urban and family problems—which played a fundamental role in their commitment to the new state. This book attempts to describe these two dimensions, which are intertwined, form a whole, and give sense to European jihadism. Following this line, one can describe the aims of this work.

The first is to portray European jihadism mainly in a particular period marked by the emergence and decline of the Islamic State in Iraq and Syria (ISIS), renamed in June 2014 the Islamic State (IS), or Daesh (its Arab acronym), mainly by its Arab opponents. The new state introduced a profound break in the history of transnational jihadism, until then dominated by networks, especially al-Qaeda. The founding of this territorial state gave

Jihadism in Europe. Farhad Khosrokhavar, Oxford University Press. © Oxford University Press 2021.
DOI: 10.1093/oso/9780197564967.003.0001

a boost to jihadism and heightened the aspiration among young Europeans whose number rose to around 6,000 so-called Foreign Fighters (those people who went to Syria to join jihadi organizations) between 2013 and 2017.

The second aim of this book is to describe in depth the subjectivity of young people who radicalized, but also their repertoire. Terrorism in the name of Islam, which we call jihadism, or any other extremism can only be fought effectively by understanding what is going on in the minds of its followers. But understanding is not justifying. It is, however, necessary to grasp the intricacies of jihadi subjectivity, which is multiple by definition, and which enlightens us both on the extremist logic of its agents as well as the shortcomings of European societies.

This book focuses also on the sociological and anthropological aspects of jihadism in order to grasp the motivation of its main actors in a phenomenological perspective. More broadly, it aims to show the complexity of jihadism, and the need to understand radical Islamism as a "total social fact" that encompasses anthropological, sociological, and political but also psychological dimensions. Jihadism cannot be understood independently of the mental and anthropological contents of its agents' subjectivity and their relationships with the global society. A comprehensive vision of the jihadi actors' behaviors in relation to their socio-economic condition and family relations is therefore necessary to elucidate this phenomenon, which an abstract view in terms of variables and parameters with no reference to their subjectivities is incapable of clarifying, although statistics and the correlation between different objective factors greatly help us to build up a conceptual framework.

This book aims at explaining jihadism by contextualizing the urban, parental, social, economic, and psychological aspects of their subjective, imaginary dimension. Imagination, becoming almost boundless through the web, migration, and globalization, had a major impact on the minds of these people. In this global perspective, the anthropology of the family is at the heart of jihadism: many young jihadis belonged either to broken families or to those in which authority was diluted or shattered, and violence was largely present—that is to say, families in crisis, marked by a shaky authority.

This book also focuses on each specific European country. To take an example, Italy did not suffer any major successful jihadi attack in the years 2013–2017, whereas France suffered a lot, the United Kingdom, Germany, and Spain being in between.

The official proclamation of IS on June 29, 2014, swelled the number of vocations. This research intends to show the importance of that event by raising the question of this new state and its role in promoting a territorially based "Islamic dreamland" (we call it the neo-Ummah). The decline of IS and, finally, its disappearance as a state in October 2017 put an end to the wide-scale appeal of jihadism for European youth, but not to jihadism itself. The caliphate was at the heart of a utopia that attracted young Europeans in search of meaning and an ideal, ready to cross swords with their elders in order to promote the new order, totalitarian but endowed with enthusiasm and a new sense of belonging, in much the same way as did Nazism, fascism, or communism, which promised a new life to those who were ready to join their ranks. It was a mass phenomenon: at least 5,904 Europeans went to Syria and Iraq during those few years (Cook and Vale, 2018),[1] and many more would have left Europe for Syria if the means had not been set up in Europe and Turkey to prevent their departure since the end of 2014. Most of those who made the journey to Syria intended to join IS. They had social class problems (most of them were from lower-class Muslim families in Europe, a minority of them from the middle classes, mostly among converts), and identity problems (many were of Moroccan, Algerian, Pakistani, Bangladeshi, and other descent, and they did not feel they were accepted as full citizens by the European societies).

I focus particularly on six aspects of radical Islam in Europe.

The first is the jihadi agents and their subjectivities, according to social class, gender, generation, psychology (normal versus depressed, psychotic, and so forth), and religion (convert, born-again, etc.).

The second raises the crisis of the family as one of the explaining factors of Jihadism, differently shaped within the middle classes and the lower-class youth of migrant origin, their ethnic background being significant (youth of Moroccan, Pakistani, Turkish origin behaved in specific ways toward jihadism).

The third relates to national differences and political cultures in some major European societies (French laïcité as a political culture distinguishes France from other European countries, English multiculturalism having its peculiar features, etc.).

The fourth explores the urban structure and what I call the "jihadogenic urban structure," which is at the heart of radical Islam in Europe, including poor districts and middle-class urban settings, for different reasons.

The fifth dimension is the age group (adolescents versus adults), their respective motivations, and the influence of preachers on them and their religiosity. Teenagers were massively lured to Daesh. Their view was influenced by the production of IS on the internet and by local recruiters, but also by their own imaginary worldview and their desires, mostly ignored by adults.

The sixth dimension is gender. Women became significant agents of jihadism during this period (around 17 percent of those who went to Syria), mostly as "jihadi brides" but also as violent jihadis among a minority of them. In their desire to join IS, their subjective grasp of feminism, parenthood, and family played a key role.

Of course, in dealing with jihadism the vocabulary is not innocent. While there is a consensus on the terrorist nature of jihadism, terrorism itself is a matter of dispute and more than 260 definitions of it have been put forward so far (Easson and Schmid 2011). On the other hand, the word *jihadism* is not universally accepted since the notion of "jihad" is regarded positively by Muslims, even though the neologism "jihadism" (jihadiyah) is pejorative both in Muslim and non-Muslim societies. Muslim theologians sometimes use the term *Kharijite* (*Khavarij* in Arabic) to characterize jihadis. A few decades after the death of the Prophet, the Kharijite opted for violence against the fourth "well-guided" Caliph Ali and killed him in 661. They used violence against those they considered fake Muslims, and whom they subjected to excommunication (*takfir*) and death. Nowadays, Muslim extremists use the same word to reject in their turn those who oppose them in the name of Allah's religion. For lack of a better word, and to avoid cumbersome circumlocutions, I use *jihadism*, while being aware of its disputed semantics. I mean by it a politico-religious phenomenon by which agents combine a radical version of Islam focused on jihad, in conjunction with violent action. The overwhelming majority of Muslims around the world reject the jihadi view of Allah's religion.

The notion of "radicalization" also poses serious problems in social sciences: some reject it outright because of its polysemy, its emphasis on a linear vision, underscoring the social and political context, and overemphasizing psychological problems. Some even think that the notion is not only useless but even harmful because of its false transparency and its exclusive stress on few aspects (Coolsaet, 2016; Sedgwick, 2010). But the expression has gained currency in social sciences, particularly because of the huge investment made by governments and research institutions in this field and under this labeling. On the other hand, social scientists have endeavored to subsume it under a social-anthropological construct, overstepping its original psychological and security-related meaning (Khosrokhavar, 2014; McDonald, 2018).

The battle of interpretations has been raging over whether radicalization is the result of manipulation, psychological and social fragility, or the consequence of the individual's sovereign decision to engage in this path. For some, social debility caused by stigmas, economic exclusion, or psychological causes are at the root of radicalization. Others believe that the "revolutionary" aspiration, or the will to change one's life as well as the life of others (willingly or through repression), is paramount in radicalization. The study of the jihadi agents (a long chapter in this book) attests to the large diversity of motives: some people with deep psychological problems became involved in IS (as well as adolescents in crisis); others, from poor, segregated districts, felt it as a revenge against those who stigmatized them; but also some middle-class people identified with what they regarded as the revolutionary dimension of IS and its aim at fighting against an unjust, imperialist, and immoral world in the name of Islam; many also became jihadis due to their imagined view of a utopian Islamic society to be erected, represented by the "neo-Ummah" (the embellished, imagined, mythologized Ummah or Muslim community, at variance with the real one). Neo-Ummah was in part the outcome of their imagination in reaction to the disenchanted life in Europe, and in part the consequence of the propaganda of Daesh on the web (thousands of video-sequences in more than eleven languages) as well as the preaching of local recruiters.

As for the role of ideology, it certainly plays a significant part in the motivation of many young adults. But the same ideology can be violent or non-violent; Salafism is an example: its pietistic version being non-violent and its jihadi version, violent, although ideologically they are more or less close to each other, with notable differences (the first stresses the importance of *Hijra*, the migration of the Muslim to a Muslim country, whereas for the second, *jihad* is paramount; the former opts for a sectarian vision, separated from the mainstream society in a hermetic community, but without the use of violence, while the latter makes violence in the name of holy war the spearhead of Islam). The two tendencies are distinct, and the second is a minority trend within the first, totally different in regard to violence.[2] More generally, religiosity (which is a subjective religious feeling) is important and will be analyzed under two headings, the neo-Ummah on the one hand and the caliphate on the other. The new religiosity reinvigorated a sense of a distinct identity among part of the European youth, in quest of a sacred meaning to life in reaction to a secular world that had marginalized religion and pushed it to the private sphere, the mainstream society having no utopian alternative to propose (the major ones, dating back to the eighteenth and nineteenth centuries, had worn out).[3]

European societies have been marked by anti-democratic movements during the last centuries. In the second half of the twentieth century, far-left movements challenged democratic regimes in Europe in the name of an imagined working class, which they pretended to spearhead, notably Red Brigades in Italy, Baader-Meinhof Gruppe in Germany, and Action Directe in France. Like them, jihadis fight against the pluralistic regimes, democracy being in their eyes "the idolizing of the people" (*taqut*), marked by the "world arrogance" (*istikbar*) that they anathematize (*takfir*) (Khosrokhavar, 2009, 2011; Al Subaie, 2012).

Jihadism displays some characteristics of social movements: it has a homogeneous ideology, a neo-caliphate political project based on the opposition to the secular world and what its followers consider to be a fake version of Islam (the Saudi style government, among others). It is a repressive movement (especially with regard to different minorities, religious or not, such as homosexuals or unrecognized religions like the Yazidis) and, in several respects, it is regressive (the status of women, Human Rights). But these features make it attractive to many young men and women (and teenagers) who look for another society, and for some of them, another belief system that would give meaning to their lives by delineating clearly between what is sacred and what is not, what is allowed and what is forbidden, harshly punishing those who transgress sacred standards.

a-Jihadism, a Total Social Fact

Jihadism is a "total social fact" (or a "comprehensive social phenomena," respective translations of "le fait social total"), the expression having been coined by Marcel Mauss: "The total social facts . . . set in motion in some cases the totality of society and its institutions . . . and in other cases a very large number of institutions, particularly where such exchanges and contracts are more about individuals." He continues:

> These phenomena are at once legal, economic, religious, aesthetic, morphological and so on. They are legal in that they concern individual and collective rights, organized and diffuse morality; they may be entirely

> obligatory, or subject simply to praise or disapproval. They are at once political and domestic, being of interest both to classes and to clans and families. They are religious; they concern true religion, animism, magic and diffuse religious mentality. They are economic, for the notions of value, utility, interest, luxury, wealth, acquisition, accumulation, consumption, and liberal and sumptuous expenditure are all present. (Mauss, *The Gift*, 1925)

By "total social fact" I mean one that involves major social dimensions: generation (particularly young people who, for the most part, are in their twenties, and adolescents below the legal adult age); gender (not only men, but also women); psychopathology (not only the so-called "normal" people but also those with more or less acute psychological problems); employment (not only the jobless or blue-collar workers, but also the white-collar and middle-class people), religion (Muslims by birth, but also converts); family (different types of families, many of them in crisis, are involved); the urban setting (few types of districts are involved); ethnicity (people with a specific ethnic background are more prone to jihadism than others); nationality (the national political culture plays a distinctive role); the geopolitical situation; and the affects (humiliation, resentment, real or imagined stigmas, empathy). The interaction between these dimensions makes the choice of few variables questionable, the description in terms of correlations between them giving only a partial picture of a complex reality.

Jihadism spread over most of the countries in the world, except in Latin America and Japan (Jones, 2015). It shook the symbolic foundations of societies: the significance of killing people in the name of jihad went far beyond its quantitative aspect and took on a qualitative meaning that magnified several times its purely numerical impact. The fact that jihadism is a vision and ideology alien to the mainstream European culture increased its monstrosity. Based on Islam and jihad and not on familiar categories like class struggle or nationalism that are endogenous European ideologies, made it the more appalling. Jihadism is in many ways different from the indigenous European terrorism, be it regionalist, nationalist (Basque, Corsican, Irish, etc.), far left (Red Brigades in Italy, Baader-Meinhoff Gruppe in Germany, or Action directe in France), or far right (neo-Nazi groups in many European countries). They are rooted in European history and are therefore "understandable," whereas Islam is still regarded as a foreign religion by European public opinion.

b-The Crisis of Secular Europe and Jihadism

One of the reasons for the success of jihadism in Europe, particularly among the migrants' offspring, born-again Muslims, and converts, was the promise to build up an idealized religious world that would make life more meaningful than within secular European societies. Daesh fleshed out this claim in its heyday by violently rejecting secularism and the lax religious attitude of many Muslims that did not match its puritanical and repressive view of Islam.

Until the third quarter of the twentieth century, secularization went hand in hand with the utopias of progress and social justice. Since then, it has been running on empty, without utopia, producing a malaise, namely that of the "flattening of meaning." It then opens the space for new forms of the sacred, which gain credibility by being repressive. Since the eighteenth century, secularization in Europe has gone hand in hand with freedom. Henceforth, the religious expresses itself in a repressive repertoire to counter the vacuum of utopia. Daesh proposed a dystopia that substituted repression for emancipation and binding duty for emancipatory right, the latter being identified with sin. It proposed an idealized future, painted in rosy tones by the adepts of the new religious revival, be it among jihadis or other non-violent fundamentalist zealots (even among Christians, in particular the Pentecostals). More generally, secularization meant people assuming their political responsibility in the name of human capacity to handle its problems in an autonomous manner, without reference to God or any supernatural force. That Enlightenment view was meaningful within the framework of human progress and a fair society, to be built in the future. Western societies in general did not evolve along those lines in the late twentieth and early twenty-first centuries, the prospect of a "just society" having receded with the growing class disparity. For many young people, the real secular view leads to an unfair society where middle classes and the poor are squeezed and upper classes become even more opulent. Both jihadism and Islamic fundamentalism propose themselves as remedies for this state of affairs. They are imaginary remedies that do not solve the problem but make mental exile from it possible. First and foremost, they propose a religion encompassing the entirety of believers' lives, not only dealing with their spiritual needs in their private spheres but also including their social, economic, and political situations—in brief, their public lives.

Daesh, with the promise of an "all-religious" life in which politics, economy, and culture were subordinated to Islam, made sense to those young people for whom the secular order meant meaninglessness and the individualistic (egocentric) lack of responsibility toward others within a life devoid of fundamental divides: between the licit and the illicit, moral and immoral. The demise of utopias in Europe (the downfall of communism, socialism, republicanism) made Daesh's dystopia (a transparent society under the aegis of a totalitarian version of Islam) more attractive. On the other hand, in Europe, human frailty became more prominent as the capacity of the Welfare State to manage individuals' lives was restrained while the economic gap between rich and poor became a chasm, with middle classes being squeezed, the promise of a better future for many of its members becoming problematic, if not meaningless, and lack of trust in the future making the search for an alternative religious society a panacea for them. Of course, secularism was perceived as somehow autonomous from the social inequality within the capitalist order that dominated the world after the fall of communism in 1989. Until then, social justice was within reach of human capacity to handle this major social issue, and the "secular order" was a political system that managed human life through the promise of more social justice and freedom, particularly within communism. After its fall, capitalism had no enemy and the unbalanced distribution of wealth became more accentuated in the following decades in conjunction with the weakening of the Welfare State.

At first glance, the link between the attraction for jihadism, the crisis of secularism, and the growth of inegalitarian capitalism in major Western countries might seem at best remote. But the demand for an all-solving religious tenet (Islam) became more attractive as the widening economic gap between social classes under the auspices of post-communist capitalism made the fascination for a religious holistic solution in the name of Islam (the only non-secularized Abrahamic religion) irresistible to many young people. They yearned for divine justice for want of human justice, unattainable in this world, owing to the unavailability of a political alternative. The lack of a "hope horizon" among the middle- and lower-class youth resulted in the infatuation with mythical solutions in light of an unjust economy that penalizes the poor and rewards the rich. The disappearance of the ternary utopias of socialism, communism, and fascism opened the way for an anomie that made attractive the ideal of a sacred society under the aegis of a neo-caliphate, which would achieve what had escaped the control of secular and democratic regimes in Europe. In the imagined Islamic State, social justice would go hand in hand with the hegemony of Islam as a holistic system that would also put an end to doubt and suspicion and usher in an era of full transparency. This autocratic global system that enclosed politics and economics under the inflated category of religion (Islam as a system encompassing politics, religion, culture, and economy according to the motto *deen wa dawla* [religion and government]) was a utopia whose fascination had been in a large part due to the unsolved problems of the young middle- and lower-class youth in Europe. They lived devoid of utopia (which meant without a sense of collective belonging projected onto the future) and were marked by the fear of an uncertain future: not only by a lack of expected upward mobility for a large part of the middle classes, but also by a diffuse anxiety at the prospect of their possibly declining social status. In its heyday (2014–2015) IS promised not only a new utopia, but also a tangible social and economic ascent for the lower- or lower-middle-class youth who joined it. In addition to this, the cult of the hero in a holy war distracted from economic problems by subordinating them to those of warrior bravery and the narcissistic image of the glorious knight of Islam.

Secularism was meaningful as long as it was coupled with a utopia of social progress and hope for a better future. The crisis of this utopia since the fall of the Berlin Wall in 1989 and the subsequent end of communism has gone hand in hand with the growing fragility of the middle classes, for whom social ascent is no longer a foregone conclusion and the fear of social demise is growing. Secularism has in turn entered into crisis and God's call has become much more credible among the middle classes as well as among the marginalized and excluded people (not only Islam, but also evangelical sects). Through IS a new Islamic order seemed within reach that would combine social justice and a cohesive community, in contrast to the loose social bonds in Europe. Fascinated by IS, young people's imaginations were shaped by the predicament in which they found themselves in uncertain democracies in which managing their personal lives had become far more difficult than in the 1960s.

Two distinct social classes were concerned by Daesh's utopia. Middle-class youth, among them converts and born-again, as well as young, disaffected Muslim youth. For the latter group, secularism meant denial of dignity to the Muslims by a Europe in which neo-colonialism was disguised under the secular view, contemptuous of Islam, the religion of the former colonies. Becoming a born-again Muslim meant reconquering dignity through opposition to a godless society. In their view, secularism was a sign of disdain toward the sons of the Muslim migrants. That is why jihadism had a provocative dimension toward secularism in their case. Among the sons of Muslim migrants, exposed to racism and Islamophobia, rejecting secularism (and particularly laïcité, as a distinctive militant French form of secularism) had a taste of humiliating the humiliators through bellicose Islamism by denying legitimacy to their "sacred" motto, namely laïcité, this secular "civil religion," opposed to Islam.

As for teenagers, secularism mainly meant denial of adulthood: the entire system disallowed them to become grown-up by unduly prolonging their non-adult status. By espousing radical Islam, they forced mainstream society to recognize their adulthood either as a result of their violence among young boys or their precocious pregnancy among young girls.

In general, different jihadi groups had specific views of the secular world, but one common denominator united them against it: the lack of "indisputable" moral authority. Secularism in its new configuration (late modernity) levels meaning and makes society a collection of loosely tied individuals, lacking unquestionable moral authority, in particular through the loss of what gave strength to the secular view in its heyday (the nineteenth century and the first half of the twentieth), namely the utopia of fraternity through justice and equality, to be achieved in the future (the motto of the French Revolution was "Liberty, Equality, Fraternity"). The quest for a sacred world in the name of radical Islam was a remedy for the loss of a secular sense of togetherness. The neo-Ummah was supposed to restore social bonds through sacred standards.

c-The Crisis of Gender Relations

Daesh was successful in alluring many young European women and female teenagers through the promise of a new gender relation based on the strong distinction between men and women. It entertained the dream of the "knight of Islam" as a husband, and the "mother of lion cubs" for their new community (the neo-Ummah, as we called it) as a wife. For men, becoming a valiant fighter in the service of the caliphate stressed their virility and underlined their manhood. Both men and women resented the deep crisis of manhood and womanhood in the Western world where the demand for gender equality obscured the sense of manhood and womanhood in their view.

The dissatisfaction with modern feminist gender relations is tangible among the European youth who went to Syria, but beyond it, the malaise of gender relations comes into the open: the new tendency toward gender equality has overburdened women with the task of managing the family and at the same time, working and earning their living (one salary is not anymore enough to sustain a decent middle-class life within modern capitalism, contrary to the 1960s). Men also feel a "castration complex," new gender relations creating among them a sense of being dispossessed of their manhood.

In late capitalism, gender relations have undermined the patriarchal family, but they have also made family ties fragile, the new self-centered subjectivity being destabilized by the exhausting relations between men and women, particularly within a family in which authority has been largely impaired. In reaction to feminism, inegalitarian late capitalism, and narcissistic subjectivities, young people embraced IS mythology of man as a valiant combatant and woman as a devout mother whose union would build a harmonious family, instead of the fragile and conflicting family of late modernity. The mythological view of the family promoted by Daesh was endeared by so many young people because of their deep disenchantment with modern family life. Daesh exploited and entertained the dream of a god-ordained society in which non-competitive relations between men and women would be the cornerstone of a new type of family, based on gender inequality. However, in this new family, the division of labor was clear and unambiguous (women ruling over the private life of the family, men governing the relations to the external world), in contrast to the modern family where everyone is expected to participate in the collective work with the disappearance of specific barriers between men and women. The quest for an idealized family relation outside the realm of Western societies projected onto a mythical neo-caliphate in Syria before these young people could reach the "land of Sham" revealed their disillusion toward the prevailing family structure. The dream of a new family, marked by a rigid distinction between male and female roles, was the promise of Daesh to European boys and girls. The myth of a new femininity and masculinity denoted a deep frustration toward gender and family relations within modern Europe. The so-called Islamic family fascinated so many young men and women because they were traumatized by the instability of modern family life, all the more fragile as the economic situation was also characterized by deep insecurity.

d-The General Political Crisis

Jihadism is a multi-faceted phenomenon. One major aspect in Europe is the social question, which is at the heart of jihadism and concerns a large part of radicalized youth who live in ghettoized neighborhoods in or near the cities and are often unemployed or involved in illegal activities in the underground economy. Added to this is the crisis in the Muslim world that has repercussions in Europe among Muslims and, in turn, converts. Still, jihadism is not only a lower-class phenomenon. It also recruits among middle classes, some from migrant communities, many from converts, although most of its members are Muslims of working-class origin in Europe.

Daesh was successful in mobilizing many thousands of young Europeans (and many more would have been enrolled, had not the European governments established institutional and legal obstacles to the departure of young candidates to Syria). This denoted the crisis of European democracies. Its manifestation in the form of departures or the aspiration to leave was dependent on a particular historical conjuncture, the creation of IS, which was regarded as the resurgence of the caliphate and the promise of a better world, both politically and spiritually. However, jihadism was one expression of a deeper crisis in Europe, that of social togetherness, social bonds. Daesh displayed it in several ways: in its symbolic foundations, but also, at the economic, social, political, and cultural levels.

The modern world is increasingly unequal: class gap has become a large chasm in many societies. IS did not intend to combat economic inequality, but the enthusiasm of young people who sought to join it had also economic undertones: precariousness among young Muslims of the poor districts in Europe, and uncertain future for the middle classes who apprehended proletarianization. Jihadism in its neo-caliphal IS configuration conjoined religion with a promise of an affluent society, at least in its heyday (2014–2015). But the most important aspect of Daesh was that it overshadowed economics with its warlike rhetoric. It instilled enthusiasm for a heroic life at the service of a sacred ideal. It made young people feel that their economic future was of little importance in front of a cause of cosmic significance, preparing for the end of times. It neutralized economic concern with noble warrior ideals for which young people offered their lives to save Islam and prepare for the future reign of God. Selfish self-care was supplanted by devotion to a cause for which absolute generosity was necessary, even more, self-evident. It was a free gift of life in the service of a noble ideal. The life dedicated to this ideal was exuberant and had an overflowing meaning, unlike the withdrawn life those young people led in Europe, at least as long as they imagined it in Europe. Once in Syria, concern about the war made the economy derisory and the commitment to it left no time to think about the distant future.

In Europe, the imagination of these young people operated as if in a vacuum, in defiance of the real situation in Syria, as if another world, freed from the constraints of reality, was possible in the face of an infinite horizon of dreamlike possibilities for a youth suffering from idleness and lack of ideals.

In other words, life in Europe was marked by its emptiness and the absence of ideals and standards, and the European crisis was deep, particularly at the political level. In the first place, politics no longer offered a utopia, nor a horizon of hope: there was no longer any political messianism (as it used to be with the utopias of socialism, communism, nationalism, and its French version, republicanism) through which society would project itself into a brighter future. Politics was reduced to the management of everyday life and no longer represented the promise of a greater social justice and a brighter future that would unite society and give people a sense of belonging. In the second place, politics no longer offered the prospect of improving individual life, as middle classes have been increasingly assailed by the fear of social downgrading, especially for their progenies, fear that is internalized by the younger generations. Politics has no longer been based on collective solidarity, neo-capitalism favoring rootless individuals looking for happiness through private economic gain. The quest for a mythological neo-Ummah by young European Muslims or converts was the dream of social unity and solidarity beyond politics, religion playing the role of an imaginary cement in overcoming the loss of solidarity. In this respect one could speak of the crisis of democracy in our contemporary world (Gauchet, 2017). As already mentioned, the widening gap between the rich and the poor, the squeezing of the middle classes who have been exposed to the flexibility of the labor market and job insecurity explains in part the allegiance of middle-class youth to Daesh, seeking status and identity through it, filling the void in their lives within European societies. Jihadi identity was in this sense an ambivalent counter-culture, in part opposed to the neo-capitalist society where "gift" has lost its meaning (the martyr accepts to sacrifice his life and give it as a gift to God and to his idealized neo-Ummah) as much as its continuing through the narcissistic promotion of the Self in terms of heroism and coverage by the media (the cult of stardom, promoted by Daesh). Fame fulfilled the psyches of these young men who aspired to attain recognition worldwide through violent action within a subculture of violence exalting the sense of revenge against an unfair society (it became an "Infidel society"). Wannabe jihadis were addicted to the cult of the stars by the narcissism of their ego, in love with their own magnified Self through TV screens (when they killed a Westerner in the name of jihad, they became headline news worldwide). Death at its center, jihadism is by definition either meta-political or infra-political, never political in the sense of proposing an alternative to the secular modernity other than through death and destruction. This aspect appealed to many young people who wanted to escape everyday life that did not offer them the opportunity to fulfill their dreams, in search of a sacred death that would free them from the burden of an unattractive existence. This was the suicidal side of jihadism, overshadowed by the killing of disbelievers.

e-Death as a Fundamental Category Denoting a Global Crisis

Jihadism is a "syndrome" of a global political-social crisis in Europe (and of course, at a deeper level, in the Muslim world). However, compared to crises Europe underwent in the first half of the twentieth century, such as fascism, Nazism, and communism, jihadism is of a much more limited scope. The Second World War was in a certain way the consequence of the shaking up of European democracies following the economic crisis of 1929 as well as the humiliation of Germany and those defeated in the First World War. Jihadism expresses in its own way the difficulty of living in utopia-less societies, marked by widening economic inequality and lack of a "sacred" principle (in other words, secularization without utopia). These societies are on one hand "commodified" (the paramount value is that which can be "sold" or "bought" as a commodity, real or imaginary) and, on the other, more and more individualistic, the individual's Self becoming at times a burden, difficult to bear for those who are at the bottom of the social ladder or belong to the middle classes, exposed to an uncertain future, and disposed to depression as the most common psychic disease of the twentieth and twenty-first centuries (Ehrenberg, 1998). People easily lose their sanity, the more so as they have to endorse many responsibilities that were assumed in the 1960s–1980s by the Welfare State. With jihadism, death that is put on show is the end of the "positive individual" and the birth of a "negative individual" who achieves his Self through an exhibitionist dying and killing: in many cases the camera carried by the jihadis films live their killing, which they then put on social media, exemplifying show-off death. This type of exhibitionism did not exist in the Northern Ireland, Basque, or Corsican terrorism. In jihadism, showing the spectacle of death is a "necro-narcissism," extolling death being the only way one can glorify the Self. Somehow life is too much filled with counter-jihadi values, holy death for the Self and an anathematizing death for the enemy becoming a means to celebrate a utopia that glorifies killing and dying and those who implement it, contrary to classical terrorism for which violent death was a means to achieve the professed ends of their organization. Jihadi neo-community (neo-Ummah as we called it) is also a necro-community.

Dying in the name of Allah for the caliphate was called martyrdom in a mixture of horror and fascination that gave meaning to the ostentatious and "self-inflated" individual, disoriented and marked by the perversion of self-esteem, somehow in the sense of Rochefoucauld's "amour-propre." Jihadi Self is all the more inflated and exacerbated as it lacks a positive link to others. Radical Islamism mobilizes categories of disparate origins, but their common denominator is the self-affirmation of its agents who discover in a violent dystopia the means to dignify their Selves by denying dignity to others. Jihadism is as much a protest against a world devoid of moral values and spirituality as it is the worsening of its major tendencies through an exacerbated narcissism that feeds on sacred principles to vindicate its misdeeds in the name of God.

Jihadism focuses on death—sacred (martyrdom) or damned (killing the Infidels)—rather than life.[4] This reflects the reversal of politics in Europe. Recognition within the political sphere is usually achieved by mobilizing life among different groups confronting each other, claiming hegemony. The domination issue has been, particularly since the Enlightenment, bound to life and its avatars, not to death and afterlife. Nazism and communism questioned the normativity of life through revolutionary violence, but they mobilized death only against their adversaries.

Jihadism is a theological-political vision in which death's significance is incomparably superior to its place in secular totalitarianism.

Nazi and communist visions were based on the primacy of life here below (earthly life) in a secular conception (moving toward a classless society for communism, a purely Aryan world for the Nazis). The death suffered (in millions) in the war unleashed against the rest of the world was only the consequence of a destructive action without this notion bearing a fundamental significance among the core ideas of communist or fascist ideologies. Martyrdom by those who wear an explosive belt and trigger it to kill others and themselves has a central meaning that cannot be found in secular totalitarian death. Certainly, among their followers one can decipher a fascination with death in the attitudes, or the criminal excesses (e.g., in the Gulag camps or those of the Jewish genocide), but again, in the ideological corpus of Nazism or communism self-imposed death is not a founding principle.

In jihadism, death, be it salvific (for the jihadi) or damnatory (for the disbeliever) is a seminal notion built into a new theology. It claims to be rooted in the origins of Islam, but in fact it stems from a "perverse modernization" in which Islamic notions are revisited and reintegrated into a death-inspired enterprise that glorifies violent death and exalts the killing of "disbelievers" and the heroic death of the true believer in reference to martyrdom that has been reshaped to serve this new death-centered worldview (Khosrokhavar, 1993, 1995, 1997, 2009, 2011, 2018; Cook, 2015; Roy, 2017).

Radical Islamism denies legitimacy to other versions of Islam, including Sufism, which opens the religion of Allah to a plurality of perspectives (among others the mystical love of God), in which violence and war often play a marginal role (there were Sufi warriors, but the major trends within Sufism exalted love of God in an ecstatic manner within closed communities).

If this regressive and hyper-repressive vision has been successful among many people in Europe, it is because it addressed a need for transgression and a new utopia among many groups who did not anymore believe in a promising future or a meaningful life in the world in its current shape. Death intervened as a cathartic operator, giving sense to the life of believers and denying it to others (the "Disbelievers") in the name of a dystopian version of Islam. The ultimate meaning of the Sacred was, in an archaic manner, the sacrifice of the Self on its altar. Since reality had no promise for the future, taking refuge in sacred death in reference to the Golden Age of Islam was a way of surmounting life's meaninglessness. Death became the repository of meaning in an inverted world where life turned out to be meaningless.

II

The Birth of the Islamic State and its Impact on European Youth

a-The Historical Perspective on European Jihadis and the Birth of the Islamic State in Iraq and Sham

Jihadism in Europe began in the 1990s with the advent of GIA (Groupe Islamique Armé), a military offshoot of FIS (Front Islamique du Salut) in Algeria, after the latter won the majority seats in the parliamentary elections in 1991 and was overthrown by the Algerian army in January 1992. GIA targeted France, suspected of having supported the Algerian military, for its terrorist attacks. On July 25, 1995, the first major terrorist attack with the assistance of people who were born or socialized in France (the so-called homegrown terrorists) occurred at the hands of Khaled Kelkal, who had lived in France since the age of five. The attack killed eight people and wounded 117 at the metro station Saint-Michel in Paris. Members of the Algerian GIA residing in France (Boualem Bensaïd and Smaïn Aït Ali) were involved with him. Kelkal had been involved in deviant activities and had served prison terms before converting to radical Islam, most probably in prison under the influence of jihadi recruiters. In Europe, a period began in the 2000s when many terrorist attacks were perpetrated, mostly by homegrown jihadis, after the seminal September 11, 2001, attacks in the US. Major jihadi acts were committed in March 2004 in Madrid trains and in July 2005 in the London bus and Underground systems. During the period extending to 2012 and including a major terrorist attack by Mohamed Merah in that year in the cities of Toulouse and Montauban in France, the inspiring organization was al-Qaeda and its offshoots.

Since 2013, a major event occurred in the Middle East. A jihadi group founded a new state in June 2014 with a territory that was, at its heights, almost as vast as the United Kingdom (around 300.000 square kilometers) under the name of the Islamic State in Syria and Sham (ISIS), and later on, simply the Islamic State (IS). This event was a sea change in jihadism, not

Jihadism in Europe. Farhad Khosrokhavar, Oxford University Press. © Oxford University Press 2021.
DOI: 10.1093/oso/9780197564967.003.0002

only in the Middle East but also in Europe and, more generally, worldwide. IS brought about a great transformation in the minds of European jihadis. Of course, al-Qaeda underwent many changes, up to nine from its birth until 2009 (Filiu, 2009), and one can extend the list even further since then. But the major sociological shift was in the 1990s, with the homegrown terrorists, mainly sons or grandsons of migrants to Europe in the 1950s and 1960s, who grew up in Europe and felt rejected and stigmatized. They acted out of anger against Europe, which denied them, from their viewpoint, recognition in terms of real citizenship and equal opportunities and confined them to poor districts and menial jobs. Even among the Muslim middle-classes, there prevailed a strong sense of denial of citizenship. Those who suffered economic marginalization and social stigma developed an unrelenting sense of hatred toward society and its standards. In 2013–2014, the newborn state transformed rancor and hate into a new hope, that of a new Muslim society in the Middle East where Muslims from all over the world could achieve recognition and become full-fledged citizens, in contrast to Europe where Islam was despised and had an inferior status, not least because it was the religion of the former colonized people.

The IS foundation was laid after the US and UK invasion of Iraq in 2003. In the jails of Bucca in the city of Garma and Abu Ghraib close to Baghdad, many radical Islamists were locked up, next to the senior officers of the Ba'ath army. This was particularly the case of Abubaker al Baghdadi, who later became the first IS caliph. He spent eight months in Abu Ghraib and in Bucca, until December 2004.[1]

On October 13, 2006, the Mujahideen Advisory Council in Iraq, consisting of six jihadi organizations including al-Qaeda in Iraq and about thirty Sunni tribes representing a large part of the population of Anbar (western province of Iraq), proclaimed the creation of the Islamic State of Iraq. In 2012, it began to expand and consolidate in Syria. On April 9, 2013, it became the "Islamic State in Iraq and the Levant" (ISIL). It was officially founded on June 29, 2014, under the name of the "Islamic State" (IS). For the Sunni Muslims (around nine-tenths of the world's Muslims), the caliphate represented the rebirth of Islam. Its disappearance in 1924 had distressed many (Pankhurst, 2013; Guidère, 2016).

Since its foundation, IS has exerted an overwhelming influence on European jihadis.

European countries, in this respect, present their own history, and they differ from each other in many respects. Each country thus has its own history of jihad, and European jihadism is influenced by what happens in the Middle East, North Africa, Bangladesh, and Pakistan.[2]

European societies had not undergone major ruptures between the years 2000 and 2014, but the number of young people who became jihadi warriors, either internally (the so-called homegrown terrorists) or externally (the so-called Foreign Fighters) grew disproportionately between 2013 and 2016 in comparison to the pre-IS period. To give but an example, in France in the decade between the years 2000 and 2012, the number of jihadis has been estimated to be around 175 (Trévidic, 2013), whereas between 2013 and 2016, it was around 1,900 (including the Foreign Fighters who went to Syria), that is, divided by the number of years, several dozen times as many. In the same period, the number of those arrested in Europe for jihadi activities went up from 110 in 2009 to 718 in 2016, according to Europol (*EU Terrorism Situation and Trend Report* (TE-SAT), 2010 to 2017) due to the passion for the self-proclaimed caliphate that mesmerized young people, somehow in the same manner that the incipient Soviet Union appealed to those with left-wing leanings in 1917.

Global quantitative data on young people who left for Syria between 2013 and 2016 show their seduction by IS. According to a 2015 UN report, vocations to become Foreign Fighters increased sharply from a few thousand in the previous decade to around twenty-five thousand in the new period of just three years starting in mid-2013. The countries of origin of these Foreign Fighters were over one hundred, including those which had never sent candidates to jihadi networks. Between March 2014 and March 2015 callings increased by 71 percent (United Nations Security Council, 2015). It was mainly due to IS, which appealed to Islamic youth all over the world.

A key element was holding a territory as a state. It fundamentally changed the capacity of this jihadi organization. Following the declaration of the caliphate in June 2014, the group was able to dispose of financial means that were far superior to those of al-Qaeda or similar organizations. Their income came not only from the banks seized in Mosul but also from the sale of oil and arms, taxation, human trafficking (the Yazidis, a Kurdish group with a religion unrecognized by traditional Islam although tolerated before the seizure of their land by IS), the sale of archaeological artifacts, and particularly a rather efficient administration put in place after the conquest of a territory (Callimachi, 2018). Its hold on around ten million people allowed the new state to implement a diversified system of levies. Its financial resources grew rapidly, and IS became by far the richest terrorist organization in history. At its peak, its annual income was estimated at around $3 billion, which allowed it to finance thirty thousand Foreign Fighters. However, as of 2015 the group had lost a large share of its revenues, from $1.9 billion in 2014 to about $870 million in 2016 (Rasheed, 2016).

One essential characteristic of IS was its apocalyptic nature. The creation of the new caliphate in 2014 after a ninety-year interruption aroused new hopes in many parts of the Sunni world, traumatized by the failure of nationalism and pan-Arabism and eager to rekindle its lost glory. Even among the European Muslims, marked by the break with the Muslim countries, and living in a secular world, the caliphate raised the hope of ending the humiliation caused by the vicissitudes of modern history, and particularly the subaltern position of Muslim migrants in Europe.

The caliphate's goal was to conquer the world and to open new vistas for the end of time. It detailed its objectives in its magazine *Dabiq*, saying that it would continue to seize land and take over the entire world until its "Blessed flag . . . covers all eastern and western extents of the Earth, filling the world with the truth and justice of Islam and putting an end to the falsehood and tyranny of *jahiliyah* (state of ignorance of pre-Islamic times that is paramount in the modern world)" (Thomas, 2015).

In its history and ideology, IS had specific features that set it apart from the other states as well as the traditional caliphate. It was an apocalyptic state; it refused compromise with other governments in Muslim countries and was moved by an absolute urge to continue the struggle, in an attitude that would be qualified as suicidal for normal states. In all likelihood, if it had waived its hostility toward Saudi Arabia, the latter might have helped it build up the anti-Shiite front against Iran, Iraq, and the Hezbollah in Lebanon. But from the very beginning, IS declared war on the whole world, showing its total intransigence—even if it came to local agreements with those at war with it, like Assad's Syria, to whom it sold oil after it took over the Syrian oilfields (Hoffman, 2016).

IS organized an army made of Iraqi Sunnis and Foreign Fighters. The number of its militias increased between 2013 and 2015: from 11,000 to 13,000 in 2013, to several tens of thousands (between 20,000 and 100,000) in 2014, and from 30,000 to 125,000 in 2015 (Fontaine, 2015). The caliph Abu Bakr al-Baghdadi was seconded by a deputy, Abu Muslim al-Turkmani (who became the second caliph after al-Baghdadi's death under an American attack in October 2019) and a cabinet of seven "ministers," as well as six governors under the leadership of the deputy caliph and three persons who served as army leaders and defense ministers (Sherlock, 2014).

Its apocalyptic nature made it the implacable enemy of both the Shias and the Sunnis. In Afghanistan, it came into conflict with the Taliban, although ideologically it was close to them. In Syria, IS waged war against al-Qaeda and its Syrian branch al-Nusra Front, ideologically almost identical with them. In its perspective, only submission (*bay'ah*, allegiance) or war prevailed.

IS did everything to wage total war against the world, to the expense of its survival as a state, ensuring its own rejection by others, multiplying "suicidal" actions at the political and military levels. Self-annihilation in a half-conscious, half-unconscious attitude was considered a contribution to the acceleration of the end of time, fulfilling the urge to hasten it by pushing toward absolute intransigence in matters regarding faith. This attitude was politically different from the states emerging from a revolution (in Russia, China, Mexico, Iran, etc.) that looked for compromise in order to ensure their own survival.

b-The Appeal of Young Europeans to the Apocalyptic Vision of IS

The apocalyptic references were numerous in the propaganda of IS, which strongly motivated many young people to join it (McCants, 2015). But apocalypticism was not only manipulation toward the recruits, it was part of the IS vision of itself. The new caliphate was not poised to institutionalize, or even refused to do so. It could not "normalize" according to the model of other states (although it "normalized" its tax system in order to warrant funding for its Foreign Fighters and urban services in Syria and Iraq). This apocalyptic state had historical precedents in the Muslim world and in the fifteenth- and sixteenth-century European religious movements (among others, the Thomas Münzer peasant movement in Germany at the beginning of the sixteenth century); it was also a product of modernity, at war with a vision centered on the secular view that had been the contribution of Europe to the Islamic world's nationalist movements (in particular Arab, Turkish, and Persian nationalisms).

The new version of Islam implied the restriction of individual freedom in the name of the political hegemony of the new caliphate. On the other hand, this limitation of freedom found favorable ground among European youth who adhered to radical Islam. The urge to repress individual freedom did not come only from IS but also from many young Europeans who felt the prevailing boundless individualism and its freedom in many respects as a burden. They needed a "neo-Ummah" as a sacred group-reference against European secularism, and they needed an inflexible authority, the Islamic caliph, to force it on the unwilling. Contrary to the traditional Islamic Ummah, the imagined "neo-Ummah" was effervescent, marked by a totalitarian ambition to impose its view on everyone in the name of the purity of faith, whereas the traditional Muslim Ummah recognized ethnic, regional, and local differences (the groups went along with each other, like the Shiites and the Sunnis; even among different Shiite and Sunni branches, mutual understanding usually outweighed the differences). The neo-Ummah aimed at unifying the world under the aegis of the caliphate by means of jihad. It sought to de-individualize people in order to subject them to a higher law, beyond the person's reach, in the name of God. We call the aspiration to a sacred law beyond the free will of citizens "repressive transcendence." Jihadi repressive transcendence feeds on the exhaustion of modernist utopias.

The attraction of radical Islamic utopias promising revenge against inhospitable European societies pushed a tiny minority of these young people toward violent action in the name of Allah, in particular after the creation of IS that galvanized them in that sense. The secular and immanent ideas that did not change the world for the better gave way to transcendent and religious views that gained credibility, supernatural forces and "miracles" vindicating religious utopias for a significant number of people.[3] In their view, radical Islam would overcome injustice and poverty, but also punish the culprits, namely the secular Westerners and their accomplices, building new societies on the ruins of the old ones. The end of time became an attractive eschatological notion within jihadism. To take but an example, Jean-Louis Denis, a visionary convert, a champion of the end of time, sent more than a dozen young Belgians to Syria who were enthralled by his views. He founded a charity for the distribution of free food, calling it "restos du Tawhid" (The Tawhid Kitchen), Tawhid referring to God's Uniqueness, the first pillar of Islam), spreading among poor Muslims in Brussels the apocalyptic idea of the end of time according to the "white minaret" prophecy: Sham (the greater Syria including Lebanon and part of Iraq) would be the scene of the ultimate war between heretics and true believers in the final battle. The story was made even more attractive by introducing Jesus, who would intervene in Damascus in the white mosque where he would fight *Dajjal* (the Antichrist in the Islamic terminology, cherished by born-again

Muslims and converts, in search of mysterious words and picturesque images). Jesus would live seven years in peace and, at his death, the war between various communities would begin and end in chaos and massacres until the Last Judgment (Royen, 2015).

Exotic and millenarian representations combined in this narrative to fascinate young people seeking thrills, miracles, and a transcendent meaning beyond mundane human history. All those dimensions were missing in the secular view of the world that dominates European public opinion.

In the Muslim world, a new apocalyptic literary genre, called "apocalyptic fiction," has developed, using many elements of conspiracy theories, especially regarding the Jews and Christians, but also Freemasons and new religions such as Bahaism, Sudanese Mahdism, and Ahmadiyya in India. It differs from the traditional Islamic views of the end of time but borrows their terminology and narrative styles. The rise of this type of literature involves new Islamist intellectuals, and sometimes traditional scholars from Al-Azhar University in Cairo. We can distinguish two types of apocalyptic literature: one that integrates totalitarian and anti-Semitic tendencies inspired by Western authors and one based on sacred numerology and interpretations that inspire the traditional apocalypse (Filiu, 2008). The two tendencies could mix, referring to the figures of the Islamic antichrist (*Dajjal*) as well as to Gog and Magog (*Ya'jouj* and *Ma'jouj*). The saga of Jean-Louis Denis' "white minaret" was a popularization of this type of literature that has significantly developed in the Arab world since the trauma of the Six-Day War against Israel in 1967, the invasion of Iraq by the United States and the United Kingdom in 2003, and the crisis of the 2011 Arab uprisings. This literature joins the mythical stories developed in the movies such as the *Lord of the Rings* or *Star Wars* where a world dies in fire and blood and another one is born in its margin, marked by heroic figures who fight injustice and evil forces. It can be linked to the military action in the video games like Call of Duty, jihadis preparing for the Islamic Armageddon by organizing training sessions in the forests of Algeria or Tunisia, or socializing, as in France, in remote rural areas or in the public gardens as with the Buttes-Chaumont cell whose members used to run and do exercises in the Parisian namesake park.

IS assumed the transitional period between the time of injustice and that of absolute justice that would be realized at the end of time, when true Muslims would go to heaven and infidels, to hell.

In Europe, the apocalyptic edge of Daesh has to be related to the end of humiliation[4] among disaffected Muslim youth, as we can see in an interview made with a French-Moroccan in his late twenties or early thirties, in a poor district in Bondy in June 2016 whom I had already interviewed in 2012 in Fresnes Prison and who somehow trusted me:

Bachir: My life is between being bored and pissed off. From time to time I have troubles with the police or the justice for some theft or trafficking, and I find myself behind bars.

Question: How do you make sense of your life?

Bachir: Islam remains the only support I have in this world. I read Islamic books in this damned prison and I feel at peace.

Question: You mean Islam gives sense to your life?

Bachir: The only thing that can give sense to my life is a world turned upside down, a new order, Islamic. Sometimes people like me dream of joining IS, there they can build up a new life. But that means breaking with the family and friends here. Some from this area went there, some died. At least IS would change the world for the better, contrary to what the French media say.

Question: But they are violent and intolerant.

Bachir: Do you think the French are tolerant? Do you think European colonialists are tolerant? Look at me. They don't like me. They accept me only as an inferior, not an equal. It is so humiliating! Even the way they look at me or talk to me is humiliating! It is violent without physical pain, my body remains intact, but my mind is destroyed. Daesh kills fast, here they kill us slowly, bit by bit. I prefer quick violence to one for a lifetime. In Syria they have established an Islamic government, and they don't compromise with the West. That is their crime in the eyes of the Western governments, not the human right, which is a pretext. Otherwise why are they so close to Saudi Arabia? Its human right record is so bad! In my view, IS is building a new order, superior to here. In France the only thing that makes sense is to look for holidays, nothing is sacred except holidays! IS is an Islamic government that is just and harsh. It's its quality!

Question: But this new order is in bad shape. They are opposed to the rest of the world. On top of that, they are harsh and uncompromising.

Bachir: They announce the end of time. Our world is nearing its end. IS makes it clear. They are losing territory, but they know it. What makes me hopeful is that this world will end, and another will replace it. In it, Muslims won't be underdogs. The French are afraid of IS, like the West, but I am not. On the contrary, I would be happy with it.

The existing literature points to these two dimensions, humiliation on one hand, the eschatological hope, on the other. The feeling of a hopeless world through the daily experience of humiliation (disaffected youth) and lack of utopia (middle-class people) gives an anthropological clue to the attraction of the end-of-time vision, to occur via IS (McCants, 2015).

The messianic story has also been attractive to another category of people, teenagers who were seeking a short-term paradise. They sometimes converted in record time (from a week to a few months) and were deluded by the unlikely IS end-of-time story.

The usual themes were Life in "Sham" (Great Syria) as in an earthly paradise (2014–2015), the announcement of the imminent end of time there, entering heaven through martyrdom, and interceding with Allah for "unfaithful" relatives and friends who did not convert to Islam. These themes were reported by a teenage girl who had left for Syria in an e-mail she sent to her mother in France:

> *My dear Mummy, I want you to know that I love you as nobody loves their mother. It's because I love you that I left* [France]. *When you read these lines, I will be far away. I will be in the Promised Land, the Sham, in security. Because it is there that I must die in order to enter Heaven. And even if you are not a Muslim, I am well aware, I will be able to save you. God will not make me suffer, I'll feel nothing, and I will find you in Heaven. They promised me. You must just believe in God. If you convert, it will be easier. But if not, I will still be able to take you to Heaven. I know you will not understand, because you are not elected. But I had access to Truth. I was chosen and I was guided. So, I know what you don't know: we will all die, punished by the wrath of God. It's now the end of the world, my Mummy. We left too much misery, we left too many injustices . . . Palestine, Burma, Central Africa. . . . And all humans will end up in hell except those who fought with the last Imam in Sham, that is, except us. It will hurt you at the beginning, I know, it's hard for me too, it's very hard. But when we meet again in Heaven, you will thank me. You'll be proud that I saved both of us. Of course, I will also take Clemence, and Dad, although he does not help you much in the household. I will also take Grandpa and Grandma, and the cousins. I hope they'll behave in Heaven and not shame me. There, mum, I do not know when my time will come. In the meantime, I am going to look after the children wounded by Bashar al-Assad, since the world doesn't care. And then I will do what the Emir will tell me to do, because the last imam sent by God is one of these Emirs. You will*

> *understand later; you will thank me. But you know that nobody loves you like me. The proof, I'm here for you. Your Adele who is so eager to find you, my Mummy, I love you so much.* (Bouzar, 2015)

In this farewell we find the following points:

- She went to Sham, because she felt safe there: if she died there, she was certain to join heaven.
- She will intercede with God to save her mother, and her entire family from hell, since they did not convert to Islam. The desire to rebuild the family post-mortem and give it consistency and harmony (which is often lacking in real life in the modern family) is one of the concerns of born-again Muslims and converts, especially teenagers. Mostly living within fragile families, they long for stable relationships, which are often lacking in their family circles.
- She reverses the role of her parents: from being protected by them, she becomes their protectors. Usually, parents are supposed to know what is good for their children; in her case, she firmly believes that she knows better what is good for her mother and her family. She wants to save them from hellfire while her mother is unaware of it in her eyes.

  Jihadism provides an opportunity for teenagers to become imagined adults at the expense of their parents, who in a sense become sub-adults. This extends, in their view, to all adults for their supposed recklessness: by not embracing Islam, they act irresponsibly and are somehow stripped of their adult status, whereas they, as adolescents, by converting to Islam, are elevated to the status of hyper-adults.
- She owes, as a duty, obedience to the emir (the military leader in Syria within IS) because, according to the eschatological narrative to which she naively adheres, one of them will become the "last imam" sent by Allah (the Islamic Messiah).

The born-again Muslim or the convert feels invested with a sacred mission involving his relatives and, more largely, his friends and acquaintances. Salvation is collective: even if the family has not embraced Islam, the intercession of the young man or woman can save them from eternal damnation.

In the same vein, Andréa Soviéri went with her stepmother to Syria, to do *Hijra* (religious emigration to a Muslim land) and settle in the land of Islam. Her presence in Sham, she believed, would save her mother who had died of an overdose, having been in a state of mortal sin: in addition to not having converted to Islam, she had indulged in drugs, which is prohibited by Allah. Andréa wished to save her mother by her allegiance to Daesh.[5]

Proselyte zeal is the consequence of this eschatological vision in which salvation is conditional on conversion to Islam in its radical version. Jihadi zealots are convinced that embracing radical Islam saves them from hell, and their dying as martyrs redeems their disbelieving families. That is why they often sent their parents missives from Syria to convert or, at the very least, to give their blessing to their already accomplished departure. In some cases, though, young Muslims were doubtful whether they could save their parents if they refused to convert to Islam. Jean-Daniel Bons sent a letter to his father, after having gone to Syria with Nicolas, his older brother: "Dad, I came to Syria to do jihad with Nicolas. . . . We will not see each other again in this world, Daddy. But if you convert, we'll meet in heaven" (Bendavid and Byrka, 2014).

Unlike Jeanne, who thought she could save her non-Muslim parents from hell by committing herself to the way of Allah, Jean-Daniel believes that his becoming a martyr does not save his parents and divine mercy does not extend to them.

Bilal Hadfi refused to follow his mother who went to Syria to bring him back to France. Instead he called her to leave her "country of Infidels" and join him to participate in the development of the Islamic State. "If I come, it's to come and look for you," he retorted. "I'm afraid you'll die and go to hell because you live in the country of kuffars [miscreants]." These were his last words before he severed all ties with her ("Sa mère raconte sa descente aux enfers," 2015).

To the adolescents and post-adolescents, IS gave the ability to become imaginary pre-adults through a rite of passage marked by physical violence, through the suppression (beheadings) or intimidation of adults or its mimetic dimension (holding the cut-off head of prisoners before the cameras), encouraging them to embrace sacred death as martyrs or to inflict pains on Infidels.

As for the young girls, the promise of becoming a "real woman" drew them to IS: the new caliphate gave them the chance to become an "umm" (mother) as soon as they set foot in Syria, precocious pregnancy being the sign of their becoming grown-ups, contrary to the feminist ideals that pushed childbirth into the age of thirties. IS also used its apocalyptic ideology to encourage them to bear children, particularly males, who would die in the future as martyrs, in the same way as their husbands, hastening the end of time. The eschatological dimension made sense to many young men and women who were looking for a meaning to life beyond death, encompassing life and afterlife in a unified view of existence (late modernity has separated life and death into two disconnected realms). The apocalyptic dimension was good news, since the world would be destroyed. The end of the world thus put an end to the separation between life and death by opening the prospect of eternal life beyond this irredeemable world. The war initiated by IS against the Infidels became the first major step to put a redeeming global destruction in motion. The meaning of violence changed, therefore, from negative to positive in the hands of the caliphate. Once integrated into an apocalyptic imagination, the worst violence was absolved and young jihadis gave free rein to their worst impulses toward cruelty, being freed from the social taboos that made human life untouchable. Suffice it to mention the case of a young couple from Germany who let a nine-year-old Yazidi girl bought as a slave die of thirst, tied like a dog in the court of their house, insensitive to her plight because of the new IS standards justifying total violence toward disbelievers, who were treated as sub-humans ("German Female IS Recruit," 2018).

IS was a crucial moment in the re-enchantment of the world for the wannabe jihadis. It gave meaning and purpose to their aspiration to do away with a complicated and unjust world according to an apocalyptic vision that proposed a simplified and transparent narrative about its end. The latter also put an end to the anguishing leveling of life through a secularization devoid of utopia that denied meaning to death and only focused on the thin layer of life exposed to insecurity and, mostly, a future without promises. To the secularized ideologies that emancipated the people from the tutelage of coercive religious frames (but had been eroded since then), Daesh opposed a repressive neo-Ummah that enslaved the individual for the sake of his or her salvation, justifying the repression of those who found themselves outside it. At the same time, young European jihadis cheerfully accepted the constraints of the neo-Ummah as a proof of their belonging to a sacred community. Many young jihadis found the new life sound and judicious, adhering to a modern version of what the Renaissance thinker La Boëtie called the "self-willed servitude." They were tired of living in a world where freedom was painted grey and where lofty ideals had been eclipsed, experiencing an identity crisis that went hand in hand with an uncertain future, with no hope for the less gifted, a world also leveled by a lack of transcendence, a purely human world devoid of sacred meaning, on the edge of inhumanity. Their sense of belonging to a neo-Ummah went hand in hand with their renouncing personal freedom and dehumanizing those who did not embrace their repressive tenets.

Unlike the 1960s generation, who fought patriarchy to emancipate the individual, the new generation that Daesh endowed with a repressive utopia attempted to do away with a freedom that had become anguishing, owing to the lack of utopia and future perspective. The Islamic theocracy enforced a coercive patriarchy that reassured this generation because it offered to their imagination a family-like community. Within a framework that functioned as an enlarged family in the dream world of young men and women, IS played the role of a "superlative father" in close touch with the neo-Ummah, which embodied a "superlative mother."

With regard to Daesh's utopia, European societies were on the defensive. They could only denounce its repressive nature, not propose another imagined community, likely to divert young people from Daesh apocalyptic dystopia. As long as secular ideologies had a utopian content, they retained divine transcendence in a new shape: they promised to achieve an ideal society in an indefinite future, substituting for God. The Christian Beyond was thus replaced by a future, extended into an unlimited time. Against the background of the mundane world of late modernity, marked by selfish individualism, the caliphate made numerous promises, at odds with secular wisdom and individualist common sense: re-enchanting politics through violence (jihad), breaking from trivial everyday life through heroism and exoticism of a warrior version of Islam, challenging the down-to-earth realism of peaceful times with the romanticism of sacred death, reshaping the family by enforcing patriarchy in the name of Allah, and reinstating sacred standards in social relations by prohibiting free sexuality (homosexuality, sex outside marriage, etc.), alcohol consumption, and the mixing of men and women in the public space. The barriers put in place were designed to end the excesses of individualism and, more generally, social anomie.

As already mentioned, the caliphate was double-faced: on the government side, it promoted a divine political order, and on the community level, it fostered the neo-Ummah, a mythified organic community that provided the individual in distress with a legitimate identity, a sacred sense of belonging that would help him or her overcome loneliness by giving up an agonizing freedom. In order to assure certainty to an uncertain and destabilized individual at the price of his or her freedom, neo-Ummah promoted unambiguous standards imposed by the caliphate, drawing a clear-cut dividing line between what was prohibited and what was authorized, the *halal* and the *haram* (the licit and the illicit). This clear-cut dichotomy was sought after by a significant part of the European youth in disarray, for whom the existence of gray areas in their daily lives and the absence of a rigid divide between right and wrong was unbearable. They needed a sacred principle that prescribed binding guidelines for them, its injunctions having to be absolutely explicit and independent of their own judgment, which was tainted in their eyes by their inability to assume a burdensome freedom. Neo-Ummah imposed a "salvaging bigotry": tolerance was associated with the sluggishness of the modern, immoral society, marked by generalized inconsistency and fluidity (Bauman, 2003), a mental instability that was usually coupled with precarious employment, and an unremitting change (of profession, more and more random), subjective freedom being felt as a burden due to its lack of objective counterpart in real life. Henceforth "good intolerance" referred to a kind of peremptorily ordained morality that God condoned against a licentious and dissolute modernity, in which freedom, precariousness, and instability (mental and material) went hand in hand.

The jihadi spirit, reinvigorated by Daesh, dismissed doubt as a sign of disbelief: doubting was not allowed, the more so as it was coterminous with social debates and their endless and often futile dialogues of the deaf, unable to prove what is right and what is wrong. The neo-Ummah showed beyond doubt what was licit or illicit, excluding debate that usually leads to nowhere. It removed the doubt residing in almost every corner of the modern psyche by repudiating counterweighing arguments in the name of the transparency of God's commandments, whose sole legitimate interpreter was IS.

Neo-Ummah asserted its universality beyond the particularistic culture of each society, the universality of jihad overshadowing the differences between different Sunni doctrines (the four official Sunni Schools). As for Shiites, they were anathematized as fake Muslims, as "Hypocrites" (*munafiqun*) who introduced dissent and disorder within Islam and deserved death.

Neo-Ummah legitimized violence, which increased in return its appeal among those who longed for revenge among stigmatized Muslims in Europe. It reassured the jihadi community by dehumanizing those who did not share their credo. Jihadism joins totalitarian conceptions of otherness: the other is demonized. Under Daesh, neo-Ummah rejected miscreants (*kuffar*) and all those who did not follow its agonistic understanding of Islam. It managed to unify under its protective wing both the excluded migrants' sons and the converts from the middle-class youth, two different groups in their psychic structure and in their patterns of behavior. Under the jihadi rule, they lived together, in the same quarters, within the same brigades (*katiba*), under the same roof. If in everyday life in France or in the UK, these two groups regarded each other with suspicion, in Raqqa and other cities under the aegis of the caliphate, they lived in symbiosis. Two social groups, strangers to each other, were united by sharing the same faith. Class lines were thus blurred in reference to sacred violence and shared ideals.

The neo-Ummah emphasized the close links between honor, joy, and a feeling of catharsis. This trilogy, on which some of the IS propaganda focused, spoke to many young people of migrant backgrounds who felt "dishonored" by the contemptuous attitude of the "Whites" toward them. They were desperate in European societies in which they found no place. This facilitated their identification with IS and the effervescent community of the born-again Muslims through the joy of belonging to the neo-Ummah, which had a cathartic effect, allowing them to recover the lost dignity by becoming knights of Islam. As for the middle classes, faced with depression linked to the loss of the horizon of hope and fear of social downgrading, in addition to the loss of a sense of belonging (the anomie), jihad opened new vistas, opposing to the uncertainty of the future in Europe the certainty of redemption in Syria, through which they would enter paradise and find sexual fulfillment and eternal, affluent life. Daesh propaganda asserted: "The cure against depression is jihad. O my brothers! Come to jihad and experience the honor we experience. Feel the joy we feel" ("The Jihadi Cure for Depression? More Jihad!," 2014).

In summary, during its rise, the caliphate attracted four major categories of people. The first and most numerous were those young males who became knights of Islam in its service; the second was made of young women, whose role was to ensure its expansion by multiplying the number of their descendants; the third category was teenagers who were recognized as quasi-adults, their promotion on social media attracting more adolescents and retarded adolescents; the last category was those with mental problems, for whom joining the Islamic State was a catharsis.

At the core of jihadism in Europe is the feeling of rootlessness and humiliation among the migrants' offshoots and a sense of "no future" among lower-middle-class converts. In both groups, anomie pushed many of them to join national armies or the police in Europe (but they failed) before adhering to IS, in order to share a strong group identity.[6]

III
Subcultures of Humiliation and Counter-Humiliation

One can distinguish three types of subcultures within the poor districts in Europe: the Slum Subculture, the subculture of religious introversion, and the subculture of violent religious confrontation. They are all marked by humiliation and discontent.

Jihadism cannot be solely attributed to the disaffected young Muslims. A sizeable minority of jihadis are converts (from 8 percent to more than 20 percent, according to the European countries[1]), as well as middle-class Muslims. Nevertheless, male disaffected Muslim youth, mostly from the first and the second generations, living chiefly in ghettoized neighborhoods, represent the major part of the jihadis in Europe.[2]

a-European Slum Subculture Proper

Slum subculture proper is the stigmatization, humiliation, counter-humiliation, and mutual rejection between mainstream society and young people who belong to the slum subculture. The latter is not only the result of the development of social relations within a specific area but the consequence of an interaction between the global society and the group, the tension between the two being an integral part of this subculture. A slum subculture is by no means one of passivity or submission to a subaltern position in the global society. Within it there are ways of escaping from social domination, individually or in small groups (like the gang members who are a tiny part of residents in the district but a meaningful minority that acts as a role model for others). The ways to escape poverty within this subculture are real or imaginary, usually a combination of both. Still, what gives the individual a space of freedom does not fundamentally change the dominated status of the local residents. Participation in an underground economy gives financial means to a limited number of individuals who run it within the poor neighborhood,

Jihadism in Europe. Farhad Khosrokhavar, Oxford University Press. © Oxford University Press 2021.
DOI: 10.1093/oso/9780197564967.003.0003

but the others will more or less be its victims. Local mafias reinforce the bad reputation of the neighborhood as a deviant area and reduce the chances for the local people to find jobs, employers being suspicious of the residents of the district.

Slum subculture is marked by a type of discontent that often boils down to individualized bouts of violence or fights and riots but does not generally lead to lasting political constructions that are likely to change the fate of its members in the long term.

Slum subculture in Europe appears mainly in specific geographic settings, namely poor, ethnic districts or neighborhoods. It includes mostly male residents who feel stigmatized and marginalized as sons and grandsons of mostly Muslim migrants (sometimes, gypsies and the so-called White trash—White downgraded people—are included). Its main characteristics, as will be extensively analyzed, are humiliation, resentment, and coping with the latter through a vision of a "wounded honor," but also lack of communication with the mainstream culture. Young men in these neighborhoods confront the police, engage in delinquent activities, and often end up in prison as multiple offenders. This type of subculture finds outlets within the underground economy, with males confronting each other but also cooperating through local gangs. However, it is also marked by solidarities based not on the legal status of the individual but on his capacity to assist others, legally or illegally (mostly illegally). At the same time, this subculture is directed against the mainstream society and, in particular, its government: discontent and rejection point to a culprit that is society and its institutions, in particular the police, but also the judiciary and, more generally, all those who wear a uniform (including firefighters). Being rejected by mainstream society, the male members of this subculture reject it, in turn, frontally.

The slum subculture is marked by a desperate, ego-driven vision: those who share it feel like they are doomed to failure, having no future and facing closed doors within a society that denies them fairness and justice. They have a deeply pessimistic sense of social change and believe that it will evolve negatively rather than positively: the rules are set against them and they can only cope with this situation by acting illegally, especially through trafficking within an underground economy or by acting violently, through intimidating others.

Within this subculture, the dominant feeling toward the global society is not emotional neutrality but hatred. Hate is based on the impression that society is hostile to you, treats you as sub-human, and is marked by double standards through which "Whites" judge you on the basis of your origin and not your abilities. The prevailing feeling is that the game is rigged, and that society rejects your demand for fair treatment and social justice. A wounded subjectivity is at the root of slum subculture, based on the colonial and more generally Muslim origin of those who belong to it. Hyper-aggressivity on the part of its male youth is a result of this feeling that induces the inability to cope with the constraints of a modern economy and everyday life in society: regular working hours, control of one's frustrations without hurting others with one's attitude or derogatory remarks, acting in a neutral manner and not hyper-emotionally. These young people raise their voices at the slightest discontent, use words and phrasing considered vulgar by mainstream culture, behave threateningly toward others or in a manner perceived as such by the middle classes, and so on). Every constraint is interpreted as a sign of humiliating, unfair treatment by the "Whites," social bias against this youth contributing to a vicious circle of prejudice by mainstream society and counter-prejudice by them. Some people living in these poor districts escape this predicament, but they pay a heavy price for it: they have to constantly overcome social stereotyping against them, work more to earn less, and accept being often reminded of their origin in a derogatory manner.

In the poor ethnic districts of Europe, male residents have few choices: either express their anger through violence, engage in fundamentalist or radical Islam, accept being impacted by the collective prejudices against them but also endure the wrongdoings of disaffected and outlawed youths (e.g., stealing cars, making a mess at night), or move out of the "ghetto" in order to join middle classes through hard work. Those who remain in the poor neighborhood either become part of a small gang to make ends meet or remain poor with a little perspective of improving their standard of living, mainly benefiting from social welfare and occasional jobs, for instance in enterprises like Uber that transports people for a small monthly earnings and long working hours. On the whole, young people living in the poor, ethnic districts blame society for forsaking them in their plight and, on top of that, for stigmatizing them for their origin, their religion (Islam), and their residence in those neighborhoods with a bad reputation. Aggressivity and hatred are reactions to this stereotyping by others.

This subculture is also marked by its defects, of which the dwellers of the poor districts are keenly aware, namely, a profoundly deficient capacity to communicate with those belonging to the mainstream culture. These young people lack the linguistic tools but also the access to behavior patterns coded as "normal" by middle classes that would enable them to communicate with others, outside their community. School is the very place where these young people should acquire the codes of "normal conduct" in order to be able to come to terms with mainstream society, since their parents, who are foreign and of the working class, do not master French (sometimes they are even illiterate) and therefore cannot fulfill this role. For structural reasons, the school system fails to carry out this task.[3]

In Europe, these young people feel ashamed of their non-European roots. Instead of being proud of their origins in order to gain self-confidence and become future citizens ready to access the middle classes, they develop a sense of unworthiness that embitters them from the very beginning. Slum subculture is as much about internalizing humiliation as it is about reacting to it via attitudes deemed excessive and inappropriate by the mainstream culture. Immersed in it, they develop a provocative attitude against the "White society": over-gesticulation, shouting, aggressivity (both real and culturally coded as "normal" in their environment), a body language that is regarded as hostile and confrontational by outsiders, a language that uses coded verbal exchange, incomprehensible to the global society and understood as being a sign of their intellectual disability and their crookedness (the *argot des banlieues* or the "verlan" in French, the "Pakistani slang" in Britain, among others). Living in segregated areas, they develop a painful sense of being put in quarantine, segregated, and illegitimate. They lack the means of adequate communication with the larger society, particularly what can be called the implicit, non-verbal as well as the explicit, verbal means of communication in everyday life.

Internalizing a feeling of intense difference and inferiority, experiencing the inaccessibility of the mainstream society, and reacting to social stigmas with over-aggressiveness, a large part of this youth will not find a "decent" job: living in enclaved poor districts, they grow bitterly aware of their exclusion now and are convinced that it will be invariably their lot in the future. Without self-respect, they cannot develop empathy for others. In order to appreciate other people, they should appreciate themselves, but they have learned the opposite: they are not worthy of respect, and their parents' past as foreign workers is a liability (in German, *Gastarbeiter*, foreign worker, has become a derogatory word). By their abruptness and lack of sympathy for others, they contribute to their own rebuff by them, their attitude being regarded as anti-social and threatening.

Not mastering the codes of the dominant culture, the male residents belonging to the slum subculture internalize an attitude of revolt against their subaltern position. They believe they are denied the status of full citizens. In reaction to this denial, partly imagined, partly real, they become provocative, mishandle voluntarily elementary codes of behavior of the mainstream society by being "rude" toward the others, spitting, calling somebody they don't know well by his first name, or raising their voice inappropriately. This is a constant complaint against them in French prisons, not only by the guards and the "White" men, but also by the generation of their parents, among those North Africans who, by their easygoing attitudes, paradoxically handle the French cultural codes more adequately than these young people who are born, raised, and educated in France).[4] They internalize the breakdown in communication with others as they cannot even put their discomfort into words, lacking the proper language, not possessing the minimum vocabulary to express their feelings, particularly their being estranged and stigmatized. Violent action is in part the result of their inability to put into words their frustrations. In prison, some of them who passed diploma or read literature and became able to convey their sentiments were able to exert more control on their impulses, according to their own accounts and the guards who saw a real change of attitude in them following their success in the exams during their imprisonment.

Generally speaking, in European countries we find identical derogatory attitudes on both sides: on the side of the majority and on the side of those who belong to the slum subculture: these expressions denote mutual rejection, with a reinforcing action and reaction, building up a vicious circle. The vocabulary stresses the denial of real citizenship to the sons and grandsons of migrants: they are called in Sweden "non-ethnic Swedes," in Germany "Passdeutschen" (those who have a German passport—but are not genuine Germans), and, even more pejoratively in the UK, the "Pakis" (of Pakistani origin or, more broadly, Southeast Asians, with a strong deprecatory nuance); they are called "Perkers" in Denmark (with the same pejoration as the "Paki" in English) and "Moros" (Arabs), with a note of irony and depreciation, in Spain. In French, there are plenty of derogatory words to qualify the sons of North African migrants: "Arabs," "Bougnoules," "Picots," and more. The "Arabs" in turn call the French "Gaouris," "Roumi," "Kafir" (Infidel), "Céfran", and "Babtou," all pejorative or ironic expressions. Sometimes the internalized sense of unworthiness experienced by disaffected young Muslims causes them to refer to themselves ironically and disparagingly by the mainstream society's designation, such as the "scum" (*racaille*) and its vernacular *caillera* (the reverse of *racaille*: "stone").

Rejection by the majority and counter-rejection by migrants' sons and a deep sense of self-depreciation facilitated the espousal of radical Islam by some of them, since the premise of dehumanization was there. Daesh's utopia was essential for them to assert themselves in large numbers in opposition to society by overcoming their sense of indignity and inferiority.

The case of women in the slum subculture is different: they do not master the cultural codes of the mainstream society, but since they are in a subaltern position within the traditional Muslim culture, they do not develop an aggressive attitude toward others who deny them equality, and their lack of violence eases their integration into the mainstream society, the more so as they are regarded by the "Whites" as being victims of Muslim men. Mainstream people develop a paternalistic attitude toward these women, offering diffuse sympathy toward them and helping migrants' daughters to access more easily employment than their brothers.[5] They sometimes find jobs within the "ethnic business," and usually they are not frontal in their attitude toward the "Whites," unlike their male counterparts. What may call into question the favorable attitude of the mainstream society toward young Muslim women is the veil, and more generally, their Islamization in the slum's areas.

Another characteristic of the slum subculture is mistrust, primarily of the government and its institutions, but also of the people of the slum area. A French citizen of Algerian origin, in his mid-twenties, told me this in an interview in June 2018, in Belle-Fontaine, a poor district in Toulouse:

Question: You have no trust in the institutions of this country: the judiciary, the police, the school, the government. . . .

Nasser: It's true, I don't trust them at all. Not only that. I don't trust either the people in my own district, unless I know them personally. Life has taught me that I'm in a hostile world: if they can, others will harm you. There is no such thing as good people. Life has taught me to be constantly on my guard. The police are racist and seek to harm the Arabs, the judiciary has thrown me in jail, it is a jungle in this country and the only people I trust are my family and few friends.

Not trusting anyone adds to the hardship of living in a society where the fundamental affective category of togetherness among these young people is not neutrality or a positive view of others but mistrust and a deep suspicion that extends to the neighborhood itself.

Another feature of the European slum subculture is the ambivalent attitude of its male members toward sexuality. The young "Arab" is tempted to have sex not only with the "French girls," but also with the "Arab girls" a block away from his home. He flirts with them while acting violently against those male Arabs who would try to seduce his sister. A relationship based on assertiveness in sexuality and the transgression of Islamic norms about other people's sisters, but also the imposition of the very same norms (that he transgresses in his sexual drive on other Arab girls) on his own sisters, are at the heart of slum subculture, at least in the so-called Arab neighborhoods in France (in Great-Britain, this attitude is less frequent and traditional Islamic respect for women is probably more entrenched in the attitude of young Asian men). Sexual ambivalence is the essence of this dual system: my sisters should behave according to Islamic norms, whereas I myself, as a male Arab, do not respect the very same rules when it comes to those Arab girls who are not my sisters. This attitude is rooted in a narcissism based on the desire to magnify a male Self that is mistreated in the real world and reduced to insignificance. The "wounded" honor finds a leeway in one's arrogance toward the girls outside the family, whereas those within it are supposed to abide by the Islamic rules concerning women's modesty and sexual decency—of course, many of them do not play the game in this way and find boyfriends outside their district, out of the sight of their brothers, in the anonymity of the larger urban world. Still, social control over girls in the European shantytowns is still alive and well, and they become punching bugs in a society where young men bear the stigmas of their origin. By personally transgressing the Islamic sexual code of conduct, these young men are asserting themselves against a society that denies them the ability to act as independent individuals. By imposing the very same codes on their sisters, they attempt to preserve their male privileges within a patriarchal family in an Islamic community that is in crisis in Europe. But this attitude gives them the illusory feeling of their male superiority in a world where their sisters often do better in school and more easily find jobs outside their neighborhoods than they do.

Within the slum subculture, male youth ideal promotes patriarchal values, in part reasserting traditional Islamic values, in part in reaction to those of the mainstream society, predominantly based on egalitarian gender values.

Caught in the trap of social relations within the slum subculture, male residents of ghettoized European poor neighborhoods feel deeply humiliated by the mainstream society. They are overwhelmed, as they themselves call it, by their hatred of society. One young man in the town of Roubaix in northern France told me ironically in February 2020: "They don't like us; neither do we [like them]!" The overwhelming feeling among the "Arabs" is that the "French" don't like them or even hate them. In particular, they think that government agencies such as police, justice, administration in general, and even those intended to help them (like firemen) are actually against them. That is why, when they are able to extract an advantage that is rightfully theirs, they think they have scored a victory against an opponent who is fundamentally opposed to them. They see only one way of dealing with people belonging to the government (particularly the police, more generally the administration): to scare them. In reality, the alternative, from their point of view, is either to scare them or to be scared by them, usually both ways at the same time. Deep fear of the police and law enforcement officers and their arbitrary dealings with the "Arabs" goes hand in hand with the desire to scare the cop and, beyond that, to frighten the whole society. These young men are afraid to go out alone outside their neighborhoods, apprehensive of police forces that might mistreat or humiliate them, in France, as well as in Great Britain, concerning for example Black people (Greene, 2020).[6] That is why they usually go out in groups, which triggers the mechanism of fear among city dwellers who face a band of young, uninhibited, unruly people who outbid each other in acting aggressively, bragging, and shouting. This happens in part because of group dynamics: the competition to act more aggressively and a body language that is perceived by outsiders as threatening make them highly undesirable, even hated. In a vicious circle, mainstream society and these young people do everything to worsen their relationship based on mutual rebuffing rather than emotional neutrality, tension being likely to degenerate into violence, particularly when they face the police. Radical Islam can be metaphorically compared to a "definitive exit from society," whereas everyday life is a temporary and progressive exit through deviance, crime, and targeted violence. In this respect, jihadism operates as an accelerator of exit, making it irreversible through total violence. The exacerbated dialectic of "being scared" and/or "scaring" finds its final response in jihadism: through it dying and killing become the last acts of a drama of fear and counter-fear, killing being equivalent to radicalized scaring, dying expressing the capacity to overcome the feeling of fear through the promise of paradise and martyrdom. A young man of Moroccan origin, living in one of the poor districts of Gien called "Les Champs de la ville" in the department of Loiret, told me in an interview in September 2018:

> *Here we feel in a prison. We live in a cut-off district, far from the town: you need a car to go downtown. The bus is almost dead. We are not numerous* [around 300 families], *the Turks* [French citizens of Turkish origin] *are*

not friendly to us, the two mosques [one for the Turks, the other for the North Africans] *are worlds apart* [mentally].

Question: You told me that you deeply hate the cops ["flics"]. *Why so much hatred?*

Answer: They hate us! In front of a cop, either he spooks me, or I spook him, there is no other way around it. Few months ago, they arrested some of my mates, they were sentenced to light prison terms [less than a year]. *They sold drugs* [mainly hashish] *and they gathered close to the abandoned sport premise that was burnt years ago. . . .*

Question: The police arrested those who broke the public light bulbs so that during the night they could indulge in drug trafficking without being identified by the cameras!

Answer: The neighborhood is ours, and the cops should not enter! This is our home. This is the only place we're home. Outside it, we are interlopers, the cops look down their nose at us, we feel damned, they check us all the time. The Whites are not controlled, only us and the Blacks. We are afraid outside our district, the cops hate us, people don't like us, to say the least. To them we are outsiders, foreigners, non-French! We hate them too! We don't live in the same world; we have nothing in common. If they could, they would send me back to Morocco [where his parents came from], *but I have the citizenship, they cannot. What they can do is fuck with me, but I do the same, fuck them!*

In French prisons, the high proportion of North African inmates is beyond dispute, but it is legally forbidden to make official statistics of them, mainly due to the norms of *laïcité* (once a citizen, your origin should not be publicly investigated through official statistics). My guess, after many years of research, was that around half of the inmates were of North African origin, mostly from the so-called poor suburbs, which is a very high proportion, Muslims in France being between 6 percent and 8 percent of the population (5,720,000; Hackett, 2017). In the United Kingdom, where we dispose of official statistics, Muslim prisoners outnumber their proportion in society by a factor of three (Khosrokhavar, 2016). In 2012, Youssouf, a French-Algerian, on remand, imprisoned in Fresnes for armed robbery, told me:

Youssouf: This is the ninth time they've put me in slammer.

Question: How old are you, and when was the first time you were imprisoned?

Youssouf: I am 26. I first went to prison when I was 16. Practically every year I've spent a few months behind bars. Sometimes, the entire year! It is part of my job! It's like the risk businessmen take! Mine is going to jail.

Question: But what about your nationality? You said that you were not French.

Youssouf: I have the French passport but France is not my country, the French look at me as non-French, the Algerians too: when I go to Algeria, they find that I am privileged with my French passport and I can go everywhere, I have free Medicare, whereas they are stuck at the gates of Europe and have none of those advantages. . . .

Question: But you have the French passport, so you are French!

Youssouf: All this is blah, blah. Islam is my only "country." I don't feel at home here. Sometimes I take pleasure in scaring the shit out of the French. I live in one of those "cités" [poor districts] where there is no job besides trafficking. It is for an Arab the only way to tell the Whites to go to hell and live like rich guys. I refuse to follow my father's path. They exploited him [as an industrial worker]; they won't do that to me. I want to live like the rich guys, and I am ready to pay the price, and go to jail.

Question: As a Muslim don't you feel guilty?

Youssouf: Guilty? You are joking! As a Muslim they deny me my right to live according to my faith, my sister or my wife cannot wear freely the hijab [veil], I cannot put on a jellaba [traditional dress] in prison. . . . They were violent in the colonies, now they are violent with "Arabs" and I just pay them back in their own coin: they treated us badly, we treat them badly!

Question: What do you think about young people who become violent jihadis?

Youssouf: These young guys take their revenge against France who despises them. They become radicals for the sake of revenge! They put us in those filthy poor suburbs like animals, nobody cares about us, and we rot there. Then, we get involved in the "bizness" [trafficking, mainly drugs] and we end up in jail. This is our second home and we get used to it. Look at these White people [Frenchmen] who are sent to prison for the first time. They are so scared, we are not, we're even proud to be put in jail: spending some time here is a sign of seriousness, we earn our stripes. The big guys don't take seriously a young man without a prison stay in his bio! The Cité [poor suburb] is where I learned to be who I am, somebody who hates them, who knows that we are at war with them, but it's a hypocritical war and nobody dares to call a spade a spade.[7]

The other testimonies, less virulent, go in the same direction: those who live in the disadvantaged ethnic districts have a deep sense of being subaltern citizens, they feel constantly assaulted by the police and beyond that, by the government and its administration. Slum subculture increases mutual incomprehension, and people lock themselves in the slums because they think the doors are closed for them to the outside world, and communication is impossible with it (which is partly true, partly false: the doors are not as open for the Muslims as for the "Whites," but they are not entirely closed, a sizeable minority of "Arabs" having joined the middle classes). In reaction they become aggressive, pugnacious, and even bellicose. Jihadism is somehow the exacerbation of this tendency toward unruliness in a society that is regarded as unfair and deeply biased toward its "Arabs." Living in an enclaved urban settlement that looks like a ghetto, makes them reject others. When some of them succeed in joining the middle classes, they leave the district, the poor neighborhood losing those who might put into question the slum subculture, a phenomenon that also boosts segregation and stigmatization effects. What is astonishing is not that many jihadis in France (and, more generally, in Europe) came from the so-called poor districts; it is that there were not many more of them within these landlocked and ghettoized areas. Slum subculture plays an ambiguous role: it breeds hatred, but it also generates ways of containing it within these enclosed spaces by creating the capacity to "get out" through the trafficking of goods and drugs (the underground economy), but also by settling freely in this enclosed world which constantly oscillates between a confined space, like a prison, and a space of socialization, through codes, rites, and specific languages (Lepoutre, 1997), marked by mutual recognition, with a touch of conflict but also of mutual assistance.

Another feature of slum subculture is the dismissal of politics as a social action. Generally speaking, the inhabitants of these underprivileged neighborhoods do not believe that they can change their lot by casting their votes or by becoming involved in the democratic game. Local elections are sometimes taken into consideration because part of the neighborhood's people benefit from them in terms of employment or subsidies. But otherwise, politics is experienced as not only inaccessible but also undesirable. This view is also shared by part of the middle-class youth, but the difference lies in the fact that slum subculture is self-centered; it does not consider the possibility of change outside of it and therefore the "national" is discredited in favor of the "local," most of the time through clientelism or family ties.

One can mention the British case, which is likely to be generalized to many European countries. In 2009, an official report stressed the lack of political commitment by disaffected youth in the UK (*Understanding Muslim Ethnic Communities*, 2009). They found substitutes for political affiliation in radical movements. Disengagement was the result of a mistrust of politics, and, more deeply, its utter dismissal. These young people strongly believed that no real change could be made by entering the political game or by voting. This trait is found everywhere in Europe among young disaffected Muslims. It is, in fact, one of the factors that encourage deviance and criminality (as a personal solution to become "rich" through illegal shortcuts), which are closely linked to jihadism: the majority of jihadis had a criminal record (Basra, Neuman, and Brunner, 2016; Hecker, 2018).

In Europe, slum subculture is imbued with re-imagined colonial memory, even if, in several cases, colonialism did not actually occur, as in the case of the Moroccans in Belgium (they were not colonized by Belgium but mainly by France, and in part by Spain). Minorities of Algerian or Moroccan origin in France, or those of Bangladeshi or Pakistani origin in Britain, or of Black African origin in France and Britain, or of Indonesian origin in Holland, are marked by this sense of direct or indirect colonialism which, in their perspective, continued in another guise after independence, while their fathers migrated to Europe. This type of colonialism becomes visible through the contempt of "Whites" for "Greys" (Arabs) or Blacks in Europe. We call this phenomenon the "complex of the ex-colonial people," a feeling that has been re-imagined by the progenies of immigrants in Europe. This perception is all the more pervasive as many of them live in impoverished and segregated neighborhoods where they develop an intense sense of being landlocked like outcasts, of being colonized once again by "Whites."

Like all mental constructs, this victimization, in part real, in part imagined, entails a stiff reaction: often a tense and aggressive attitude that accentuates segregation and non-communication with the mainstream society in a vicious circle of dismissal and counter-dismissal. In view of the fact that Europe colonized a large part of the world, new forms of racism are often translated into a language reminiscent of colonialism by those who either were colonized or identify in an imagined manner to it. This can be compared to what has been called "internal colonialism" in Latin America after independence (Gonzales Casanova, 1963). The major difference between the two is that in Europe we are dealing with a population resulting from a recent immigration (around half a century ago), in a large part from the former colonies, which was not the case of "internal colonialism" in Latin America (the minority that migrated and colonized Latin America mixed with the population and has a dominant position, not a dominated one, as among most of the migrants' sons in Europe).

The main affect of the ex-colonial people is humiliation. They overdramatize this feeling and give it a tragic content (it becomes a stumbling block for developing a more neutral view of Self and Others). From the perspective of those living within poor districts and steeped in slum subculture, there is no way out. The colonial background, social stigmas, and their own sense of powerlessness and despair pushes them to an uncompromising attitude which reinforces the prejudice against them and in turn validates their assumption of an irrevocable predicament. In the enclaved neighborhoods where segregation is experienced as a life of pariah, the half-imagined, half-real feeling of continuity with the colonial past is overwhelmingly present. For a tiny minority, jihadism seemed an escape from humiliation and indignity when IS proposed them a life of glamor and pride.

In many respects, slum subculture in Europe bears similarities to the so-called culture of poverty in the United States. There are, nevertheless, major differences between them. Elijah Anderson's view on the "code of the street" in Philadelphia's Germantown avenue (Anderson, 1999) can be put in contrast to the poor subcultures in Europe. In the latter case, violence is directed inside but also outside the community. Of course, inside violence toward other residents of the poor district areas exists in Europe, but violence is also significant toward the "outsiders," the "White men," the French citizens regarded as neo-colonialists who impose their humiliating views on the sons of Muslim migrants relegated to poor quarters, and also toward the government agents.

Demands for assistance from the government are an important dimension of slum subculture in Europe. The government is as much hated in its agents and officials as it is called to the rescue by the local population. In the US, the federal government is often too far away to be the target of the residents' demands.

Right from the beginning (Lewis, 1959), the American perspective on the culture of poverty has been rather silent on government. In Europe, since the government is present through the welfare state in the poor urban areas, not only crime but also social protest and violent action is in part directed toward it, its agents, and its institutional presence through its buildings (police offices, social housing buildings, bus stops, voluntary associations centers that are subsidized by the municipalities, and the like).

Social housing in Europe plays a dual role: it reduces social poverty, but it contributes to the concentration of the poor not only in the same block but also in the same building. It also puts the government at the center of the claims of the inhabitants, in comparison to the US where social housing is marginal and the welfare state, less developed. Violence becomes visible through damaging the buildings belonging to the institutions where the very same poor people live. Their anger often shifts toward the government, due to its supposed insufficient support.

In France, social housing, social security for all, and a degraded but genuinely existing education for all alleviates poverty and, in part, influences the subculture of poverty in the poor neighborhoods and gives their residents more self-confidence about the legitimacy of their revolts (social justice is also a strong motto in French republicanism). Paradoxically, the "poor" are more prone to rise up in France than in America because they benefit more from welfare opportunities than their counterparts in the US and are therefore less poor than them. The government also offers them a pole of opposition through the ideology of *laïcité* that forbids scarves at government schools and in the public sector and makes illegitimate (although not illegal) showing religious insignia in public. Generally, in the United States the Federal Government is not as tangibly present at the local level as in most European countries (and particularly in France), and partly for this reason, it has not become a pole of frontal opposition by minorities. The more tolerant attitude toward religion in the US compared to France is another factor that mitigates religious radicalization there.

b-Subculture of Religious Introversion: Salafism and Tabligh

It is mainly through religion (especially Islam, but also, as a minority case, Pentecostalism) that some young men and women express their new attitudes. They break their symbolic ties with the secular society and join fundamentalist groups, mainly the Salafists and the Tablighis (Tabligh wal Da'wa). In doing so, they turn their backs on secular values of the mainstream society. Religion becomes a medium for the reversal of their values. We call it a subculture of religious introversion. In the slum subculture proper, the individual feels oppressed by society's denial of his dignity. In the subculture of religious introversion, sectarian ties transform non-participation in global society from a negative value into a positive one. They turn indignity into dignity by rejecting the dominant secular values that impose stigmas on them. Anomie is a major characteristic of the slum subculture. In the subculture of religious introversion, strong ties with the imagined Islamic community that we call "neo-Ummah" put an end to anomie. Unbridled sexual desire and difficult access to women are a source of frustration in the slum subculture proper.[8] In the new subculture, puritanical Islam makes the lack of access to that type of sexuality a positive value. From now on, the boundary between the group and society goes through the restriction of sexuality: it has to be religiously lawful and licit (*halal*). Believers of the new version of Islam reject the unrestrained appetite for sexuality that marks the slum subculture, for which sexual bulimia often replaces unattainable middle-class status. In slum subculture the young "Arab" is tempted by the sexual relationship not only with French but also with North African girls next to his block. At the same time, as we have already mentioned, he acts violently against North African males who would court his sister. Now, the rule is Islam, not the culture of honor, nor the Algerian or Moroccan habits and customs. Fundamentalist Islam puts an end to ambivalence in sexual matters. The young male "Arab" must submit to Islamic law. At the risk of a crisis in the family, his sister must also comply with the Islamic model of managing sexuality. She follows it more willingly because it is no longer the whims of her brother but a sacred principle, Islam, that governs her sexual behavior as well as that of her brother.

One should not lose sight of the fact that only a tiny minority of the disaffected youth joins jihadi movements. More and more, in poor districts of Europe, some of the marginalized young Muslims follow non-violent Salafism (called pietistic or scientific Salafism). As a specific subculture, it fosters a sense of community that is not set in violent opposition to others but results in sectarian attitudes that separate them from the mainstream society. In France, in several poor districts, Salafists have gained the upper hand, the municipality and its secular institutions having been more or less marginalized. They have succeeded in establishing a puritanical version of Islam based on the separation of men and women. The few "cafés" that are still open in that area do not serve alcohol; women do not go to them either. In these districts, "halal butchers" and "halal supermarkets" replace the old ones, women without veils becoming rare. . . . One pietistic Salafist living in La Reynerie, a poor migrant district of Toulouse, expressed his wishes in August 2017:

Question: What is your project?

Karim: My dream is to migrate to a Muslim country with my wife and child so that I can live according to Islam, do my daily prayers, avoid women who are "naked" [i.e., not veiled], *and raise my children far from the eyes of the Kuffar* [disbelievers, extensively applied to non-Muslims in a pejorative sense].

Question: What do you have against life in France?

Karim: In France, state-funded schools spreads kufr [disbelief], *boys and girls are mixed in a sinful way. They look at each other lewdly, in an illicit way* [haram]. *They are taught that God should not interfere in human affairs. Men and women are equal, polygamy is not allowed, daily prayer is not tolerated in public. My wish is to go to a Muslim country where haram* [illicit] *acts are forbidden and halal ones are allowed. Hegira* [*Hijra*, migration in conformity to the ideal model of the Prophet of Islam who went from Mecca to Medina] *is my wish.*

Question: You can't live according to Islam in France?

Karim: This society perverts my daughter, who is mixed with male children at school and does not differentiate the licit [halal] *and the illicit* [haram]. *My wife tries to protect herself against sin every minute when she goes out. TV, radio, media—they all spread sin. . . . We have a small community of true believers in this district, women do not go out unveiled, they do not go to the cafés. There aren't so many left anyway, one or two closed down, we have our halal stores and those who sell pork or alcohol have disappeared. We have our own TV satellite dishes, and I have forbidden my daughter to look at the French channels. We have a small community, but it is still far from perfect.*

Salafist identity is based on conspicuous dressing and "conspicuous non-consumption" behavior. Hardcore Salafists refuse the consumer society by rejecting TV, the amenities of modern life, namely pleasures and comforts in an open society and in particular, sexual freedom. For them, the repudiation of the secular way of life is not discreet, but ostentatious. Salafists assume a conspicuous attitude as *nouveaux pauvres* (newly poors), in the same way as the *nouveaux riches* display their wealth. In the name of their faith they reject dominant social values, be it gender mix or modern leisure. They embrace asceticism instead of hedonism, often try to sleep on the rough side (refusal of the bed) and use a piece of wood (*siwak*) as a toothbrush, in imitation of the Prophet of Islam. Their religious values are set against those of a society that promotes hedonism and secularism, Salafists exalting asceticism and anti-secularism as conspicuous signs of Islam, opposed to the Infidels. Among them prestige is acquired by conforming to the ideals of frugality. Since most of them are from lower classes, they have no choice but to be sparing, the difference residing in the fact that they assume it in a proud manner as stemming from their own initiative, instead of passively enduring poverty in private as a disgrace as people do in the slum subculture. Salafists are "prodigiously" frugal. They make deprivation the cornerstone of a way of life that is meant to be the opposite of that of the mainstream society.

Salafism is, in a large part, the religion of the poor and stigmatized people. It transforms deprivation into a standard for a pious life: living without TV, sleeping preferably on the ground like the Prophet, refusing to take part in a consumer society, rejecting what is already inaccessible (the comforts of the middle classes), making impure what is mostly out of reach, denouncing the turpitude of secular societies, and building up walls around the community in order to live in an alternative society with strict Islamic norms, among which are not smoking, not drinking alcohol, not having sexual relations outside marriage, marrying a member of the community rather than someone else, and developing exclusive social relations within the community. The *de facto* segregation of the poor ethnic districts becomes the *de jure* condition among Salafists who feel "elected" and lead a rather secluded life in conjunction with other fellow Salafists.

The so-called pietistic Salafism is in most cases an alternative to jihadism. It makes it possible to live at peace with a sinful society, the choice being made not to fight the Infidels but to exclude them from one's close contacts. Anti-secular attitudes are expressed through a way of dressing, conspicuously rejecting physical contact between men and women (e.g., a handshake), gender segregation and total veils (burqa, niqab, sometimes multiple veils) becoming a way of underlining their distinctive features against the heathen secular society that surrounds them. Still, in few cases, some of the future jihadis went through pietistic Salafism, their number being low, the path to jihadism being usually distinct from that of pietistic Salafism.

Salafists value life, which is worth living and is not marked by the aspiration for sacred death. This is the main difference between them and the jihadis. Radical Islam displays death as a conspicuous sign of Muslims' superiority over Western Infidels: not being afraid of death is an ostentatious manner of asserting one's belonging to a community based on faith, against a godless society. Both Salafism and jihadism display their otherness by exposing their new identity publicly: the former by stressing their belonging to a community of believers that rejects the values of the secular and consumer society, the latter by promoting death—a sacred death for God's Combatant (the *mujahid*, he who performs jihad), death and Hell for the Infidels. In this way they indulge in an over-consumption of death instead of opting for a consumer's life.

Both radical Islam and pietistic Salafism provide a bond between their members who are at loggerheads with the mainstream society, the first through violence, the second by creating an enclave fostering a distinct subculture that raises a wall between them and the majority.

In their majority, jihadis are prone to neglect the ritualistic dimensions of Islam. Their death washes their sins at the service of God. In their eyes, their transgression of the religious standards is a minor sin in regard to the major act of dying as martyrs for the sake of Islam. Salafists, on the contrary, are eager to live in this world, and therefore, their distinctive feature is their puritanical attitude within a sectarian version of Islam in which they meticulously observe the ritualistic aspects of religion. Jihadis are usually the more relaxed toward religious prohibitions as they end up sacrificing their lives for Islam's sake (some young people partied before their departure to the front lines or attacks in Europe, consuming alcohol and even dancing and flirting with young girls). The acceptance of holy death frees, in a way, the wannabe martyr from the constraints of orthodox Islam.

Pietistic Salafists and jihadis do not usually mix in spite of their ideological proximity. They are mostly distinct, and jihadi paths are distinct from the pietistic ones. In some rare cases, pietistic Salafism ended up in jihadism. Adam Lotfi Djaziri, the perpetrator of the attack in the Champs-Elysées avenue in Paris on June 19, 2017, was a member of a Salafist group. The son of a Tunisian father, Mohamed Djaziri, and a Polish mother, Edfij Paflantic, he was born in 1985 in Argenteuil in a northwestern Paris suburb.

He was the father of four children and belonged to a Salafist group, in which members followed a rigorous version of Islam. Before ramming his car into a van of gendarmes, he pledged allegiance to IS in a letter sent to his brother-in-law. He was the target of an Interpol research file issued at the request of Tunisia in 2013. He had been on the French police security watchlist (fichier S) since 2015 for his links with radical Muslims. In 2015, he traveled to Turkey with his family. As a gold merchant, he professionally justified his stay there while getting in touch with IS members. The family lived in isolation, solidarity between its members tightly woven because of their religious rigorism. This family model is in contrast with that of a large majority of jihadis in France where de-Islamization is often in an advanced stage, especially in the so-called poor suburbs. Family solidarity is strong in this type of fundamentalist family, again unlike most of the jihadi families in the disadvantaged districts, fraught with internal dissent and violence. Djaziri's father works in the pharmaceutical industry and his mother is a nurse, both middle-class. With a clean criminal record, Djaziri's trajectory was distinct from most of the young jihadis of the poor districts in Europe who usually have a heavy criminal record.

c-Subculture of Violent Religious Confrontation: Jihadism

Jihadism represents a subculture of absolute violence in the name of radical Islam. It targets not only specific persons but groups, and beyond them, the entire society, moreover, the entire world. Its scope is not the district where the individual lives (that would be, for instance, the case of gang violence within a slum subculture). Group solidarity in this subculture is not defined in terms of spatial proximity but via what we call a neo-Ummah, marked by its imaginary character and its universality. This subculture transforms individual's "unruliness" into universal transgression, legitimized by radical Islam. It reverses the major vectors of everyday life within the poor districts:

- From inferior (he is stigmatized and poor) the young man becomes superior (he is a believer, the others being Infidels).
- From judged and condemned by the judiciary to judging and condemning others through the verdict of radical Islam.
- From restricting oneself to the geographic limits of the local community to a boundless Islam that declares war on society and beyond it, on the world.
- From "nobody" to a prominent person scaring the others through violent action.

Jihadism transforms indignity into pride among those people who share the slum subculture.

In a slum subculture, violence is allowed at the individual level for personal or collective gains (small gangs or antagonistic groups who defend their turf against others or, simply, who fight for their honor against those who belong to other districts or towns). Stigmas are internalized and occasionally can erupt and result in violent action against those considered as outsiders. The motives for violence are non-ideological, non-religious. Violence generally results in the quest for prestige, in disputes against rival groups or the police, or in festive occasions (like burning cars on Christmas in poor districts in Eastern France). It has also its root causes in attempts at earning money in an underground economy, or for symbolic prestige among those seeking status.

In a subculture of religious introversion, mostly represented by Salafism or Tabligh wal Da'wa, violence is mostly symbolic, rarely real. The group seeks to achieve its domination over a neighborhood, or a geographic area within a poor district, and organizes not only religious sectarianism but also sometimes a parallel economy based on religious ties among the group members. Salafism rejects mainstream society and its values, replacing the ideal of a secular society with puritanical Islam that reshapes social norms in a nonviolent opposition to the secular ones. Salafism can go hand in hand with an underground economy, justifying its attitude by the fact that living among "Infidels" allows Muslims to act in ways that would have been forbidden within a genuinely Muslim Ummah.

In the subculture of religious violence, contrary to Salafism, violence in the name of jihad becomes the central means to achieve sacred values, martyrdom being regarded as the highest ideal. A radical attitude that makes compromise with the mainstream society impossible prevails in the minds of radicalized Muslims. In contrast to slum subculture, violence is not mainly instrumental; it is not promoted for personal gain but aims at achieving the goals of an imagined neo-Ummah that transcend particular interests. Ideology in its rudimentary theological form, inspired by hatred of society, is the justification for this antagonizing attitude in the name of a holy total war against Infidels.

As already mentioned, within the poor districts in Europe one finds not a single subculture, but at least three. The tie between the second and the third is Islam but it is not the same version. They are ideologically close to each other but they differ in their relationship to violence. Within a subculture of religious introversion, violence should be avoided, and the withdrawal into a sectarian introvert group is a means of escaping contamination by the larger society. Jihadism is a subculture of resentment in that it does not only intend to end social stigmas but also imposes reverse stigmas on others. What the jihadis seek is not to gain status outside the slum subculture, but to break out of it through violence in order to build a new, enlarged community in which they would become the elite (the neo-Ummah). Bearing in mind this imagined community, they do not hesitate to eliminate those who do not share their vision. Death is dual: holy death for the jihadi who dies for his faith and damning death for the Infidels who oppose the message of God. In addition to building a religious world on the ruins of the secular one, jihadis intend to end their disarray in the face of a meaningless life by embracing a meaningful death through martyrdom. A major reversal through religion takes place in their minds: the change of a meaningless secular life into a meaningful holy death by means of an Afterlife in which the martyrs will be redeemed by God. Honor, reputation, and status that play a major role in the notion of disputatiousness (Wolfgang and Ferracuti, 1967) within the culture of poverty and honor (close to the slum subculture) are reversed through holy death: self-realization occurs not in this world but beyond and above it, in an imagined afterlife that gives sense to the key notions of the Last Judgment and Heaven. Jihadism is a new religiosity based on a radical change of attitude toward death in the twentieth and twenty-first centuries.

Contrary to common sense, although the ties between the Salafist and jihadi subcultures are ideologically strong, they present major differences in terms of involvement in violence. The path to jihadism is usually distinct and some of those belonging to the slum subculture join the jihadi one, but those of the Salafist subculture are usually quietist and generally do not join the jihadis.[9]

Jihadi as well as Salafist introvert subcultures make substantive changes to slum subculture by adding religious values to it. They break off ties of "disputatiousness" (fight for the status within the group) by enlarging it far beyond the district.

Slum subculture is mainly imposed by the mainstream society. It is based on adjusting to segregation, economic exclusion, and stigmatization (even by revolting against it). Salafist and jihadi subcultures have an undeniable voluntary dimension. To begin with, their members take the initiative to join them. In slum subculture, people are somehow acted upon; they react to stigma in a way that deepens the domination effect upon them. In Salafist and jihadi subcultures, members become agents; they opt for voluntary segregation (Salafist subculture) or utter violence (jihadi subculture) in order to put into question their status within the slum subculture. Salafist and jihadi subcultures express a change of scale and meaning: society is declared illegitimate and the means to achieve the group's ends is not primarily motivated by personal gain, self-esteem being achieved through a new religious subjectivity. The latter is based on a counter-secular view expressed through Islam, a religion regarded as alien to the Western civilization by a large part of European citizens. It is precisely this dimension that makes it attractive to disaffected youth: appealingly religious because it is counter-secular, viewed as violent in the name of God in reaction to stigmatization, and because it embodies counter-values to the dominant non-violent European culture. Through it the members of the neo-Ummah join a counter-European imagined community that puts religion at the center of the individual's personal and social life.

Slum subculture bears the imprint of the urban ghetto: it accentuates the closure and segregation imposed by society on the poor, ethnicized districts. This subculture makes the neighborhood look like a place of confinement where residents are on the verge of suffocation but also where they feel secure, protected by friends and gang members as well as by the architecture of the buildings where they can hide from the police or confront it. The introvert Salafist or Tablighi subculture turns the imposed closure and segregation into a self-imposed, voluntary one. People felt separated from the mainstream society through a barrier imposed on them by the latter that made them suffer. They felt as if they were victims of social injustice. Now, within the Salafist or Tablighi community, they ask for this barrier, to prove their religious authenticity in front of a society made of Infidels. In brief, what used to be a compulsion becomes an aspiration. But both slum and Salafist subcultures share the characteristic of not being systematically violent. In contrast to them, jihadi subculture makes violence its main hallmark. It also breaks away from the closure, imposed (slum subculture) or claimed (Salafist subculture), and opens the way to an open-ended community that intends to include the entire world, led by a religious leader, the caliph. Opposition to the society becomes radical and violent; it denies legitimacy to it and declares war in the name of a radicalized Islam.

While quietist Salafists confine themselves to living their faith, mostly in the segregated space of European shantytowns, jihadis break down the spatial enclosure and open up a new space, marked by absolute violence. This is the only way, according to them, to end the ghetto life and its confinement, this time in the name of a liberating religiosity that emancipates them but enslaves others to its repressive rules.

Islam becomes the bearer of a new identity that declares war on secular society, not only because of the hatred accumulated during the years living in the "ghetto," but also for the sake of a new utopia that changes the mindset of the born-again Muslim, even if he belongs to the middle classes and did not hate the mainstream society before joining the ranks of jihadists. Jihadism breaks down mental barriers that enclose the poor, ethnicized district residents in the slum subculture. It opens the way toward a new identity at war not only with the local, but also national authorities, and beyond that, the world. A repressive utopia based on the counter-values of secular society takes away the individual from the specific urban setting where he felt confined and puts him into an imagined open community (the jihadi neo-Ummah) where he pledges allegiance to the caliph and declares war on a society to which he was ascribed without a sense of belonging. Violence is legitimized this time not in the name of one's position within the gang or in opposition to the police but in reference to a religious view that makes impossible compromise with a secular society.

In the European poor districts, the question of the "sense of community" (Cantillon, Davidson, and Schweitzer, 2003) is a major one. When it comes to the slum subculture, it is a sense of distorted community that prevails, in which solidarity ties are not working properly. For instance, the Algerian and Moroccan communities lack strong bonds; they are usually tied together by negative feelings toward the "Whites," namely despair or resentment, rather than positive ones that would enable them to cooperate closely in business as do the Turkish, "Chinese," or Portuguese communities who enjoy strong ties that bind their members together. The notion of slum subculture does not apply in general to the Turks in Europe: they act cohesively toward each other (sometimes they exploit each other) and try to build up a better future, without being beset by the feeling that all the doors are closed and only through transgression of the law can one succeed, which is one of the distinctive features of the slum subculture. The latter mainly concerns North Africans in France, and Pakistanis, Bangladeshis, or Black Africans in Great Britain. Due to the lack of strong links within their communities, some young people shift toward the Salafist or jihadi subcultures as an alternative to the defective community in which they live. Missing strong community ties, sons of North Africans or of Bangladeshis or Pakistanis[10] look for an alternative community, respectively the Salafist and the jihadi, both marked by an imaginary construction of a new community in religious terms, the neo-Ummah. The community within the slum subculture areas is mostly disorganized or in bad shape. Looking for another type of community is a largely shared attitude among the youth in these neighborhoods. Of course, mothers, and sometimes social workers, try to promote new cooperation within these districts in order to alleviate social disorganization, but on the whole, the change in the attitude of the new generations, in particular toward Islamic communities that are notably different from the prevailing ones, is a sign of exhaustion among those communities. They look beyond, adopting a religious horizon that is unfriendly or even antagonistic toward the secular trends within European societies, but also critical toward the ethnic communities to which they belonged.

The dream of a brotherly society with strict norms respected by everyone (the neo-Ummah) is totally at odds with everyday life of these young people within the slum subculture. That is why a fraternal community where people are united in the name of an idealized Islam is such a strong motive among them. It was one of the reasons for their departure to Syria to join the new caliphate where the new ties were to be built.

More generally, jihadism, this "Islam of rupture," is based on the invention of an identity that breaks all ties with the surrounding world and opts for a dream-like community, devoid of the evils of mistrust and fear, made of authentic and pious Muslims who are at war with those who do not share their view. They refuse to endorse French, English, or German identities—on the contrary, they feel anti-French, anti-English, anti-German; nor are they Arabs, Pakistanis, or Turks, being in denial of their parents' identities that were traditionalist, quietist, and passive in their eyes. Identifying with Daesh, they aspire to be exclusively Muslim, nothing else, at war with others. But a minority also come from the middle classes and their attitudes change into an agonistic religious view after they reach Syria and espouse Daesh's views.

In the United Kingdom, Javed, from Derby, had the same view as his French counterparts. He was jailed for six years in 2007 after he called for the murder of American and Danish people at a demonstration in London against cartoons depicting the Prophet Mohammed in an insulting manner:

> *I was born in this country, I went to nursery, infant, and secondary school, college and then university in this country. But am I British? Absolutely not. I am a Muslim first and foremost. We will never be accepted by the Kufr* [Disbelievers] *so we should never pander to their whims or support their actions like some so-called Muslims have been doing.* (Bracchi, 2017)

A British jihadi, Siddhartha Dhar, expressed the same view, declaring himself a Muslim to the exclusion of any other belonging:

> *[I don't] . . . really identify myself with British values. I am Muslim first, second and last.* (Casciani, 2016)

An Algerian in Fresnes prison close to Paris, interviewed in March 2013, uttered the very same view:

Question: Can you give me your bio?
Mahmood: I am of Algerian origin.
Question: How do you define your identity: French, Algerian, or Muslim, or all of them at the same time?
Mahmood: I don't care about being French or Algerian. I am neither French, nor Algerian, I am a Muslim; this is my true identity.
Question: But your parents were Algerians and you have a French passport!
Mahmood: You know, in my life, I never felt French. Nobody accepts me as French. To the administration I am an unruly kid from the slums [*cités*]. *They think I'm Algerian rather than French. And many young men like me waved the Algerian flag during the football matches between Algeria and France, not because they felt Algerian, but to piss off the French, otherwise they aren't Algerians: when they go to their parents' town* [*bled*] *in Algeria, they don't understand people there, they don't speak their language, they feel ashamed, they discover they are neither French nor Algerian. Islam is our only bond to a meaningful world.*

Islam becomes an exclusive identity, neither that of one's parents nor that of where one was born or educated. Radical Islam is the empowerment of those who have been denied belonging to the country where they lived by the "White" majority, in their view. Through it a transgressive Self adopts an arrogant view of others (they are *kuffar* [Infidels]) for having himself suffered from their "arrogant" attitudes. Its arrogance is in a large measure a counter-arrogance, but it goes beyond it by denying humanity to them through radical Islam.

d-From Negotiated Recognition in Life to Forced Recognition in Death

Intense, internalized feelings of unworthiness and yearning to live in a provocative manner made these young men seek not legitimate recognition (inaccessible in their eyes) but illegitimate recognition, in the dialectic of recognition and its denial, whose theory was initiated by Hegel and further developed by contemporary social scientists (Honneth, 2000, 2007). They therefore longed to become, not "positive heroes," admired by the mainstream society, but "negative heroes," hated and yet glorified all the same by the media who assure their universal ill fame (fame all the same, in their eyes), based on their monstrosity and their superlative violence (Khosrokhavar, Le nouveau Jihad en Occident 2018). IS provided them with a positive appraisal of their attitude by legitimizing it through radical Islam. Their attitude was also that of a double denial: not only the West was rejected, but also the Muslim world. The first was where they felt not at home, having been treated as unwelcome foreigners by the mainstream society. The second was where they parents came from, where they were also frowned upon as non-Algerians in Algeria and non-Pakistanis in Pakistan. In general, Jihadi identity antagonizes the entire world besides the only place they felt at home, the Islamic State in Syria and Iraq, a pariah country they glorified because of its outcast nature that was a harbinger of the end of times. There, they felt a sense of belonging because IS rejected the West and the East, this double dismissal corresponding to their "wounded" identity based on neither here nor there (neither French nor "Arab," neither English nor "Pakistani," or, for Black converts, neither British nor Jamaican).

For them, their status as a negative hero was a token of their recognition, through fear and trembling, by the same societies that had previously despised them. From then on, they proceeded in an active rather than passive manner. Daesh transformed passivity into activity, the contempt suffered by their ego into the fear instilled in others, their undignified insignificance into a proud notoriety (negative fame) through terrorist acts that pushed them to the forefront of the world media. The recognition they were looking for was reversed: since they could not be recognized for good, they should be acknowledged as evil in the eyes of the "Whites" whom they regarded as heathens, terrifying them instead of inspiring admiration, by breaking off with non-violence, the dominant value in mainstream Europe.

The jihadi "negative hero" invented, so to speak, a new configuration in the dialectic of recognition and denial: as he was refused recognition as a genuine citizen by the mainstream society, he did his utmost to achieve recognition through monstrous acts and espousing the opposite of non-violent values of the mainstream society. A key feature of his negative attempt at recognition was inspiring dread instead of wonder, wishing to be noticed by excessive manners whose surfeit denoted the will to break social standards and widen the gap vis-à-vis the mainstream society through heightened hatred. The emergence of Daesh bolstered the wish to become a negative hero and a hated though feared terrorist, which provided a positive recognition of these negative values within a new country. The caliphate legitimized them.

Another trait of the jihadi's will to negative recognition that was bolstered by Daesh was stressing and exhibiting the irreconcilable antagonism between him and the others, pushed to the extreme: only death would be the intermediary, nothing in life bridging the gap between him and those representing mainstream society. Sacred death in front of a secular society for which life is the ultimate value makes up the complexity of this type of "recognition coerced on others": the refusal to be recognized unless the others totally abdicate, leaving no room for compromise or even negotiation. The negative hero forced others to recognize him as the embodiment of their counter-values and, on top of it, imposed death on them as an illustration of those death-centered values. Radicalization, in this situation, denotes denial of the shared bonds with society, a desire to live in a totally different world, Islam becoming the icon for this "absolute otherness." Attempts at recognition are customarily based on the will to find a common denominator by forcing the adversary to an "honorable" compromise via threat or violence. Jihadism is the denial of any bonds with others who become arch-enemies. The only bond is that of total submission, put into practice by Daesh worldwide.

In the dialectic of recognition, jihadis embody a particular figure: they refuse to recognize the adversary as a partner in future negotiations and intend to carry the war through to the end, including the death of Self and Others. This contradicts the figure of master and slave as described by Hegel in his famous *Phenomenology of Spirit*. According to him, the slave pushes to death and the master abdicates so as not to die. In jihadism, the combatant of faith rejects all agreements, war is that which goes to the end, to the death of oneself and of the other via an apocalyptic attitude for which the end of times is paramount. Peace is not on the agenda, the values of agonistic death replacing those of peaceful life in the name of an eschatological future without concession to the world of life here below.

Jihadism introduces a high dose of pride in the soul of a youth that thinks dignity can be achieved only by oppressing the majority, in retaliation against their being mistreated as descendants of the former subaltern humanity. They focus on sacred death (martyrdom) as a means for being recognized in their superiority (whereas in everyday life they suffer from a feeling of deep inferiority).

Their exposure to deadly dangers in the war zones in Syria flattered their wounded egos (they henceforth considered as inferior those citizens who avoided danger). In 2013, in Fresnes Prison, a French-Moroccan man, probably in his late twenties, jailed for a hashish-smuggling operation of over a ton between France and Morocco, deeply marked by the stigmas of his origins, expressed his ideas in an indirect manner:

Mohammad: As my mate said, they humiliate us, put us in a hole in these poor housing estates [HLM], *separate us from the rest of the population, put us in prison, look down on us, think we have no pride. . . . But Islam gives us pride. That scares them. They fear death—we don't. We rely on Islam, they are afraid of us; they no longer despise us, they believe we are reckless and violent. We know where we're going, and after death we go directly to heaven while they go to hell!*

Question: Can you tell me when you became aware for the first time of humiliation as something unbearable?

Mohammad: I was young, around 16 to 17 years; I was not a genuine Muslim at that time; I didn't do my daily prayers; I drank beer and sometimes even more: I took booze and smoked pot. I did like the White boys. One night I decided to go to a nightclub. I took a shower, put on my best clothes, combed my hair. I wanted to have some fun. The White kid in front of me got in, but when it was my turn, the security guard did not let me in. The irony is that the bouncer was himself an "Arab." He was a big man and they had given him that job. He didn't tell me, but he was told not to let "Arabs" in. An Arab would be embarrassing to others. I drew two conclusions: first that Arabs are good only to get inferior jobs like the bouncer or the unskilled worker, and second, when it comes to sharing the rights, they deny them to the Arabs because they are inferior to others [entry to a nightclub being one of them]. *They denied me access to white girls. That was for me a breaking point. Laïcité and Republic* [republicanism] *that promised equality were dead. Another chapter of my life had opened.*

Question: Was it the first time you experienced injustice?
Mohammad: Of course, it wasn't the first time I'd been discriminated against, but this time it was too much.

Another young Muslim from Seine-Saint-Denis stressed his sexual frustration as a denial of equality (interview in April 2017):

Ali: Either you find a job outside your neighborhood and there you go out with non-Muslim girls, or if you go out with a Muslim girl, you have to marry her! Women have become stricter in the name of Islam nowadays. Outside, there are few nightclubs, and usually, they find excuses not to let you in. As an "Arab," they don't want you, because they are racist.
Question: But don't they behave sometimes in an unruly way?
Ali: Arabs are not always behaving well. But they are crazy because the others drive them crazy! In twenty-first-century France, I'm having trouble finding girlfriends. . . .
Question: Does it lead to radicalization?
Ali: It adds to the frustrations: they pile up. My guess is that some radicalized Muslims had this type of experience.

Through Islamization the individual recovered the lost pride, reacting to the denials (in this case, the right to get into the nightclub) by avoiding nightclubs. A secular society that refuses access to free sexual life (the nightclub) to the sons of migrants faces fundamentalism (Islam forbidding nightclubs) or jihadism (Islam fighting against Infidels who allow nightclubs) in the name of anti-secular values (jihadism and Salafism are prominent anti-secular creeds), denying thus legitimacy to secularism. Extremist and fundamentalist versions of Islam seduce sons of Muslims as an "anti-secular" way of living provocatively against a hypocritically secular society that denies them access to free sexuality under the pretext of their unruliness (which is sometimes real). Here too, the imaginary dimension plays a major role in the dilemmas the "Arabs" are facing in front of those who seek to protect themselves against their "excesses," be it in reference to sexuality or other issues related to their encounter.

In fact, in many poor districts in France and more generally in Europe, the opportunity to meet girls is shrinking. Three decades ago, there were around 4,000 nightclubs in France. Their number shrank to around 2,200 in 2014 ("

Les discothèques perdent du terrain en France," 2014). And when it comes to letting in "grey youth" (*gris*, people of North African origin), right or wrong reasons abound to refuse them entry: besides racial prejudices their attitude toward the girls is regarded as aggressive by the latter in the nightclubs. When it comes to the Muslim girls, they either try to find their boyfriends outside the district among the non-immigrants (in France), or their families arrange their marriages, but not so many meet in nightclubs. The access to girls has in this way become more complicated than before for those who do not relate through the web. Mohamed Merah[11] had sexual problems related to the access to the girls and had turbulent relations with prostitutes. Chérif Chekatt, according to an officer (with whom he engaged in informal talk during an exchange in Strasbourg few days after his attacks in December 2018) also suffered from sexual problems.

In another case, in prison, I met a young man, in his early thirties, of Pakistani origin, imprisoned for jihadi activities, who candidly revealed that he was a virgin and that the society of men was for him a substitute to his sexual problems (February 2013, Fresnes Prison). The family intended to find him a spouse but due to his legal troubles (he had been involved in trafficking and had pending legal problems related to jihadism), "decent" Pakistani families refused to give him their daughter. Among some traditionalist families, this type of problem emerges because the access to the girls is restricted, sometimes barred; the individual ignores how to relate to girls, not knowing how to start relationships with them, woo them, and eventually end up having sex. IS made relations outside marriage possible with prostitutes (mainly enslaved Yazidi women who were coerced into prostitution), but also through marriage with the available girls (they met in *maqarr*, places where unmarried girls and women stayed), or through the imaginary access to virgins in paradise after death. Violence can also fulfill sexual desires as a substitute, with Syria at war under Daesh offering many opportunities for its practice in its cruelest forms.

An analysis of the cases of three young men, Karim, Adil, and Rabi, gives an insight into what we have called the subculture of religious confrontation or jihadism. It explains why these young people left for Syria to work at the service of Daesh. They were the first to leave Lunel, a town in southern France, with a population of 27,000 in 2013. After them, more than twenty young people followed suit from the same town. Seven were killed in Syria, including Karim. Hamza lived close to a small shop run by Karim and his brother Saad. The two friends spent long hours discussing the Arab

Revolutions in the Middle East, the warning signs of the end of time in Islam, and the problems of French society: "I did a technician's diploma (BTS) in accountancy. All native French with the same diploma found a job [*taf*] and we, the only two Arabs of the class, didn't find any. . . . Arabs find jobs (only) for manual work," said Hamza to the investigators (Le Devin, 2015). There is a strong sense of stigma and social unfairness in his words.

Hamza put Karim in touch with the network of Johan Juncaj, an Albanian close to Mourad Farès, one of the main recruiters of French Foreign Fighters. Before being formally identified by the Intelligence services, Mourad Farès and Johan Juncaj held Facebook pages in which they praised holy war and invited young men to join jihadi groups.

This type of radicalization is based on reversing humiliation into a radical form of counter-humiliation. Humiliating the humiliators is the dream of many young people belonging to the slum subculture. They feel their life destroyed by the overbearing attitude of a mainstream society that regards them as inferior. Deviance becomes the major way to reject their social class as they refuse to start with underpaid jobs to finish, like their parents, with an insignificant retirement pension, synonymous with unworthiness in their eyes. They want immediate access to middle-class status. The purpose of delinquent activity is not only to bring those from below into the middle classes, but also to take revenge on society for the humiliations which are not only of economic nature but are rooted in the daily lives of the sons of migrants. This is why this delinquency has a provocative side that White people's delinquency does not usually have. It is about belittling a society for which the sons of immigrants have been regarded as "less than nothing," like "insects," as a young man in prison told me (see also Dubet, 1987, 2002).

By reacting to humiliations, in a vicious circle that often goes crescendo, these young people come to exaggerate them, or even give them a disproportionate meaning, the feeling of being humiliated turning into paranoia. Everything can become a pretext for humiliation, potentially or actually. The slightest glance, the most benevolent criticism, insignificant attitudes can be over-interpreted in the sense of an existing or future humiliation in a mental register in which humiliation becomes omnipresent, even in the many cases where it is not aimed at by the others, or according to institutional logics that suppose the expectation or possibility of failure, such as an army or police entrance exam. Radicalization is certainly a reaction to real humiliation, but it is often exacerbated by a disarrayed imagination that finds a touch of humiliation in everything that makes up the fabric of collective life.

e-Aggressiveness and Humiliation: The Easy Transition to Jihadism

Outsiders put forward one major characteristic of the male youth living in the poor districts and belonging to what we call the slum subculture: their aggressiveness. In Fresnes Prison, a "White" middle-class man in his late forties, imprisoned for embezzlement, described them in a disparaging manner, expressing more or less the viewpoint of the mainstream society and its stereotypes toward them:

Question: You told me about the youth from the poor districts and their characteristics. Could you describe them in few words?

Alain: In this prison I don't feel as if I am in France. Most of the prisoners are from the poor suburbs. In my section there are only a few "Frenchmen," the others are from the "cités" [another name for the poor suburbs]. *They behave in a way that is closer to the Arabs than to the French. They are aggressive and fight each other for no good reason, but they quarrel with the others as well, the guards, the other prisoners, anyone they don't like for some reason. They don't talk, they shout. Their vocabulary is limited to a few hundred words. Here in prison, if you have a claim, if for instance you wish to see a doctor, you must write it down and give it to the guard. These people are illiterate and can't write. From time to time, they ask me to do it for them. At the time, they are grateful, but they forget it quickly. They ask me for cigarettes, many don't have the means to buy them, but they refuse to work in prison to earn some money. For them, working is beneath them. They are lazy. When they meet you, they don't say hello to you, they haven't learned how to say it. Instead, they yell at each other and at you if you simply look at them. They remain idle during the entire day: they get up late and sleep late and trust no one. One day, they are on good terms with the guards; the next, they insult them for no reason. I should normally be against the guards but to tell the truth, I feel sorry for them."* (Fresnes Prison, October 2012)

This is a stereotype that one hears often and like many of them, there is a grain of truth in it: they shout instead of talking; their gesture is abrupt; they easily resort to verbal and even physical abuse if an outsider stares at them, because they feel offended and may react violently; they refuse to work because they can't stand working under a "White" man's command. One of them told me that it reminded him of colonial times and especially, of the exploitation of his parents by the French at the factory. While this aggressiveness is real, it is in part exaggerated by the "Whites," attributing to them an "aggressive nature" while they use their own subcultural codes and, for their part, are distrustful of the "White men." In prison, one of the constant complaints of the guards, as well as the other prisoners, is the anti-social demeanor of these young men who behave unpredictably, ignoring what it means to act normally toward others, using a disrespectful language, calling people even in their first meeting by their first name, adopting a familiar language toward them,[12] and being constantly defiant. In brief, their overall picture by the people from the mainstream culture denotes their inability to discipline themselves, their impoliteness, and their refusal (in fact, inability) to communicate with others by violating basic codes of manners. Their behavior makes normal relations with them impossible, at best cumbersome, according to them. In prison, the others avoid them, and they have ties only with other inmates behaving according to the codes of the slum subculture and belonging to the poor districts (Khosrokhavar, 2016).

This was acknowledged by Qasem, of Moroccan origin, who was jailed for violence against his younger brother and parents. In prison, he registered for correspondence courses and obtained the bachelor's degree (baccalauréat). He started reading novels and short stories. It was an opportunity for him to do some soul-searching. He told me:

Question: Why do the poor-city kids have such a bad reputation in prison?

Qassem: It is a long story. The gist of the matter is that they never treated us fairly. As a child, I didn't know how to talk about my frustration, my father was illiterate, he spoke colloquial Arabic and a basic French he had learned on the job at the factory. So, he could not help me speak or read French. At school, I was in trouble with the authorities because we did not live in the same world, and we didn't understand each other. I was aggressive. It was true, but the reason was that my parents did not care for me; we expected no bright future, no good job, and we didn't know how to talk, and explain our problems. I lived in a poor area in the Quartiers Nord of Marseille where my role models were drug dealers and they showed me that violence alone pays off. I was also aggressive because I was immature, and nobody cared for my education. It is ironic that through correspondence courses in prison I have learned to control more or less my impulses, because I have been reading a lot during the last three years, for a simple reason: I have nothing else to do. Otherwise, life is so boring behind the bars!

Question: You talked about aggressiveness in the poor suburbs.

Qassem: Being aggressive is part of the way people behave in the poor neighborhoods. It is their way and also because it is the only way to protect themselves. It's sadly true that behaving in this way separates them from others. People avoid them because they become easily violent. (Interview conducted in Fresnes Prison, March 2013)

Qassem recognized the dual role of aggressiveness: it is in line with the cultural code of the slums and it is also a way for them to assert and protect themselves in the poor districts from others who might otherwise encroach on their domain and try to exploit them. At the same time, behaving violently isolates, recognized Qassem. He went on and on about his childhood setbacks and tirelessly repeated his problems in an inhospitable society and an environment that prepared him in no way to live peacefully with others:

Qassem: I was being abused. I wasn't lucky enough to be in a good family with a caring father and a loving mother. She was the occasional cleaning lady. He was a janitor at Renault [French automaker]. *My parents were struggling to make ends meet, they didn't understand the culture of this country and didn't teach me how to behave. What I learned was on the job, at school with children of poor foreigners who came from many countries and didn't know either how to behave.*

Question: So, do you believe that it is a family problem?

Qassim: My family didn't pass on any good device to me for relating to others, and the poor neighborhood where I lived made me feel like I was on an island, separated from the others, locked up with people like me in a social housing unit where everyone was poor and everyone had problems with their own and with others. Nobody taught me how to be normal, and I learned to defend myself only by getting aggressive. I showed my teeth and believed that nice people were weak people, and I was of course strong! I live in a hypocritical society that always rejected me and never gave me a chance to redeem myself.

In Europe, a large part of the Foreign Fighters who enlisted under the IS flag or other jihadi groups came from the disaffected youth, or what a sociologist called the "disaffiliated" (Castel, 2007)—that is, those sons of migrants who feel uprooted and rejected by the mainstream society. They live in poor ethnic districts and are steeped in slum subculture. They take for ideal those successful gang leaders, riding in SUVs, wearing brand shoes, and exhibiting ostentatious but also provocative consumption in a society in which they were supposed to be eternally at the bottom in status and social class. Through trafficking and theft, they sometimes become rich, but also, future prisoners. The male youth cultivates within this subculture the idealized picture of ostentatious wealth and the ability to spend lavishly before the half-envious, half-admiring eyes of their peers. The transfer of this identity from delinquency to jihad requires major shifts, but also preserves some features like the narcissistic character of the Self who seeks to overcome inferiority by "shining" and squandering money and roaring his car, often stolen, which is then set aflame to erase the traces of the robbery, but also to make an impressive spectacle in the eyes of the gang members and the admiring young bystanders, or by becoming a jihadi. In the latter case, instead of money he squanders the lives of the disbelievers, featuring himself in video clips on social networks much in the same way as he boasted by publicly humiliating policemen or public authorities before his radicalization. Someone like Larossi Abballa, the killer of a policeman and his wife in Magnanville in France on June 13, 2016, videotaped himself on the spot, transferring directly the sequence to his Facebook page. Or Mohamed Merah, who videotaped himself murdering Muslim soldiers and a Jewish father and three children in Toulouse and Montauban in March 2012, then sent the sequences to the TV channel Al-Jazeera to replay it.

Radical Islam rejects citizenship, which the disaffected youth believe is a fraud, since in their everyday life they are denied recognition as equal citizens by "White" people or in their relationship with the public administration. In their encounters with others they experience this denial of citizenship, which they then reject the more easily as they feel they are already ostracized. That is why they fully approve of the rejection of their European nationality in radical Islam. Some even burned their passports in front of the camera to show how little they cared about their national ties. IS became a pole of attraction still more as it promoted violence in order to establish a new order in which Muslims would gain the upper hand in a counter-colonial manner through holy war. Those who colonized would be colonized within the new order as neo-dhimmis[13] to whom equal rights were denied in the name of the traditional view of Islam (but *de facto* tolerance established by Islamic tradition was absent from the new rules implemented by IS).

An almost perfect model of jihadi involvement according to the preceding description is illustrated by Amédy Coulibaly, a Black man of Malian origin exposed to racism. He was thirty-two years old when the French police shot and killed him in January 2015 after his killing of a policewoman and the attack of a kosher supermarket. He had been sentenced to more than eighteen years in prison before his last attack. Born in Juvisy-sur-Orge, in a southeastern poor suburb of Paris, into a Malian Muslim immigrant family, Coulibaly was the seventh child and the only boy among ten children. He grew up in a housing estate, La Grande Borne, in Grigny, a poor district in the vicinity of Paris. He was nicknamed "Doly of Grigny." He obtained a qualification as a technician (BEP) in hi-fi equipment, but he interrupted his training to study for the baccalaureate (high school diploma), leaving school at the age of twenty. Starting deviant activities at seventeen, he was convicted five times for armed robbery and at least once for drug trafficking. His father died while he was in prison. He obsessively hated the police. This was due to the death of his accomplice and best friend, Ali Rezgui, who was killed on September 17, 2000, in Combs-la-Ville by a police officer during a robbery in which Coulibaly took part. Hatred of the police is very common among the youth of the poor districts in France, in part due to police racism, in part because many of them engage in illegal activities and often confront the police, their disrespect as well as their violence culminating in aggressiveness toward all those who wear a uniform (even firefighters). Their relationship is fraught with mutual hatred, each one trying to corner the other, the police using harsh methods after their arrest, including humiliating body searches and insults, and disaffected youth stoning the police and throwing bottles at them, and even sometimes shooting at them, chasing them in the maze of their neighborhood.

In 2004, Coulibaly was sentenced to six years in prison for armed robbery. In Fleury-Mérogis, close to Paris, the largest prison in Europe, he met Chérif Kouachi (one of the two brothers who killed the *Charlie Hebdo* journalists in January 2015). He converted to radical Islam in prison at the same time as Chérif. He also met the al-Qaeda recruiter Djamel Beghal there, who was in solitary confinement in the cell above him.

After he was released from prison, Coulibaly succeeded in finding a short-term work contract at the Coca-Cola factory in Grigny. He worked there from November 2008 to September 2009.

In 2008, during his incarceration, he organized a clandestine shooting of a documentary denouncing living conditions there, signing it under his pseudonym, "Hugo la masse." He dedicated it "to those who will do all they can in order never to go to jail and those who will do everything to never be thrown there again." After his release, excerpts from this documentary were featured in a 2009 TV broadcast (*Envoyé Special*), in which he was interviewed. Inspired by this documentary, a book by Omar Dawson and Karim Bellazaar was published, with a mixed French and English title, *Reality Taule, au-delà des barreaux* (Reality-Prison, Beyond Bars) in 2009, featuring Amédy Coulibaly with his photo on the back cover (Plummer, 2015; Lazard et al., 2015; Bronner, 2015).

He married Hayat Boumedienne on July 5, 2009, in an Islamic religious ceremony. On July 15, 2009, along with about five hundred other young people, Coulibaly met the French President Nicolas Sarkozy, whose government promoted youth employment. Ten months later, in May 2010, the police arrested him, finding in his flat ammunition and letters seeking false official documents. In December 2013 he was sentenced to five years in prison for supplying ammunition to set free from prison the jihadi Smain Ait Ali Belkacem, in a plot in which the Kouachi brothers were also involved. However, Coulibaly was released early from prison, in March 2014. He was required to wear an electronic bracelet until May 2014.

Coulibaly's biography summarizes almost all of the features of jihadis from the poor districts in France and, more generally, Europe: coming from a poor immigrant family, stigmatized as a Black and a Muslim, living in social housing, being a school dropout and a deviant, hating the host society and particularly the police, becoming radicalized in prison along the lines followed by many young men with the same social profile, and ending up committing violence in the name of radical Islam. He had also the narcissistic attitude of many jihadis from the same background, looking for notoriety through social media, seeking world prominence through violence, aspiring to join the jihadi star system worldwide by being at the same time hated and celebrated as a "negative hero." For him, the only possible recognition in the world was through violence in the name of jihad that frightened Western societies.

f-Humiliation and Radical Islam

Humiliation is presumably the major anthropological ingredient of radical Islam in Europe, particularly among the sons of Muslim migrants, whether they are disaffected youth or middle class. A tiny minority of them joined Daesh.

We can distinguish two types of humiliation. First, people living in the poor ethnic districts who share the slum subculture, suffering from economic exclusion and cultural stigma; but also middle-class Muslims, whose discrimination in employment has been widely studied in Europe (Adida et al., 2013; Valfort, 2015, El Karoui 2016; Dugan, 2014; Manchester University, Centre on Dynamics of Ethnicity, 2014; Dobson, 2014). They suffer from everyday Islamophobia, global reproaches (for instance, "Muslims are terrorists"), or harsh criticism (remarks like, "Islam and democracy are irreconcilable"). Globally, Muslims feel humiliated in their daily interactions with the mainstream society. Racism plays a significant role in this type of humiliation, and one can speak of "cultural alienation" among middle-class Muslims (Khosrokhavar, 2020). Their humiliation is not as extensive as among disaffected Muslim youth. What is at stake in their case is to preserve their economic status, achieved through hard work. They are not as desperate as the disaffected youth who live in a hopeless predicament, both economically and culturally.

Middle-class Muslims usually have their feet on the ground and show more patience and less acrimony toward mainstream society than disaffected Muslim youth. However, they often accuse society of neo-colonial bias toward them, while doing everything possible not to exacerbate tensions, except among a small fraction of jihadis.

The case of the disaffected youth is different. They suffer economically and culturally from their marginalization and feel like they're in the hot seat, being the target of racism and Islamophobia. Their imagination amplifies them, extends them to the whole society and, above all, portrays their Selves as total victims with no recourse except through violence or by breaking the law. This holistic picture of racism and Islamophobia does not adequately reflect the complex reality (not all Europeans are racist, and not all social relations are fraught with Islamophobia). It results in a feeling of victimization ("everybody is against us"). Humiliation within this mindset is total because racism is regarded as universal and ubiquitous (social prejudices and, more generally, racism is widespread within the mainstream culture but not to the extent they imagine it). It ends up becoming an obsession.

This type of humiliation, by its very nature, afflicts the ego in its intimate nature, and self-concern becomes obsessive. Since everyone is against him, the Self locks himself up in order to protect himself. From then on, empathy becomes impossible, since it implies identification with others in their humanity, whereas the deeply wounded Self is dehumanized. He projects his dehumanization onto others and cannot understand them in reference to their mutual humanity. In other words, the embittered individual focuses exclusively on his own discomfort in order to seek a respite. In this predicament, he is blinded to the others' pains. For instance, if Palestinians endure repression under Israeli occupation, or Indian Kashmiris from the Indian army, their pain is akin to that of the Self who suffers from racism in France ("Arabs" versus the Palestinians) or in the United Kingdom ("Pakis" versus the Kashmiris). If Syrians suffer under Assad's regime, their distress is similar to those of the Muslims in the European poor districts who experience Islamophobia. It is almost impossible to envisage any empathy to other people's suffering without referring to the victimized individual's own pain: the obsession of the Self mentally under siege makes reflexivity well-nigh impossible. As we shall describe it extensively, geographic segregation in poor areas means mental imprisonment in a fortress that becomes a breeding ground for total victimization: the Self is in a desperate predicament, there is no way to escape one's destiny as a poor, the migrant's son is locked up in a neighborhood that is governed by the ruthless law of the strongest (the only way to succeed is trafficking, but not everyone has access to it and it is reserved for a minority of thugs who usually keep the neighborhood under their sway). Ghettoization is not only physical (being trapped in a suburb poorly served by bus service) but also mental (there is no escape, the very idea of getting out to refresh one's mind becoming remote, even meaningless), the minds of young people being haunted by a lack of future perspective. Slum subculture plays a key role in this victimization process. One way out is to project one's own hatred onto all mankind: no empathy with others, only the obsession with a Self, wounded by racism and a sense of unfairness that justifies violence against the mainstream society. A specific version of Islam sustained by an eschatological state made possible to mentally overcome ghettoization by building up an imaginary community, to be erected through violence (the neo-Ummah). Mainstream society, and beyond that, the world, became through Daesh the imaginary space where the grief of this distraught youth was projected. It was not the real world that the European disaffected youth was unaware of in all its complexity, it was an imaginary theater where their humiliation and resentment were staged, and against which they intended to retaliate through violence. They wanted vengeance on Europe (and more generally the West and its Arab allies) for all the contempt and humiliations they had suffered.

Daesh managed to use their malaise to lure them to Syria, giving them the chance to realize their dreams of retaliating against Europe, and by extension, the world.

Yassine, a French jihadi, in his communications from Syria with a French journalist through the internet, said: "Islam has restored our dignity because France has humiliated us" (Thomson, 2014, p. 25).

The case of Nasser, in his late twenties, who refers to the agonies of the Palestinians and the Muslim world in general, is symptomatic of this type of attitude (interview in October 2017 in La Reynerie, a poor district in Toulouse Mirail):

Question: You talked about humiliation. You're not the only one suffering from it. A lot of people around the world are exposed to it.

Nasser: I live in these poor districts ["cités"] and I can tell you that I deeply feel humiliated. It's with me all the time. The hardest is that it is all the time there, at the bottom of my everyday life. I suffer when I go to the town hall to get a document: the civil servant looks down at me; in his face I can see that he hates me. When I go to the social housing office for some reason, the same thing happens. The police [les flics] *are even worse; they treat me as less than nothing.*

Question: But you're just as aggressive with them!

Nasser: Mine is plainly justified! They treat me badly, and I know that they are 100 percent biased against people like me. They are racist, against those like me, Muslims, sons or grand-sons of Algerian workers, jobless, living in the "cité" [poor district]. . . .

Question: Is there anything in particular that hurts you? The Palestinians suffer also, the Kashmiris in India, and they suffer much more than you!

Nasser: I suffer every day from being in this damned country, from dawn to dusk, all the time, it is the same as being a Palestinian in Gaza under the yoke of the Israeli army, supported by the Americans, the French, and the whole West. Our suffering is the same, they feel pain like me, we belong to the same suffering humanity. Arabs, all over the world, suffer from bad governments, the police, the Westerners, the White men [les Blancs]. . . .

Question: But the suffering of the Palestinians is different: they are facing the Israeli army, you are not facing the French army, the Israeli speak another language, belong to a different nation. . . .

Nasser: You get it all wrong! I speak French but for them my language, my words, my slang [verlan, reverse words], *my way of speaking* [specific to the slum subculture], *means our French is different. It is a bad French to them, the so-called poor-suburb slang* [*argot des banlieues*]. *They are as harsh as the Israeli army; they are even more dangerous. At least the Palestinians know that they are facing an enemy. Here, we have the illusion that the French are not our enemies but our well-meaning friends, although few people still believe it nowadays. As for my nationality, they call me "Frenchman* [only] *on passport"* [on paper]; *that means I am a fake Frenchman, not a true one. The Palestinians, the Arabs suffer like me, we are "bastard Frenchmen." Sincerely, I don't feel French, I am a Muslim, not even an Algerian.*

Question: You seem to believe that there is no escape for an Arab in France. There are successful Arabs in this country, and they have joined the middle classes, even if it is more difficult for them than for ordinary Frenchmen.

Nasser: Successful Arabs are either yes-men [*Arabes de service*] *or they pull strings* [*au piston*]. *An Arab cannot succeed in this country without swindling. Look at those who become radical Muslims. They have no choice, it is the only way they can get revenge, and become worthy in their own eyes.*

Pointing the finger at the police as a means of repression of "Arabs" and not for their protection is a recurring fact in the interviews I have conducted over the years. It sometimes ends up with an attempt to kill them specifically.[14]

Social workers who are in touch with this disaffected youth often feel powerless in front of them, as one of them confided to me:

> *Before, "young people"* [*les jeunes*, a "polite" denomination for the disaffected youth of migrant descent] *used to ask us a lot, they were much more demanding. Now, they don't do it anymore, they think that the future has no prospects for them, it is empty. They are no longer demanding. Before, they asked for many things, now they say: you can't do anything for us; we are not citizens, we are nothing and your help is void: you promise, and nothing comes out of it. Besides, you can't do anything for yourself either. You have a precarious job, without security, and you want to help us? That's the last straw! You should help yourselves first, before you think of us!* (Interview conducted in Maubeuge, January 2020, district Les Provinces Françaises)

Beyond a certain threshold, the future becomes pointless and cannot change because of the lack of a horizon of hope. Moreover, for these young people it is a world where everyone has to take care of themselves, as they learned in their poor neighborhoods where solidarity and mutual aid are more a myth than a reality. They do not understand the concern of social workers for them beyond their own problems, unable to empathize as described previously, but also because for them social workers are themselves at the bottom of the social ladder.

A second type of humiliation had spread among young middle-class converts, in which empathy was a major component, at least at the outset. They acted empathically against the suffering of Iraqis under American occupation after 2003, or Sunnis under Bashar al-Assad in 2013. There was a humanitarian component to this type of humiliation, which was rooted in "humiliation by proxy": young converts felt humiliated in the face of Western hypocrisy toward the Syrian Sunnis who suffered without the European governments lifting a finger to help them. At the same time, there was a deep sense of anomie among a large part of middle-class youth seeking identification with an imagined warm Muslim community, in contrast to the cold nations they lived in.

Initially, there was no hatred of others among the middle-class Muslim youth (converts and middle-class Muslims), unlike those stigmatized young, disaffected Muslims who hated society. It was an empathy toward Muslims being abused that first translated into humanitarianism and then adopted violence as a legitimate means of achieving justice. In that crucial respect, their subjectivity was not identical to that of the disaffected youth: it was not a reaction to racism and social exclusion, the major focus being the others and, at the same time, the quest for a warm community for the Self (the neo-Ummah), unlike poor Muslims in disadvantaged neighborhoods whose action was first and foremost based on retaliation against a humiliating society regarded as inhospitable, racist, and Islamophobic, Daesh giving them the golden opportunity to achieve that goal.

These were two distinct processes of humiliation, the first being based on an existential substratum ("I suffer because I am humiliated and racialized"), the second on the internalization of the suffering of the members of the community to which one belongs ("I suffer to see Muslims humiliated, their humiliation becoming mine"). The first was self-centered, the second, other-centered. In each case, IS assumed a different role: it was the means to conquer dignity (the disaffected youth), the means for the individual to fight against repression of Muslims and at the same time overcome the malaise of anomie (middle-class Muslims and converts).

However, Muslim middle classes did not suffer solely out of empathy for Syrians or Palestinians. They also suffered from the way mainstream society treated them. Unlike young people from poor neighborhoods, they were patient, so as not to jeopardize their hard-won socio-economic status, despite the discrimination they suffered at work. Since they were economically integrated, they grudgingly accepted stigmas, not without rancor, although they felt French, contrary to the disaffected youth who rejected Frenchness. This was the case of Taoufik, thirty-eight, an executive:

Taoufik: The Arab-Muslim citizens deeply feel humiliation and injustice. We are French and contribute to the wealth of this country: we pay taxes, and we have children here who believe in the values of equality, freedom, and fraternity [the motto of the French Republic]. Besides that, they [Frenchmen of non-Muslim origin] treat us not only as strangers, but sometimes also as potential terrorists. This is shocking and hurtful. . . . People behave differently towards French Muslims and other French people. Two different attitudes! I see it in my work. They don't talk to me the way they do to native Frenchmen [Franco-Français]. I have friends of Arab-Muslim origin who showed up for a job. They were graduates [from good universities] and wore suit-tie. But, as soon as the person announced his name and surname Hassan, it went wrong. . . . And his native French counterpart, whose name was François, had no problem getting hired. I myself have experienced harassment, racist insults. I am not saying that I am a Muslim, I am not even saying that I am Arab [that is, of North African origin], but people conclude it from my facial features [faciès] and my accent. (Interview conducted in June 2013 in Seine-Saint-Denis with a middle-class Frenchman of North African origin)

Humiliation is thus common to the middle-class and lower-class Muslims, but it is much deeper among the latter who do not take part in social and economic life and are excluded from it. Among jihadis, a minority were middle-class Muslim.

The loss of political meaning is also essential among the middle and lower-class Muslims. Middle classes were attracted to Daesh, which positioned itself beyond politics (Islam trumped politics, religion making social unification possible) and also included "infra-politics," that is, everyday relations that would be devoid of the humiliation to which Muslims were exposed. Among the disaffected Muslim youth, politics didn't mean anything essential. It was usually beyond their cultural horizon and they did not engage in it (those few who did it were considered as traitors who justified neo-colonialism by taking advantage of it). Daesh proposed a religion that replaced politics, which satisfied these people, since politics had been unable to achieve a society without humiliation and on top of it, Islam made them feel like an elite whose members would become knights of Islam, without undergoing a complicated political process.

For the disaffected youth, two types of historical past played a key role in their symbolism of revenge. The first was the case of the former colonial countries like the United Kingdom and France. For the sons of migrants from the former colonies, especially those living in poor districts who felt simultaneously the pinch of poverty and social stigmas, colonial contempt was still there: behind the guise of citizenship, they faced un-avowed racism due to their origins. After independence, their parents migrated to the country of the former colonizers to work in their industry, due to the shortage of manpower in the 1950s and 1960s in Europe. They were treated as inferior, but they accepted it as foreign workers, the same attitude continuing toward their children, according to the latter. One can speak of a pervasive transgenerational humiliation that was passed on from parents to children and grandchildren, one that young boys felt intensely in the former colonizer's society (the girls' situation was different, particularly among those who secularized: they generally found themselves better treated in European societies as compared to their parents' country, where women are treated as inferior). To take revenge on a society that colonized their parents and continued to despise and humiliate them seemed legitimate to them, even if only a tiny minority of them went to extremes and opted for radical Islam. In French prisons, in some interviews Muslims strongly expressed these views. One case among others was an "Arab" French, in his early thirties, imprisoned for drug trafficking in the prison of Lille-Séquedin in north-eastern France, whom I interviewed in February 2012:

Kazem: I do not allow them to treat me like my parents: my father was in his twenties when he began to work here and after more than thirty years, he was left with a ridiculous small pension and a crippled body. I want to live independently, and I don't want a Gaouri [native Frenchman in a pejorative sense] bossing me around and giving me orders. I have no choice but to become a drug dealer. This provides me with enough money to live on comfortably. Prison is part of the game.

By joining IS, those people sought to exact vengeance for the humiliation inflicted on their parents and grandparents who did not retaliate due to their traditional mindset, suffering from stigmas without protesting against it. Another illustration was the interview in January 2013 in Fleury-Mérogis Prison with a Harki "Arab" (Algerians who collaborated with the French army and fought the Algerian independence movement in the late 1950s and 1960-61). He was put in prison for several crimes. He was from Bondy, a poor, northeastern Parisian suburb, and had studied at the university for a year or two before dropping out:

Question: You said you are from Bondy, a poor suburb the media blacklist so often!

Saeed: I am from Bondy, one of those poor suburbs that the media slander all the time, but I don't think life there is that bad. I hate the medias that denounce it and add insult to injury for us [they contribute to stigmatize us even more]. *That makes life more difficult for us. Ask young people from Bondy who look for a job. The employer refuses to hire them because they are "Arabs," but also because they come from the notorious Bondy.*

Question: Why do they do it in your opinion?

Saeed: This is a long story! It is the story of colonization and decolonization. We were colonized and manhandled; above all, at the end, we were taken hostage as "Harkis," between a rock and a hard place. My parents were hated by the French as Algerians and by the Algerians as collaborators ["collabo," a pejorative term meaning, since the Second World War, cooperating with the German enemy—in this case the French Army against the Algerian Independence fighters]. *My father took part in the repression of the insurrection by the Algerian people against the French army* [in the late 1950s]. *We are of Algerian origin, but the Algerians here hate us, they hate even the children of the Harkis who have nothing to do with their parents' past. Some said to me: your mother slept with the French, you are a bastard, "ouled haram"* [see, for a similar view ten years earlier in another French prison, Khosrokhavar, 2006]. *The French also look down on us, we are "Arabs," not the sons of soldiers who fought with them and suffered death, particularly after they left Algeria and abandoned many of us there, to be killed by the Algerians. We are hated on both sides, by the Algerians and by the French.*

Question: But colonization was painful all over the world, and in particular in Morocco, Tunisia, and elsewhere.

Saeed: Colonization was much more painful in Algeria than in Morocco or Tunisia. In Algeria it lasted 130 years, in Morocco and Tunisia much less. In Algeria they took the land of the people, took their dignity, gave French citizenship to the Jews [the Crémieux Decree in 1870], *and denied it to the Muslims, to divide and rule. After Independence, the same story began, this time in France. I am a "French citizen on paper" as they* [the extreme-right in France] *call me, and not a real Frenchman.*

Question: But your father accepted to side with the French army against those who fought for independence.

Saeed: I am also angry at my father: he sided with the French colonizers against his own people and now, I am paying for his acts. The Algerians here know it and by word of mouth, they spread to others that I am the son of a Harki, a bastard in their eyes.

Question: Why are you in prison?

Saeed: Because I don't let them exploit me like my father, they can't humiliate me like they did with my father. My father worked hard here in the textile industry and was poorly paid. He lost his health working for very little pay. I want to live like the middle classes, not as a poor guy, despised on top of it. I prefer to be under lock and key rather than living as a poor. I am acting on my terms, not theirs. I want them to know that I will not let them abuse me. I accept prison, but I don't let them exploit me or humiliate me. It is my game, not theirs; although I pay a heavy price and have spent years behind bars, it's worthwhile.

The drama unfolds in three acts from the perspective of this son of Harki (but more generally among many second-generation "Arabs"): the French stigmatized and colonized his ancestors in Algeria, enrolled his parents in the French Army to fight against the independence fighters there and once they came to France, they exploited his parents in their factories, and now they deny dignity to their sons. The same scenario, in less dramatic terms, applies to the British people and their colonial attitude toward the Bangladeshis, Pakistanis, and Black Africans as well as their children. Humiliation becomes complex, imaginary ingredients mixing with the real situation. In interviews with French "Arabs," many of them said that their situation in France was akin to the Palestinians in the occupied Palestine. In the same vein, in the UK some "Pakis" believe that their lot is similar to the Kashmiris in India (marked by the military crackdown against the Muslims in the Indian part of Kashmir). This comparison is based on two premises: the first is the similarity between the Muslims' situation in France or the United Kingdom and their predicament in the Middle East or Southeast Asia. Objectively, the resemblance is dim, but subjectively, for many young Muslims who become aware of the predicament of the other Muslims through the internet or TV, this imagined similarity is "obvious"; it is more than a humiliation by proxy, it is "real" humiliation. The second point is that since in those regions Muslims act violently in response to the violence of non-Muslims (the Palestinians against the Israeli army, the Kashmiris against the Indian army), European Muslims should act in the same way. That justifies their violence. In both cases, the comparison is based on an imagination that flouts reality. In the same way, jihadism is based on a frenzied imagination that bends reality according to its worldview in defiance of its complexity, only in relation to a humiliation that crosses the border of time and extends from the colonial past to the post-colonial present, with an acute sense that the future will be no different from the present and the past in this regard.

Jihadism being a phenomenon of a tiny minority, humiliation framed by a tormented imagination is transcribed into action by IS, which makes it possible to move on to violence with reference to a religious register (the injunction to perform jihad, *fardh ul ayn*).

The second case in regard to colonialism concerns countries like Belgium, which did not colonize Morocco (where an important Moroccan community resides). Among the second- and third-generation children of Moroccans, a "neo-colonial" feeling has developed: in their view, they are treated as if their community had been colonized in the past, being humiliated by the Belgians, denial of dignity and humiliation being the main accusation against them. I call it the "as-if humiliation": Belgians behave toward Moroccans "as if" they had colonized Morocco, Belgium being similar to France in this respect in the eyes of the disaffected Muslim youth in Belgium. In Belgium in 2017, in our discussions, young Belgian-Moroccans blamed the Belgians as colonizers of Congo in Africa, which they extended to their case in spite of the fact that Belgium did not specifically colonize Morocco; in Germany, young Turks blamed society for behaving toward them like the Nazis toward inferior races or the Kaiser toward Eastern Europeans.

In most European countries, a large proportion of Muslims live in poor ethnic districts. The colonial image returns, this time in a more humiliating way because it develops in an egalitarian world: Muslims experience their lives governed by a neo-colonial order where ghettos are not only places of indigence but also of cultural unworthiness. They also live a "double non-belonging" (neither North African nor French, neither Pakistani nor British, neither Moroccan nor Belgian . . .) as a drama. In these neighborhoods, a feeling of colonial divide is internalized, imaginatively amplified, making these young people unable to develop a more relaxed or neutral attitude toward others, in order to seek constructive solutions to the social prejudices that make them suffer. They are convinced that a fatality hangs over them in a world where humiliation and stigmatization go hand in hand, causing the indignity of Self, but also hatred and aggressiveness toward others. In France these feelings are more accentuated because of cultural and political secularism (*laïcité*). The sons and daughters of the colonized people regard it as the last avatar of French colonialism. Words such as *hogra* (a mixed feeling of inferiority and contempt), *ghahra* (resentment, helplessness), and *nakira* (invisible, without identity, non-existent in the eyes of others) express this sense of inferiority.

Delinquency is of course a means of joining middle classes by deviant action, but it is also a way to get back at a contemptuous society. It becomes the icon for the refusal of a postcolonial inferiority by a twofold transgression: first, non-observance of the code of legality (acting in an unlawful manner), second, dismissing rationality through a festive mentality: they squander in a single night the monthly salary of a worker in alcoholic drinks and other ostentatious expenditures after a successful traffic deal or robbery. An interview conducted in Cité des Indes close to Sartrouville (Ile-de-France), with a French-Algerian in March 2018 is symptomatic of this attitude. I had met him in prison few years before, and he had been recently freed from prison, famous for his hold-ups and robberies:

Question: You seem to have earned a fortune in your hold-ups. Why, on earth, did you then work in prison for a miserable salary? Your prison inmates told me that you did so because you wanted to make believe that you were ruined, while you had made millions!

Kamal: I know the gossip, but I did not put aside money for a rainy day. My lifestyle was different from normal people. When I was young, I spent in a single night a few thousand Euros in a nightclub. That was the sign of my success, but also, a way of sending a message to the French: I can afford what you cannot!

Question: You mean, there was a provocative side to it?

Kamal: This fact of life, the others are unable to understand it! I had to prove to myself that I was better and higher than the "White" people. This was part of my claim against them: you exploited my father with a miserable salary, you forced my parents and myself to live in a ghetto [in a poor suburb] *so that I couldn't do serious studies, I am from a poor working class family from the Algerian colony. Now I am here: in a way I colonize you, I trample on your laws and get richer than you!*

Sometimes, after a successful attack, I'd spend in a few hours what people earn in six months. On top of it, my lifestyle made the others jealous, and earned me the respect of my colleagues. I also had to pay lawyers and that was also very expensive.

Question: Now you have been freed from prison, but other indictments could come, your life is somehow in tatters, at least from the average people's viewpoint.

Kamal: But I lived intensely, I lived the way I wished, right under the nose of the French. If I had chosen the normal path, I would earn minimum wage, my life would be just like my parents', and that wouldn't be a dreamlife. It is true, I have paid a heavy price, and I have overspent my last dime.

Question: This is somehow desperate, isn't it?

Kamal: Some of my colleagues, at the end of the road, choose a heroic death: they kill a cop in the name of jihad, and get killed in the shooting. They do it because they feel there is no way out. They choose to die as a star of jihad, otherwise they would spend the rest of their life in prison. They claim to fight for jihad but they are not religious: they do not follow the sharia laws, and they do it because they want to finish their life on a high note and perhaps earn the favors of heaven. On top of it, they try to fuck [niquer] *the French by scaring them and killing cops who make life miserable for them. But this is not my exit.*

Kamal underscores what I have called "fake jihadism"[15] or desperate jihadism. In many cases delinquency leads to jihadism in the name of radicalized Islam, without any religious content.

IS was regarded by some European jihadis as the ideal Muslim country where they could feel at home, beyond humiliation, able to practice freely their religion without being reminded of their belonging to a stigmatized minority. A British jihadi of South-Asian origin, Siddhartha Dhar, expressed it clearly in a video he posted on You Tube, describing the IS's caliphate as "a dream for all Muslims worldwide. We can finally have a sanctuary where we can practice our religion and live under the Sharia. It is a big, big thing" (Casciani, 2016).

Generally speaking, jihadism enables one to refuse an identity that has already been denied by the mainstream society (Frenchness, Britishness, etc.). The disaffected youth who turned jihadi, turned down what was already disallowed, namely French, English, German, Belgian, and other identities, going much further in the logic of denial by radicalizing their reaction. Before joining jihadi tenets, their subjectivity was marked by a deep sense of self-hatred, close to the "Jüdischer Selbsthass" (Jewish Self-hatred) attributed to the German Jews at the turn of the twentieth century. In fact, German anti-Semitism blamed Jewish self-hatred on Jews, marked by resentment and an inability to appreciate themselves, when in fact it was one of the consequences of the stigmatization of Jews by German society. Similarly, the self-hatred of the "Arab" disaffected youth is a consequence of European racism. The Muslim transforms self-hatred into "hatred of others" through jihadism. The first (self-hatred of the "Arab") is secular, the second (hatred of others), religious; the first is marked by an internalized sense of unworthiness, the second by the projection of this unworthiness onto others as disbelievers. Jihadism is the metamorphosis of the first onto the second under the aegis of Daesh by those who suffered from racism and Islamophobia.

Jihadism is a proud refusal of Europeanness by the sons of migrants who were refused as Europeans by mainstream society. They achieve it through violence. For humiliated Muslim Europeans, jihadism is a counter-humiliating posturing, based on a recovered pride. As for the middle classes, jihadism is the quest for status against a background of social decline, recovering a lost sense of pride through an agonistic religiosity that promises a bright future, if not in this world, certainly in the other (heaven).

1-Humiliation at School

Humiliation of the disaffected youth begins at an early age at school. There, young sons of migrants (the case of daughters is different and rarely ends up in jihadism, most of the jihadi brides being converts or lower middle-class Muslims) learn to feel inferior to the middle-class boys who can choose the main track, whereas they are mostly confined to vocational options due to their mediocre rating. Even if some of them get good grades, school authorities discourage them from following the long courses that require several years of study. From there, their careers are mapped out. The school system also humiliates the sons and grandsons of immigrants by putting them together in deprived areas: they go to the same school, due to their geographic location (within most of Europe, students are assigned to the schools within the district they live in, if their parents choose non-private schooling). They are from a wide variety of different countries, almost all of them from the Third World, without encountering native students, French, Danish, Dutch, or English, whose role would have consisted in socializing these young people by introducing them into the mainstream culture with their mores and customs that the latter could imitate. One can speak of "school ghettoes" and "apartheid" at school (Félouzis, Liot, and Perroton, 2005; for European countries with the same type of structural problems, see Breen et al., 2010).

There is a paradoxical situation: dozens of different cultures are present in the poor ethnic districts with the major exception of the mainstream (French in France, British in the UK, Germans in Germany, and so on). Young children learn the mores and manners of each other with a major deficiency: the society's mainstream culture is lacking, and those few "White" children whose parents have not been able to put them at better schools outside the poor district align themselves with the others by adopting what we have called the slum subculture, in which the main ingredient, national culture, is missing. Slum subculture gives birth to a de-socialized youth who begins by behaving differently and ends up by rejecting the mainstream culture that they have not internalized, for want of any young mediators at school, being unable to behave according to the middle-class code of conduct. Becoming a "normal" French, English, or, more generally, European citizen in the future becomes difficult, these young people lacking the knowledge of how to behave according to the unwritten patterns of conduct in day-to-day relations with other nationals. What these young children miss is an Ariadne's thread to lead them out of the urban and mental ghetto by indicating how to conduct themselves "normally," according to the mainstream culture. The specific body language developed by these youths, feared and rejected by the mainstream culture, is a reaction to the lack of knowledge of the middle-class way of life as much as a transgression in order to call attention to its inaccessible codes and the frustration resulting from it. To give few examples: in a poor suburb, Les-Champs-de-la-ville close to the town of Gien in France, in a government-sponsored school (*école publique*), more than 90 percent of the pupils were of non-French origin in 2018 and the few French natives adopted the slum subculture rather than the mainstream French culture. In the city of Toulouse, in the poor neighborhood of La Reynerie within the district of

Le Mirail, the major government school is, as it is in the nearby district of Bellefontaine, in the same situation: pupils of many nationalities and cultures mix together, and students who master mainstream French cultural codes are missing. The result is a resentment-filled, do-it-yourself subculture. Teachers are overworked and usually unmotivated, regarding their unrewarding task, unattainable school programs result in high proportions of dropouts. National TV is, in turn, bypassed by satellite dishes, and more and more, the internet. A major deficiency in socialization becomes part of the identity of these young wannabe French citizens who have problems in dealing with elementary French cultural codes, mostly tacitly learned through interaction between young native children and their family standards, within the middle-class French society. The same assessment can be generalized to other parts of Europe. Different ragtag cultures find Islam as a common denominator, in part against the secular French culture, and in part because Islam is the only frame of reference that unites the majority of these people, mostly from Muslim countries. Those who are not Muslim are all drawn to the religion of Allah from an early age at school, being thus "pre-Islamized." Later on, many will convert to Islam, to the astonishment of their parents.

Many drop out of school before they graduate. Young men gather for long hours until late in the night in the open air, mainly close to the social housing units where they live, in a corner of the district or beside their buildings. Some of them communicate through the web and give up gathering in the nearby street corners. They kill time, often between young men, not socializing with girls, except for sex, which is strictly regulated if they adhere to a fundamentalist brand of Islam. Boredom is the secret of their socialization, away from the mainstream culture, and part of their transgressive acts are caused by tedium, living in a block of buildings, insular and cut off from the town or the city, or within an inner-city deserted by the middle classes.

Lack of socialization according to the mainstream standards sets in motion the dialectics of humiliation, counter-humiliation, aggressiveness, rejection *of* others in consequence of being treated as second-rate citizens, and their being stereotyped *by* others as unsociable people.

Young boys develop an anti-school subculture, as Colin Lacey (1970) and Paul Willis (1977) reported a few decades ago. The main difference is that the young working-class boys in the 1970s were acting against school standards because they knew they wouldn't have a chance of accessing white-collar jobs and would be able to secure only manual jobs when they left school.

Nowadays, it is not so much the unskilled jobs, but membership of deviant groups that motivates them (unskilled jobs have largely disappeared due to the new technologies). School curriculum does not enable most of them to embrace a middle-class career, it simply lets them choose pathways ending up with lower-paid jobs under the supervision of native citizens (the so-called Whites). They hate it because it reminds them of colonial times, and the type of discipline it requires exhausts them (regulated presence in the office and a social behavior that is alien to their mental universe). They reject it and aspire to a kind of job in which they are the boss: for instance, working for Uber as a driver offers them autonomy in regard to hierarchy, or being self-employed avoids the contact with the "White" boss. School is where many young people in the poor districts develop an unruly attitude as troublemakers, not believing in its ideals, having little respect for teachers who are there for lack of an alternative (once they can leave these districts for middle class areas, they do it gladly). Young boys are well aware of the dead-end jobs to which they are destined, even if they succeed at school. A minority enters university (Truong, 2015), obtaining the diplomas required for white-collar jobs, but this does not easily open the vistas for them, due to their origin, their name, their accent, and their body language (with the same diploma, Robert has far more chances to get a qualified job than Mohamed, as already mentioned).

For most of them, schooling does not lead to upward mobility, given their social and cultural handicaps. Their parents are unable to help them because of their lack of fluency in European languages or, even more seriously in some cases, due to their illiteracy. Even if they do not drop out of school, the latter's poor quality in their district, and their low grading within the elitist school system in many European countries, makes it improbable for the majority of these young children to climb the ladder and gain access to higher education, and beyond that, good jobs. In brief, school environment in poor districts is not conducive to fair competition in learning and usually does not foster social promotion. In general, the school system in Europe reproduces class divides, particularly among immigrants' progenies, rather than facilitating their upward social mobility, with some notable exceptions.[16] Bitterness and a strong sense of injustice follow these young people, often de-socialized, who refuse to do low-level work for a miserable wage, both because they refuse to follow the path of their parents and because of their inability to enforce upon themselves discipline at work. Daesh provided this youth with a golden opportunity to get out of boredom and to find a sacred calling in contrast to their total lack of vocation in their neighborhood, and to ward off social insignificance by inspiring fear in Europe.

2-Jihadis and Social Housing

Social housing reduces poverty by providing decent housing at an affordable price for low-income social categories. But its expansion has perverse effects, one of them being the concentration of not only poor but also stigmatized people, extended into many generations. High ethnic concentration creates not only frustration but also a deep sense of being apart, of living in a ghetto, of having been confined and even put under house arrest there, male residents developing slum subculture, a subculture of deviance and rancor. Provocative attitudes and ostentatious anti-civic behavior become part of their identity, particularly among young men who are convinced that there is no future for them in the mainstream society. As already mentioned, this type of urban district becomes a scene of deviant actors who believe that only through illegal action within an underground economy can they achieve upward mobility. They usually end up in prison.

Social housing contributes to a high concentration of social defects in poor districts in Europe. Many jihadis are not only from disadvantaged districts but also from those with a large number of social housings, many of them living there.

For lack of statistics, we analyze concrete cases in France, the United Kingdom, and Belgium, combining sociological and anthropological observations.

Amédy Coulibaly, the killer in the kosher supermarket in January 2015, was born in Juvisy-sur-Orge, a southeastern suburb of Paris, into a Malian Muslim immigrant family. He was the only boy among nine sisters. He grew up in a housing estate, La Grande Borne, in Grigny, a southern poor suburb of Paris, which is a vast social housing estate of 3,685 homes, in the territory of the communes Grigny and Viry-Châtillon, in Essonne. Around thirteen thousand residents live there. Hosting a fragile and precarious population, and classified as a sensitive urban area by the authorities, the Grande Borne is notorious for its deteriorated security situation and the extreme gravity of the criminal acts perpetrated by some of its residents. The general protest movement in November 2005 in France did not spare La Grande Borne, where some of the toughest confrontations with the police were recorded.

Following more than thirty carjacking attacks, in October 2016 nineteen hooded men violently assaulted four police officers, and their cars were set afire. Two policemen were seriously injured, one of them remaining in a coma for several days. A subsequent inquiry by the police uncovered a drug trafficking cell; sixty-two kilos of cannabis resin were confiscated. The rate of unemployment in Grigny is 24.1 percent, and it is even higher in La Grande Borne (more than twice the average French rate). A large community of Malians, many with a large number of children (between ages four and fourteen) live there. Grigny is one of the most disadvantaged communes in Ile-de-France (Cour des comptes, *Rapport public annuel*, 2019). More than three-fourths of the residents live in "priority districts" (the poorest districts with acute social problems), the social housing quarter La Grande Borne being in that sector of Grigny, which makes up the poorest district in Ile-de-France, the medium yearly income being €8,892 compared to €22,639 in Ile-de-France. In an official report (*Rapport sur l'évaluation et l'orientation des politiques publiques*, July 2016), Grigny was described as belonging to a category of territories suffering from "social and territorial apartheid.". The inter-ministry mission painted a dramatic portrait of a town without a city center and divided between two sets of large social housings. According to it, Grigny suffered "the omnipresence of local crime, which imposes its 'curfew' at the time when drug trafficking begins."

This kind of district, in which massive social housing concentrates poverty, ethnicity, delinquency, a high rate of school dropouts, and violence is more favorable to jihadism than normal districts.

Bilal Hadfi, a French national, the youngest terrorist in the Paris attacks of November 13, 2015, resided in Belgium. He lived in social housing in Neder-over-Heembeek with all the major problems of ethnic concentration, social disadvantages, and mental separation from the larger society.

Rachid Kassim, a major French jihadi recruiter, of Yemenite father (Mohamed) and Algerian mother (Leila), was born in the town of Roanne, where social housing (HLM) constitutes 34 percent of the housing stock. He lived in a poor district called La Bourgogne.

The disadvantaged neighborhood of Abrivados in the town of Lunel was the departure point for many Foreign Fighters who died in Syria in 2014. This quarter, with a large social housing area, wields the highest concentration of burglaries in the town (90 percent in 2014). Twenty percent of the housing stock consists of low-income social housing, and its 8,400 inhabitants were mostly unemployed or marked by precarious employment. From there, many young people went to Syria (Froelig, 2014).

Mjølnerparken, which wields the highest percentage of social housing in Denmark, is one of Copenhagen's "ghetto" neighborhoods. It is a haven for poor migrants, who make up 92 percent of its population. On February 14, 2015, the Palestinian-born Danish jihadi Omar El-Hussein, twenty-two years old, attempted to kill people at the Krudttønden Cultural Center. He was born and raised in Mjølnerparken (Chrisafis, 2015).

The members of the Strasbourg cell which sent young people to Syria in 2013 and 2014 were from poor ethnic neighborhoods. They were mainly from La Meinau district in Strasbourg, where unemployment exceeds 20 percent according to the French statistical organization INSEE (twice the national average) and constitutes one of the largest social housing complexes in the region.

Ismaël Omar Mostefaï was born in Courcouronnes, Ile-de-France, where unemployment and poverty rates are particularly high. He spent his childhood in the poorest district of the city, Le Canal, in a social housing flat.

The Buttes-Chaumont cell sent young people to Iraq to fight against the Americans in the year 2000. Its members were from the 19th district of Paris. Some of them dwelt in the social housing (HLM) building, La Cité Moderne.

Herouville in Normandy has some of the characteristics of the poor districts in France. It hosts a population of North African, Black African, and southern European origin. It has a high rate of youth unemployment and delinquency in its poor districts. This is particularly the case of Belles Portes, where 43 percent of dwellings are social housing units. Several people accused of terrorist acts have come from this quarter, hence the nickname "Normand Lunel" (Lunel in southern France having had the highest number of Foreign Fighters in 2013). Among these young people was Reda el Ayachi, who went to Syria and was killed there.

In Nice, the district of Ariane has many social housing dwellings and is classified as a priority urban area (ZUP), and since November 2012 is a priority security zone (ZSP). Its ten thousand inhabitants are mostly young and unemployed or have precarious, underpaid jobs. Ariane is one of the neighborhoods with a "high level of insecurity" according to a classification of the Ministry of the Interior (scale 4, the highest level). Among its radicalized young people was Omar Omsen, one of the major French recruiters for jihad, who lived in Ariane with his parents.

Ismaël Omar Mostefaï was born in 1985 in a family of five children in Courcouronnes (Ile-de-France) where unemployment and poverty rates are particularly high. He spent his childhood in the poorest district of the city, Le Canal, in a social housing flat. His father was Algerian, his mother Portuguese, converted to Islam. At a young age, he was having problems at school and was considered a difficult pupil by his teachers. His youth was marked by the rivalry between two neighborhoods of Evry, the Canal and Aunettes, as it is in many poor suburbs in France. The killing of Romuald, a youngster of the Canal, by a band of Aunettes gave rise to pitched battles, with the frequent use of knives and sometimes guns, and caused some deaths and injuries in the year 2000 among them. In a video made before the attacks of November 13, 2015, and put on social networks on January 24, 2016, Mostefaï beheaded a man with a knife and became a notorious jihadi worldwide.

In Savile Town, a suburb of Dewsbury, West Yorkshire, Sidique Khan, the leader of the group that perpetrated the metro and bus attacks in London in July 2005, was living in a council house, as was Hammad Munshi, who was arrested in 2006, carrying bags containing products needed for manufacturing explosive belts. Munshi's younger brother, Hassan, and his neighbor Talha Asmal, both seventeen years old, joined IS where Asmal became the youngest English suicide bomber to blow himself up in Iraq.

The Merah family (Mohammed Merah was the killer of Muslim military and Jews in 2012) lived in the social housing Raphaël in the district of Izards in Toulouse (Domingo, 2021, forthcoming).

Social housing in combination with other factors has a prominent significance in the drive toward radicalization through the concentration of populations that eventually share identical features, not only economically and socially but also culturally, contributing to the slum subculture, and beyond it to the jihadi subculture.

g-Beyond Humiliation

In many European poor neighborhoods, humiliation spirals into sheer violence. The death of young people in their clash with the police or in their confrontation with each other (or from two poor districts) for seemingly trivial reasons (the susceptibility of one side or the other) is not exceptional. In the French *banlieue*" or in poor ghettos in Copenhagen or in London, the experience of violence (particularly stabbings in London), either from hearsay or through direct involvement, is more common than in middle-class districts. In some cases, the death of young offenders by police leads to "police bashing." Some young jihadis have been direct witnesses to their friends' death confronting the police or have directly observed police violence or rough handling against them. Amédy Coulibaly (the killer of a policewoman and people in a kosher supermarket near Paris in January 2015) a few year earlier had witnessed his friend Rizgui being killed by the police. Others, like Larossi Abballa (who killed a policeman and his wife on June 13, 2016) and Karim Cheurfi (who killed a policeman on April 20, 2017, in Paris), were antagonized because of alleged police violence against them. Being a Black man (Coulibaly in France, and Michael Adebolajo and Michael Adebowale, killers of the soldier Lee Rigby on May 22, 2013, in London) and a Muslim often leads to tense situations with the police. Many young men belonging to the slum subculture develop a tough anti-police, anti-system attitude, having witnessed this type of traumatizing event (death of a friend) (Truong, 2018). Violence in its diverse forms becomes somehow routine, taboos surrounding violence and death fading because of the environment in which they live.

Sometimes, non-violent people emerge among them who develop new skills for acting peacefully (empirically observed cases in some French districts), but these are at best exceptional cases and as a rule, the experience of police violence ends up in despair or in exasperation against an unfair society, leading in turn to more violence. Sometimes, women, mostly mothers, become agents of peace within poor ethnic ghettoes: they act courageously by resisting dealers or young thieves, mainly through denouncing them to their mothers or families, mobilizing community resources, avoiding the call to the police, as in a poor Parisian suburb, Grigny (Truc and Truong, 2017). But these cases are quite rare.

Fascination with violence may become a way of life. Young men enjoy it, transgressing the dominant values based on non-violence, "doing dirty things" (*faire le sale,* as Truong [2018] calls it), dehumanizing the victims but also, in the meantime, dehumanizing themselves as well. An essential means of overcoming self-depreciation is to adhere to radical Islam. Through it, violence in its most extreme form becomes religiously licit and the individual feels vindicated in perpetrating it because of the sacred status of the Islamic norms, interpreted in an extremist way by jihadi groups, at the apex of which was IS.

As already mentioned, violence is not only related to humiliation, but also to the frustration of not being able to verbally express one's dissatisfaction or anguish among many young men belonging to the slum subculture. Once involved in deviant action, this inability becomes a positive feature: their silence becomes meaningful (threatening, disapproving, intimidating), their inability to express their feelings is understood by gang members as a positive trait of their character, adding to their prestige. The less they talk, the more they act violently, and the more they are feared as tough guys by the gang members, and the more they are appreciated as seasoned bosses. Not speaking becomes a virtue. In acting violently, these young men become even more impulsive, no mediation between their affects and the verbal expression being possible due to the paucity of their vocabulary, also shared by their accomplices. Jihadism provides them with a prefabricated language that makes unnecessary any reasoning or justification. Jihadi language is either incriminating or legitimizing in a Manichean way: it legitimizes violence of a self-righteous Self toward a guilty Other and therefore, adopts the previous channels of non-verbal violence by giving it a justifying voice. Dichotomous notions like *kafir* (Infidel, plural *kuffar*) versus Muslim, *Taqut* (the non-legitimate government or society) versus *Qest* (the idealized Islamic government dispensing justice), licit (*halal*) versus illicit (*haram*), and notions that have a dichotomous meaning such as *al wala' wal bara'* (enmity against non-Muslims and friendship with genuine Muslims), *jihad* (the holy war against the disbelievers), and *jahiliyah* (fake Muslims in reference to the pre-Islamic period) become a substitute for the absence of thought and reflection and poor semantics. Jihadi worldview is Manichean, it gives a black-and-white picture of reality and dispenses with nuanced views of life that would require a subtle and versatile vocabulary. It supplants a genuine lexicon and is a blessing to those young men who are unable to express their feelings in a personal manner. For the lack of an individualized language, the jihadi glossary substitutes the illusion of a sacred terminology that gives a black-and-white picture of the world, Islam becoming a pretext to sanctifying a dualistic, impoverishing vista of life, in contrast to the traditional Islamic worldview. To quote but a single example, traditional Islam sets out five levels with subdivisions between what is absolutely forbidden (*haram*) and what is allowed or necessary (*halal, vajib*): those acts that are rather acceptable or recommended (*mustahabb* or *mandub*), those that are rather to avoid (*makruh*) and divided into the explicit (*tahriman*) or implicit (*tanzihan*) ones, or those that are neutral (*mubaah*). Jihadi mindset often reduces this complex categorization to a dual, Manichean distinction between what is right and what is wrong (*halal/haram*). In the same manner, in the post-prophetic era, traditional Islam looks at jihad as a defensive action against those who attack Muslim territory (*fardh al ayn*, personal duty), the other cases falling within the jurisdiction of a less binding duty, according to one's capacity (*fardh al kifayah*). Jihadis declare war on the entire world under the first leitmotiv, ignoring the fact that Muslims are not under threat of invasion in most parts of the world. Radical Islam dispenses with discussion and debate, it declares them unnecessary or even harmful, and is close to the view of these young people who have not learned to cope with frustrations through arguments and counterarguments. Violence caused in part by the poverty of their language and their disability to voice their feelings through words finds an outlet with jihadism, which legitimizes it by a rudimentary vocabulary that forbids discussion in the name of religion. Radical Islam, through its ideology, allows for an exclusively punitive action, justifying extreme violence beyond any thought. In the Koran, one finds contradictory expressions toward violence. In some verses Muslims are commanded to act violently against disbelievers (for instance in the Surat Repentance), in some others tolerance is paramount (killing unduly a single person is assimilated to killing humanity in its entirety, 5:32). The jihadi version of Islam favors the agonistic verses of the Koran against those that preach tolerance, even against the Unbelievers (for instance the Surat *kafarun* that assert tolerance, against the verses of the Surat Repentance, such as 9:14) or some verses of the Spoils of War (for instance, 8:60) that preach violence against non-believers. (It is true that the dominant tradition has given precedence to the latter over the former.) In general, in the Koran, jihadis grant absolute privilege to those verses that promote violence. This vindication of violence in the name of the sacred word of God is reassuring to them, given a complex world that the crude and simplistic language of the basic jihadis fails to elucidate. Instead of dealing with the complexities of life in a nuanced way through a subtle hermeneutics of the Koran, they use violence as the key to open all closed doors.

In summary, violence has a cathartic function against humiliation for those who cannot find an autonomous symbolic expression, be it in language or in other ways, such as personal creativity.

On the other hand, radical Islam is an opportunity for many young Muslims to challenge the weakened patriarchal authority within the family in the name of fighting humiliation and subservience. They blame their parents for having a primitive, even a false sense of Islam, for being passive

Muslims, dominated by the European secular culture that pushes them to become "French Muslims" (or European ones), instead of being just true, uncompromising Muslims, proud of their religion. An anticolonial component comes into play, exacerbated by the imaginary dimension of colonization: according to this view, parents continue to behave like colonized people in the country of the former colonizers, and it is time to question their docility, even their servitude with respect to a country that dominated their ancestors, exploited their parents, and stigmatizes their children. It is a tragedy spanning over several generations (at least three) that takes place in the imagination of young European Muslims in search of a dignified identity that would allow them to overcome a long history of indignity (in France the Algerian colonization of 1830, in the United Kingdom that of India in the eighteenth century).

In summary, young Muslims blame their parents for not being genuine Muslims, for being ashamed of their Islamic identity, and for not being proud of their religion in the face of arrogant Europeans. The authority of the father is thus challenged in the name of a more inflexible understanding of Islam by the sons who criticize the submission of their elders to the "Whites" and adopt an attitude of transgression and confrontation in the name of Islamic values, particularly among those who belong to the slum subculture.

To give an illustration of this attitude, I take the case of a second-generation French-Algerian who started college but interrupted it before graduation. He became an armed robber due to family ties and, as he said, for the "lure of money," ending up in prison:

Question: You criticize your parents for the way they practiced Islam.

Karim: My parents, with all due respect, had a false knowledge of Islam. If they were true Muslims, they would have rejected French arrogance and their laïcité. What is laïcité? A way of denying respect to us, Muslims. They are hypocrites. In Algeria, the same people who proclaimed laïcité in France in the nineteenth century used Islam to impose their authority to the colonized people and maintained religion and defended Catholicism. Jews became French citizens because they were not Muslims [the Crémieux Decree in October 1870 declared the Jews, but not Muslims, in Algeria French citizens]. *Our parents were too submissive, they were exploited and on top of it, in awe of the French. My generation has questioned this admiration and claimed an Islamic identity in the face of their religion, laïcité.*

Question: The French criticize fundamentalist Islam as putting into question laïcité.

Karim: They use laïcité to colonize us a second time: in their view people like us can never be genuinely secular [*laïc*]. *Even if we renounce Islam, eat pork, take off the scarf, drink wine, commit adultery, in brief, if we become like them in every respect, they will still say: "These guys are fake, they are not really secular! They are only Frenchmen on their* [administrative] *paper." If we abide by Islam and refuse to kiss their women on the cheek, or shake hands with women, or drink beer or wine, they say: "You see, they cannot be secular, they cannot be good republicans, good Frenchmen!" I, for one, know that they'll never accept me as French. My name is Karim, and it's not a French name at all, it is once and for all "Arab." But they are wrong if they think they can stamp on my pride because I don't give a damn about their accepting me or not. That is their problem, not mine! I live here and I fuck them* [*je les emmerde*]*!*

Interviewer: But then, there is no room for compromise!

Karim: Compromise is long gone. They don't accept us. We aren't Frenchmen in a true sense, we are non-citizens, and I take note of that. I became an armed robber because I had to settle a score, that was my payback. Otherwise, I had started university. I wanted to do something and show them concretely that I hated them. I was tempted to join jihadi groups, but it required a lot of sacrifice.

Question: Why do so many "Arabs" become jihadi? Is it ideology?

Karim: People of my kind don't become jihadi for ideological reasons, but because they have a grudge against society. The "Whites" deny our identity and do not respect our religion or the way we are. They are not tolerant but claim the contrary while blaming us for not being tolerant.

Question: What has Islam to do there?

Karim: Islam is my life and the French cannot trample on our pride and dignity through laïcité. We are Muslims, and this goes beyond any secular norm. . . . Up to a few years ago I was not religious at all. I have become so and don't ask any more for "integration" as they call it, which denies our faith, our past, our roots. . . .

Question: Have you heard of Merah? [Mohamed Merah killed, in March 2012 in Toulouse and Montauban, three Muslim soldiers and three Jewish children and their father.]

Karim: He killed Muslims who joined the French army and were sent to kill other Muslims in Afghanistan and elsewhere. They had acted against

> *Islam: God has forbidden that a Muslim kills another Muslim, particularly if the French colonizer orders that. I find Merah's acts justified but killing children, Jewish or not, is not acceptable to God. He shouldn't have done it, Islam forbids it.* (Interview conducted in the prison of Fresnes, November 2012)

Many movies in France show the association of hatred, poor districts, deviance, and violence. *La Haine* (The Hatred), a black-and-white film by Mathieu Kassovitz, released in 1995, was one of the first. Since then, those focusing on the "Arab" or Black offenders are legion and more than 150 movies up to 2019 dealt with the problems of the disaffected youth ("Mes 150 films Banlieue, jeunesse, délinquance préférés", 19 December 2019). The latest one, *Les Misérables*, released in December 2019, describes violence and drugs in the poor districts of Seine-Saint-Denis, close to Paris, mainly among "Arabs."

In general, a large proportion of young Muslims in Europe find fault twice with their host societies: first, the public opinion treats them like colonized people, stigmatizing them as being unable to be adult and modern, unfit to become genuine citizens, in spite of the fact that they are, legally speaking, holders of European passports; second, they put Muslims in a quandary: on one hand they are supposed to be citizens and therefore, Muslims only for the sake of their souls (due to their intimate persuasion). On the other, the same people ask Muslims to condemn jihadi violence *as* Muslims. Did they ask Irish people to condemn the IRA (Irish Republican Army) for its violence, or the Corsicans for Corsican terrorism? Do they ask French people to condemn French violence against Algerians during the 1960s war of independence? Why do they ask Muslims to reject publicly jihadi violence, assuming they might be bad citizens? (This view was put forward by a middle-class French-Algerian in a discussion a few days after the July 14, 2016, jihadi attack in Nice, in southern France).

Young Muslims no longer tolerate being socially invisible but claim visibility *as* Muslims, even ostentatious in order to compensate for the lack of recognition in the past and in the present. They reverse the reserved attitude of their parents by a provocative show-off in order to teach a lesson to the Europeans (and particularly the French with their specific brand of secularism, *laïcité*), even to the left-wing people who defend in principle Muslims as a dominated minority but whose prejudices against Muslims puts them on an equal footing with the conservatives. "White" Europeans are suspected of being fundamentally driven by the same mindset as the hard-core colonialists, even though some of them show understanding toward Muslims and their plight in the colonial past. In France this new type of attitude is illustrated by a group called "Les Indigènes de la République" who claim that both right and left have a colonial attitude toward Muslims, although for different reasons, and that one should "decolonize" society, "deracialize" it (*déraciser*, a neologism), right and left altogether. The new radical Islamic religiosity, on the other hand, incorporates revenge and self-assertion in order to break with the colonial legacy, reversing the logic of contempt and condescension, identifying non-violence and softened morals with lethargy and lack of genuine ethics. It calls into question the secular, supposedly integrative and tolerant culture that is in reality intolerant and stigmatizing in their opinion. The latter is regarded as the continuation of colonization through a system confining Muslims in the "here below" in denial to God, locking them up in the secular straitjacket of "White" culture (despicably called *dunya*, this earthly world, opposed to the *akhira*, the Hereafter). In short, the secular world becomes the immanent world of colonization, Islam offering an escape from secularism and colonialism in reference to the transcendence of God, recovering a proud identity that was denied to Muslims by colonialism and is nowadays, by secularism. Secularization, the ensuing freedom of religion, and the autonomy of the individual in European societies are viewed as an attempt to denigrate Islam and humiliate Muslims. According to this view, secularization restricts life only down to the material world, excluding heaven, pushing toward godlessness, and thus denying legitimacy to Islam and Muslims. They become violent in the name of their lost dignity and its reconquest through radical Islam and its antagonistic values to those of a secular Europe.

Through jihadism, slum subculture reverses stigmas in the name of a culture of confrontation tinged with Islamic religiosity. Nasser, a French-Algerian citizen in his early thirties, convicted for armed robbery and put in jail in Fresnes, described to me in 2013 in a remarkable analysis disaffected Muslims' predicament and the role of radical Islam not only in reversing stigmas (Goffman, 1963) but also in achieving self-respect through compounded violence against a humiliating society:

Nasser: I'm in prison, but it's the life of all of us.
Question: What do you mean by that?
Nasser: I mean for the sons and grandsons of North African migrants [Maghrébins], prison is our second home; we start our adult lives in prison,

and we bury it here. Not that we are innocent, I don't have a problem acknowledging that I committed those robberies—but I didn't commit all those that the French justice blames on me. . . . Still, "White" society imposed deviant life on me. My father worked for a small salary in the heavy industry, my mother was a housewife, she occasionally worked as a cleaning lady to help my father, whose salary was not always enough to feed my four other siblings and myself. I refused to live in poverty, I wanted a new life, avoid the hard work of my parents who brought home just enough to live on.

Question: But exploitation is a fact of life shared by many other Frenchmen.

Nasser: But my story has its roots in colonization: my grandparents were colonized, French colonizers confiscated their land, they were humiliated by the French who took not only their land but also their pride. They despised them while exploiting them. The story of people like me extends to many generations treated inhumanly by the French, without any sense of regret, even long after independence.

My father had health problems like many Algerian workers after so many years spent in the factory. He became asthmatic after breathing long hours in the polluted factory air. I wanted to live like you, middle-class people, those with money, who make themselves look important in front of people like us, as if we didn't exist. We cannot be proud, either of our colonial past, or of our illiterate parents, or of ourselves. Nobody appreciates us, and people like you despise us, even if they pretend they don't. . . .

Question: But I don't despise you!

Nasser: Not you in person, but people like you. Jihadis have changed the situation!

Question: But what has this to do with jihadis?

Nasser: Well, now, when people like me kill people like you by blowing up their explosive belt or shoot them in the name of Allah, we are taken seriously. You despised us, now you are afraid of us, and from now on, there is no room for contempt, only fear. Contempt has changed sides. Jihadis make fun of those who are afraid to die and they know they will kill and die. With them contempt has switched sides: we despise you while previously, you despised us.

This remarkable analysis shows how contempt and humiliation are at the heart of one of the major models of radicalization as analyzed in this chapter, whose aim is to overcome the insurmountable sense of inferiority and "misrecognition" by the mainstream society. To act in order to humiliate the "White man" has become an irresistible impulse: it is not only the desire to overcome contempt and to become like others, but the will to reverse contempt and humiliation, to despise and show it in an ostentatious manner to those who despised the sons of migrants. It is more than a reversal of stigmas, as Goffman observed. It goes beyond it, through "showing off" one's contempt, enjoying it publicly and putting it on display in a script in which death is a major constituent. Killing and dying in a self-righteous manner—in an exacerbated manner—goes far beyond the Goffmanian dialectic of reversing the stigmas; it is the desire to put an end to the confrontation by killing and being killed, closing the chapter of life and opening a death-centered worldview.

What Nasser says also underlines the fact that compromise and mutual understanding is henceforth impossible: for him, whatever "White" people do falls under the logic of contempt toward people like him: either they are lying and cynical, or they are naïve and gullible. Communication is impossible, only confrontation prevails. Once in this slum subculture, for most people there is no way out: it shapes their lives and imposes on them an agonistic view of social relations.

For Foreign Fighters, joining jihadi movements freed them from the obligation of being orthodox Muslims, the important thing being not to scrupulously follow religious rituals but to engage in the service of the caliphate as a combatant of jihad (*mujahid*). This is what one French jihadi expressed by saying that he was the soldier of the IS, not an (ordinary) Muslim ("I was Daesh, not a Muslim") (Seelow, 2018). For him, acting under the IS banner freed him from submission to religious orthodoxy. This put an end to the supremacy of their parents, who pretended to know better than them ritualistic Islam. They denounced their parents' religion, which was compromised by their submitting to the harmful Western culture: older Muslims sometimes were secretly drinking. On the whole, they were lax in the practice of the five daily prayers, their mothers did not cover their faces with tight veils, men shaved in defiance of the tradition of the Prophet who did not trim his beard, and so forth. Young radicalized Muslims questioned their parents' submission to a Western world that was, in their opinion, an avatar of colonialism. Rejecting the "docile" Islam of their parents was also tantamount to rebutting a past that had bowed down to the colonial rule. To them, the West was the "mother of all vices" (*Umm ul fissad*), as a Salafist told me in an interview in prison in 2013 (Saint-Maur prison in central France). In particular, the creation of Daesh in the Middle East gave an impetus to the desire for self-assertion among the new generations of European Muslims. Their "will to power" found an outlet in the new caliphate that combined pride and might with a radical version of Islam whose main target was the confrontation with the "arrogant" West (*istikbar*) in the name of their reconquered dignity. In this respect, the social context of jihadism in Europe is paramount. Among the new Muslim generations, many suffer from joblessness (contrary to their parents, who were employed in industry as unskilled workers) with no hope for the future. Stigmatization, added to segregation in poor districts, deeply abases them. Jihadi propaganda through IS became the best means for developing counter-humiliation strategies. Against a background of humbling, they discovered self-respect through radical Islam: "White" people became unworthy due to their secular and therefore heathen view marked by the fear of death, jihadis being able to demean them by their acceptance of death as martyrs. They acquired a noble identity by inspiring dread in White people, their new Self touching the sublime, in their opinion. Of course, God was the paragon of sublimity, jihadis sharing in it by debasing Western Infidels who had rebelled against Him.[17] But their experience of Sublime was distinct from the purely aesthetic view, which begins with a feeling of awe toward a boundless beauty, whereas the jihadis' feeling was based on a relentless fight against the heathen enemy, putting their life at stake and giving them a sense of acting for a sublime cause, overcoming the colonial past and a "hopeless" present by transcending the fear of death. Sublime became the holy war, but this version of jihad had its roots in resentment and a wounded Self, suffering from stigmas and a deep sense of having been shamed. Sublime became the experience of being invulnerable by leaning on God and overcoming the fear of death while inspiring it to others. It was a narcissistic feeling of empowerment by God's decree and, in part, an "infinite" capacity to take vengeance against a hostile Europe that had become the land of the pagans. Holy death (martyrdom) versus an unholy one (the death of the Infidels) became the Janus face of the Sublime: on one hand, the sublime lack of fear of death and acceptance of martyrdom that created in them a sense of self-esteem that they sorely missed; on the other, the mean fear of death among the Infidels that expressed an infinite negation of sublimity on their part.[18].

In the United Kingdom, society does not impose a secular model of citizenship as restrictive as in France. The acceptance of Islamic clothing even in the public administration (in the police the tolerance for headscarf and turban, even among policewomen and policemen) in the name of multiculturalism makes relations with Muslims less confrontational. Islam as an identity thus takes on less contentious contours than in France, where official secularism (*laïcité*) as an intangible principle denies recognition of their religious status to Muslims and the followers of other religions in the state apparatus. Still, British multiculturalism is denounced by migrants' sons as fake, the domination of the White British over others being implemented, in their view, through a strategy of "avoidance": the "Whites" do not marry non-Whites and the rate of mixed marriages crossing the community boundaries is low—in fact, far lower than in France (9% vs. 27%; Office for National Statistics 2014; Gabizon, 2010[19]).

For fundamentalist Muslims and jihadis, multiculturalism leads to a denial of Islam's legitimacy. Its minority status means for them its inferiority within a hegemonic secular English culture. That is why those who become secular and don British identity, like Salman Rushdie, join the British anti-Islamic mainstream culture, which thus reveals its true nature in their eyes.

More generally, second- and third-generation sons of Southeast Asian origin suffer from ambivalence between ethnicity and religion. They are treated as "Pakis," and Islam is regarded as an additional version of this subordinate position in an English society, which is moving toward an overwhelming secularization and an "à la carte" religiosity. Islam is experienced by the non-Muslim majority as a holistic religion that fiercely resists secularization and rejects individualized faith, which are signs of commitment to modernity, to which Islam is reticent. As a counterpoint, Muslims experience the conditions imposed by mainstream society to their religion as a roundabout way of making them subaltern and marginal. In contrast to the frontality of French racism and Islamophobia in the name of *laïcité*, its British counterparts offer a soft form of marginalization that remains no less stigmatizing. There is a British distancing toward the former colonized people that resurfaces with Islam. They split off from members of former colonies by cunningly appealing for recognition of different communities, on a par. However, Muslims' recognition by the mainstream society is experienced by them as a way of separating the former colonizers from the people of the former colonies. Radical Islam assumes this separation, this time with pride and self-proclaimed religious superiority, which, prior to their joining jihadis, was experienced as a sign of their inferior status. The extremist version of Islam rejects both religious tolerance and the separation between different communities by setting out to unify society under the banner of Allah, whether the majority endorses it or not. Stigmas are thus overturned in a radical way: Islamists do not so much ask to be treated on an equal footing with others, they demand that others voluntarily or under duress submit to the religion of the minority, in the name of Islam's absolute superiority.

h-A Cumbersome Freedom and the Need for Sacred Norms

For IS, a Muslim's duties go far beyond his freedom and, above all, those freedoms acquired through the secularization of society are null and void. Modern freedom is another name for idolatry: it substitutes the individual subject who wishes to legislate in his own name to God and his commandments. "Sacred duties" (*fardh ul ayn*), theorized as imperative personal obligations that are absolutely compulsory, supersede individual freedom. In the past, Muslims subscribed rather loosely to these duties and they usually were not strictly put into practice, the Muslim world not being unified, and competing states not in unison either. Jihadism is by far more intolerant than past Islamic traditions with the probable exception of the Kharijites (Khawarij) who emerged during the reign of the fourth "well-guided" caliph, Ali, who reigned from 656 CE to 661 CE and was killed by a follower of that sect. What is noteworthy is that in European jihadism, the language of duty is far more attractive to young men and women than that of freedom, in contrast to the 1960s European youth who were the main agents of the May 1968 movement in France. There has been a major change in the "spirit of the age" (the Hegelian *Zeitgeist*), if we compare their mindset in the 1960s and in the wake of the twenty-first century, particularly regarding the meaning of freedom. Among part of the contemporary European youth (not only Muslims), freedom has become suspicious, in part because under its guise the progressive withdrawal of the Welfare State has been accomplished since few decades ago. On the other hand, the fear of indistinction (between men and women, young and adult), sexual deregulation (homosexuality), and family instability have become paramount. Jihadism proposes a mythical solution to this multiple crisis. Young European jihadis prefer repressive norms in the name of God that give sense to their lives to a freedom that robs them of certainty and stability. What distinguishes the current generation from the 1960s is that they suffer from a lack of standards and are scared of their almost infinite but rather useless freedom. They do not know where to draw the line: the patriarchal family is moribund, authority within the family is at best diluted, sexual freedom extends to the same-sex relations and beyond—in brief, nothing seems sacred or untouchable. Youth movements in the 1960s fought against patriarchal family, state authority, gender inequality, and restrictions to sexual freedom. Egalitarian families, gender equality in legal terms, and loose family structures were achieved as a result of these movements. Nowadays, people enjoy an almost boundless freedom in matters touching family and sexuality (homosexuality has become legal, lack of marriage in couples is widespread, changing sexual partners has become a private matter, gender reassignment is within reach). Feminism has freed women from the yoke of patriarchal authority, but it has also contributed to the weakening sense of male and female identities in the name of gender equality, particularly among fragile teenagers, and overburdened women with housework, child rearing, as well as wage labor.

Daesh particularly targeted teenagers, unsettled by the blurred figurehead of father and mother within the modern family. For many of them, freedom was of a negative rather than a positive nature; it meant family breakdown, authority crisis, and the eclipse of the tutelary figures of father and mother insofar as second marriages multiplied them in the roles of stepfather and stepmother in increasingly intricate and confusing configurations. Freedom became also threatening as it heightened the risk of a life devoid of solidarity, gradually turning into the loss of social ties and the isolation of the individual.

In all those cases, a sense of a loss by the younger generations, teenagers and adults, was exploited by IS, promising a new world in which the instable modern family would be replaced by a stable neo-patriarchal one and a desecrated democracy by a sacred political regime (the caliphate), shielded from the uncertainties of political pluralism. The latter was deemed illegitimate, as much because it was a *Taqut* (an idolatrous government that usurps the place of God in its legislative dimension) as it gave the impression of disorder and powerlessness toward criminality, transgression of social norms, and disrespect for sacred values (for instance, the desecration of the Prophet of Islam by the Scandinavian caricaturists, followed by those of *Charlie Hebdo* magazine in France). In opposition to democracy, with its lengthy processes and its inability to make quick decisions, IS offered its capacity for prompt repression in the name of the sacred, Islamic law. Against the slowness of the judiciary in democratic Europe, marked by endless procedures, it offered the celerity of the sentence in its tribunals that applied the uncontested Shariah (Islamic laws).

To put an end to endless discussions and negotiations in the modern family and society, a youth in disarray looked for sacred norms, beyond dispute. Their aspiration was exploited by Daesh. As already hinted, in the new generations' freedom has become more of a burden than a boon. In the modern world, in many ways, freedom has become synonymous with loneliness and a lack of solidarity: freedom of divorce results in easy separation and children's disarray; sexual freedom exposes people to new illnesses (AIDS, among others); solitude and despair due to the loosening of parental authority pushes teenagers toward a desire for transgression, having no model to follow: father and mother have turned into old brothers and sisters and are devoid of undisputed authority, in particular in stepfamilies with the multiplication of parental figures.

Another factor, as important as family change, has been the worsening of social conditions, in particular in the field of employment. It makes freedom a source of anguish, in particular among those exposed to the new rules of "flexibility" in labor relations, which is more of a servitude than an emancipation. Those left alone and jobless, and in general those with no social back-up against the blind market forces in the name of economic "freedom," intensely feel the lack of protecting standards. Daesh presented an alternative to this anguishing exposure of the individual to the stringent rules of the market: social promotion and individual heroism, and beyond that, the certainty of redemption in the Hereafter.

Individualism has culminated in the globalized individual assuming many areas of his social, emotional, economic, and cultural life, which crush him under their weight. The negative sides of freedom push him to despair and depression, whereas the positive dimensions—to choose one's job, to live in economic stability, to take advantage of one's right to benefits from the Welfare State in order to achieve creativity in culture and leisure—have faded away. Self-depreciation, a feeling of deep mental instability, and a sense of being inept and ineffective are commonly shared among middle-class youth (they usually attribute to their own faults their failure in life within a globalized economy).

During the glorious days of Daesh, involvement in jihadism was in many respects a remedy against the ills of this modern freedom that leaves the individual helpless and distressed. IS's version of jihadism contributed to a renewal of self-confidence, the person attributing to others what he considered up to then to be his major defects, burdening himself with them previously and feeling mediocre. Through Daesh, the fault changed sides. The jihadi became guiltless and the pagan, godless society became guilty. That freed the Self from the distressing feeling of helplessness by relying on an imaginary neo-Ummah, through which his hidden talents would develop and, in particular, his heroism would be rewarded. The sense of self-depreciation would disappear, once he would put himself at the service of the new Islamic government, the caliphate bringing him prestige and a strong sense of righteousness. This occurred in sharp contrast to the young man's concrete situation in Europe, in which he was either nobody (the disaffected youth) or someone with a very modest prospect of future promotion (most of the middle-class young men). Exposure to the test of sacred death by staging jihad brought self-esteem to these young men and led to a laudatory acceptance of themselves as valiant knights of Allah in their fight against the Infidels.

IV
Jihadi Actors

IS jihadism attracted several new categories of male and female actors, sometimes newcomers (European teenagers, for instance). During the crucial years of 2013–2017, when IS was born, established, thrived, and then declined, most of these actors identified with the new State that epitomized in their minds the rebirth of the caliphate and the dawn of a new world.

The main link between them, as will be shown in this chapter, was the aspiration to a future other than the one they had come to expect in their society as well as a sense of a meaningful and sacred mission, which consisted in fulfilling the utopia of a universal Islamic State. An unbridled imagination, often with contempt for reality, but in search of a new world, inspired them.

Jihadis who joined IS were young. In a sample of 1,200 individuals who left Western countries between 2012 and 2015 for Syria and Iraq, 14 percent were under eighteen years of age, 27 percent were between eighteen and twenty-one, 26 percent between twenty-two and twenty-five, 17 percent between twenty-six and twenty-nine, 9 percent between thirty and thirty-five, and 7 percent were thirty-six years or older: those aged between fourteen and twenty-five years made up 67 percent of the total, two-thirds of the jihadi actors (Perliger and Milton, 2016).

In this section we consider jihadi agents in regard to social class (disaffected vs. middle-class youth), gender (male vs. female), age (adolescent vs. adult), mental status ("normal" vs. "pathological" cases), born-again versus converts, preachers and recruiters versus their targets, institutions such as prison, and the role of the jihadi star system—that is, those who achieved fame for their warlike deeds in the imaginary pantheon of jihadism.

a-Jihadi Actors and Social Classes

In terms of social classes, we can distinguish three types of jihadi actors:

Jihadism in Europe. Farhad Khosrokhavar, Oxford University Press. © Oxford University Press 2021.
DOI: 10.1093/oso/9780197564967.003.0004

1. People of immigrant origin, living in ghettoized poor districts in European cities (the so-called Muslim disaffected youth), sharing what we have called slum subculture.
2. Middle-class Muslims who suffer from stigmas despite their economic integration. Their humiliation pushes some of them toward radical Islam.
3. Middle-class or lower-middle-class converts looking for a "warm community," as opposed to their "cold" national societies.

1-Disaffected Youth

As already mentioned, disaffected youth suffer economic exclusion and cultural oppression simultaneously. The rate of unemployment is by far higher among them than in the average population. Most of the Foreign Fighters who left European countries for Syria and Iraq were unemployed.

In France, Belgium, and Holland, jihadis had a lower level of education than the average citizen. In France, the percentage of people holding a higher education diploma who went to Syria and Iraq was around 8 percent, while the national average was around 38 percent; in Belgium the rates were 7 percent and 40 percent, respectively; in Holland, 22 percent and 37 percent. The trend was not similar in other countries, where there were no significant differences: in Germany, respectively, the numbers were 27 percent and 28 percent, in the United Kingdom, 43 percent and 40 percent .[1] In the preceding jihadi sample, only 11 percent had a specialized job, the others being either unemployed (35 percent) or having temporary, low-qualification jobs. A comparison with the overall population reveals that a large part of them are unemployed: in Belgium, among the Foreign Fighters 68 percent were unemployed compared to 8 percent in the general population in 2014; in France, it was 44 percent against 11 percent; in Germany, 17 percent against 4 percent (while the educational level, as we will see, was not notably different from the national average); in the UK the numbers were 32 percent against 6 percent, and in Holland, 17 percent against 7 percent (Perliger and Milton, 2016).

The disaffected youth are unable to act according to the mainstream cultural codes and are imbued with a slum culture that shows the gap between society and the ethnic poor neighborhoods where they live. In reaction to their dual marginalization—economic as well as cultural—they develop a provocative attitude, boasting about their "Otherness." Their insurmountable differences with others and the fact that they do not act according to the mainstream cultural codes creates misunderstanding and antagonism between them and the mainstream society. Since they regard the gap as unbridgeable, they adopt a defiant attitude that leads to their further exclusion (they are considered to be irrecoverable, irrevocably de-socialized from the perspective of the mainstream society). Their inclination to join jihadi forces was studied in the preceding chapter, which discussed the transition from the slum subculture to the jihadi subculture.

We can also mention the case of split identities, between two polarities (e.g., French vs. Algerian; English vs. Pakistani) or even three (divided identities between the Berber, Arab, and French or Berber, Arab, and Belgian [or Dutch]). A few examples highlight their mental state.

Mohamed Bouyeri, who killed the Dutch filmmaker Theo van Gogh, showcases the torn identity of sons of Muslim migrants. Radical Islam played the role of a unifying principle that mended his split identity through violence against those who, in his view, had broken it. He did it in the name of the sanctity of the new religious identity.

Bouyeri was born in 1978 in Amsterdam into a family of Moroccan origin, the second generation of Berbers. His Berber descent is an important feature in the phenomenon of radicalization of young Europeans of Moroccan descent: the Berbers were manhandled by King Hassan II, who intended to get rid of them because they represented largely the *blid al siba* (the land of rebellion) in Northern Morocco (the Rif mountainous region). They demanded political autonomy and recognition of their language (Amazigh) and culture, which the Sherifian kingdom denied them. Sending them to Europe was, in this perspective, to keep opponents and insubordinate people away. In Holland, their number is estimated at 300,000 out of a population of 391,000 of Moroccan origin (CBS StatLine, December 2017).

In Europe, whether in Belgium, France, or Holland, Berbers have been caught in a plurality of inaccessible, denied identities. In North Africa, to be a Berber is to have an identity distinct from that of the Arabs, and mostly despised. The individual is driven by a sense of intense domination by the Arab regimes that impose on them an "internal colonialism" and seek to quell their urge for cultural and political autonomy. In Europe, the new generations coming from the Berber regions (particularly the Rif in Northern Morocco) do not feel primordially Moroccan, although they usually possess Moroccan citizenship, because of the repression of their parents by the

Moroccan central government, the so-called Makhzen. They do not feel European (Belgian, French, Dutch . . .) because they feel like they are being treated as second-class citizens (Buruma, 2006). While their Berber parents were more secularized than their fellow Arabs, they fall back on a rigid version of Islam that makes a virtue of the war against the "Infidels" (that is, Western powers but also the Arab governments that repressed their parents).

In 1995, Bouyeri graduated from high school and tried to continue at Nyenrode Inholland College in Diemen. After five years, he gave up his studies without having graduated. At an early age, he was known to the police as a member of a group of troubled youth of Moroccan origin. For a time, he worked as a volunteer at Eigenwijks, a neighborhood organization in the suburb of Slotervaart in Amsterdam. He began to radicalize shortly after his mother's death from cancer and the new marriage of his father in 2003. The al-Qaeda attacks of September 11, 2001, in the US and the war in Iraq contributed to his radicalization alongside his family trauma. He began to follow strict Islamic rules in their Wahhabi version. As a result, he could perform fewer and fewer tasks at Eigenwijks, where he refused to serve alcohol or take part in activities involving women. He gave up his job. He let his beard grow and started to wear a *djellaba* (a traditional dress, hooded cloak). He attended the el-Tawheed Mosque where he met other radical Muslims, including the terrorist suspect Samir Azzouz, a high school student. With them, he founded a radical group called by the security forces the Hofstad network. Bouyeri split up with his parents in 2002 and rented a studio in the western district of Amsterdam where he hosted a group of young Muslims under the guidance of a Syrian in his forties, Redouan al-Issar, who became the ideologue of the group. In early 2003 Samir Azzouz was arrested in Ukraine, seeking to enter Chechnya. He was sent back to Amsterdam, where social workers and teachers tried unsuccessfully to assist him in his final exams. A few months later, Spanish intelligence informed the Netherlands that they had intercepted communications between Azzouz and a Moroccan in Spain suspected of having participated in the suicide bombings in Casablanca in May 2003. It looked as if Azzouz and several others were planning a terrorist attack. The Dutch authorities found components of a bomb in his possession. The group members were arrested, but shortly after, they were released for lack of evidence. Issar was deported to Germany.

On November 2, 2004, Bouyeri shot dead Theo van Gogh and, at the end, cut his throat. Van Gogh was known for his harsh criticism of Islam and the multicultural society. At his trial Bouyeri unambiguously asserted that he would again act in the same way if he were released. He expressed no remorse and showed no guilt feelings. In his view, killing Van Gogh was legitimate according to the Islamic commandments: "There is a law that obliges me to cut off the head of anyone who insults the Prophet," he declared.

Bouyeri, who adopted the pen name of "Abu Zuhair" for his writings and translations, mastered Dutch relatively well, and his open letter to the public that he pinned on Theo van Gogh's chest was rather well written. It contained a farewell poem in which he described himself as a dead martyr for his faith, as he wished: "This is my last word, riddled with bullets, baptized in blood, as I wished." The poem was followed by jihadi slogans and a letter about Ayaan Hirsi Ali, the Somali woman who was at the time a member of the Dutch parliament and had written the screenplay for Theo van Gogh's latest film, "Submission," marked by a virulent criticism of Islam. He called her heretical and at the service of her "Jewish masters," these followers of the Talmud who, according to him, dominated Dutch politics. He declared war against her, the United States, Europe, and especially Holland. Bouyeri was sentenced to life imprisonment.

His Dutch poem entitled "Baptized in Blood" is an apology of exhibitionist martyrdom through violence, inflicted on oneself and others:

> This is then my last word . . . / Pierced by bullets. . . / Baptized in blood . . . As I hoped.
>
> I leave a message . . . / For you . . . the fighter . . . / The Tawhid [God's unicity, the first principle of Islam] tree is waiting . . . / Longing for your blood . . . / Make a purchase . . . / And Allah gives you space . . . / He gives you the Garden (paradise) . . . / Instead of the earthly debris.
>
> I also have something to say to the enemy . . . / You will certainly die . . . / Even if you go on tour all over the world . . . / Death is lurking . . . / Chased by the Knights of the Dead . . . / Coloring the streets in Red.
>
> To the hypocrites [fake Muslims] I finally say this: / Wish DEATH or else shut up and . . . calm down [sit].
>
> Dear brothers and sisters, I am approaching my end . . . / But this certainly does not end the story.

This poem has four major topics. The first is the self-promoting image of a martyr, suffering painful death; Bouyeri's expected death would send a message to others, friends and foes alike. To the friends of Allah, the message is that of hope in an otherworldly blissful life in which paradise will be their abode. To the enemies, it is the threat of death at the hands of Muslims like him. To those "hypocrites" (Muslims who spread disunion, *fitna*, that is, who do not share these radical views) he promised also death in case they do not "shut up." Martyrdom, death at its center, is for Bouyeri the principal message of Islam. His religiosity is death-centered and Manichean, like that of many people before him, beginning with Iranian martyrs during the long war with Iraq (1980–1988) who wrote their wills and poems, promoting holy death as their ideal (Khosrokhavar, 1995). This view is in frontal opposition to the mainstream culture in Europe, characterized by a life-centered hedonism and a secular view of existence. Islam, as opposed to the West, is marked in Bouyeri's view by its reversed values. To secular societies that despise them in their opinion, people like Bouyeri are "in" and "out" at the same time (they are in, living and socializing in Europe, but they are not accepted as full citizens), and in their own perspective, they feel neither in nor out. He found in radical Islam a principle that fused the disjointed parts of his identity by rejecting his belonging to Europe and promoting violence against those who were disrespectful toward the Prophet of Islam. By making the apology of an exhibitionist martyrdom in his last words, Bouyeri referred to a counter-secular dimension of radical Islam in a European society where death is pushed to the extreme limits of invisibility. His conception of death was hyper-visible in his poem, even ostentatious. His version of Islam subordinated life to holy death and he declared enmity with those who never considered him their equal. In reaction to a life that was unbearable to him, he inflicted an unbearable death to the others.

2-Middle-Class Jihadis

The mental landscape of young, middle-class jihadis is different from that of the disaffected youth. While the latter suffer from a lack of recognition by society and are trapped in a self-deprecatory view of themselves, the former do not cope well with the humiliation imposed on them by society despite the fact that they fulfill their duties as citizens (having a job, paying taxes, behaving according to the law, etc.). In the case of the disaffected youth, we are faced with the denial of citizenship by society. They transform it, via jihadism, into a rejection of citizenship. In the case of the middle-class youth, it is a wounded citizenship, a gap that seems at times unbridgeable despite the fact that the individual behaves according to the canons of middle-class standards, with small differences (such as not eating pork, not having the same attitude toward sexuality, nor adopting a fundamentally secular behavior in their personal life).

To this we must add what might be called the post-colonial suspicion. No matter what the Muslim does, he is confronted with his past, which he does not control, and which is ascribed to him as a liability: mainstream society does not recognize him as an anonymous citizen but as a Muslim, suspected of entertaining sympathies with radical Muslims. This post-colonial suspicion toward the sons and grandsons of Muslim migrants finds a response within the slum culture by rejecting the "White man," but middle classes do not have a ready-made answer to it, especially since they want to live like everyone else, apart from minor differences (wearing the scarf, avoiding alcohol, etc.), whereas disaffected young live usually isolated in housing estates within impoverished and ethnic neighborhoods where they do not mix with mainstream society. Social proximity with mainstream society and liability toward the burden of a past that is lived through as being still alive in everyday life make middle-class Muslims miserable.

One should not lose sight of the fact that among the European Muslim middle class there is a widespread feeling that they are second-class citizens, exposed to the prejudices of "Whites" and their Islamophobia. On top of it, they do not enjoy the same employment opportunities as other citizens. Empirical research by sociologists largely confirms this subjective feeling of inequality (a "Mohamed" with the same diploma as "Robert" has a fraction of the latter's chance to find an equivalent job; Dobson, 2014; Dugan, 2014).

A major reason for joining Daesh among middle-class young people, converts as well as the born-again Muslims, was humanitarian. Indeed, the desperate situation of Syria, where a protest movement against the Assad regime ended in 2012 in a bloodbath by his government, and the intervention of the other countries (Iran and Russia on Assad's side, Saudi Arabia and the Emirates on the side of the Islamist opposition) pushed young Muslims to assist the victims in Syria by means of what they considered legitimate violence. In the first wave of departure to Syria, from 2012 to 2013, the jihadi dimension was rather marginal among the middle-class Muslims. One can quote this middle-class convert in his early twenties, who was tempted to go to Syria in 2013 (the interview took place in April 2014 in a voluntary association in the 19the district of Paris):

> *I was tired and sick of injustice: Muslims were killed in Syria and nobody cared, despite the lofty words by the* [French] *government. I wanted to do something, help these people who were left alone. . . . Humanitarian assistance was powerless, these people needed more than doctors or medicines, they needed to be defended against Assad's bloody regime.*

Another Muslim middle-class student from Seine-Saint-Denis (a northern Parisian suburb where numerous disaffected Muslims live), who was kept by his family from going to Syria but was deeply indignant of the hypocrisy of the Western governments, believed that helping Muslims trumped other considerations, not only for Islam's sake but for sheer human-rights reasons (February 2014):

> *In Syria, Palestine, Afghanistan, Pakistan, India, almost everywhere in the world Muslims are being abused, and nobody cares. Israelis kill Palestinians, they hold hostage two million Palestinians in Gaza; in India (Kashmir) Muslims are under military rule and suffer from dire social and political conditions; in Afghanistan, Americans occupied the country after the Russians, they invaded Iraq* [in 2003] *and caused so much suffering. . . . Muslims need help not only in the name of Islam, but also and above all in the name of human solidarity, human rights; they need humanitarian assistance but we deny it to them because of the geo-politics and the world power as it is. Israel does whatever it wants and if you denounce it you are anti-Semitic. I wanted to go and help my Syrian Muslim brothers, but my family got wind of it, my mother cried, and I didn't have the courage to hurt them. A friend of mine did it, the family was not aware and once in Syria, he called them. He died as a martyr few months later.*

With the creation of Daesh, the process of ideologization began in the second half of 2013 (Daesh was officially created in June 2014, but many months prior to its proclamation as a caliphate it was already attracting Muslims from all over the world). The aspirations of these young people were manifold. As already mentioned, many no longer had confidence in their future in Europe where family life was destabilized, the Welfare State was on the wane, the distinction between men and women was put into question, social utopias had lost their credibility, and the ties had loosened among citizens for lack of common ideals. The identity that gave a new sense of belonging was Islam, the more so as it filled with pride those who suffered from the syndrome of the colonial past. This was the case of this young middle-class man, who had received a suspended jail term for attempting to go to Syria in 2013 (the interview took place in September 2016 in Paris):

Question: Why did you attempt to go to Syria? Wasn't it because of your own situation? You said that you wanted to build a new life for yourself.

Sadiq: We live in a country where the future they promise is bullshit [“*de la merde*”]: *our future is at best a badly paid job. We make a mediocre living, dream of a better life, and know full well that it is out of reach. My parents have a rather decent life with a pension that allows them to live free from want. In their youth it was easy to find a good job; mine will be worse. They had job security, in my case there will be none. I have a shabby university diploma that will not open to me many doors. I feel cheated, although I have a small job that gives me enough to live on, without high expectations. And what holds me here? No ties, nothing serious or deep; people are selfish and we are strangers to each other. It's a society where solidarity is dead or dying. . . . To me it makes more sense to be a Muslim than French. They* [the French people] *hate us and that is why they reject Islam. I must simply ignore my Muslim origins to be French, and they will never accept me entirely. Still, I am not like the youth from the poor suburbs, my parents are secular, and they are alarmed by my new ties to religion.*

Question: What about your French identity?

Sadiq: I don't believe anymore in French identity; Islam makes sense to me, it helps me belong to the community of believers. I'm not alone anymore, and on top of it, I am proud to be a Muslim.

Not only are the middle classes in an increasingly precarious situation, but suspicion reigns between the “dangerous classes” and the middle classes, between the secular and the Muslim citizens. More and more, in Europe the dividing line is between Muslim and Secular, Islamic fundamentalism on the one hand, a secular way of life on the other. This dichotomy replaces, at least in part, that which was between dangerous classes and normal citizens in the past. Islamic fundamentalism becomes the epitome of the dangerous classes.

For this young man the tragic thing is that there is no common ideal, no shared utopia. Of course, this does not entail joining jihadi groups, but IS proposed a utopia that fascinated many young people like him, in search of it.

This is what a middle-class professional (computer specialist) of North African origin in his middle thirties, rather in good economic conditions, maintained in an interview in Paris in October 2016:

Saïd: Islam makes me close to those who submit to Allah. What spiritual bond do I have in common with others?

Question: Your father, you told me, was a Communist.

Saïd: My father was a Communist, he was Algerian, but Islam was only his faith, not his link with other citizens. A minority among the Algerian workers in this country joined the CGT [the communist trade union]. *Communism was my father's real bond with France, but also with Algeria and the rest of the world.*

He believed that we could create a classless society where no one would exploit anyone else, nor be exploited by them. That idea united him with the labor movement in France. Because of that view my family did not have a problem with French identity. Other people were socialists, others still found meaning in republicanism. Today, nothing of that sort makes sense, there is no bond. People are living in their solitary confinement.

Question: Your father's stance was social: he fought for a classless society. What is your take?

Saïd: This was his utopia. But to me he was wrong. The problem is not so much a society without class differences. For me the problem is to live without being hassled by my origins. My father thought that with a communist society all these problems would vanish. But I am still the target of social prejudice, my face, my accent, and my past follow me and I cannot get rid of them. Racism and Islamophobia are on the rise and I feel it every time I talk to other people. For my father, anti-Arab racism was due to class society. In his dream, once they achieved a communist society, it would disappear. Now I know that racism is there and it won't disappear, and the classless society was a dream.

Question: You talked about Islam and how important it is to you.

Saïd: Islam makes my life meaningful. It is more than it was to my father. For him the social realm was autonomous, people had to build their society according to their views and God had nothing to do with it. God was a kind of personal bond for him. He was a communist and a Muslim, but their realms were different. For me it is much more. I feel that there is a God to whom I am accountable for my deeds and my social life depends on Him. I don't feel alone, something relates me to those who share this religion with me. Islam provides a sacred meaning to me, something that is lacking in society.

Question: How do you live your religion in this country?

Saïd: The French hate Islam, just like the rest of the West. Islam has become the whipping boy, and racism against it is on the rise. Palestinians are oppressed by the Israelis, the Arab world is oppressed by the West, and Islam is the new enemy. Their hatred is pushing Muslims to radicalize: a girl with a simple scarf is a fundamentalist, whereas the naked Femen [a movement of young women who show their more or less naked bodies in protest against religion or other causes that anger them] *who desecrates a mosque* [they demonstrated topless on April 4, 2013 in front of the Mosquée de Paris] *is regarded with indulgence. A French Muslim who joins the Palestinians to defend them against the Israeli army is a terrorist, a French Jew who goes to Israel and cracks down on the Palestinians as a military in the Israeli army is a hero. We pretend to defend human rights but Saudi Arabia and other despotic governments who are our allies but who repress their own people do not outrage us. Muslims are rejected and despised almost everywhere, and that is why they radicalize. Sometimes I am tempted to declare war to our society, even though my economic situation is good, and I can't complain about it. But sometimes I wish I could join jihadi groups like this top scientist, Adlène Hicheur, who worked at a famous European nuclear laboratory in Geneva (CERN) and sought to punish the French army for its involvement in Afghanistan. As a Muslim I am angry at the French, but also English and American armies who fight Muslims for the sake of their geopolitical interests.*

Saïd's father submitted to the French principle of laïcité (France's version of secularism), according to which Islam was a private matter; religion did not mobilize him, what mattered was class struggle, although he was a devout Muslim. But to Saïd all those ideals were dead, and the only thing that made sense was Islam. He was outraged to see Muslims being mistreated all over the world, France and more generally Europe being complicit with America in their repressive policies toward Muslim countries. Still, Saïd mentioned the predicament of Muslims in France as much as their plight in other parts of the world as the root cause of his indignation. He did not mean that he would one day engage in jihad, but he nevertheless pointed to the fact that Muslims' predicament all over the world can be a major concern for European Muslims who are upset by their fate and the complicit European governments in their tragic fate. Some might seek to punish them by joining jihadi groups. For this category of Muslim, it is governments and not societies that are to blame.

A second category of young, middle-class Muslims or converts was those who were weary of an unexciting peace and a boring, aimless everyday life in Europe. Since the end of the Second World War three-quarters of a century ago, Western Europe has lived in peace. The Syrian war exalted their will to a heightening life, somehow of Nietzschean nature. These people were no longer satisfied with the dull status quo of the everyday life, unsurprising, uneventful, and mundane. A European youth deprived of utopia looked for thrills that would shake up boredom and enliven them through warrior exaltation and virile heroism. This young convert, who dreamed of leaving France for Syria but was prevented by his family, still entertained the dream of going somewhere to wage holy war in 2015:

> *Our life is boring as hell. It has a flat pulse. There is no excitement, nothing noble. The only thing worthwhile is to get rich, to consume this or that, and pick up girls to fuck* [*baiser*]. *I need something more thrilling and more heroic. Sometimes I also need to be out of the ordinary. The war in Syria excited me, I saw the video footage of some young men wearing Ray-Ban glasses, posing in front of their four-by-fours, and proudly showing off their machine guns. They defied death and killed the nasty soldiers of the Assad regime. If the guy dies in the battlefield, he will go to heaven; if he survives, he becomes a hero and the girls will be in love with him.*

The routine of a life without a calling can push toward a warrior ideal that might bring a new sense to life. The words of Hassan, one of the members of the so-called Pompey (Portsmouth) Lads who went to Syria in 2013, is also indicative of the boredom and lack of noble vocation among those young people of Muslim origin who felt woefully aimless in their daily lives:

> *Sometimes I just get sick of generic life. I'm living in the West to eat, study, work, pay tax, sleep. #Slave.* (Saner, 2015)

This category included a large proportion of middle-class youth, looking for adventure in order to escape boredom and emptiness, due in part to the lack of a unifying utopia in society that would point to a common goal to achieve. The festive effervescence of war and the intensification of life would make them forget the vagaries of an uncertain future and a pointless present. It would engender a generalized joviality blurring the frontiers of life and death, the possible and the impossible, the predictable and the unpredictable. It would be a sensational concrete utopia, able to unite the present and the future in an intensified and festive manner, a cheerful violence being its glue. These young men exorcised the anxiety of a risky future and a monotonous present through the thrills of war.

The urge to engage in a deadly game in order to join an "effervescent community" was a revolt against the "coldness" of the national community in which the individual was, in their view, left to his own devices, isolated and lacking a strong sense of belonging. The jihadis' imagined neo-Ummah provided a reinvigorated sense of togetherness to these young people, otherwise bereft of hope, fearful for their possible debasement in the future, and bored to death in their everyday lives. On one hand, at the individual level prevailed their sense of economic fragility; on the other hand, at the global level, nothing noteworthy was happening, things had lost their meaning, middle-class youth being squeezed between an unpromising future and a dull present.

In many cases, young people expressed their desire for heroism, if only to escape this daily routine that wears out by its monotony, heroism being experienced as a break in the weave of a harassing uniform daily life where everything repeats itself tirelessly, meaninglessly. War in Syria allowed their positioning as potential heroes. This heroism was projected into an imaginary future that contrasted with the insignificance of the Self who, in the peaceful West, should wait indefinitely to find few opportunities in lifeless societies, while living within families that have been destabilized by half a century of feminism and cultural egalitarianism, in the meantime the meaning of being a man or a woman slipping away. Shortcutting this long and hopeless wait for a brighter future within European societies became possible by the holy war in Syria under IS aegis. They were becoming potential future heroes and were already starting to dream about it, long before they even set foot in Syria. Confronting death opened the prospect of a glorious future in this world if the would-be hero survived, and salvation if he died.

A direct or indirect influence of the Muslim Brotherhood on some of the middle-class European Muslims tempted by radical Islam can be detected through their disillusions with democracy, human right issues, and the predicament of the Muslim countries, victims of Arab autocracies, American hegemonism, rentier oil states, and Israel. The international situation pushed some toward radical Islam. A Franco-Algerian sympathizer of the former UOIF (Union des organizations islamiques de France that changed its name to Musulmans de France [MF]), in his late twenties, working as a computer programmer, expressed his temptation to join the jihadi movement in 2014 (this interview took place in Paris's 18th district in October 2013):

Kazim: I was a member of UOIF, but I dropped out because they are unable to take a courageous stand on the so-called Islam of France. I was for a democratic Islam that would come to power through democratic means. Egypt opened my eyes to the reality: Morsi was elected democratically [as President of Egypt in 2012] *but was overthrown* [in June 2013] *by a military coup. While Muslims respect democracy, others do not, and throw them out. I was ready at some point to join jihadis in Egypt, because I was angry against the military there, but reality got the upper hand: what could I do there without knowing Arabic and the ground? . . . In France too, Muslims who are respectful of the secular norms but ask for tolerance on the issues like scarf, are stigmatized. Respect by the Muslims is not paid back by others. . . . I am angry, and now I understand those young Muslims who join jihadis after so many setbacks.*

Question: You told me that as a technician, you had to fight constantly against "Arabophobia."

Kazim: An Arab, in the public opinion, cannot be a good technician. He is only good for manual work that does not require a great deal of intelligence. I have to prove to every new customer that I am as good as my French colleagues. I have the same degree as them, but in my case I have to convince them of my competence, whereas for my French colleagues, it goes without saying. These prejudices become unbearable in the long run. Add to this the fact that with each new jihadi attack people look at you as a potential terrorist, or their accomplice. This sometimes leads me to side with jihadis, purely out of provocation. I understand why they revolt and seek to fight against French society in which they lived. We are treated like a fifth column and sometimes some of us may be tempted to go in that direction and do harm in return for what they do to us.

It is noteworthy that engineers make up a large part of jihadi recruits. In the Muslim world, it would be 44.9 percent (out of the 207 recorded cases of jihadis who had a university degree); and in the Western world, 45.1 percent (out of 71 radical Islamists in the sample with university degrees; Gambetta and Steffen, 2016). This peculiarity can be attributed to the lack of social mobility (they get neither financial return for their long studies, nor social recognition for their scientific capacity). One can also mention the mentality of engineers, in search of order and method in a world that lacks them. In Europe, Muslim engineers and technical managers tend to espouse the jihadi cause, in part because of social disregard toward them: despite having acquired similar diplomas to their middle-class colleagues of European descent, they have to prove they are as good as their non-Muslim colleagues. The struggle against social prejudices makes the lives of sons of migrants in Europe exhausting.

Disaffiliated people and middle-class members show similarities, but also differences, in the way they become radicalized. To illustrate this, we have chosen two interviews, one with an individual belonging to the slum culture, the other, from the middle classes. In March 2013, in the largest European prison, Fleury-Mérogis, a Franco-Algerian, probably in his early thirties, expressed in an interview his dream of martyrdom in an unambiguous manner:

Ahmed: You know, those who die as martyrs in the battlefield are heroes in this world, but also "friends of Allah" [awliya Allah] in the other. If they accept to die in the path of Allah [fi sabil illah], they will be eternally redeemed for their sins, and they'll go straight to Heaven.

Question: You seem fascinated by martyrdom. You are still young, a long life to live!

Ahmed: My life here is a mess: I am in prison for theft and trafficking among others, and once out, it's going to happen again because I don't know what else to do, and once more, they'll put me under lock and key. I have no choice.

Question: In your view it is your fate and you couldn't do anything to change it. In my view, this is the case of those people who do not respect themselves.

Ahmed: I have no great respect for myself but I hate those who have put me in this mess. My life is over, it's mapped out. I have nothing to add to it. Martyrdom opens the doors to heaven, and it also brings self-respect. In the same vein, jihad punishes those who are responsible for the suffering of people like me by killing them. I don't join the jihadis, but they do me a favor by punishing the Whites in my place. They're doing the job I can't do.

Question: Who are the culprits in your situation?

Ahmed: The White men. They lock us up in poor districts. Right from the beginning, we had no future. I took part in robberies, hold-ups, trafficking. . . . There was no other way round.

Question: You mean that you were not to blame at all?

Ahmed: I was also responsible, but it was peanuts compared to them: I was put in a one-way street, there was no way out. Or else, I had to live like the poor, and I couldn't accept that. I was already discriminated against as an "Arab"; on top of that, being poor was impossible, I couldn't be doubly mistreated, or else, I would kill myself!

We find a close association in this interview between a present without a future, the desire to die gloriously as a martyr, the longing to be redeemed by God after the misdeeds committed by the individual in the past, and the quest for punishment for those who put him in this desperate situation—namely, the mainstream society, another name for the "White men."

The feeling of being a second-class citizen, exposed to social prejudices and not having the same opportunities as the other people, is widely shared and empirical research confirms it almost everywhere in Western Europe, mostly among the disaffected youth, but also among the Muslim middle classes. In a prison close to Lille (Lille-Séquedin) in northern France, a guard of North African origin expressed his dismay in an interview in February 2013:

Karim: I have a bachelor's degree in law and despite that, I couldn't find any better job than this one. I am largely overqualified. My friends, "White" Frenchmen who got the same diploma, found good jobs in law firms and earn three, four times my salary.

Question: Why?

Karim: Why? Only because I was an "Arab". This is the country of equality, liberty, and fraternity (the motto of the French Republic)! But in reality, we are not equal; I am inferior to any Frenchman with the same qualification. If I apply for a job, I bet that all the "Whites" will get it before me, even if I'm better. I'm rotting in this prison because they don't easily find "White" candidates for this thankless job. Since they need and there aren't enough candidates, they take "Arabs." They don't value me for my competence, and my origin bars me from qualified jobs.

Question: Some prisoners told me disparagingly about the Arab yes-men who become guards to make life even more unbearable to them in prison.

Karim: I'm all the more depressed because most of the inmates are "Arabs". This is the absolute proof for the "Whites" that Arabs are scum, and their place is in prison. The prisoners also hate me, they treat me as a sellout to the French government, the former colonizer who still cracks down on "Arabs"! I am the "Arab fool" [Arabe de service]: the personnel despise me for being an Arab and Arab prisoners hate me, because I am an Arab guard who imposes on them the rules of the "White" men. All of this for a miserable salary that is so much below my qualification!

Karim firmly believes that he was unjustly denied equality with others because of his Arab origin, and this is a common feeling not only among disaffected youth but also middle-class Muslims, which is confirmed by empirical research in Europe, as already mentioned.

3-Examples of Middle-Class Jihadis

Middle-class youth became jihadis despite the fact that they did not suffer economic exclusion. Among them, the case of Abdelhamid Abaaoud is noteworthy. He was the son of Omar Abaaoud, one of the symbols of Moroccan success in the district of Molenbeek, close to Brussels, in Belgium. His father came from Morocco and worked in the Belgian coal mines, but he gradually built up a fortune and acquired two clothing stores, offering his family upper-middle-class living standards. The eldest son, Abdelhamid, ran one of the stores. The six children of the family spent their holidays in Morocco, in a villa acquired after the father's financial success in Belgium. Despite their social standing, Abdelhamid was in legal trouble in 2002; he committed petty theft with his brother Yassine, and was condemned to short prison terms between 2006 and 2012. They could not understand that people despised them in spite of their middle-class status. The petty "Whites" who had a lower economic level than theirs scorned them even more. They found the world upside down, since "Arabs" had succeeded where they, the Whites, had failed. They were not only at the bottom of the social ladder, but also below the "Arabs," which was, strictly speaking, unbearable to them. This fostered a kind of racism that was even more vicious than that which normally prevailed against Arabs from the lower strata, who were accused of living off the Welfare State. These well-off Arabs paid more taxes than they did and were no longer "parasites"—on the contrary, they "entertained," as it were, the lower-class Whites. This shattered the self-image of many people belonging to the so-called category of "White trash." They resented these Arabs who had become wealthy in defiance of their "natural place" as lower-class people in a "White" society. If they had become rich, it is because they had usurped the place of the Whites.[2] This attitude was not limited to a few isolated individuals, but to a large part of the mainstream society, for which "Arabs" were not citizens in their own right. They were treated as upstarts, illegitimate in their status as *nouveaux riche*. Added to this was the success of the father, which robbed the sons of the sense that they had achieved their social status by themselves. A way was open to them to give meaning to their lives by transgressing social norms, to steal while they did not need to—in short, to imitate young Arabs from poor neighborhoods in order to give themselves a plausible identity as outcasts. In fact, they belonged neither to the Belgian, nor to the Moroccan, nor to the Berber society, neither to the lower, nor to the middle classes: they belonged to nowhere.

Besides deviance, another way out of the malaise was Islam. In a secular Europe where Islam has a poor reputation, claiming to be a Muslim is already in itself a sign of transgression, as is deviance in another way. Fine European public rhetoric on religious freedom soon meets the test of a harsh reality, namely the more or less marked ostracism of Muslims in the mainstream society. Even for the average Muslims, of whom Nilufer Göle speaks (she calls them "ordinary Muslims"; Göle, 2015), the modest claim to Islam leads to suspicion. Whether at the individual, institutional, or corporate level, being a Muslim is a rather negative point and is frowned upon, even though legally a Muslim woman cannot be condemned for wearing a headscarf or a Muslim man for refusing alcohol or for not shaking hands with women. As for the new generations, adhering to Islam is experienced as a violation of the unwritten laws of the secular European societies (in France more, in Great Britain or Germany, less). Islam is experienced as a transgression and that is why many young people display it in a much more exhibitionist, even provocative way than their parents. On the basis of the suspicion that Muslims are not sufficiently secular, young Muslims, whether middle class or economically excluded, use the religion of Allah to mark their rebellion in the face of a society that does not fully accept them and makes them feel it in their everyday relations. They turn a religion suspected of separatism vis-à-vis European modernity into one that challenges secularism head-on and rejects the worldview of the mainstream society. In short, through it they challenge society and make Islam the emblem of their revolt against it.

For Abdelhamid, joining the Muslim community was the other side of his transgression toward Belgian society, where he did not feel welcome, quite the contrary. In his case, defiance was expressed both through deviance and through Islam. He projected himself into a mythical Islamic identity as an alternative to a double denial: neither Belgian nor Moroccan; neither Belgian nor Rifian (from the Rif region in Northern Morocco, populated mainly by Berbers speaking Amazigh, a non-Arab language); neither middle class nor lower class. His case is not exceptional. Even though belonging to the middle classes, many second- and even third-generation migrants' sons feel the humiliation of not being regarded as genuine citizens by others. Paranoia sets in. Not only do they feel the contempt that many people (but not all) show them, but they experience it obsessively everywhere, even where it does not exist, in the neutral gaze of a passer-by, in contact with others whom they suspect to be biased toward them without any tangible evidence. . . . They build up, in a morbid way, a stereotype image of Europeans (French, Belgian, English. . .) who, they believe, reject Muslims. This in turn pushes them to be more aggressive and sets off a vicious circle of rejection and counter-rejection that ends up, in few cases, in jihadism that operates as an ultimate dismissal of mainstream society. Deviance, prison, and embracing radical Islam while they are imprisoned constitute a frequent cycle among second- or third-generation Muslims in Europe. Abstract data showing the high rate of deviants among the jihadis (Hecker, 2018; Basra, Neuman, and Brunner, 2016) do not explain this anthropological phenomenon.

According to his father, Abdelhamid was radicalized during his stay at Forest in 2012, a prison with harsh living conditions, close to Brussels. In early 2013, he left for Syria but returned in September of the same year to Belgium. He left the country again in January 2014, accompanied by his young brother Younes, a thirteen-year-old teenager. IS used the latter in its advertisements as the "lion cub of the caliphate."

Abaaoud's case is emblematic insofar as he felt he was treated as inferior despite his belonging to the middle classes. Humiliation was all the more unbearable because it had no tangible basis, as he did not behave in accordance with the role models of the slum culture; he was rejected simply because he was the son of a migrant, even though the latter was successful. Prison played a significant role, especially because many European prisons impose inhuman conditions on prisoners, in small, crowded cells where two or even three prisoners reside, some of them sleeping on the floor on a mattress because there is no room for an extra bed (Khosrokhavar, 2016). Forest Prison used to be one of them. The high proportion of Muslims in many European prisons pushes them toward radicalization: they believe that they are locked up mainly because of their migrant origin.

The Abdeslam brothers' case resembles that of Abdelhamid Abaaoud in many respects. Their parents, working-class migrants from Morocco, achieved upward mobility in Belgium. The father, a Moroccan citizen born in Oran in French Algeria, lived in Aubervilliers in the department of Seine-Saint-Denis, a poor suburb of Paris, before moving to Molenbeek-Saint-Jean in Belgium, a poor district close to Brussels. Previously a worker, he became the owner-manager of two shops in Molenbeek (his income exceeded an annual €100,000 from 2012 onward). As for the mother, she is a Berber (Amazigh), belonging to a non-Arab ethnic group, mistreated in Morocco.

The family achieved economic rise and lived in a bourgeois building facing the town hall in Molenbeek. Nevertheless, the children had identity problems. They lived under the paternal roof except for the older brother who left it after his marriage. Of the three brothers, two became delinquent and, later, jihadi. Salah Abdeslam was arrested for being involved in petty criminal activities and was put in jail for a short period of time. He lost his job as a technician at the tramway depot in Ixelles because of his prolonged absence due to his imprisonment. From December 2013 he became the manager of the bar "Les Béguines" in Molenbeek, which was closed by court decision after drugs were found there. The case of Brahim Abdeslam is not fundamentally different. An electrician by training, he married in 2006 and divorced in 2008. Between 2005 and 2010 he was convicted several times for theft, fraud, and traffic offenses. He then became the owner of the bar "Les Béguines," his brother being its manager. The distinguishing feature of the two brothers was their Moroccan origin and their life in Molenbeek, where staying in what was sometimes called "little Morocco" among numerous Moroccans widened the gap between them and the mainstream society.

Even Muslim middle classes bear the stigma of their origin, and everyday life in an ethnic neighborhood (where the proportion of migrants, unemployment, delinquency, leaving school, and imprisonment is high) creates identity malaise. Instability and foul feelings are rooted in the lack of recognition by others (not being recognized as a Belgian in Belgium, nor as Moroccan in Morocco). It is also an internalized duality felt as a split identity, the more unbearable as the shame of not being what one is supposed to be is part of the daily experience for one's ethnicity, facial features, accent, gestures, and religion. Radical Islam puts an end to the fracture within their identity and bestows them with a strong and stable Self rooted in the Sacred, which ends the suffering. Of course, many people with the same characteristics do not join jihadi groups. Like all terrorism, jihadism is a minority phenomenon. Still, in this specific case it is grounded in debasement and identity crisis. One can suffer from the latter without being subjected to the former (the case of many Eastern Europeans in France or in Britain). When identity crisis and humiliation go hand in hand, however, one can more easily become violent. IS transformed passive humiliation into active antagonism.

Another case is that of Najim Laachraoui, born in Ajdir, Morocco, who was raised in Schaerbeek, near Brussels, where he attended a Catholic school from the age of twelve to eighteen. He was a serious pupil and never failed in his exams. Later, he lived with his parents, brother, and sister in the middle-class neighborhood of Terdelt. From 2009 to 2010 he studied engineering at the Université Libre de Bruxelles, without graduating, and from 2010 to 2011, at the Catholic University of Louvain where he was considered a good student. He worked on the tarmac of Brussels-Zaventem airport from 2008 to 2012.

He was radicalized in the years 2008–2009, between the ages of seventeen and eighteen in contact with the preachers of the Ettaouba mosque in Evere, one of whose imams was incarcerated in July 2014. He attended their conferences and had been under the influence of a certain "Emponz B."

In February 2013, Laachraoui moved to Syria and joined Daesh, adopting the name "Abu Idris al-Beljiki." He was wounded by a bullet in the fight against Al-Nusra Front, a rival group affiliated with al-Qaeda. In December 2014 he paid tribute to Bilal Nzohabonayo, who was shot dead in an attack against the police in Joué-les-Tours: "He understood very well that Muslims were living in a situation of total war," he tweeted ("Attentats," 2016; Balboni, 2016).

Laachraoui was the older brother of the European taekwondo champion Mourad Laachraoui, who had no ties with him. Their cases were similar to that of Richard Dart (the jihadi) and Robb Leech, his stepbrother, the filmmaker. This was also the case of Mohamed Abdeslam, who was not involved in the jihadi adventures of his two brothers, Salah and Brahim.

We find thus two distinct models: the first, in which brothers together join jihadi groups (Tsarnaev brothers, Kouachi brothers, Bakraoui brothers), the second in which the brothers split up in regard to radical Islam, some joining jihadi groups, the others refusing to follow them.

Contrary to the poor-district model, where young pupils quickly leave school and opt for a deviant model leading to prison, Najim Laachraoui lived in a bourgeois neighborhood; he even began university studies and had no problem with justice before his jihadi commitment. His case is that of a split identity and a new Islamic personality. The latter becomes all the more uncompromising as it is intended as payback for humiliations suffered, and sometimes magnified in an imaginary way.

Bilal Hadfi was the youngest terrorist in the Paris attacks of November 13, 2015. Born as a junior in a family of four children, of French nationality, he lived in Belgium. At a very young age he lost his father, who was buried in Morocco. He lived in a social housing complex in Neder-over-Heembeek and studied electricity at the Dutch-language "Anneessens Funcks" in Brussels. In July 2015 he moved to Forest in the Brussels suburbs. Like many young people, he led a non-religious life before radicalizing. He called himself "Billy Hood," practiced taekwondo, was a football fan, and posed shirtless on Facebook while making the sign of the US West Coast rappers. In 2014, he quickly radicalized under the influence of an extremist imam, and made a trip to Syria, opting for the noms de guerre "Abu Mujahid al-Belgiki" and "Bilal al-Muhajir." Back in Belgium in July, he posted a plea on his Facebook page to launch attacks against Westerners, calling them "infidel dogs." The school he attended sounded the alarm, especially after the Paris *Charlie Hebdo* attacks in January 2015, but the authorities did not take those warnings seriously. However, he was put on the file of radicalized people by the Belgian intelligence services.

He did not live in poor ethnic suburbs or neighborhoods with a delinquent past. Of immigrant origin, he suffered from the father's absence and was torn between numerous identities (Moroccan, French, and Flemish Belgian identities), being stigmatized for being an "Arab." His middle-class status enhanced his ability to identify with abused Muslims in the Middle East, beyond his own personal situation. As hard as empathy was for disaffected youth (as we have already described), it was easy for middle-class Muslims, the humanitarian vocation playing an important role. The affiliation to Islam gave meaning to the war against Western Infidels who treated Muslims in a still-colonial manner, stirring painful memories among European Muslims. He participated at the age of twenty in the November 13, 2015, attacks in Paris and was killed with two other accomplices while triggering his explosive belt after being denied access to the Stade de France, causing no other casualties. His attack looked like a suicide.

Charaffe el-Mouadan, aka "Aba Souleymane," was born to Moroccan parents in 1989 in Bondy, a town in Seine-Saint-Denis, close to Paris, where sons and grandsons of North African migrants live in poor ethnic districts. He spent his youth in Drancy, also in Seine-Saint-Denis. Jobless, he enrolled in the employment center and managed, at the same time, to receive a consumer loan of a high amount (€20,000), which he used to buy hiking equipment for his departure to Syria.

In October 2012 he already had been arrested while preparing to leave for Afghanistan, but he was left free under judicial supervision. Finally, in August 2013 he managed to get away to Syria with his wife and two children. He developed, like many other European jihadis, a "web-narcissism": he posted photos of himself, one of which is one-on-one with his horse, but also scenes in Syria and Iraq, including a photo with the younger brother of the Belgian jihadi Abdelhamid Abaaoud. In his tweets he recounted his daily life under the nom de guerre "Abu Souleymane." In one of them he declared that no one was innocent in France, everyone being complicit in the government of disbelievers and, therefore, a legitimate target for attack.

Still, his family had lived in a detached house with their eight children, and at school he had been rather a good student, the family showing no sign of external crisis. From a lower middle-class family, he had failed to preserve a middle-class status and was in low-level temporary jobs. His parents had managed to climb the middle-class ladder, but he had slipped down. The combination of loss of status, undignified identity, stigmas, and the quest for a meaningful life made him hate France, not to the point of being willing to carry out attacks against it, but enough to leave it for good and put himself at the service of the caliphate. There, he thought he could realize his dream of being a knight of Islam, and finally assume an identity of his own—instead of being torn between a French identity that France denied him and a distant Moroccan identity that he refused and that the French wanted him to carry at all costs. For him, being a born-again radical Muslim meant dismissing both identities and adopting a third one that would give a sacred unity to his split ego. That is why, unlike his parents, he wanted to be a total Muslim, and sought to prove it to himself by fighting against Shiite infidels (the Alawis) who repressed Muslims (the Sunnis) in the service of the idolatrous regime of Assad in Syria. The quest for a mythical Islam that would redeem his dignity by declaring war on Infidels of both Syria and the West led him first to leave for Afghanistan, and then for Syria. Dying there while fighting for his faith seemed more dignifying to him than living in humiliation, carrying a broken and unrecognized identity in a society that had never accepted him on a par with the "Whites."

The London Boys cell had many middle-class members. They grew up in a small section of northwestern London and were initially moved by the civil war in Somalia where Islamic militant al-Shabaab had conquered a vast territory. One of the prominent members of this group was Bilal al-Berjawi al-Lubnani (aka "Abu Hafsa"). He was born in Beirut in September 1984. His parents took him to London where he grew up in St. John's Wood, a residential neighborhood in Westminster. In 2006, he took part in military activities in an al-Qaeda training camp in Mogadishu. In February 2009 he traveled with his Egyptian friend, Mohammed Sakr, to Kenya. In October of the same year, they went to Somalia. Al-Berjawi was trained at another military camp in Baidoa, a town in southwestern Somalia. His citizenship was revoked in 2010 by the British authorities. On January 21, 2012, he was killed by an American drone outside Mogadishu. He is considered a close associate of Fazul Abdullah Mohammed, the chief of al-Qaeda operations in East Africa. They helped build a jihadi network from the United Kingdom and East Africa linked to al-Shabaab in Somalia. They were also involved in providing funds and equipment for terrorist purposes. Mahdi Hashi, a Somali-born Briton who had left northwest London for Somalia, was captured and held at a US base in Djibouti in August 2012. He was then sent to the United States where he was sentenced to nine years in prison. At the age of twenty-six, he had traveled from Britain to his native Somalia to join al-Shabaab, which planned to establish there an Islamic state.

In Somalia, Hashi was linked to the American jihadi Omar Hamami and his group of Foreign Fighters as well as other associates in al-Shabaab's suicide bombing program. The latter became famous in jihadi circles in the West for his rap videos. Hashi's family had emigrated to Britain accompanied by their six-year-old son Mahdi, escaping civil war in Somalia in 2000. He grew up in London. He went to Egypt and Syria as a teenager. In 2010, he returned to Mogadishu where he got married and had a child. Hashi's British citizenship was withdrawn shortly before he was sent to the United States in 2012 to be charged for terrorist acts.

At least three members of the London Boys network were banned from London by order of the British courts. One of them, Ibrahim Magag, born in Somalia, was transferred to the West of the UK in 2009. He returned to West London in 2012 after the travel ban was lifted, but he remained under control of justice by an electronic tag. He got rid of it and absconded to Somalia. There he followed the military training in al-Shabaab camps.

The London Boys were mostly of Somali origin, but some of them were also of Lebanese and Egyptian descent. What bound them together was the shared feeling of not belonging to the English society. They suffered from the cold and distant individualism toward the sons of Muslim immigrants in a so-called multicultural society which, in fact, kept Muslims (and particularly black Muslims) at arm's length instead of including them as equals in society. Dark-skinned and Muslim, they felt rejected by White England, which ostracized them in the name of a hypocrite respect for other cultures. English multiculturalism kept them at bay in their difference while French monoculturalism sought to force the "Arabs" into a stifling, unattainable resemblance. They intended to create a new state in the name of Islam in Somalia, to participate in it as protagonists, whereas in England they were insignificant non-beings, locked in their differences. They also sought revenge on English politics, enslaved to the United States and marked by contempt for Muslim countries.

A notorious jihadi of middle-class background was Muhammad Emzawi, called "Jihadi John" by the British press. He was a prominent member of the jihadi British cell nicknamed "The Beatles" by hostages in Syria (they let their hair grow long like the members of the Beatles). He took part in the beheading of American journalists James Foley and Steven Sotloff, the American aid worker Peter Kassig, the British aid workers David Haines and Alan Henning, the Japanese military contractor Haruna Yukawa, the Japanese journalist Kenji Goto, and twenty-two members of the Syrian army, between August 2014 and January 2015. He was born Muhammad Jassim Abdulkarim Olayan al-Dhafiri in 1988 in Kuwait. The family, of Iraqi origin, lived in the city of Al Jahra before moving to the United Kingdom in 1994 when he was six years old. They settled west of London. Emwazi attended St. Mary Magdalene's Church of the UK Elementary School and later Quintin Kynaston School. In 2006, he went to the University of Westminster to study information and management systems. He graduated three years later. At the age of twenty-one he worked as a salesman in a computer company in Kuwait and was considered by his boss as the best employee of the company. "Jihadi John" appeared in a video as a Foley assassin. He was killed by an American drone in November 2015.

Fouad Belkacem, the founder of "Sharia4Belgium" is typical of the individual with a Muslim immigrant background who had the capacity to join the mainstream society but was unable (or unwilling) to do so because of the humiliations suffered by him and his fellow Muslims and a sense that the secularized world was, by its very nature, against Islam. Belkacem was born in April 1982 in the Flemish part of Belgium in Rumst. He was the son of a middle-class couple, his mother working as a sworn interpreter in Arabic, Dutch, and French and his father being a car salesman. His parents were not Salafis, nor did they believe in a radical view of Islam. His older brother was working in his father's business and after high school, Fouad also started as a car dealer, until his business went bankrupt in 2003. In that year he became a practicing Muslim, adopting the name "Abu Imran."

In the meantime, he had been convicted many times in 2002, 2004, and 2007 for burglary and was also involved in car scams, forgery, and tax fraud. In 2007, the Tangier court requested his extradition because he was sentenced to ten years in prison for drug trafficking in Morocco. In 2009, Belkacem challenged the headscarf ban in high schools, but was arrested during a demonstration in Antwerp on September 3 due to his aggressive behavior with the police, and was convicted on April of the same year.

Belkacem is multilingual, speaks French, English, and Arabic, but prefers Dutch, his movement Sahria4Belgium having a hard core of thirty people, mostly Flemish, living in Antwerp. It is there that his association had most of its followers. His itinerary was that of a middle-class delinquent who passed through the prison cell.

Unlike France, where radical Islamists adopt a discreet attitude, in Belgium Fouad Belkacem combines arrogance with a boastful proselytism that he displayed in 2012 at a conference in Molenbeek on behalf of the association Sharia4Belgium, of which he was the founder:

> *Do not think that we have a drop* [gram] *of respect for you, for your lifestyle, for your way of thinking or for your system. We have our religion which is superior to your religion, we have our system which is superior to your system, and we have our values which are superior to your values. . . . If you don't want to accept the sharia that will dominate you, move, go to the North Pole for example. Either you accept it, or you leave, it's very simple!* (Otreppe, 10/02/2015).

This type of statement, also made by Choukri bel Ayd in the UK, reverses relations between minority and majority: the majority must leave if it does not conform to the religion of the Muslim minority or, according to other European Islamists, pay a religious tax (*djiziya*) to Muslims, which would confirm their supremacy. This voluntarily overbearing attitude rings hollow among most Muslims, but, among radicals, it refers to their desire to reverse the inferiority experienced as the sons of migrants into an ostentatious superiority. It does not mean overcoming the inferiority complex, it simply means reversing it into a superiority complex through bragging and a provocative attitude.

Fouad Belkacem's association Sharia4Belgium was behind the departure of dozens of young people to Syria, around 10 percent of young Belgian Foreign Fighters ("Sharia4Belgium Trial," 2015). Forty-five members of his group were sentenced to prison terms for terrorist activities. Belkacem was condemned to twelve years in prison in February 2015, and the other members of his group received from a few months to fifteen years prison sentences. On October 7, 2012, he announced the dissolution of his association. Belkacem married a Moroccan-Belgian woman in jail in June 2017. On October 23, 2018, the Antwerp Court of Appeal repealed his Belgian nationality. He had a mix of middle-class and some disaffected jihadi features: he did not live in poor ethnic districts, went to school, and had good living conditions. But he became involved in illegal activities and ended up being radicalized.

Among the middle classes of migrant origin, sometimes humiliation and double standards create an explosive mixture: they do not even find the excuse of being at the bottom of the social ladder, which would make plausible the stigmas they are subjected to, and they sometimes express their indignation by adhering to radical Islam. To a disdainful society they exhibit their defiant attitude of arrogant Muslims.

The egalitarian image of the Self in modern society comes into conflict with the disparaging picture that society enforces on Muslim individuals.

By espousing an uncompromising version of Islam, Belkacem attracted young Muslims, even converts. They discovered in his self-confidence via his radical Islamic values a remedy against the doubts that assailed them about their place in society. His firm stance made them feel that they had finally pierced the mystery of life. His bellicose attitude against society gave them the assurance that they had discovered the cause of their misfortune. Most of the recruiters or preachers have a strong personality and their charisma fascinates young people, often suffering from a shaky personality. They seek certainty as embodied in a strong character that can satisfy them emotionally, making them suffer less from the existential ills that overwhelm them and against which they find otherwise no relief. Belkacem gave them self-confidence and enabled them to criticize society in the name of jihadism instead of doubting and not trusting in their ability to overcome their shortcomings. In brief, Belkacem, as a charismatic leader, allowed them to free themselves from their internalized sense of unworthiness and rise above their insecure personalities.[3]

4-Jihadi Rappers

Some jihadis were rappers, amateurs or professionals. This is a rather common phenomenon among extremist groups. Neo-Nazis have relied on rap to further their cause, including the "Nipsters" (neo-Nazi hipsters), a group of young neo-Nazis who borrowed certain aspects of hip-hop music. We can mention the case of the Dutch Marouane B. of the city of Arnhem who went to Syria in 2013 to break with his past (trouble with the police and justice) and appeared later in a propaganda video of IS. He was involved in beheadings in Syria but claimed his innocence in interviews in which he spoke of his motivation, which was to help Syrians against Assad's repressive regime. He wrote various rap lyrics to apologize to his mother, the only person toward whom he felt guilty: "Mom, I have often been in trouble, sorry, I hope you can forgive me"; "Mom, mom, I'll always go back, but do not worry, I'm in the mum race, I still love you up to the [last]day I live"; "It hurts so much that I cannot be with you / she is what she is [the mother], he is so difficult [the rapper] / I love you and the rest cannot change me" (Smit, 2017).

Some, on the contrary, renounced rap, such as Elvin Bokamba-Yangouma, a member of the Cannes-Torcy cell who converted to Islam, attending every day the Torcy mosque to pray there. Others continued to rap in an Islamic way by adopting the "nasheed" style, Islamic songs without musical instruments, such as Jean-Michel Clain. Once in Syria, he started singing songs of war (*anasheed*, the Arabic plural of *nasheed*) in French. The German rapper Deso Dogg can also be mentioned, who took the name "Abu Talha al-Almani" or "Abu Maleeq" after joining IS in 2014. He was killed by American air attacks in January 2018.

We can also mention the following cases to further illustrate the participation of rappers in jihadism: Abdel-Majed Abdel Bary, an Anglo-Egyptian, rapped under the name "L Jinny." He is the son of Adel Abdel Bari, an Egyptian suspected of sympathizing with Usama Bin Laden, the head of al-Qaeda, and was extradited from the United Kingdom to the United States in

2012, accused of having played a role in the attacks of American embassies in Africa. He was part of the trio of English jihadis nicknamed "The Beatles" by their hostages.

Ibrayma Sylla, born in 1980, was a former robber and rapper, having spent several years in prison, including a twelve-year sentence in 2005 for robbery. He sometimes called out dawn prayers from his Fleury-Mérogis cell, waking up and angering other inmates. His proselytizing worried prison authorities. He was released in 2012 and was tapped by authorities who suspected him of preparing an attack. They discovered in his phone conversations the plan of an attack. He sang: "Make your crusades, we make jihad; in all our countries you will recall your embassies." Or, even more threatening, "We shoot at the ministers in the state, at the guys from the BAC [anti-crime squad]; we will kill them without mercy. . . . The bodies, you will find them in the lakes." He was an admirer of the French jihadi Mohamed Merah, and intended to follow in his footsteps. He planned robberies to finance his jihadi agenda.

Most of the jihadi rappers are migrants' sons and they express their spite and hatred toward a "White" society they believe they don't belong in. Disaffected youth living in stigmatized and ghettoized neighborhoods in European countries are predominant among them. Some of them managed to join the middle classes through their music, but the hatred of the "White,", "neo-colonial" society remained long-lasting.

b-Women and the New Jihad

In the West, before the civil war in Syria in 2013 and the genesis of Daesh in 2014, few women were involved in jihad. There were converts, like the Belgian Muriel Degauque, or those like the Americans Colleen LaRose (nicknamed "Jihad Jane") and Jamie Paulin Ramirez, who tried to kill the cartoonist Lars Vilks for having drawn the Prophet of Islam in a disrespectful manner, or Samantha Lewthwaite (called the "White Widow") from the United Kingdom. From 2013 to 2015, there was a large increase in the number of women involved in jihadism: they totaled 1,023 (around 17 percent) out of 5,904 people who left Western countries for Syria (Cook and Vale, 2018). They were often from the (lower) middle classes. Few of them came from the poor districts, in contrast to the majority of young men, and few of them had criminal records, unlike men (Basra, Neuman, and Brunner, 2016).

One can distinguish two types of women among them: those who sought to become the wives of jihadis (called "jihadi brides" by the media) and married Foreign Fighters, and those who sought to become jihadi agents, ready to use violence against the "Infidels." The vast bulk were jihadi brides, jihadi women being a small minority, if only because IS did not give them the opportunity to act like men in Syria. Once there, they had to primarily marry jihadis, military activities being reserved for only a small minority of them in a brigade called Al Khansaa.

In Muslim countries, women usually took part in the jihadi attacks in order to avenge a family member such as a husband, a cousin, a brother, or a father, murdered by the security forces, as was the case of the "Black Widows" in Chechnya. Or they accompanied their husbands, as with Sajida al-Rishwai in November 9, 2005, who unsuccessfully tried to detonate her belt in Jordan. In Europe, feminine jihadism occurred in a new way, and family vengeance was not the motive for their action. Rather, it was a new identity influenced by more than half a century of feminism that paradoxically pushed them toward choosing their path either as an act of love, or seeking adventure, or looking for a new feminine role in stark contrast to that of their mothers.

Some post-adolescent young women found a way of becoming "adults" through the war, which assumed the role of a rite of passage for them. The older sister of a young teenager (fifteen years of age) who left for Syria described in these terms the latter's mindset (the interview took place in a voluntary association dealing with youth problems in Ile-de-France in November 2016):

Question: Why did your sister go to Syria?

Sarah: My sister Nicole was impatient. She thought she had become a woman and desired to be a real woman. She yearned for children. My mother told her: "You are too young to have a child. I became pregnant when I was in my thirties. You must study, find a job, build your future before getting pregnant." But Nicole insisted that she wanted to be a woman, and be recognized as such. She was ill at ease with her adolescence, and thought that our mother did not understand her wish to be a woman and a mother. She went to Syria, not because she was radicalized, but to achieve her goal of becoming a mother.

The attempt at becoming precociously "genuine women" through pregnancy and giving birth to children was associated with another one, namely, restoring the patriarchal family in which the distinction between men and women would be fully asserted. Feminism and the contemporary evolution of society have blurred the distinct identity of women and men from their point of view. They thought that modern egalitarianism sought to transform men into women and to erase the difference between them, and feminism intended to eliminate gender distinction. Paradoxically, in line with modern trends to promote empowerment of the individual as a person in full possession of his faculties, these teenage girls sought to become adults before they were old enough, and they believed that this could not be achieved but through acceptance of the insuperable difference between men and women. That is why they accepted the gender division imposed by IS as a means of realizing the dream of their imagined womanhood, before moving to Syria and facing the harsh reality there. Still, leaving Europe for Syria was popular among adolescent and post-adolescent boys and girls because it would end the anguishing predicament of being neither a man nor a woman in the European post-feminist societies where the gender distinction had become problematic in their opinion.

In a 2017 interview with a young man and a young woman (nineteen and twenty-one years of age, respectively) from a middle-class family in Paris whose sixteen-year-old sister had joined Daesh in 2015 as a young convert (they had no news from her anymore), they said:

Robert: I don't seriously know anymore what it means to be a man. My father is not a role model for me, he divorced my mother and I don't like him particularly, he was mean towards my mother. But she too, married a man whom I don't like so much. . . . It is difficult to be a man nowadays. I guess before, people knew what it meant to be a man, a father, but not anymore!

Isabelle: I would say roughly the same thing as Robert about being a woman. We often discuss this matter together. We are from a divorced family, but I find my mother faultier because she did everything to make my father angry. As a feminist from the 1960's generation, she found some kind of glory to stand up to him on almost every topic. She wanted to be a man and my father refused to be a woman. Both were sticklers for principles and their marriage was jeopardized because of their selfishness, even though they loved each other. My mother taught me to stand on my own two feet, and not to depend financially on men, in brief, to be like a man. This anguishes me because I also am a young woman and contrary to her, I would like to have a child in my early twenties, not in my mid-thirties like her. My sister who became a Muslim and wanted to marry a jihadi in Syria told me once that she dreamed to be pregnant at the age of 15! She wanted to be a woman, not a man, a woman in the sense that she desired to be a mother and only a mother, and not in competition with men, nor in search of equality on the job market. She didn't want to be a substitute to men. I sometimes feel that we are becoming unfit to live in a genuine family. We are doomed to divorce sooner or later, because we have our big egos. My sister Odile suffered. She was traumatized by the divorce of my parents and looked for something more substantial, a family with strong ties. This seems backward, but it isn't as much as that. My mother told us that she had fought for equality, but Odile wanted a patriarchal family in which she could have children, nothing but children, a family in which father and mother would be different, and play their role without endless haggling and fighting! The problem is that I understand Odile's views and in a way I share them! At the same time, I refuse to have my future husband decide for me! It's a dilemma, isn't it?

Robert: The guy who seduced my sister was in Syria. He sent her pictures of him, in a brand new four-wheel drive, a machine gun in his hand, like a superman. This also seduced my sister. She found that a man had to be virile, capable of fighting, a kind of Rambo who fights to death, and nothing should frighten him. She was looking for a man, and she felt that being a man and being a woman are different. She was upset that in our society that was not anymore the case.

Interviewer: You mean that she was looking for a stable patriarchal family and wished to be a kind of traditional woman, devoted to her children rather than being equal to men, in particular in the labor market?

Isabelle: She accepted a patriarchal family that would protect her against the instable family she had experienced with our parents. She also wanted to be a woman in a romantic sense, being nothing but a woman, somebody who would bear children and enjoy family life as a mother, who would be respected by her children and her husband. Daesh had glorified women by telling them that they would be the pillar of the community, they would bear lion cubs for Islam, and they would be respected because of that. That made her happy. She did not want to live in this society with an uncertain family and a life in which she should work her fingers to the bones [trimer] and raise at the same time her children, while the father and the mother divorced. She paid a heavy price for her dreams.

Among those who went to Syria or intended to do so (but were prevented by the European governments), some intended to restore their image as genuine "women" as opposed to their mothers, who had become "quasi-men" by adopting attitudes that undermined their female identity. Those who failed to join IS harbored a strong hatred against society. Some of them tried to set up autonomous female cells. This was particularly the case of a group of five women who were in touch, three of them attempting to detonate a car in September 2016 near Notre-Dame Cathedral in Paris in order to kill as many tourists as possible. Among them, the nineteen-year-old Inès, the youngest and yet the leader of the group, attacked a policeman who sought to arrest her and wounded him in the shoulder with a knife. She was classified in an S file (meaning "security" concern) by the police for having attempted to join IS, and was reportedly in touch with Hayat Boumedienne, Amédy Coulibaly's Islamic wife (he had committed the attack against a Kosher supermarket near Paris in January 2015). In a letter in which she pledged allegiance to IS, she declared that she wanted to avenge the death of Abu Mohammed al-Adnani, Daesh propaganda minister, killed in Syria in September 2016 by US drones. Her father was known for alleged Islamic proselytizing.

Another member of the group was the twenty-three-year-old Sarah, who had tried to join IS in Syria. She intended to marry a Foreign Fighter before her departure, to facilitate her joining Daesh. She wanted first to get in touch with Larossi Abballa before his deadly attack in 2016 against a policeman and his wife in Magnanville in the Yvelines, during which he was killed. She then tried to get close to Adel Kermiche, who later slaughtered a priest and was killed by the police in 2016; finally, she opted for Mohamed L. A., arrested in the Paris region, a brother of Charaf Eddine A., who was already in police custody for his ties with Larossi Abballa. For these young women, marriage was regarded as a facilitator for their departure to Syria, the union with a man being subordinated to the fulfillment of their aspiration to join the caliphate. The third female activist was Amel S., the oldest (at thirty-nine). Unlike the two others, she was unknown to the police. She was the mother of four children and was a security guard in a supermarket. In 2014, she made the decision to take the full veil and was forced to give up her job. A fourth suspect, Ornella G., a twenty-nine-year-old convert, accompanied the group. She unsuccessfully tried with Ines to set afire the gas bottles. She ran away when she saw plainclothes policemen.

Another case was that of a teenager named Safaa Boular, her sister, and her mother. They set up the first all-female terror cell in the UK and were arrested in April 2017 (Casciani, 2018), just before their attack.

Female jihadism challenges traditional feminism that rejects violence. Jihadi action exalts violence in an attitude that derives simultaneously from feminism, post-feminism, and anti-feminism. The feminist dimension lies in women's self-assertion and their ability to act without a man to lead them and provide them with legitimacy. To be sure, Rachid Kassim suggested to the French female cell members violent action through the encrypted messaging application Telegram, and the jihadi Naweed Hussain in Syria influenced Safaa Boular through the promise of marriage and gave her instructions. Still, the "patriarchal" vision of Islam could not convince young women to act alone, without the background of European feminism that pushed them to act in a self-assertive way, as autonomous agents. The implicit feminist tenet here, at odds with mainstream Western feminism, contests men's monopoly of violent action. At the same time, young women and teenagers are fragile and sometimes, they are motivated by escapism, a flight from reality: the British Safaa Boular belonged to a broken family with a disturbed Moroccan mother who imposed on her coercive religious attitudes after having become a fundamentalist Muslim, the young girl suffering also from diabetes. Her older sister, her mother, and Safaa became accomplices in a jihadi plot that could have become really deadly, had not the intelligence services neutralized their plan to make an attack in London. Between self-assertion and self-delusion and manipulation by recruiters, mainly through social media, the combination can be explosive.

In the jihadi movement, violence has become over time not a fact only admired by some women, but also implemented by a tiny minority of them.

1-Convergence and Divergence with Men: Feminism and Its Avatars

The push factors that attracted girls and women to Syria from 2013 to 2016 bore similarities to those that drew men there.

First, women constitute a significant proportion of workers and employees in Europe since two generations, following the progress of feminism, the shaking up of patriarchal family, and the legal benefits arising from gender equality. As a result, they feel even more intensely as men the pangs of job insecurity and fear of the future, due to their disadvantaged position in the employment market (in Europe they generally earn 20 percent to 30 percent less than men for the same job). In a Europe bereft of utopia where the sense of belonging has been weakened in many ways (the increasing fragility of the family, the weakening of the nation-state, the loss of primacy of politics), jihadi women have been drawn to the dystopia of radical Islam, attracted by its promise of a caring community (in contrast to the "selfish" individualism of European nations) and a restored patriarchal family (a reassuring non-egalitarian family rather than the destabilizing modern family based on an anguishing, incomplete gender equality). Men shared the regressive utopia of a neo-patriarchal family, looking for a new type of household to surmount the crisis of modern family, especially, the loss of male supremacy. Many young women had grown tired of playing the man's role without fully benefiting from the male status (in particular in terms of job security and salary) and being at the same time a mother in the household (in addition to outside work). Longing for a clear-cut dividing line between men and women in their lifeworld became an aspiration: to be a "total woman" facing a "total man," the division of the tasks being clear-cut between them, men providing subsistence by working outside home and the women taking care of the family and, in particular, children. Obviously, all this was in the imagination of these young women before they left for Syria. Once there, the harsh reality challenged their irenic view of gender division, which was a travesty of an inequality that was offensive to a modern mind. A minority of young women accepted the new situation, so traumatized were they by the instability of the modern family and its endless quarrels in Europe.[4]

The volatility and fragility of the family, even if it is experienced differently by men and women, has the same root: the primary anthropological cell of society is no longer stable in the face of the uncertainties of modern life and the multiplication of family models (heterosexual versus same-sex family, different types of stepfamilies, single-parent family, formal or informal family that lasts as long as the couple accepts to live together. . .). Family "à la carte" puts the burden on the couple, man and woman alike, who must negotiate their mutual roles, stepfamily conducing to a split authority, divided between biological parents and stepparents in a non-formal way, to be worked out specifically in each concrete case by the partners. The splintered authority between the biological father and the stepfather on the one hand, the biological mother and the stepmother on the other, contributes to this growing sense of unease, subject to endless bargaining between husband, wife (or the two members in the same-sex couple), and children. The dream of marriage with a "knight in shining armor" who might die after a few months was easily internalized by many young women who ventured into Syria because in their minds marriage had already been affected in its stability and put to the test of a disruptive modernity. At least, during the short lifetime of the husband, they would be assured about family stability, shielded from the vagaries of modern life under the supremacy of the caliphate, hoping that the husband might survive the war.

The joy of being part of a new, effervescent Muslim community (although this would prove an illusion after few months' stay in Syria for many of them) was a strong motivation for young women to join Daesh. The "knight of faith" was the counter-model to the "de-virilized" man to whose trivialization both feminism and the loss of his role as the exclusive financial provider for the family had contributed. Many of these young women were driven by the romanticism of love that re-idealized men rather than by adherence to the political ideal of an anti-imperialist Islam or the desire to protect Muslims against secularization, both of which played a decisive role in motivating Muslim men to join IS.

Finally, there was a quest for norms and even discipline among both men and women, a need for an authoritarian guidance that would give meaning and direction to their lives. For men, this was particularly the case among those who sought to engage in the police or the national army in Europe, before enrolling in Daesh. As unsuccessful candidates at home, they turned to jihadism outside. There were also instances of female cases, like Hasna Aït Boulahcen, who dreamed of joining the French army (Rey-Lefebvre et al., 2015).

Another shared ideal between young men and women was the aspiration to reach paradise after death, in an otherworldly existence, beyond the dissensions of modern life. A young Swedish woman who fled from Raqqa in Syria to Turkey and then to Sweden after the death of her husband there, described her motivation in these terms:

> *When you go this way, you don't think about the worldly life, like I can have a good bed. You don't care about these things. You just think about the fastest way I can die and go to heaven.* (Hakim, 2016)

While men and women shared some aspirations for their reshaped relationship in a neo-patriarchal family within the new Islamic State, other characteristics separated them. To begin with, their relationship to death was different in most cases, even though some jihadi women would have liked to die as martyrs in the same way as men. Many girls died in bombings in Syria, but overall, the female death rate was far lower than the men's, and in their overwhelming majority, they did not die fighting the enemy. What often awaited women was the death of their husband, a period of mourning (lasting around three months), and then a possible marriage with another aspirant. There was an urge for afterlife in an escapist attitude for those afraid of life in this world, who aspired to attain felicity by bypassing anguishing ordeals that await young people confronting an uncertain future. To an existence doomed to the vagaries of an increasingly unsettled world, some preferred post-mortem bliss. Martyrdom resolved a dilemma among Muslim young men: they escaped the heavy responsibility of being agents in their own lives through a felicitous death.

2-Fascination for Coercive Standards

Jihadi women, like their male counterparts, yearned for a community that would give a strong meaning to their lives. The dystopia of Daesh was repressive and regressive but promised organic bonding with each other within a close-knit, imaginary Muslim community (the neo-Ummah). It was highly attractive to many young men and women in Europe, where social cohesion has waned, due to the decline of social organizations (like trade unions or political parties promoting working-class ties) and social utopias[5]. Daesh reversed the trend and proposed coercive norms as a new utopia that would cement social life at the cost of personal freedom. Women were even more receptive to this idea, due to their fragile life in which they had to be mothers and working persons at the same time. The more restrictive the standards were, the more reassuring they became, at least before women experienced real life under Daesh in Syria. Rigid norms played a heartening role for the anomic individuals, coercion replacing integration in a mythological manner.

This was particularly the case for Saïda, born in the early 1980s in a non-practicing North African family to a French-Algerian mother and an Algerian father. Her parents divorced when she was thirteen. She blamed her father for not raising her as well as her brothers and sisters. In high school, she was having a hard time keeping up with classes and turned to Islam, influenced by her friends. She tried to pass the national police entrance exam in order to fight against pedophiles, drug dealers, and other law breakers. She failed, despite receiving good grades, because she did not show a medical certificate of good health. Later on, she attributed to Allah's favor this failure that had kept her from attending a male environment, in her eyes forbidden (*haram*) to Muslim women. She married a Tunisian Salafist despite her parents' opposition, learning about Salafism (the "Salafiyya") on Google in order to be a good wife to her future husband. She also found answers to her questions on Islamic forums. She had fits of depression that she attributed to the sins she had committed prior to joining Salafist Islam. Not only did she yearn for rigid norms, but she also felt guilty for not having followed them prior to her conversion. This type of aspiration is prevalent among the pietist Salafists who long for *Hijra* (that is, leaving Europe for a Muslim country), in contrast to the jihadi Salafists who consider holy war as the only way to warrant their redemption. Both are in search of restrictive norms, absolute certainties, a faith that will frame and give meaning to their lives. While wearing the full veil (illegal in France since October 2010), Saïda was stopped by the police and, after a quarrel, she spent a night in prison. For her, the will to build another life with a set of self-imposed restrictive norms was a paramount existential question. The Salafist neo-Ummah filled the void in her life but stripped her of her free will, although the restrictions were decided by her. Without a veil, she felt "naked," exposed to the gaze of those to whom the sight of her body was religiously forbidden. Like many young women, she did not end up in Syria, but within France the nostalgia of a Muslim land in which strong ties would go hand in hand with piety loomed large in her imaginary world (De Féo, 2019).

For men, jihadi norms restored their former patriarchal power over women and put an end to their feeling like fallen gods in gender-equal societies. For them, repressive standards had another meaning as well: putting an end to the democratic chaos in modern societies where punishment has become complicated for lack of godly judiciary standards and the absence of bodily punishment like cutting hands or stoning for incest. Instead, imprisoning the culprits, as many of those young Muslims belonging to the slum culture had experienced, robbed them of their life. For women, the insecurity of modern life caused by the dual pressure on them as mothers inside their homes and workers outside, pushed some of them to desire the return to a mythologized past when women reigned in the household, leaving the hardship of providing for the family's needs to men. Daesh played on both of these myths of male supremacy and females' role as a mother through its intense propaganda machine that exploited exoticism in order to seduce young Europeans: what was "traditional" (patriarchal family) became exciting through its "novelty" among young people who had experienced post-feminist relationships and egalitarian gender relations and had only naïve notions of tradition.

3-Women and Violence: From "Total Muslims" to "Negative Heroines"

The relationship to violence has changed in the new generation of women in the West, if we take as witness jihadism and, in particular, the enthusiasm of women toward it. Even today, violence remains largely the preserve of men: the female prison population was around 4 percent in France and 6 percent in the United Kingdom in 2017, and domestic violence has its roots mainly among men (90 percent), women playing a marginal role (around 10 percent). However, women's imagination regarding violence has changed. The proportion of women who went to Syria was high (17 percent, or 1,023 women out of a total of 5,904 people) (Cook and Vale, 2018), many of them being jihadi brides (they intended to marry jihadi men), a minority of them aspiring to become jihadi actors, as already mentioned. If we compare this figure with the other extremist movements, this proportion is one of the highest, except in the far-left movements like the Baader-Meinhof gang in which the proportion of women exceeded 50 percent and at times reached 60 percent (Neumann, 2016) or the Red Brigades in Italy, in which 30% of the members were women (B. Cook, 2006). In the IRA in Northern Ireland, there were 5 percent women (Gill, Horgan, and Deckert, 2014), and 6.4 percent of the members of the ETA Basques were women (Reinares, 2004). Given how women were treated by Daesh, their high number reflected their fascination with jihadism as well as the dreams of adolescent and post-adolescent girls, divorced from reality.

Some of the women who joined Daesh bore particular traits, especially their quest for "de-Westernization" in order to embrace Islam more thoroughly, but also in order to become born-again Muslim women. They felt that Western civilization was totally perverse and sinful and prevented them from identifying fully, absolutely, and totally with the neo-Ummah which, in their eyes, embodied happiness in this world and bliss in the afterlife.

For them, the West was first and foremost a reign of total secularization, the profanation of religion in the name of the supremacy of human beings dethroning God, the annexation of the public sphere by a non-religious (or anti-religious, in jihadi view) system of reference that made impossible life under the aegis of Allah. Leaving Europe meant escaping the all-secular public sphere where "female naked bodies" (in their view, women without a veil) reigned supreme. Shedding all occidental traits and habits became a prerequisite for recovering a "full" Muslim identity for these men and women.

In an interview in Toulouse in June 2016, the brother of a young woman from a secular French family explained how his sister had converted to Islam and had become radicalized under the influence of a local preacher, leaving France in 2015 in her twenties for Syria in order to become a "total Muslim":

> *She said that everything in France was sinful: in the street, her veil annoyed other people who gave her a dirty look, and that made her furious. But since other women did not wear the hijab and some men had their arms and sometimes their legs exposed, for her the entire society was corrupt and perverse. At the family table, wine and even non-halal meat was unacceptable to her. She sometimes told me: I feel ashamed to be a French woman. I am not free to be a proud Muslim, but on top of that, other people dress and behave in a way that makes me feel uncomfortable all the time. My dream is to migrate to a Muslim country, forget about France, and embrace fully my Muslim identity. I am ashamed of being French, and more so, of belonging to the Western world. You will all go to hell for your sinful behavior!*

Women and men of this category, whom I qualify as "total Muslims," look for a unified world in the image of the uniqueness of Allah, entailing the subordination of all spheres of life under the protective wing of religion, whose commandments were imposed by the caliphate, even to non-Muslims. The secular world seems monstrous to them because it has broken off its ties with God, having banished God from their existence and usurped His place. By denying any transcendence, hyper-secular European societies create a void in the mind of those individuals who feel the need of a sacred entity that would provide them with absolute standards.

To the female total Muslims, feminism in the West desecrated patriarchal family, brought the social roles of men and women closer together, and barred the path to motherhood. The desire for early motherhood among young women or adolescent girls who went to Syria (or intended and were prevented to go) was set against the feminist model. It was a reaction to the generations of feminist mothers and grandmothers, marking the yearning to recover a more intimate sense of womanhood rather than a desire to become equal to men or fight against men's supremacy. In their attitude, anti-feminism played a major role.

Another step was taken in jihadism with the figurehead of what could be called "the negative heroine" who went beyond the "total Muslim woman" in terms of her radicalization. She was the feminine counterpart of the male "negative hero" (Khosrokhavar, 2015). Her mindset was an explosive mix of feminism, anti-feminism, and post-feminism: her will to act hid her tormented character. The jihadi negative heroine sought to embody the counter-values of society in a violent manner. Like the negative hero, her male counterpart, the more violent she became, the more she was legitimized in her own eyes, inversely proportional to her being delegitimized in Western societies. She endeavored to punish the West through violent action. She also intended to recruit new female adepts to strengthen IS. The number of these negative heroines was rather small. In contrast to most of the young women who intended to marry a knight of Islam, their yearning was to take up arms and fight against the miscreants (the entire West) in order to defend radical Islam. In Syria, the "mujahidat" were not allowed to operate in the battlefield during the reign of IS. In Europe, some of the women who were prevented from joining Syria turned their anger against society. This was the case, as already mentioned, of the young women who tried to blow up a car in the tourist district of Notre-Dame de Paris in September 2016. The Boular family (the mother and the two sisters) in London, arrested in April 2017, intended to blow up the British Museum.

Women thus oscillated between the dream of love, the desire to break with a morose everyday reality, the yearning for building up a God-ordained family beyond the fragility of the modern household, and the aspiration to recover their female identity by reinforcing their differences with men. A tiny minority among them intended to act as combatants in the battlefield or to attack their own country through violent acts as jihadi negative heroines.

4-Examples of Radicalized Young Women

Sally-Anne Frances Jones, born in Greenwich, southeast of London, in 1968, aka "Umm Hussain al-Britani" or the "White Widow according to the media, belonged to the category of negative heroines. Before her conversion, she was a guitarist in an all-female rock band and occasionally sold L'Oréal perfumes. She lived on welfare benefits in a council house in Chatham, Kent. Her messages were clear: "My son and I love to live with the cutters!" She made violent statements, in sharp contrast to the mainstream non-violent culture in Europe: "You Christians, you all need to be beheaded with a beautiful blunt knife and be put on the rails in Raqqa. Come here and I will do it for you!" (Kern, "Britain's Female Jihadists," 2014). She became a propagandist and a notorious IS recruiter. She was the leader of the secret Anwar al-Awlaki battalion's female wing. She was responsible for the military training of European female recruits, or *mujahidat* in Syria. They would then be instructed to carry out suicide missions in the West, although there is no evidence of her leading the jihadi women into the battlefield.

She had two children and made the trip from Kent to Syria with her youngest son Joe, born in 2004. There she became the second wife of the English hacker Junaid Hussein, the head of the "digi-jihad" brigade, who was killed on August 25, 2015, by American drones. Sally Jones was heavily involved in social media propaganda to attract young, English-speaking women to Syria, particularly by Twitter, and remained the first woman to act in this regard on social media in the name of IS. She undoubtedly belonged to the jihadi star system. The more she took part in IS propaganda, the more ruthless and extremist she became, the narcissistic spiral of fame and more fame through "unconventional" attitudes (extremism in her case) operating fully in her case. In her mind, fame became "notoriety," that is, negative fame, which is a major characteristic of the negative hero or heroine.

Another jihadi negative heroine was a young twenty-one-year-old medical student who put on social networks an image of herself holding a severed head. The woman named on Twitter "Muhajirah Bint Usama" claimed to be a doctor (she was a medical student, in fact) acting on behalf of IS. At her side were two children. The image was accompanied by the message "dream job, terrorist doctor!" accompanied by the symbol LOL, (meaning "laughing out loud"), combining irony and extreme cruelty, associating medicine and death, a counter-image of the medical calling whose purpose is to save lives and not to inflict death (Pleasance, "British Jihadi Medical Student," 2014). She was linked to the al-Khansaa all-female brigade, which chastised women who were non-compliant with Islamic modesty in Syria. The members of that brigade ran, with the assistance of another English jihadi woman, Aqsa Mahmoud, a whorehouse where young enslaved Yezidi women were forced to prostitute themselves to the IS military. The new jihadi order allowed transgression of moral taboos, in reference to the archaic rules of Islamic justice, reinforced and made even crueler through the media effect and the urge to be "scandalous" in order to attract the attention of the public. Still, associating in an ironic fashion the cut-off head of a prisoner with a doctor's action would not be in conformity to the traditional Islamic views. This attitude is rather a "perverse" consequence of the modern transgressive behavior against dominant moral norms, in the West as much as in the Muslim world, reinforced by the social media effects (the more scandalous, the more famous).

Another case of jihadi negative heroine is Maria Giulia Sergio, nicknamed "Lady Jihad" by the Italian media (Marone, 2016). She was born near Naples and was the second daughter in a modest Catholic family. In the year 2000, the family decided to settle in northern Italy. After school she enrolled at the university and did part-time jobs to finance her studies. In 2007 she converted to Islam and adopted the name "Fatima al-Zahra" (the daughter of the Prophet). According to her, the web played a significant role in her conversion. An Italian of Syrian origin, Bushra Haik, helped indoctrinate Maria and some other Italian women. At first, her parents did not approve of her conversion, but eventually, she managed to convert them all. Gradually, she began to wear the *niqab* (total veil) and declared herself a victim of religious persecution in Italy. The creation of IS in June 2014 opened up new vistas for her, and she decided to join it. In order to migrate to Syria, she married on September 17, 2014, an Albanian by the name of Aldo Said Kobuzi, in order to avoid marrying someone she did not know, once she was in Syria. Four days after the wedding, the couple left Italy for Syria and settled in Aleppo where Kobuzi's sister joined them, and they became part of the Albanian community of Foreign Fighters who had taken up residence in that district. Maria had an irrepressible desire for action, and she took part in military training even before the creation of the al-Khansaa all-female brigade in Syria. She explicitly expressed the desire to join in the fighting and die as a martyr, earnestly learning Arabic for the sake of her Islamic integration. To convince her family members to join her in Syria, she played on psychological levers: "Hijra [migration to Syria, land of the caliphate] is [religiously] compulsory. It does not matter what you think, it does not matter. You must come here to save your soul from hell and that's all [that matters]!"

Her older sister was interested in the ideological aspects of radical Islam, and after her divorce, she was looking for a Muslim husband. Her father and mother were less enthusiastic. Out of love for their daughter they agreed to go to Syria to join her. The prospect of a higher standard of living enticed them as well (she promised a washing machine to her mother). In July 2015, the Italian police arrested her father, mother, and sister to prevent their departure to Syria. After their arrest, Maria gave an interview to the Italian press, defending IS as a Muslim "perfect state," justifying the beheadings and rejecting human rights violations.

The case of Maria Giula Sergio reveals the rather rare transition from Islamic fundamentalism to jihadism. Long before her Syrian trip, in October 2009 she took part in a TV show in which she defended Muslim women's headscarves and the necessity to accept a "pluralistic [cultural] system" in Italy. Shortly afterward, she wore a full veil and, in September 2011, she signed a petition for its social approval, co-signed by her sister and mother. Her radicalization, like Emilie König's in France, was due to a sense of religious persecution, especially with regard to the headscarf.

Another negative heroine with a feminist streak is Samantha Louise Lewthwaite. The media called her the "White Widow," and she was one of the most notorious female converts of the jihadi constellation. She held a prominent position in the jihadi star system.

She was born in 1983 into a military family (her father was a soldier). After high school, she entered the School of Oriental and African Studies in London but failed to graduate. In 1994, the divorce of her parents threw her into despair, and she became closer to her Muslim neighbors, whose family ties were stronger than the Christians' in her eyes. She converted to Islam at the age of seventeen. She later met Germaine Lindsay in London in the protest movement against the 2003 war that Britain was to take part in. She married him religiously in October 2002, the act not being legalized. Three years later, on July 7, 2005, Lindsay blew himself up in the London Underground and killed twenty-six people. Lewthwaite was then eight months pregnant (they already had a first child of fourteen months). She claimed she didn't know anything about the subway attack. In 2009, she gave birth to another child with an unknown father. Then she disappeared and went to Tanzania or Somalia with her children. She married Hassan Maalim Ibrahim, a military leader in al-Shabaab jihadi group.

According to the Kenyan and English police, she was involved in several attacks (in Mombasa in 2012 and in Nairobi in 2013) and would even be the leader of a jihadi cell that targeted tourists in Mombasa in December 2011. Her alleged presence in the coastal city of Lamu in Kenya, then in Syria in

2014, as well as her death announced by the Russian agency Regnum, could not be confirmed. She was prosecuted in absentia by the Kenyan courts for possession of explosives and plans for an attack. Lewthwaite was an alleged member of the jihadi al-Shabaab group in Somalia and was accused of being one of the protagonists of the bombing of a Mombasa bar in 2012.

By her actions carried out under multiple pseudonyms and her fleeting presence on multiple scenes, Lewthwaite has become a major feminine star of jihadism in the Western world.

c-Jihadi Converts

Converts who became involved in jihadism were of two distinct social classes: a majority of lower-middle-class or middle-class young men and women; a minority of lower-class youth, mainly from Black Africa in Britain or French youth mostly living in the poor districts and influenced by the slum culture. The proportion of jihadi converts was ten times higher than that of the Muslim converts in Europe (Neumann, 2016).

Most jihadi converts in Western Europe are young men with a criminal record (Basra,, Neumann, and Brunner, 2016; "From Criminals to Terrorists and Back?" 2019). However, these data must be contextualized to take on a social meaning. Many Black people belonging to the former British colonies suffer from stigmas and police harassment (a phenomenon that is general in Europe against sons of poor migrants) and job discrimination (24 percent of applicants of White origin received a positive response from employers versus 15 percent of the minority ethnic applicants with identical CVs and cover letters) ((Siddique, 2019). The "colonial complex" (even in societies which did not colonize the migrants, for instance Moroccans in Belgium), makes life painful for the Muslim youth. The family becomes more fragile, particularly among working-class people, migration to Europe stretching thin its cohesion and weakening ties with the extended family and friends in the country of origin. On top of it, being a non-Muslim in a neighborhood with a high proportion of Muslims (poor ethnic districts in Europe) makes it difficult to live with Muslim friends without sharing their habits and customs (fasting in Ramadan, not eating pork, not drinking alcohol, not shaking hands with the other gender. . .): this pushes toward conversion in order to be in unison with the environment, the more so as there is a common ground, namely the humiliation due to being foreigners with colonial background despite religious difference: Pakistanis (Muslims) and Nigerians (Christians) in the United Kingdom; North Africans (Muslims), Gabonese (mostly Catholic) and Congolese (mostly Christians) in France. Sharing the same sense of inferiority makes conversion somehow "natural," particularly while living in the same poor districts in which Islam has become, de facto, the religion of the majority of the residents. The media display a derogatory picture of these neighborhoods that add to the stigmas attached to ethnic youth. "Slum Islam," exhibited by the media, bears the mark of this rejection. The role of Islam as the religion of those who feel oppressed or rejected cannot be assumed by Christianity or Judaism: Islam, through jihadism or hyper-fundamentalism, voices the rebellion against humiliation, this opportunity being unavailable in today's Christianity, regarded as the religion of the "White" and "dominant" people among the Muslim populations in Europe. On the other hand, Christianity as the religion of former colonizers is suspected of being a means to dominate the downtrodden Muslims. Last, in the poor districts where these people live, Muslims are the majority and non-Muslims, a (tiny) minority. Non-Muslims usually leave the district while the Muslims' proportion increases.

Women who joined IS made up a significant part of the converts. In January 2016, roughly a third of those who went from France to Syria were women: 220 French women in January 2016, one-third of them being converts (Guéguen, "Les Femmes dans le Jihad," 2016).

Among them, adolescent or post-adolescent girls were numerous. A convert girl aged sixteen whose parents had prevented her from going to Syria by having her passport withdrawn by the police, challenged her mother's feminist values as the latter reported to me. Her daughter refused to talk directly to me as a man, in the name of Islam, exchanging with a foreign male being religiously improper (*haram*, impure):

> *Whenever I pointed to her premature wish to become a mother, my daughter would retort to me: my body belongs to me, I want to bear a child and be a woman. You tell me that I should wait because I am a teenager, but I am a woman, I'm different from you: you became pregnant at 32, you worked hard in an office and were exhausted to run at the same time family life and work. That's why you didn't take enough care of me and were sometimes so grumpy! I am not interested in your way of life, I want to have a home, children around me, a family, a husband I can trust and love, who would work and provide me*

with financial means to raise our children without having me to work outside. For me Syria is where my dream could come true: I would marry my friend (from Belgium) and be happy as a woman. You stopped me; I will never forgive you. (Interview in Toulouse in June 2018 with a middle-class mother whose daughter had converted to Islam in a matter of few weeks—or perhaps more, since the parents had no access to her hidden private Facebook accounts—and wanted to join IS for the sake of marrying a young Belgian who lived there as a Foreign Fighter)

The same mother continued:

She finds fault with gender equality. She says that it eliminates the difference between a man and a woman. For her, men and women complete each other, and God has created them different. She wants to be a 100% percent woman and men don't interest her otherwise than through marriage, having children, and a close-knit family. Our history of feminism and the fight against gender inequality leaves her indifferent.

Another girl was fascinated by jihadi men. From Syria, a young Frenchman had contacted her through the web and seduced her into joining him there. The social worker who was in touch with her after she failed to leave France gave me the following account:

She wanted to be a "woman" and found in general Islam very "sexy" because the young man was very restrictive and told her: "I don't want you to show your beauty to others, I don't want you to talk to other men, your beauty is mine, your voice is mine. . . ." She found that she was more desirable to him than other men, and he liked her better. For me [as a social worker], *he just wanted her all to himself, without taking into account her freedom as a woman; he was worried that she was in touch with other men; he was selfish. She told me that the Salafists who were the most restrictive in that regard made her feel like a real woman and desirable for her spiritual qualities, since she did not show her face or body. She believed that she could take the initiative because she would behave as a woman, and her beauty, hidden to the non-authorized males, seduced Muslims. The young jihadi who wooed her into marriage made her feel great because Islam was not contaminated by this shallow gender equality, as she told me.* (Paris, November 2016)

Her sense of being a woman seemed lost in her daily life with the "White" non-Muslims, men and women being leveled through the egalitarian gender culture, which was deeply frustrating to her. Islam and, more radically, jihadism of the young Frenchman of North-African descent who courted her through the web "re-womanized" her, rejecting the "de-womanized" identity that was imposed on her through gender equality. This mythologized new identity was seductive before most of them set foot in Syria. Once there, many became disillusioned, the gap between their "dreamed-of" Islam and its real jihadi version being unbridgeable. But most of them could not return home.

Radical Islam reassured young European convert boys and girls by inscribing gender difference into a sacred register in which men and women played asymmetrical roles, reintroducing a fictitious transparency and a clear-cut divide, appeasing the modern anguish of gender indistinctiveness among them. That was one of the major causes of their conversion to Islam, based on an anxiety that was not shared by many other girls and boys. Mostly from secular families, they opted for Islam because it provided an answer to their existential problems that secularism was unable to resolve. The afterlife in paradise soothed the angst caused by the uncertainties of the present time through the assurance of eternal bliss by submitting to the demarcation line between the licit (*halal*) and the illicit (*haram*). The need for this separation, in the name of sacred values, is essential to those longing for restrictive norms and clear-cut taboos.

Before their departure to Syria, the fascination among young European teenage girls of their imagined "Daesh-type family" was rooted in the quest for a counter-model to the modern family that is marred by instability and authority crisis. In the West, the disappearance of patriarchy has given birth to new kinds of family whose common denominator is the "negotiated" authority between their members. Authority is not anymore a given, as was the case up to the 1960s. The lack of a frame of reference combined with the expansion of new technologies (the web, the mobile phone. . .) that take teenagers away from parental oversight, open up new areas of autonomy for them. The new freedom is anguishing as well, adolescents feeling anxious about not living in stable, close-knit families, being at the same time in search of freedom to assert their imagined adulthood. They have mixed feelings about being freed from the yoke of patriarchy, on one hand, or abandoned and uncared-for in broken families, on the other. The largely idealized picture of neo-patriarchal family enticed them, before their one-way trip to Syria. They looked for a new type of family that they would build themselves, devoid of the defects of the modern family in which too much freedom and too much instability as well as too few norms and taboos made life insecure.

The rapidly converted girls (mostly between few weeks and few months) were looking for men who were the antithesis of those they met in their everyday lives, marked by the loss of their former superiority, equality with women having "de-virilized" them, the dominant egalitarian culture robbing them of their manhood (in contrast to the Islamic warrior male that would restore man's virility). Teenage girls were looking for exceptional men who could be trusted (contrary to the adolescent boys around them, who just wanted to have sex), supermen who would not be intimidated by danger, who would naturally carry insignias of the imagined knights of Islam: machine guns, SUVs, and the proud air of someone who would kill or get killed without flinching. Their heroic nature reassured young women, anxious to idealize their future husband. Conversion to Islam became a way to assuage their anguish and open up new vistas for a family life that would be free from the stresses of modern couples. They would find a valiant husband whom they could trust. The "extraordinary" knight would guarantee the couple an intense life, away from the monotony and boredom assailing many modern couples after few months of marriage. Of course, the couple could be shaken by the death of the husband in the battlefield, but at any rate *boredom* would not besiege it.

For hours, girls looked on the internet to find a suitable young man who would become their husband and who would come from Europe, while men used social networks to search for women, trying to seduce them according to "Islamic norms." Women journalists contacted young European jihadis in Syria, pretending to be a young convert woman ready to migrate in order to see how male jihadis tried to seduce young girls (Erelle, 2015).

Some young women sought to become celebrities like men, to raise themselves above anonymity. The jihadi star system needed feminine figures that stood out for the quality of their propaganda on the web and for their curt, even cruel, character. This was the case of Samantha Louise Lewthwaite (in the UK), Maria Giula Sergio (Italy), and Emilie König (France), each of whom made a name for themselves in the global jihadi network and enticed young girls to Syria.

Allah's religion in its dual fundamentalist and jihadi versions attracted many young people who felt forlorn in the European societies in which anomie was the main cause of disarray within a secular framework that brought no answer to their subjective needs. In my interview with a thirty-two-year-old middle-class convert to Islam in 2014 in Créteil (close to Paris), this view was expressed in an explicit manner:

Abdelkrim [aka Frédéric]: Before converting to Islam I felt a void in my life. I had my friends, and especially my girlfriend with whom I had been for five years. But I felt like a stranger, around me life was colorless. Something was missing that I couldn't name.

Question: Are you from a religious or secular family?

Abdelkrim: I am from a secular family; my parents didn't go to church and I didn't receive any religious instruction. I was a Catholic with no religious identity. A friend of mine had converted to Islam a few years before. We discussed from time to time and he used to say that Islam was more to him than a mere religion. He said that he was living with others in a way different from ours, believing as he did in the Ummah. He gradually introduced me to the Islamic tenets.

Question: Why Islam and not Christianity?

Abdelkrim: I read the Koran and found it meaningful to me, contrary to the New Testament that gives no clues to the concrete problems of life. Islam tells you clearly what is forbidden [haram] *and what is allowed* [halal]. *It clearly distinguishes God from man, unlike Christianity, which has its man-God in Jesus. I need to know that there is a God and that I must submit to him for my salvation. One must submit to God and not be bound to him through love, according to Christianity. Submission to God means following his laws and commandments in order to be among those who will be saved. It is as simple as that!*

Question: So, you became a Muslim!

Abdelkrim: One day I told my friend that I wanted to convert to Islam. He introduced me to an Imam who was very kind and who had a rational explanation for what is forbidden in Islam like alcohol or drugs and what is compulsory like helping financially the deprived through alms and Islamic taxes [zakat]. In the ceremony [of conversion] *in the mosque, there were some fifty people who encircled me and when I recited the Shahadah* [recognition of the unicity of God and the prophethood of Mohammed], *there was a thrill among them and at the end my emotions burst into tears—they were so enthusiastic! I wasn't alone anymore, there were "brothers" who were with me, I was not forlorn! I could talk about that for hours! God is unique in Islam, this is transparent, contrary to Christianity in which God is triune. In Islam God is beyond me and this is reassuring!*

Question: But in the modern world, with the progress of science and the acceleration of history, it is difficult to submit to pre-modern norms.

Abdelkrim: In our world, science and technology promise everything and there is no need for God, until the day someone dear to you dies or you catch a cancer and are not sure to be cured. This leaves you alone, and science is unable to reassure you that after death there is a sense in life. Islam gives me a sense through a God who is beyond me and who imposes on me a moral attitude. The secular republican moral that I learned at school did not make life meaningful to me, it was not convincing at all. Through Islam there is a red line separating right and wrong, licit and illicit [halal, haram]. . . . *This pushes some young men into jihad: they declare war against those who do not respect the red line.*

Although Abdelkrim is not tempted himself by jihadism, he "understands" those who take up arms against the Infidels. The quest for limits and the need for inflexible norms and rules have elected affinities with jihadism, but there is, of course, no causal relationship between them.

What pushes young people to convert to Islam is the loss of the sense of life within modern Europe, Islam becoming for many young converts the only legitimate "strong religion" (Almond, Appleby, and Sivan, 2003) on the market, due to its opposition to a materialist, secular, and hegemonic Western world, combining this-worldly and otherworldly concerns, for which it proposes more or less utopian (or mythical) solutions.

The weakening of the national communities in Europe that were historically linked to the nation-state pushes also toward alternative identities. Fundamentalist or radical Islam proposes, according to the taste of those who look for a substitute identity, a new meaningful world, apart from the materialist Western civilization. Identity crisis is also due to the creation of the European Union that robbed many of the privileges of the national governments, without creating a European identity. The new European governments have become more or less empty entities, and under their rule, middle classes are financially squeezed and, contrary to previous nation-states, they provide no meaningful identities to the citizens.

1-Examples of Jihadi Converts

As a rule, converts develop a special relationship to their adopted religion. European jihadi converts launched attacks in their own countries since the end of 2015, when access to Syria became difficult. At that time, Daesh encouraged jihadis to stage their attacks at home rather than attempt the increasingly risky journey to Syria. Turkey stopped them at the Syrian border and sent them back to their country, exasperating young people who attempted assaults at home. They wanted to punish their own country for preventing their departure to Syria, but also for their government's involvement in the war against IS. Several young men were in this category. We begin with Adel Kermiche. He was a young convert (he called himself, among names, "Abu Jayyed al-Hanafi"), born in 1997 in Mont-Saint-Aignan near Rouen, a town in northwestern France. He grew up in Saint-Etienne-du-Rouvray where his parents live and was radicalized via the internet, by Rachid Kassim, a member of the IS, born in France (his father was from Yemen and his mother, from Algeria). In 2015, Kermiche's various accounts on social networks showed the extent of his radicalization. He professed radical Islamic views. On his Facebook page he made no secret of his jihadi views and he was known to the Intelligence Services. On his Telegram account, to those two hundred people who received his encrypted message he announced: "You take a knife, you go to a church, you make a massacre, bim! You cut off two or three heads and it's good, it's over" (Garcia and Pham-Lê, 2016; "Saint-Étienne-du-Rouvray," 2016). On two occasions in 2015, Kermiche tried to leave for Syria. The first time, while crossing Germany, the authorities sent him back to France. He was under judicial review for "criminal conspiracy in relation to a terrorist enterprise." A few months later he tried again to go to Syria and reached Turkey, where he was arrested and on May 22 he was sent back to France where he was put in prison. He met there his "spiritual guide," unknown to the authorities, who inspired him: "In prison my sheikh [Fleury-Mérogis] gave me ideas," he said. He then adopted a seemingly moderate stance and told the magistrate that he deeply regretted his past and had renounced his attempts at jihad. He reported on his professional projects, particularly in the medico-psychological field. His parents pledged to follow him closely in his work at the municipal recreation center. While he devised his plan to kill people in the church of his town, he seduced many young Muslim girls to whom he promised marriage. These two apparently contradictory attitudes (feminine conquests, projected fake marriage, and martyrdom at the same time) are common features among many jihadis who intend to become future martyrs. They think they have to satisfy their sexual desires even by cheating, God forgiving all their sins after their sacrifice as holy warriors.

Abdel Malik Petitjean was the accomplice of Adel Kermiche in the attack against the church of Saint-Étienne-de-Rouvray. Born in 1996 in Saint-Dié-des-Vosges, he was adopted by Franck Petitjean who ensured his education until his divorce from his wife in 2011. He lived with his two sisters in a stepfamily. His nominal father, after divorce, settled in Bordeaux and lost contact with his adopted son. In 2015, he obtained his high school diploma (baccalauréat) and carried out temporary assignments. He episodically participated in the religious ceremonies of the local mosque in Aix-les-Bains, where his mother resided. Unlike Adel Kermiche, whose radicalization was known to those around him, Abdelmalik remained discreet and his mother had no knowledge of it, nor did the people he attended or the authorities of the Chambéry-Savoie airport where he worked as a porter during winter holidays. It was a "silent radicalization" in contrast to the "loquacious radicalization" of his accomplice Adel Kermiche. He was shy and introverted, unlike Kermiche, who was expansive and boastful. Subsequently, he tried to move from Turkey to Syria under the name of "Abu Omar" and was arrested by the Turkish police on June 10, 2016. He was sent back to France the next day. Up to then, he had had a clean criminal record. After that he was recorded as "S" (someone with "security" problems, according to the police file), before assisting Adel Kermiche in the murder of Father Hamel on July 26, 2016.

Kermiche and Petitjean tried to leave the country to reach Syria. Their attempts having failed, they took offense and turned their anger against their society. They were influenced by jihadi agents outside (the charismatic Kassim, among others, who resided in Syria) or inside the country (the "sheikh" or the "spiritual guide" in prison to whom Adel Kermiche referred).

As for Richard Dart, he joined Islamic extremists in contrast to his half-brother, Robb Leech, who desperately sought to dissuade him. The two middle-class brothers lived in Weymouth, in the UK with their parents who were teachers. Richard could have enjoyed a quiet, middle-class life. But he chose another path. In London, he was drawn to the radical ideas of al-Muhajiroun, led by the charismatic cleric Anjem Choudhary, assisted by the convert Siddhartha Dhar. At the age of twenty-five he converted to Islam and grew a long, thick beard, following the example of the Prophet. Richard quickly formed a trio with Jahangir Alom, twenty-six, a former police assistant (after failing to return to the British army in 2006 for medical reasons, he became a police assistant in 2007, before relinquishing it in 2009), and Imran Mahmood, twenty-two and jobless. The three lived in Greater London. They were arrested at the airport on their way to Pakistan and were sentenced to prison terms for their involvement in a terrorist act: Alom was sentenced to four years, six months, Dart to six years.

The trio reveals another fact, the brotherhood of arms between the converted English citizens and the sons or grandsons of migrants, which does not exist as a rule in everyday life, each community leading its own life. With radicalization, a counter-citizenship arises between people who otherwise would not have been together, even to the point of fraternity of arms. jihadi fraternity facilitates cooperation and even affectionate relations between the "White," middle-class people (like Richard Dart), and the sons of migrants, of working-class origin, often unemployed (like Imran Mahmood). The invisible boundaries that existed in everyday life were thus crossed by "brothers in religion" who sympathized and combined forces to fight the common enemy, namely the "Infidels"; jihadism sometimes redraws the boundaries of class and ethnicity.

There is a common trait among converts: they need to prove the sincerity of their faith to others. They often became more radical than other jihadis, Daesh promoting them within its organization, without consideration of their ethnic origin, except in its highest ranks. Converts thus benefited from fraternal relations with radicalized Muslims who no longer regarded them as "White" people, and Daesh granted them high ranks within its organization, some of them achieving the status of "Emir" within its military hierarchy.

Finally, another striking fact shared by radical converts and other extremist Muslims was the perception of "decadence" and loss of moral values in modern society. According to them, modern society was in a state of decay regarding its moral values, especially in relation to homosexuality, which they believed was pushing them toward Sodom and Gomorrah. The consequence of this perversion would be the destruction of the Western world by God, who would inflict on them the same punishment that He had meted out to these two cities, according to the Koranic account. In the two films produced by his stepbrother, Robb Leech (*My Brother the Islamist* and *My Brother the Terrorist*), his jihadi brother Richard Dart complained that in Britain the dominant culture had become more and more homosexual, men and women dressing identically, women walking half-naked (Leech, 2011, 2014).

Between the cases of converts (from another religion to Islam) and born-again Muslims (those who return effusively to a radical version of Islam) one finds a third type, more ambiguous: those whose fathers or mothers were Muslim and the other parent was of another religion (usually Christianity) or secular, even atheist. In their case, opting for Islam is a special choice. They are neither born-again (they were not for sure Muslims before), nor converts (they had some relations to Islam through one of their parents). A number of people in this category that I met in prison had chosen Islam, first because their Catholic father or mother had been loosely practicing or not practicing at all; second, because through Islam they were able to show their difference with the mainstream society that had rejected them by putting them in prison (Khosrokhavar, 2016). This was the case of Peter Chérif ("Abu Hamza," his Islamic name), born in 1982, a notorious jihadi in the 2000s. He is a member of al-Qaeda in the Arabian Peninsula (AQAP). His Afro-Caribbean Catholic father died in a car accident when Peter was fourteen. His mother, Myriam, born in Tunisia, was a moderate Muslim. She did not mind living with non-Muslims. After the death of her Catholic husband, she lived with Johnny, from Guyana, also a non-Muslim. Before becoming radicalized, Peter was known for armed robbery and drug trafficking. At twenty, he tried to join the French army to fill the void of authority (as was the case of some other young people who became, later, jihadis), but due to an injury in 2002, he had to renounce it. He then took refuge in religious practice, embracing Islam in 2003. Farid Benyettou, the leader of the radical Buttes-Chaumont network in Paris, instructed him in radical Islam. In 2003 he indoctrinated the Kouachi brothers, the perpetrators of the attacks against *Charlie Hebdo* magazine in January 2015. In his case we find the combination of stigmas due to his mixed Black and North African origin, the crisis of adolescence, the death of the father, deviance, drug trafficking, family crisis, and his final radicalization by a guru (Farid Benyettou). In December 2018 he was arrested in Djibouti and extradited to France. He explained his radicalization by the crisis of his family: his brother in prison, his mother critically ill, and on top of it, the disappointment of not having been able to join the French army (Dubois and Labrouillère, 2008). Family crisis, as we shall see, plays a key role in the radicalization of a significant number of jihadis in Europe.

The cases of the converts Adebolajo and Adebowale illustrate the combination of mental problems, social stigmas, the blurring lines between lower-middle-classes and the lower classes, and their identifying with a radical version of Islam as a result of the multiple crisis they were undergoing. They are two Black British citizens of Nigerian origin, brought up as Christians. On May 22, 2013, they attacked and killed the British soldier Lee Rigby in southeast London, to avenge the death of Muslims by the British army.

Ten years earlier, in 2003, Adebolajo had become a supporter of the Islamist outlaw group al-Muhajiroun. He studied sociology at the University of Greenwich and took part in Islamist demonstrations including in Kenya, where he went with his British passport. He was arrested and expelled to Britain. He was arrested several times in Britain by the police and incarcerated for fifty-one days following his assault on two police officers in November 2006. Married and the father of six children, he drew the attention of the British General Intelligence (MI5) by his radical statements and his general attitude.

As for Michael Adebowale, he converted to Islam while an adolescent, taking classes at the same university as Adebolajo. His parents divorced in his childhood. As a child, several times he ran away from home, and as a teenager he became a member of the "Woolwich Boys," a gang of young people, mostly of Somali descent, who were drug traffickers; this gave him a sense of belonging, as a substitute for his broken family. At the age of sixteen he suffered a nervous breakdown when one of his drug-trafficking friends was killed in the city of Kent by a paranoid drug addict who believed that his victim was an al-Qaeda sympathizer. He converted the following year to Islam and adopted the Islamic name of "Ismael." In 2008, he was stabbed twice in attacks and in 2009 he was sentenced to fifteen months' imprisonment for drug trafficking. He had been diagnosed with post-traumatic stress disorder and underwent psychiatric treatment. After the murder of Lee Rigby, he claimed that he heard the voice of "spirits" (*jinn*, creatures more or less baleful in Islam, invisible, who can take the shape of plants or animals and are able to take possession of the soul of the Muslim if he is not vigilant). In his view, they were capable of mentally possessing him. These voices, according to the psychiatrist, dictated to him in Nigerian accent what he had to do and ordered him to reconvert to Christianity, which he did before converting back to Islam, because it would have allowed him to fight more effectively against those malevolent spirits. His psychotic symptoms were amplified by a massive use of cannabis. He lived in a deprived area (poor district) (McDonald, 2018). He was under the spell of Adebolajo, who had switched from delinquency to radical Islam. Both were Black, from Africa, and both suffered from racial prejudices. Islam allowed them to become members of a neo-Ummah in which their offending past was erased and they were cleared of all wrongdoing. Jihadi Islam provided them with a new identity through which they could settle their score with a "White," humiliating society, punish it, and raise themselves to the position of a judge who meted out the condemnation of Lee Rigby. Until then, they were judged and convicted by the Whites. The path that leads from delinquency to jihadism makes it possible to reverse the position of the judge and the accused. Conversion to radical Islam, in the case of disaffected individuals suffering from racism and living in a situation of precariousness and illegality, assumes an anthropological meaning: it enables them to achieve an imaginary elite status, and to impose through violence their standards on society. The counter-humiliating posturing via radical Islam is evident in Adebolajo's case. As for Adebowale,[6] who suffered from paranoia, Islam offered him the opportunity to better withstand the onslaught of the demons that were gnawing inside him and dictating to him to act against his will. Adebolajo led the group and found in Adebowale an accomplice who understood him instinctively, one suffering from his condition as a lowly black delinquent, the other from a mental illness that made him seek support in the person of his friend and mentor. Adebolajo needed Adebowale so as not to be alone in confronting White society, the second relied on the first to find a respite from the evil that was eating away at him and against which he saw no other solution than to escape into violence.

The case of Siddhartha Dhar, born in 1983 from a Bangladeshi-speaking Hindu family in London, shows the attractiveness of radical Islam for a young man whose revolt expressed itself through religious means. In his late teens he converted to Islam and took the name "Abu Rumaysah al-Britani." He became a speaker of the al-Muhajiroun, a group banned under terrorism legislation in the United Kingdom in 2005 but which continued its activities under different names. He regularly attended demonstrations against the US, Israel, and Arab regimes or against democracy and for the establishment of a Muslim theocracy in the United Kingdom. In a Daesh propaganda video dated January 2016, a masked young man, most probably Siddhartha Dhar, shot dead five hostages. He made a reputation for his cruelty by beheading prisoners between 2014 and 2015. He was called a New "Jihadi John" after the former was killed by a drone strike in 2015 in the city of Raqqa. In a YouTube rant, Dhar railed against the West and Shia Muslims. His conversion was a long-lasting one. Adolescent, after the death of his father, he converted to Islam and imposed on himself puritanical rigors: he refused to watch TV and listen to music, he slept on the floor, and warned his mother that he could not love her because she had not embraced Islam. He stopped studying and became a seller of inflatable castles for children. He supported the al-Muhajiroun, which was declared illegal by the British authorities. According to his sister, it is above all the fear of dying as a disbeliever (Hindu) and the desire to secure a happy eternal life after death that was the cause of his conversion to Islam (Robinson, 2016). In 2014, with his pregnant wife Aisha and his four children, he fled to Syria and joined Daesh, despite being on bail for his support of the banned extremist group al-Muhajiroun. His wife Aisha, thirty years old, seemingly helped her sister, Zahira, thirty-three, to flee to Syria with her children, her husband being totally unaware of their departure. To attract people to Syria, in May 2015 Dhar wrote a forty-six-page Travel Guide (Casciani, 2016) that reads: "If you thought London or New York was cosmopolitan, then wait until you step foot in the Islamic State, because it screams diversity." Further, he wrote: "In my short time here I have met people from absolutely every walk of life, proof that the caliphate's pulling power is strong and tenacious."

He also reassured on food, mentioning Snickers, Bounty, Kinder Surprise, Cadburys, and good coffee, all of them easily found under the Islamic rule in Syria. He denounced what he saw as Western depravity: "You will not find classes promoting interreligious homosexuality, evolution, music, theater, [dialogue] and the rest of the nonsense taught in non-Muslim schools. The delicate spirit of your children will be well preserved in the caliphate."

He belongs to a sizeable group of people who felt deeply hurt by the turn of Western mores, especially the legalization of homosexuality and tolerance toward sexual differences and atheism. Secularism, in his eyes, relativized and desecrated everything.

The case of the brothers Bons illustrates the role of fraternal relations in conversion to radical Islam. Jean-Daniel Bons (age twenty-one) and Nicolas Bons (age thirty) went to Syria to reinvent their lives. They defended their views in exchanges through the web with their family. They yearned for a more agitated, less conventional life than that which their father had in store for them. From Syria they contacted their brother Vincent on Skype to tell him that they were doing humanitarian work and were taking care of the wounded people. Among the two brothers, there was a great desire to believe in the Afterworld, in a transcendence that would be different in its nature from the mundane everyday life. As with many young converts, their new religiosity made them feel safe. In Syria there was an end-of-time atmosphere, martyrdom opening the prospect of eternal salvation. In June 2013, the two brothers were authorized to accompany the combatants on the front. One day, Jean-Daniel wrote to Vincent on Skype: "Today, I was almost killed by a sniper ball. It went right next to me, lol [laughing out loud]. I passed near death. And you know what? It did not scare me. God says, 'Once you are on the path of jihad, I will erase the fear from your heart.' Well, He kept his word" (Bendavid and Byrka, 2014). One may wonder by reading this testimony if Jean-Daniel had perhaps taken Captagon, an amphetamine inhibiting fear. Still, jihad was as much a will to wage war as to procure a paradise insurance in order to overcome the anguish of death. A deadly mystique was created that gave sense to life in the extreme ordeal that inevitably led to death. In this predicament, God became a constant, obsessive presence: in the face of death, Jean-Daniel was not afraid, supported by the invisible presence of Allah.

In the Bons family the departure to Syria of the two half-brothers meant rebuilding the family as a fraternity outside their broken family, away from the divorce and remarriage of their father. The two half-brothers who went to Syria intended to build a fraternity on the fringes of their family that could not give them the opportunity to unite. Unable to do so in life, they realized it in death. Instead of killing each other, as did Abel and Cain, they offered themselves as sacrificial victims on the altar of a religion that allowed them to achieve unity through their own deaths. Their jihadi brotherhood renewed family ties through exposure to death and unanimity in this ordeal. The reversal of life and death denoted the impossible realization of the Self in this world and the flight in the Afterlife as the only means for self-accomplishment. Their alternative version of life in secular France was holy death in Syria in a brotherhood that rebuilt family life there through martyrdom, torn apart in France.

The case of Jérémy Bailly shows the impact of family crisis and psychological defects on radicalization. He was born in Sarcelles (Val-d'Oise in Ile-de-France), as the only son of a taxi driver father and a bookkeeper mother. They divorced later. They were middle-class and did not belong to a poor social milieu. Both were agnostic, with no religious practice. He grew up in Torcy, suffering from the lack of support from his parents, and used to spend holidays in Cannes at his aunt's house. At twenty-two, he was arrested for hashish trafficking. He was in quest of religious certainty and showed interest in Rastafarianism, spending also time with Jehovah's Witnesses. During this period, he attended Islamist militant groups and, at the age of twenty-three, converted to Islam (Toscer, 2012). He practiced a fundamentalist Islam, calling himself "Abderrahmane," dressing in a djellaba (hooded cloak), and praying five times a day in a prefabricated mosque in Torcy. He met Jérémie Louis-Sidney and befriended him. Together they read *Inspire*, the online magazine of al-Qaeda in the Arabian Peninsula. He converted to Islam his next-door neighbor, Kevin Phan, who was then seventeen. Bailly was Louis-Sidney's lieutenant; he was in charge of the religious "doctrine" within the group and made the link between the mosques of Cannes and Torcy. According to some reports, Bailly suffered from megalomaniac delusions (Vincent, 2017). For some time, he was convinced he was bewitched, possessed by jinns, and clamored for a "rokya" (Islamic citations of the Koran to free from bewitchment, and by extension a person who performs it) to undo the spell (Bui, 2017).

d-Juvenile Jihadis

Underage youth who went to Syria in the years 2013 through 2016 accounted for a significant minority of European Foreign Fighters. Among the 5,904 people who went to Syria and Iraq, between 1,229 and 1,502 were minors (between 21 percent and 25 percent). Teenagers were seduced by the prospect of a "neo-patriarchal" or "post-egalitarian" family that provided young men with a reinvigorated sense of manhood and young women with a strong motivation for motherhood. Men and women imagined assuming their sexual identity without competing with each other within the neo-Ummah. Longing for a new kind of family had its roots in the modern family crisis. It was caused by the insecurity and the fragility of the modern household. In the poor districts, the reaction to the waning gender distinctions has been the hardening of the men's identity (machismo) and women's exclusively female identity (particularly through veiling, sometimes total veils like *burqa*). Even among the Muslim middle classes, and particularly converts, gender is at stake and the new patriarchal trends are riding high among fundamentalists, expressing men's malaise but also women's anguish in Europe. IS, well informed by its European supporters who had already migrated to Syria, used their agony to entice young men and women to Syria via its propaganda machine (its numerous video-sequences or its publications in around eleven European languages).

Adolescent and post-adolescent males in the poor Muslim districts in Europe have more difficulties coping with the challenges of gender equality than their middle-class counterparts (Lagrange, 1999) due to the slum culture and the fact that girls often embark on more promising careers than boys, who remain jobless in their confined neighborhoods.

Adolescence, as an invention of modernity, in its essential features dates back to the beginning of the twentieth century. An age of transition, of discomfort, but also of sexual change (puberty), it is marked by multiple forms of transgression, ranging from self-destruction and suicide to revolt and violence. The "Apaches" in France were the historical example of the nineteenth century's turbulent working-class adolescents becoming delinquent. They were repressed by juvenile courts created at the beginning of the twentieth century.

Until the 1970s, adolescents mainly revolted against the rigidity of the social system, repressive school hierarchy, patriarchal family, and the political regimes in which fathers or grandfathers (gerontocracy) held power.

The nature of today's jihadi transgression is to a great extent different from that of the 1970s. It is not so much a repressive system (the school, the university, the institutions, as in the 1960s) that is targeted but the lack of social norms, the loss of the sense of being a "Self," the feeling of a useless or even burdensome freedom. The aspiration is toward "good repression" and against "bad freedom" (against sexual license, homosexuality, gender equality, transsexuality, alcohol, drugs, and so on), but also against freedom at all (freedom of speech, of religion, of mores, etc.) in the anti-modern movements like jihadism. The latter shares with populism or alt-right movements many features, sexual "disorder" and lax social standards being also targeted by them.

On the other hand, jihadism, among teenagers and post-adolescents, borrows features from the ordeal rituals. Violence is a rite of passage and teenagers love it because the danger, pushed to its paroxysm, gives them an intense feeling of existing not only as would-be adults, but also, momentarily at least, as super-adults, even like almighty demigods. The question is why adolescent revolt is projected onto Islam and why a repressive version of Allah's religion presented such an irresistible attraction for so many young people during the Daesh period, between 2013 and 2016 (they would have been far more numerous without the restrictions imposed by the European states on their departure to Syria, in agreement with Turkey from mid-2014 onward). One answer lies with IS propaganda machinery. Daesh's propaganda was far superior to that of the West. It created, via thousands of video sequences in many languages, a strongly manipulated imaginary about the romanticized life in Syria, particularly about what was dubbed "five-star" jihad.[7] On the other hand, Christianity and Judaism are not able to mobilize believers to the same extent for "sacred" causes, due to the advanced stage of their secularization, whereas Islam, which has been experiencing secularization for around a century, shows strong counter-secularizing, radicalizing tendencies, to which a significant part of its followers adhere.

In Europe, before the establishment of Daesh in Syria and Iraq, jihadism appealed mostly to young adults who subscribed to it by ideological conviction but also in reaction to stigmatization (North Africans in France, Pakistanis and Bangladeshis in the UK, etc.). Adolescents were not on the list of jihadi candidates, and al-Qaeda did not welcome them. Between 2013 and 2016 they made up a significant minority of the aspirants to jihad. Middle-class girls, often better educated than their male counterparts, were among the candidates all set to go to Syria.

Several categories can be distinguished among the wannabe teenage jihadis: those who suffered family problems (parental violence, parents' painful divorce, imaginary or real rape in the family) (Bouzar, 2015), and who were manipulated by gurus on the web or were lured by friends already in Syria who encouraged them to join them or, more rarely, by self-radicalization through the web[8] (Neumann, 2016). Adhering to radical Islam offered them the opportunity to live a collective catharsis that helped them overcome, at least momentarily, their trauma and filled them with euphoria. By joining IS they drowned out their anguish in the group that offered a cathartic environment and enabled them to cover up their trauma. They became born-again, giving up their former individuality and the suffering attached to it by espousing the collective "We" of the sectarian group that submerged their anguish, and desensitized them vis-à-vis their subliminal pain.

However, this model is not universal, and many young people did not particularly suffer any tangible psychological discomfort. To them Daesh opened up new vistas for their personal initiative and allowed them to achieve their "will to power," to self-assertion in a Nietzschean sense. In the same vein, for some of the teenagers it was essential to enter the adult world at an early age. By joining the caliphate, they realized their dream of becoming precocious adults, overcoming the handicap of being an adolescent, that is, neither a child nor an adult. It has become increasingly difficult to achieve financial independence after school and to become an adult in the full sense of the word in a Europe where youth unemployment is more or less structural, especially among those with no university education. Young people sometimes remain financially and mentally dependent on their parents until the age of twenty-five and beyond, imbued with a sense of being good-for-nothings. Daesh gave them moral and financial support and restored their sense of dignity and pride: they were not only individuals but beyond that, heroes.

The "revolutionary" identity of the youth at the service of Daesh was also noteworthy among some jihadis (Atran, 2016). They became revolutionaries in order to change their identity, helping to erect a new world, that is, a paradise on earth that opened a new horizon of hope to create a utopian, vibrant community (the neo-Ummah). The latter was imagined to be harmonious and virtuous at the same time, in addition to their excitement and euphoria of fighting its enemies. The socio-political phenomenon was based on a new imaginary, manipulation by Daesh playing also its role in its promotion. In the old Europe, young people have to queue up to painfully gain access to the higher levers for the most gifted among them. It is no longer a land of opportunity for those young people who want to become quickly "someone" without being gifted in computer science or the web, to stand out for qualities that do not have many buyers in Europe, namely being fearless, fighting, and facing death. These qualities could only be valued in war, not in peace, and Europe does not give these young people, often from working or lower-middle classes, access to the higher spheres of power. IS was the government that allowed young men to become "Emirs," to earn their stripes in war and to move seamlessly into elite status (although the highest level was reserved for the Arabs). They put the revolution in the name of Islam at the service of their ambition to jump up the social ladder through their bravery and fearlessness on the battlefield. These qualities were distrusted in Europe. In the war for the glory of Islam, they served as much for their personal fame as for the grandeur of the caliphate.

Girls looking forward to marrying knights of Islam, and boys aspiring to become heroic warriors, shared the same attitude which proceeded from the same logic: passing abruptly to adulthood, becoming recognized as grown-ups, and bypassing the insurmountable restrictions European economy and society imposed on them in their quest for early recognition.

Wearing the veil was, for many girls, especially among converts, a sign of their revolt against the secular society. By donning it, sometimes in its integral version (*niqab* or *burqa*), they further underlined their rebellion in a concealment of the body that had all the hallmarks of an exhibitionist act: they over-displayed their wish to express their desire to be themselves against the dominant norms by means of a hermetic veil, or even by its multiplication (several veils superimposed on top of each other). Islam legitimized a transgressive self-assertion that went as far as voluntarily enclosing oneself in a solitary retreat.

Some young girls, who were obese or fearful of not being beautiful enough, locked themselves up in the veil to conceal their lack of beauty from others, finding a justification through Allah's religion. Others affirmed the primacy of the Sacred over social norms. At any rate, their veil was not a sign of passiveness, archaism, or traditionalism. It sometimes denoted regressive attitudes, but always in the name of the supremacy of the Sacred which they imposed on themselves by extending it to others. Daesh promoted the veil as a sign of feminine "emancipation" from a Godless world that it condemned for its heretical character. Adolescent girls made this attitude their own, which was in line with their mutiny against a society already desecrated, mainly by the loss of paternal authority, the mother's authority being challenged by these young girls who sought to create another family, patriarchal in opposition to their mothers' feminist model, which they found unstable and devoid of meaning.

By leaving for Syria they achieved the ideal of individuality that has been for centuries a major aspiration in the Western world. Since they left their families against the wishes of their parents, they felt already autonomous, acting against the will of adults, becoming quasi-grown-ups through their transgressive act. Among teenagers, individuality has been fraught with major obstacles that have gone crescendo in the last decades, due to the prolonged educational cycle and the difficulties in the employment market. The economic, cultural, and psychological predicaments have created a paradoxical situation: on one hand, never has individuality been more assertive than nowadays in terms of aspirations and dreams; at the same time, its concrete realization has been accompanied by sometimes insuperable obstacles due to the evolution of the Western society, the length of studies, the ever-delayed opportunity to earn a living, and so forth. For European teenagers, middle-class as well as lower-class (for different reasons), it is by far more demanding to become an "individual-in-reality" than it was a few decades ago (in the 1960s there were plenty of jobs), and at the same time, adolescence is a trying age, during which the youngster is torn between a childhood that is over and an adulthood that is out of reach. Among other things, they try to achieve individuality through the virtual world, excelling in video games and developing their skills in those matches that allow them to feel like "somebody." The transition of this "somebody" from the ambit of the virtual world into the real one became possible by departure to Syria and exercising violence, really or through mimicry, within IS. A few decades ago, particularly in the 1970s, the economic situation in Europe allowed young people to become financially self-sufficient and mentally autonomous through a culture of defiance and revolt against the patriarchal family and market economy (leftism, feminism, May 1968 in France). Nowadays, the overdue adulthood remains unattainable for many youngsters otherwise than through violence, institutionalized paths toward normal citizenship through the economy being inaccessible or fraught with major obstacles. At the same time, in substitution to the real world, the internet and more generally, new social technologies have made adulthood possible through one's imaginary deployment within the virtual world, the latter becoming sometimes even more attractive than the real one, the so-called gamification making possible an access to the world that oscillates between the imaginary (plenty of resources) and reality (scarce resources) (Brachman and Levine, 2010; Ungerleider, 2011; McDonald, 2018). But this new style of gamification operates in the opposite direction of what is usually meant by this notion: not so much applying game design and principles in non-game contexts to improve productivity, learning, and more generally, efficiency, but to compensate for the failure of the ego to thrive in the real world, by plunging into the virtual games. The virtual world shields from the unattractive real one. Gamification, in this sense, finds its translation into reality only through transgression and violence. It brings sense to the Self looking for "individuality" through new rituals (Hong, 2015) that imply acting within the destructive realm of hacking or manipulating. It provides the means for an individual to accomplish his aspiration for prominence by leaning on his superiority against others, in particular by imposing on them his own rules in what is universally considered as illegitimate (the hacker gets the upper hand and dominates the website of the hacked, knowing full well that he is acting illegitimately and unlawfully, according to the prevailing standards). Male adolescents become "super-adults" much in the same manner in the battlefield in Syria as in their playing video games, creating an imaginary realm in which they can assert their will to power. In a way, the virtual world makes possible the rise of teenagers to an imagined adulthood and beyond that, to the cherished "big individuality," the icon of the Western ideal of life in a way that is lived as half-real, half-virtual. The frontier between the two becomes hazy and pushes to violence in part because of the intertwining of the two realms. In these situations, violence is usually accompanied by a "cruel humor," distinct from the dark humor: the crueler the act, the more humorous becomes the young jihadi on the web, largely trespassing the confines of irony within common decency. Cruel humor is the enemy of dark humor, the former referring to a grim context that is unyielding, denoting lack of compassion and inhuman ruthlessness that dehumanizes the victim, pushing the executioner toward more inhumanity by his refusing to acknowledge the ghastly character of his act and by giving it a falsely playful turn, of which he is fully aware. Cruel humor goes hand in hand with denying humanity to the victim.

In the twenty-first century, becoming a full-fledged individual in the real world has become far more difficult than it was in the 1960s–1970s in terms of employment or remuneration (a salary is not enough to support a family). Legally burdened by the responsibility to be an individual but socially deficient (scarce, temporary, and lower-paid jobs for the middle class, lack of autonomous life financially speaking for many young men and women who depend on their families even in their twenties or thirties) has made individuality a difficult task to achieve even for those beyond the age of eighteen or nineteen, of whom many are subjected to a forced post-adolescent status. The universe of the internet remains highly virtual even at the apogee of the "gamification," but going to Syria and exerting violence was hyper-real and helped heal from the malaise of being caught in the imaginary world of gamification where the boundary between the real and the imagined is fuzzy. There, young men who psychologically looked like protracted adolescents fully became individuals through their violent deeds, regarded as heroic by the jihadis, as misdeeds by the rest of the world.

In general, the internet increases risk behavior through a new kind of sociability among young people. While exchanging with their peers in their web-friendship, face-to-face relations become unnecessary, narcissism becoming viral via sharing the same types of attitudes (anti-Semitism, Islamophobia for the far-right fans, conspiracy theories encompassing events like the 9/11 attacks in the US or the January 2015 Paris attacks against journalists, and so on). A closed web-subculture takes shape that is based on the span of time spent on the keyboard and the types of communication through Twitter, Facebook, Tumblr, and Instagram. Old rites are converted into web-culture: girls display pathological attitudes through eating disorders, scarification, and suicide attempts that easily spread to their peers through social media. Boys put games on the web in which they tighten a noose on their necks and suffocate, sometimes succumbing to death; rape rituals find their way into social media; and so on.

Among boys and girls, one of the characteristics of these rites is their shared experience in close circles: the goal is not so much to display them to the global society as it is to show those young people who belong to the same subculture, eager to acquire the recognition of their peers (hence the violence in schools or rites of hazing) (Breton, 2015).

Daesh provided an opportunity to extend those rites from the peer group to a global audience by recourse to the social media and a status through the IS propaganda machine, leading to a recognition of the individual, exploiting his mental problems to promote the new caliphate. It also translated virtual games into reality through exponential violence. Violent or even cruel acts at the service of Daesh were experienced as a supplementary excitement by many teenagers who still lived in the imagined world of intensified relations in which they recklessly trespassed the frontiers of what was possible, like deadly speed in driving the cars in the videogames and sometimes, in reality. Adolescent dreaming played an essential role in their commitment to Daesh. The latter offered them the means to convert the real into an attribute of their imagination by exercising violence, whether real (killing by shooting prisoners) or symbolic (holding the severed heads of executed prisoners).

The Syrian adventure embodied a transition from non-existence to full existence through violence for many young people, adolescents and post-adolescents alike. Romance and exoticism also played a role in their imaginary. Next to adventure, the desire to be with friends, the glamor of belonging to a military elite added to the lure of jihadism. The available statistical data point to some of these dimensions. A 2010 biography of sixty-two "homegrown terrorists" in Canada and Europe revealed that some of them accepted to use violence at home while others refused. What distinguished the two radical groups was the aspiration of the first to adventure in contrast to a calm and measured existence as the ideal of the second (Bertlett, Birdwell, and King, 2010). This analysis is in line with the findings of another 2005 study that distinguished between novelty-seeking individuals and the others (Victoroff, 2005). Sense of adventure as well as seeking novelty can be easily translated into violence through the virtual world.

Not only youngsters intended to become grown-ups through jihadism, but more radically, they sought to reverse the hierarchic relationship within their family: in their eyes, their version of Islam was far more authentic than their parents' who practiced an adulterated religion, submissive to the "Whites." The parent/child reversal through a radical Islam referred to the denial of legitimacy to older generations but was also propelled by the aspiration to become adult against their parents who symbolically blocked, by their sheer existence, the legitimacy to the new mindset. It was not a revolt against patriarchy—on the contrary, it was an attempt at reestablishing it through religious credentials by setting aside the already deposed father who had lost, long before, his authority within the family. The opposition was not so much to the father, it was to the already demised parents, to their religiosity, in brief, to their existence shaped by the colonial past, and their following a routine devoid of strong emotions and utopian vocation. Young people dismissed them in order to replace them with a more ferocious but also more assertive father, the caliph, who symbolized the triumph of the superlative father and his return to a world that had become fatherless.

The case of Omar Diaby, called "Omar Omsen,"[9] who indoctrinated a generation of young people in Nice, a major city in southern France, illustrates this new mentality. Of Senegalese origin, his family is a follower of Tijani Islam, from the Tijaniyya brotherhood. The founding chief is regarded by his followers as the only master (which is perceived as idolatrous by Salafists). His doctrine is influenced by Sufism (Islamic mysticism), it speaks of *fana* (the annihilation of Self through his absorption in God) and *baqa* (a mode of living that allows one to reach a state of enlightenment while externally conforming to the prevailing religious standards). These notions tinged with Islamic mysticism are frontally rejected by radical Islamism. Omar became a follower of jihadism and broke with his parents' Sufism. He committed to Islamic rigorism and insisted on hell to intimidate young people in his poor district in Nice. In the years 2012–2013 he insisted on *Hijra* (departing to the land of Islam following the example of the Prophet who migrated from Mecca to Medina) to encourage young people to join Syria. In his mind, the exodus to the land of Sham (Great Syria) meant jihad. He thus threw a bridge between pietistic and jihadi Salafism.

The caliphate gave the opportunity to Western male and female adolescents to assert themselves in ways that previously were exclusively reserved for adults.

Girls became a major stake in the strategy of seduction, on one hand because European jihadis sought them for marriage in Syria and Iraq, on the other hand because showing their virility was through the multiplication of female conquests according to a principle legitimized by traditional Islam (polygamy) or even Western global culture (mistresses or concubines). These young men fostered their self-image as "super-virile" and they translated it into different cultures by moving between them: officially through Islam, but also through different Western cultures to which young girls identified, in order to seduce them. As for the latter, their desire to be a mother often went beyond sexuality itself: they looked for a man who would give them the opportunity to fulfill their dream of motherhood. In this way, they could take possession of their girl-woman body precociously, fulfilling thus their aspiration to become grown-ups through a stable family. Among many of them the urgent desire to be a mother exceeded the aspiration toward romance and love. In this respect too, jihadi youth were different from the unbridled 1968 protesters who asked for love and rejected war and patriarchy (their slogan was: "Make love, not war").

By joining IS, girls and young women turned the matriarchal into a "sororal" order, in which young women of the same age, the "sisters" in the broad sense, overruled mothers. Adolescent pregnancy among European girls in Syria had its original features. In Western societies which these girls came from, teenage pregnancy is often associated with social problems such as low level of education, poverty, and immaturity. This type of pregnancy usually occurs out of wedlock and carries social stigma. This was not the case of the female teenagers who went to Syria. They were not school dropouts, they weren't immature compared to their peer groups and did not suffer social stigma in their majority (Thomson, 2016). Most of these young girls were not from lower-class families; they often belonged to the lower-middle or middle classes. They intended to offer ("donate" as a gift in the sense of Marcel Mauss, already analyzed) to the Muslim community their future children who would become members of a cohesive community in which hearts would beat in unison, in contrast to the soulless societies from which they came. In short, they longed for an imaginary neo-Ummah in which the Sacred (Islam) would give meaning to collective effervescence.[10] By giving birth to children, they wanted to be recognized as full members, the child brought to the world corroborating their ties with their imaginary community. Once in Syria, some of them fulfilled this desire and gave birth, between the ages of fourteen and seventeen, to their offspring who in principle should indefectibly bind them to the Muslim community, led by the caliph. But the cherished dream often did not match the reality experienced on the ground, and many of them were disillusioned after a few months in Syria. Some were able to flee and rejoin their parents back in Europe, others lost their lives; a minority, more radicalized, went to the end of their commitment and preserved intact their link to the neo-Ummah under the aegis of a declining caliphate. For the most part, these young women could not be qualified as jihadis in the same sense as men: for most of them, their mind was not set on a violence perpetrated by themselves (although they usually did not object to it, and even approved it when committed by their future husbands), their major aim being motherhood in a new family, free from the uncertainties of the modern household. In this perspective romanticism, exoticism, the search for a trusted "knight of Islam" that would change the family's nature by making it less fragile than what they had experienced with their own parents, and the quest to be a "woman," just a woman, trumped other considerations, ideological or ethical. Their desire was less the will to destroy the old society than to build a new community that would replace the "cold" and impersonal nations where they lived, a new community sealed by an imaginary Islam, marked by strong solidarities, endowed with a deep sense of belonging and a unanimous social cohesion. Their imagined neo-Ummah was mainly in reaction to the anomic European societies in which they lived. The problem of "donating" their children to the Muslim community was put in new terms in their minds. Through it, they imagined themselves as agents of a new society, in which giving "for free" and receiving in the same way made the difference with the "cold" and "selfish" Western societies in which egoism and mercantile relations marginalize genuinely altruistic attitudes based on generosity and authentic charity (Caillé and Grésy, 2014; Khosrokhavar, "La jeunesse féminine dijiadiste," 2018).

For these teenage and post-adolescent girls, reinvigorated patriarchy was tied with another phenomenon: to alleviate their emotional dependence on the husband, who was destined to die on the battlefield. They experienced a relationship distinct from an ideal of love based on total identification with the beloved partner. They married a man either through the web before leaving for Syria or once there, through the latter's visit to the *maqarr*, the place of residence of women who sought a husband. The man's destiny was different from the woman's, his fate being sealed by martyrdom, putting him in a kind of Otherness that made intense love improbable (or, when that occurred, it would extend into heaven). In this type of conjugal relationship, the husband became an adjuvant to procreation, an instrument to expand demographically the Ummah, providing the woman the opportunity to offer her children to the Muslim community as a "gift" in a sense different from the European societies (the "gift" of one's child to the neo-Ummah was primordially a sign of belonging to it, rather than an individual decision to become pregnant, exclusively based on one's own preferences). The young woman had to prepare to live after the death of her husband in the war, internalizing the future in the absence of a man who would, sooner or later, disappear as a martyr. She also internalized the prospect of a possible remarriage after the death of the first husband in jihad (the case of Huda Muthana from the US, who married three times while in Syria, each time after the death of her husband at the war front, points to this fact). Having to remarry another husband after the disappearance of the first one imperceptibly created a new model in which the place of the husband was relativized due to his most probable early death. The main goal was to preserve the neo-Ummah and to expand it by multiplying the number of children, and to help build a mythical cohesive community, free from the dissensions of the modern world.

Young girls' leaving for Syria (or their attempts) should also be understood in the context of group dynamics. Often a young girl in a school was manipulated by IS via video clips on Facebook or by a recruiter who contacted her and convinced her to leave for Syria or to carry out violent attacks on the spot. Once in Syria, she would encourage her friends and relatives to join her. Some of them would follow her in the spirit of imitation or competition. Sometimes from the same school or through ties of friendship, some would leave for Syria (Shamima Begum, age fifteen, a British citizen of Bangladeshi origin left the UK in February 2015, accompanied by her two friends, Amira Abase and Kadiza Sultana, and joined IS in Syria).

But manipulation can be successful if it strikes a chord, and what was paramount for them was the perspective of a romanticized life within a new community in which they could live away from the splits and fractures of the modern family. In the mythical dreamed-of family, their precocious womanhood would be recognized as well as their will to be an adult with a husband relieving them of the burden of earning their living. It would release them from the pangs of working outside, letting them devote their entire lives to their children. They longed to return to their imagined feminine nature after a century of feminist struggle for women's rights.

1-Examples of Jihadi Teenagers

A few examples will illustrate the mindset of the male and female jihadi teenager.

On April 25 of each year, Anzac Day commemorates the battle of Gallipoli in which Australians and New Zealanders successfully fought the Ottoman army in 1915, during the First World War. In April 2015, a fifteen-year-old

English teenager was charged with planning a terrorist attack on Anzac Day in Australia. He had manipulated an older Australian into beheading police officers during the celebrations. Living in Blackburn, about 30 kilometers from Manchester in the UK, he sent thousands of messages over the internet to an eighteen-year-old Australian, Sevdet Besim, claiming to be his elder and encouraging him to lead an attack on behalf of IS. Through his e-mail exchanges he let himself sound like a seasoned jihadi. They were put in touch by an Australian recruiter for IS of Cambodian origin, "Khaled al-Cambodi." The English teenager's plan was to kill as many Australian police officers as possible, by driving over them and then beheading them with a knife. He had suggested to Besim to attack a lonely person at the first opportunity to behead him and thus learn how to do it. The discovery of the plan of attack prevented many deaths in Australia. At Besim's home, the Australian police discovered a knife and a message of martyrdom recorded on his cell phone.

As for the young Englishman, he had entered the jihadi universe via the web. His Twitter account was attended by twenty-four thousand people, making him a celebrity within the jihadi community. At school, he bragged that he could kill one of his teachers, threatening also other students in his class. He was sentenced to life imprisonment with a five-year lock-in period to ensure his de-radicalization.

This case is significant in many respects. First, the teenager had convinced another young man who was four years older than him that he was an adult and an experienced jihadi, which confirms the yearning of many would-be jihadi adolescents to become grown-ups through radical Islam. Then we find his quest for celebrity in the service of jihad through the web. His Twitter account ensured him great success, with several thousands of other young people following him, thus allowing him to become a star in the radical English-speaking Islamist milieu. The radicalization of this middle-class teenager gives an indication of the capacity of the web to build the premises of a jihadi community in sharp contrast to the atomized individualism of modern society. He locked himself into this world within a virtual community that was in opposition to society—in short, he created a virtual jihadi environment, in which violence was a major component. The appeal of this virtual jihadi milieu became irresistible, while he was suffering a major disease (a degenerative eye). He asserted himself as a leader, reversing the "natural" hierarchy (he assumed a leading role by pretending to be older than the Australian he manipulated). His example illustrates the fact that jihadism for many teenagers is the means for an accelerated transition from adolescence to adulthood. The web played the role of a melting pot: it transformed a subgroup into an effervescent agonistic community through the virtual support of thousands of youngsters around the "star" who promoted the holy war through it. Gamification played a significant role, mixing reality and fiction in the imagined world of the web-community around the radicalized British teenager.

The case of a young girl named Camille is also meaningful. While conversing with another teenager, she expressed frustration because her passport had been confiscated by the police who had become aware of her attempt to leave for Syria. She then attempted to concoct a scheme for an attack, following an idea suggested to her via the internet by a nineteen-year-old convert who had left for Syria. She sought to become an adult by assuming the role of a negative heroine, instilling fear and horror in society. Questioned by the police, the girl did not make any secret of her desire to follow in the footsteps of Mohammed Merah, the killer of three Muslim military men and four Jews (among them three children) in the French cities of Toulouse and Montauban in 2012:

Camille: Yes, yes, an attack like Merah or blow everything up in kamikaze. Make a shootout like he did, kill adults, especially against Jews. . . because I was fed up being blocked in France. My project was more a shooting than suicide bombing, it's hard to find explosives in France, although I never looked for it. If it were easy, France would have exploded a long time ago!

The investigator: What does Mohamed Merah mean to you?

Camille: I am going to give you an example. There are some who want to do everything like the singer Rihanna; well, I want to do everything like Merah. (Seelow, 2016)

Camille does not share the ideals of the other girls. She identifies with the jihadi Mohamed Merah. She viewed him as a role model that she intended to follow across the gender divide. She expressed the desire to act like male adults. Daesh offered this type of teenager the chance to become an adult by means of violence against others.

We witness also a new avatar of the "spectacle society," described by Guy Debord more than half a century ago (Debord, 1967), which we call "apocalyptic spectacle society," mixing cruelty, joviality, jocularity, a sense of total irresponsibility, immaturity, virtuality, and a deep narcissism. Death becomes part of the game, treated in a playful manner: the spectacular is paramount, a phenomenon which shakes the public and leaves no one indifferent, promoting the individual who commits the violent act to the rank of an international star, regardless of the reprehensible nature of his acts. Only the apocalyptic picturesque counts. This same young girl, chatting with her friends, mixed fun with tragic facts, including her own disappearance in the massacre in a touristic district or a Jewish neighborhood:

Camille: Well, I'm going to blow me up as a kamikaze in France Insha'allah [God willing], *if I cannot leave* [for Syria].
Fatima: What is "kamikaze"?
Camille: You blow yourself up with a bomb. . . .
Fatima: Are you going to do that? If I cannot leave (for Syria), I do it with you. . . .
Camille: We will blow the government boom boom boom! We are mujahidat [religious female combatants].
Fatima: Real Mujahidat hahaaa . . . We recite the shahada [the Islamic profession of faith], *we hold our hands together and we blow up.*
Camille: Yeah, the best is at the Eiffel Tower.
Fatima: Yes, but there are a lot of Muslims there. . . .
Camille: Bah, we will target a Jewish neighborhood.
Fatima: Yes! In Lyon there is a district, only Jews live there.

This new "show" is generally inspired by the cruelest acts on YouTube (like killing people in an explosion and being killed at the same time, beheading and holding cut-off heads with a smile in front of cameras), and crude jokes (like selling parts of a body as a butcher's piece ironically presented to prospective buyers in a video).

Teenagers discern the meaning of death and violence rather in a mimetic manner. Among them, the "gamification" of death obscures its seriousness. The death of others, if they are "disbelievers," that is, the adults who do not play the game, is no problem. As for oneself, the gamification of martyrdom carries the adolescent in an imagined paradise that takes him away from the pangs of real life. Taboos are lifted in the gamification of jihad and martyrdom, among them, the prohibition to kill.

Teenage girls admired young jihadi women who claimed to be capable of beheading heretics. In tweets, they celebrated the beheading of Peter Kassig, former US soldier and humanitarian, in November 2014:

> *So, I watched the latest video of IS. Oh my God! I love them! Sharia = Justice! Thank God. Many beheadings at the same time, God is great. I was happy to see the beheading of this Infidel. I just rewind this part of the video. God is great! I wonder what he thought before his beheading.* (Saint-Jullian, 2016)

Through violence, teenagers are sure to be taken seriously by adults and in some ways, they take themselves seriously by committing it, realizing thus their dream of becoming grown-ups through monstrosity.

At the end of 2016, a twelve-year-old German-Iraqi boy born in Germany tried to blow up nailing machines in Ludwigshafen in Germany. On two occasions, on November 26 and December 5, 2016, he failed to detonate the same craft machine, first at the Christmas market, then at the town hall square. He reportedly attempted to join Syria and an IS member encouraged him via the internet to commit an attack at home rather than making a journey, because of travel restrictions since 2015. Too young to be criminally prosecuted, he was entrusted to social services.

The autonomy gained by the new generations through the web makes remote manipulation easier, making the immature child feel like a precocious adult, breaking off with childhood without going through adolescence. The Iraqi provenance of the family undermined parental authority, their knowledge of German being rudimentary, and the child sensing their confusion in a society whose culture they did not master. New values were internalized by him at school that belied those of his parents, undermining thus the traditional family's mores and culture. He found himself between a rock and a hard place: betraying his parents resulted in guilt feelings, and opposing the school system made him a stranger among his friends. One way to escape this dilemma was to reject both his parents' as well as mainstream society's values, and this was achieved by Daesh, due to its shrewd use of video sequences that enticed young people. The youth culture promoted by the new caliphate both rejected the parents' standards and the European norms and values and became the more legitimate as this dual dismissal was accompanied by the self-assertion of a child or a teenager who gained self-esteem by this double denial of legitimacy and the opening of a third way through violence, in opposition both to his parents' and society's standards.

Traditional Islam recognizes two other monotheistic religions, Christianity and Judaism, as legitimate "religions of the Book," with a lower status (*dhimmi*) for their followers, if they happen to live in a Muslim country. Other religions are regarded as idolatry or as false religions by the traditionalists. Salafism (and its jihadi version) holds an intolerant view of other religions. This was particularly evident with IS cracking down on the Yazidis, a religious group mainly of Kurdish origin living in Iraq, whose men were often executed, and whose women were treated as slaves. Overall, attacking non-Abrahamic religions was considered a pious act by Daesh. Three teenagers born in Germany (sixteen years old at the time of their action) and influenced by jihadi propaganda, placed chemicals in a fire extinguisher purchased online, and detonated it on April 16, 2016, in front of a Sikh temple where a wedding was being celebrated, wounding three men. The boys had met on social networks, through WhatsApp messaging service, and were communicating within a larger group of young people, intent on killing "Infidels" (*kuffar*). These adolescents aimed at becoming super-adults by doubly breaking the law: first by fabricating homemade bombs, then detonating them, injuring few Sikh men, considered as idolatrous. In doing so they invented a "rite of passage" that paved the way for them into adulthood by abusing the Infidels. It was, in fact, a reinvented, even reverse rite of passage: through it they did not suffer from violence (which is usually the case of martyrs) but imposed violence on others in an unlimited form through death. In so doing, from minors they became majors, forcing their dictates upon others who were desecrated as adults and punished as Infidels. Subduing others and submitting them to violence points to the fact that authority is shaken in modern society, non-internalized by children and teenagers.

In December 2013, two teenagers, ages fifteen and sixteen attending secondary school at the Lycée des Arènes in Toulouse in southern France, decided to do jihad and travel to Syria to fight Assad's regime. In a few days they organized their trip: one of them stole the credit card of his father to pay the plane tickets, and they approached on Facebook Mourad Farès, one of the main French recruiters in Syria, to be drafted into his brigade within al-Nusra Front, an al-Qaeda subsidiary. On January 6, 2014, instead of going to school they took the bus to the airport. In Syria, they became quickly disappointed, conditions being extremely harsh. They decided to return. Their families met them in Turkey, and they returned to France on January 25 and 27 of the same year, just a few weeks after their departure. On January 31, they were indicted for criminal association in relation to a terrorist organization in France. It is noteworthy that the initiative to go to Syria came from the two teenagers who contacted a major recruiter in Syria, and they did decide to come back, after experiencing the dire conditions there. Adult features were already there: they just intended to take the decision to leave for Syria, and their return showed their capacity to gauge the situation and to change their minds, a sign of precocious adulthood.

Subjectively, the modern condition means that one can freely choose one's own way of life. For these young people it meant that they could decide when they would enter adulthood, whereas institutionally it is the objective age that counts. The illusion of infinite freedom shared in particular by teenagers in contact with the virtual world of social networks as well as the subjective feeling of autonomy, means that they internalize few constraints and take all kinds of freedom for granted, which is synonymous with dismissal of authority. The crisis of this authority, which is increasingly devoid of legitimacy, leads to the denial of social constraints by an unbridled subjectivity that recognizes only its own sovereignty. Internalized constraints lose legitimacy as they become scarcer. Without a sacred principle, the supremacy of the individual in the name of modern individualism, even among immature people (adolescents, or individuals with mental problems), becomes a conundrum in some minority cases: for example, within a family in crisis or parents of subaltern culture who are discredited in the eyes of their children. The way is open to all kinds of excesses, jihadism being one of them, linked to the subject's feeling of omnipotence, who can dictate his views to others in the name of his supposed religious legitimacy. This unlimited subjective freedom often ends up in tyranny, through its sheer impulsive, inconsequential exercise.

Not all radicalizing people engage in the path of jihad. In many cases, those who fell under the spell of a group or an individual were able to escape their ascendancy. In 2012, a young man named Bora turned twenty-three years old. Of Turkish origin, he grew up in Reeperbahn, a Hamburg street known for prostitution and other illegal activities. His mother sold Tupperware and his father ran a store. Like many second-generation young people, Bora had identity problems.

Meanwhile, a young man named Djamal lived with his Lebanese Muslim parents, and worked at his father's booth, selling falafel. His father divorced his mother while Djamal was in high school, his grades suffering as a result. He dedicated himself to reading works by great philosophers but did not find an answer to the existential questions that worried him. He started to drink. In 2009, at the age of nineteen, he embarked on jihadism and gradually became a jihadi recruiter, well before the creation of Daesh in Syria. His mother remarried, this time with a German convert to Islam who had a better knowledge of Allah's religion than the young Djamel (Gezer, 2012). He felt humiliated that a German was more cognizant of his ancestral religion than him, which once again displayed the arrogant superiority of the Westerners over Arabs.

Bora and Djamel shared the same feeling: they felt bad about themselves and wanted to do something to take their minds off their malaise. Both could have continued in the footsteps of their parents, which would have ensured them a middle-class living standard, but they chose another path, more exciting, which filled their lives with meaning and, above all, gave them a taste of revenge against a society where they felt an intractable and penalizing difference vis-à-vis the majority. They met in the old Hinkelstein bar where radical leftists had gathered in the 1980s. In those years, students and ideologists denounced capitalism, the alienation of the middle classes, and the deception of the ruling classes. The situation had dramatically changed since then. In the twenty-first century the bar became home to ideological debates and recruitment for Islamic radicals. The new clientele was looking for answers in the Koran and not in Marx's *Capital*. Arabic calligraphy adorned the walls, and Persian rugs were hung. Young people smoked hookahs and endlessly talked about religion—for instance, what was religiously allowed or forbidden, how to fight against the enemies of Allah, and so forth. In this bar, Djamal met someone who invited him to join the debate within an Islamic group. He was then asked to recruit young people for the Hamburg branch of Hizb ut-Tahrir, an Islamist organization that advocated the caliphate as the Islamic political model for addressing the evils of modernity. It was banned in Germany since 2003 but continued to recruit illegally. This gave purpose to the life of Djamal, who discovered a true vocation and became deeply involved in it. He was enlivened by a proselytizing faith, far from his insignificant status as a falafel salesman in his father's shop. He traveled through the internet, listening to the speeches of Pierre Vogel, one of the most famous Islamic fundamentalist preachers in Germany.

Bora, in search of meaning, was an easy prey for Djamal. While in the cafe for video games and smoking the water pipe, he met Djamal and his group and was fascinated by them. Instead of talking about women and sexuality, they discussed the meaning of pious life and God in relation to the big bang and the theory of evolution, bringing these issues back to Islam and its miraculous ability to answer them adequately through the verses of the Koran, which announced them long before modern science had discovered them. In their minds, this proved in turn that Islam was the ultimate religion

(Christianity could not answer, according to them, those questions through the Bible). Djamal and his group tried to indoctrinate Bora by occupying all his time and hobbies and by being around him all the time, so he wouldn't have a chance to distance himself and think critically. The group was cosmopolitan, consisting of some Georgians who had converted to Islam and adopted Islamic names, a young man from Sri Lanka, and an Armenian who knew by heart many Koranic verses, among other things. Their union around Islam fascinated new recruits, who discovered an additional reason to join the Islamic fraternity within a fusional, closed Ummah. Haunted by the discomfort of not feeling completely German ("ethnic Germans," directly or indirectly, reminded him of his origins), Bora found Islam in its radical version to be a substitute to the denied German identity. He felt he finally had found the Truth in a community modeled on the Ummah of the Prophet. In it, it was great growing a beard that strengthened the sense of belonging to the community as well as the difference with non-believers who had closely shaved faces. Not only did their behavior as a whole strengthen their feeling of belonging to the imagined neo-Ummah, but it also deepened the difference with others, underlining in passing the privilege of being part of an Islamic circle that brought them close to God.

The language itself bore the traces of this religious swing: instead of "guy" or *keum* (slang of the French suburbs) or "Digger" (in German neighborhoods), they used *akhi* ("my brother" in Arabic and Turkish). The word "cool" (in German slang, *geil*) was changed into *macha'allah* (God willing).

Things began to turn sour when they began to ask Bora for a part of the profit of his father's shop as an Islamic tax. He grew suspicious of them. As for Djamal, his own doubts became more significant when the members of the group began to lecture him on the fact that it was necessary for him to leave the country of the disbelievers and join a Muslim country while they themselves stayed there and showed no willingness to leave. He gradually stopped hanging out at the bar where they used to meet him. After a while, he felt free from the spell of the group.

In this case, radical Islamic indoctrination was not successful. Of Lebanese origin, Djamal did not belong to the excluded people and did not suffer like the North Africans in France or the so-called Pakis in Britain from the postcolonial alienation syndrome (Lebanon was not colonized by Germany, but more recently by France). One could also argue that community ties among the Lebanese are far stronger than those of their Moroccan or Algerian counterparts.

On January 11, 2016, Yusuf, a fifteen-year-old Turkish high school student of Kurdish descent, a good pupil and a delegate of his class, attempted to kill a Jewish teacher in Marseille by stabbing him with a machete. In general, the Kurdish community is distinguished by its fight against IS, unlike Yusuf who claimed, during his custody, his allegiance to it. He was radicalized on the web. His attitude was primarily marked by a desire to transgress. He claimed to endorse Daesh propaganda, which made the demonization of the Jews one of the pillars of its ideology. By attacking a Jew, he opposed not only the French society but also his Kurdish parents and community, who sided with the West in the fight against IS. Joining Daesh allowed him to bypass an anguishing alternative: belonging either to his parents' Kurdish community or to the French one. A third possibility had opened up that allowed him to assert his own fictitious identity as a grown-up jihadi in revolt against a world that coerced him into the straightjacket of split identity in conjunction with a crisis of adolescence. Transgressing by denying legitimacy to those who restricted him in his claim for subjective supremacy made him an adult in his view, the more so as Daesh mirrored in his eyes the status of a super-adult hero by acting in a spectacular manner (attacking a Jew brought him notoriety in Europe, given the historical background of the Jewish genocide during the Second World War).

Yusuf was caught between many cultures, divergent in many ways, that of his parents and that of French society. His case was even more complicated, since there was also his Turkish nationality in addition to his Kurdish identity and the opposition between the two (Kurds claim their distinct culture repressed by Turkey, and sometimes even their independence). The management of these three kinds of belonging exceeded his ability to cope with his multiple identities that marked, in fact, a fractured ego. He was caught between different cultures, often incompatible in their forms of sociability (e.g., kissing a woman while separating, whereas in Muslim culture men usually kiss each other while taking leave, but also the sense of honor regarding sexuality and gender). He was uncomfortable in all of his identities and looked for a way out of their diverging values, French society promoting individualism and his parents' culture glorifying the Kurdish community, first against the Turks, then against Daesh, in the perspective of a national state to be built in an indefinitely protracted future. The family lost ground in his case due to his parents' inability to give coherence to the contradictory groups' ternary identities (Turkish nationality against Turkish identity, Kurdish identity without Kurdish nationality, French identity without recognition by the mainstream society). Choosing Daesh, apart from the familiar side of Islam, also allowed Yusuf to consolidate his identity around a well-defined corpus of attitudes and behaviors, and to endow himself with an exceptional sense of existence in reference to the heroism of the knights of faith. The choice of Daesh unified Yusuf's fractured identity: from now on, he was neither a Kurd nor a French, nor a Turk, nor a teenager; he was an "adult on standby," belonging to Daesh. The latter helped him overcome his split identity as well as his discomfort with being an adolescent, an age of unending transition, mostly to nowhere.

In another case, Quentin, whose nom de guerre was "Abu Omar al-Faransi," was born into a middle-class family of left-wing Catholics. His father, of Haitian origin, sold cosmetics and his mother was a customer manager in a health magazine. His older brother, Yannis, was an engineer and worked in Switzerland.

In March 2013, Quentin embraced Islam, attracted by its simplicity and clarity. He credited the Koran as the only religious book compatible with modern science, and even predicting major scientific discoveries, a point of view he had found in the popular Islamic literature on this topic. His radicalization occurred gradually, through self-imposed prohibitions: no alcohol, no participation in the funeral of his grandmother, no family diner if wine was served. He stopped playing piano and broke up with his girlfriend and had to give up his job as a seller because of prayers at unauthorized times .(Vidalle2016). His departure to Syria caught his family unawares. He used to attend a mosque that had ties to the radicals (Roy, 2017).

His radicalization was primarily linked to a spiritual quest and also a demand of justice for the Syrians (he told his mother that she would have been happy to have someone defending France in case of an attack by foreigners). The Islamic dichotomous vision separating God and man, licit and illicit, and right and wrong, removed his anxiety in a world where gray areas far exceed those of black and white. The Manichean dividing line seduces those who would like to repudiate doubts and embrace certainty in order to surmount anomie, a malaise due to the lack of standards. Quentin desperately sought a sacred principle to cling to, and radical Islam became even more attractive as it was repressive, drawing a clear divide between believer and Infidel, friend and foe. The need for an unmistakable, absolute certainty in sacred terms lightened the burden of individual choice, what's forbidden religiously freeing him from having to choose. The repressive norms that jihadism applies to social relations attracts many young people who are afraid of their own liberty and need the endorsement of sacred standards to overcome their doubts about their uncertain future and a life without canons within fragile families.

Islamic spirituality in its mystical version (Sufism) is totally discredited in fundamentalist circles. It does not give Manichean certainties, the need for massive, repressive, doubtless certitude being the major need of this generation, devoid of the confidence of the former generations who firmly believed in socialism, communism, or the ideology of indefinite progress.

Young people's religiosity like Quentin's feeds on a deep dissatisfaction with a world marked by the lack of utopia, dominated by social injustice and purely material values. As they suffer from a loss of meaning and a lack of standards, mysticism (Sufism) does not suit them. What they are after is not spiritual bliss but religious stringency coupled with intolerance and the will to cross swords with the world to assert themselves as knights of faith rather than explorers of spiritual values.

The case of a teenager of Turkish origin with family problems, Yussuf, was described by his mother, Neriman Yaman, in a book in German, *Mein Sohn, der Salafist: Wie sich mein Kind radikalisierte und Ich es nicht verhindern konnte* (My Son, the Salafist: How My Child Radicalized, and I Was Unable to Prevent It; Yaman, 2016). The -thirty-seven-year-old Turkish woman, born in Duisburg, Germany, to a family of small traders, recounts the radicalization of her son at the age of fourteen, including the way he followed Salafist Arabic-language preachers on the internet, joined a group that distributed free Korans on the street, and married a teenager wearing a *burqa* (total veil). He already had followed a program led by German authorities that had failed to de-radicalize him. Her statement joined that of many desperate parents: "As parents, we were helpless." This also confirms the crisis of authority within Muslim families, among single parents (the mother, alone, catering to the son), as well as the inability of de-radicalization mechanisms within European states that do not take into proper consideration the anthropological situation of the families and the multiple identity crises of teenagers.

Linda Wesel, sixteen, lived in the small town of Pulsnitz (8,000 inhabitants) near Dresden in Germany. Her radicalization took place on the web, like that of some other girls in Europe. Unlike most young boys, radicalized girls are rather good students and do not come from the lower classes but from the lower-middle or middle classes, converts as well as Muslims. The divorce of Linda's parents made her miserable, like a myriad of young girls. The new life of her mother with her stepfather pushed her to seek in radical Islam a solution to her family problems (Hall and Fagge, 2017). Her Islamization was concomitant with her withdrawal from social life. Online she met a jihadi, with whom she forged a secret bond through her second Facebook account, unbeknown to her mother. Like many teenage girls, she was able to hide her radicalization from her mother. In 2015, she was even confirmed in her Christian faith by a pastor. During Ramadan, she pretended to be on a diet, but her friends realized that she had changed: she was fasting, wore long clothes, listened only to prayers in Arabic, and refused to listen to the rapper Bushido's songs, as she usually did. After stealing her mother's credit card and buying a plane ticket for Turkey, she crossed the border and entered Syria. She married a Chechen jihadi and was called "Umm Mariam." In Iraq, she allegedly took part in military training and manipulated weapons, killing, according to her, Iraqi soldiers. In July 2017, she was found in a tunnel with other women in Mosul.

Linda's case is one of rapid radicalization, expressing the revolt of an unhappy teenager in a new family that she did not deem acceptable to her, with a new half-sister (her stepfather's daughter) and a mother whose attitude she did not understand anymore (divorce with her father, concubinage with another man). The dream of another country where she could get married and avoid the family drama she was suffering from was her main purpose in leaving for Syria. In the beginning, jihadi ideology was not her main concern; the quest for a family free from dissension was. She was looking for a community at odds with a modern world based on the principle "every man for himself or every woman for herself" (as her mother did it, by divorcing and marrying a new husband, disregarding her obligations toward her progenies), a selfish world that excluded a community worthy of the name. The search for an imaginary Muslim community (the neo-Ummah) was one of the key drivers for young Europeans who joined IS. Within it they were looking for new bonds between individuals, putting into question the heartless European individualism.

Linda later turned to violence in the fight against Kurdish soldiers, after the probable death of her husband. She also wanted to prove to herself that she was capable of violence in the same way as men, becoming a jihadi feminist.

Our next case is that of "Umm Umar," an English woman of Bangladeshi origin who left Britain and went to Syria (Jaffer, "The Secret World of Isis Brides 2015). She grew up in a part of the country where there were few migrants and even fewer Muslims. Other children often hit her at school because of her distinctive veil and her face, violently reminding her of her "non-White" origin. They sometimes spat on her face in the bus. She felt hopelessly alone and alienated. A journalist was able to contact her, follow her trajectory, and debate with her: "My God," she said. "I hated Britain so much!" While she intensely loved her mother, she did not regret the suffering she inflicted on her by leaving for Syria because she considered her act a religious duty that transcended family obligations, the caliphate in Syria being at war against Infidels. "Umm Umar" joined the Islamic State of which she had an irenic vision. To an English society where she felt miserable, she contrasted the caliphate, which gave a sacred meaning and a vocation to her existence.

The idealized *dawla* ("state," short for *dawla islamiya*, the Islamic State, IS) before the arrival of the wannabe jihadi or jihadi bride in Syria often did not stand up to the reality. Everyday life was much more mundane than the idealized portrait these young people drew in their imaginations before joining Daesh. In Syria, "Umm Umar" sought a husband and fell on a young Englishman from the Bangladeshi village of her parents. A few months later, he died in combat. She became a martyr's wife and was celebrated as such. She was proud of her husband and after a period of mourning (three months) resumed her work in the *Hisbah*, the brigade of mores, reaping otherworldly merits (*ajr*) by investing herself full-time in it. For the Syrians her role was repressive, her lack of ties in Syria making her more inflexible, and her action the more unbearable to the secularized Syrian women.

Her departure to Syria was significant in many ways. She was abused as an isolated Muslim: in her English city, being veiled was demeaning, not because of the high number of followers of Allah who would push toward racism, but due to their very small numbers. Isolation created a sense of suffocation as a misunderstood and rejected Muslim. Moreover, there wasn't a Muslim community supporting Umm Umar. Her case displays the wide variety of causes for the radicalization of Muslims, Islamophobia playing a key role.

Léa was fourteen years old when she left France for Syria. She was a good pupil in a Parisian school, an impressionable and sensitive girl (Seelow, 2016). Her parents were of Algerian origin; her father was secular, and her mother did not wear a veil. Since 2014, Islam in its fundamentalist version attracted her; she sought to wear the *jilbab*, a long robe that covers the entire body except the face, against the will of her parents. On June 18, 2014, she took the train to Amsterdam while her friends were having lunch at the school canteen. She took a flight to Istanbul the same day and, after many hours of bus travel, a smuggler conveyed her to the Turkish-Syrian border and drove her to Raqqa, the capital of IS. Her future husband welcomed her there, a twenty-two-year-old man. The letter she left to her parents was explicit: she wanted to get on with her life, to act in a way that was at odds with family values. She already behaved like a pre-adult who did not understand her parents' opposition to her choice: she was fascinated by Islam and its eschatological dimension, all of it in a counter-secular attitude: "You suspect nothing, but in 10 hours I will be gone. Part of this country doesn't let me practice my religion properly, in complete freedom.. . . I'll take the flight to Sham (Greater Syria), the holy city located in Syria. . . . I'll go to a holy land where we will be resurrected on the Day of Reckoning. I am leaving because my happiness is to build my life according to my religion and not to be pressured. Because dad refuses the jilbab and you refuse it I am leaving school."

In this story, the somewhat naive return to religion, the so-called blessing of living in Sham, and the Last Judgment are recounted as an evidence. On the other hand, French laws regarding the veil are experienced as an assault against Muslim women and an attack on their bodily integrity: "My body, I want to cover it [total veil] and they won't let me in this country," said another young convert during an interview in 2016 in Bondy, close to Paris. She continued: "I'm not comfortable without a veil [total veil, *niqab*], it's like I'm naked, and I'm ashamed in the face of God." A ban on the full veil and the stigmas attached to veiled women by the media are regarded as reasons to leave France and make *Hijra* (exodus). IS manipulated this sense of shame and indignation and the willingness of women to migrate to a Muslim land by insisting not only on their being allowed to wear the hijab in Syria, but also on the merit they would gain in wearing the full veil (*niqab*, *burqa*). The manipulation by Daesh is particularly evident in this slogan, where Daesh had a young woman say this distorted L'Oréal advertising slogan: "I am a veiled girl, because I'm worth it."

Léa was influenced on the web by a recruiter, Abu Saad al Maghrebi, from Nîmes, a town in southern France. She was also in contact with several other girls with whom she formed a closed community, marked by mutual complicity and the quest for the same ideal: to leave France, find a husband, give birth to children, become recognized as a grown-up, and break with a life devoid of sacred values. Lea is not only a victim, she is also a half-immature, half-dreamy individual who imagined life under the caliphate in Syria attractive and endowed with sacred meaning, in contrast with the routine of everyday life in families where authority is in crisis and the excess of freedom makes illegitimate every obstacle to self-assertion. Léa was critical toward

France for forbidding the veil, but living under the aegis of IS where it was imposed to women seemed natural to her.

Her revolt against her parents was a teenager's transgression against the slackened standards of a secular society. Her aspiration was to realize her desire to wear the veil, but also to end her disarray at the lack of restrictive norms (the obligation to wear the hijab according to Islam was a positive point in her view). She was desperate in a secular society where nothing seemed sacred and immune from questioning. In short, she suffered from the absence of sacred standards that should be untouchable at least as much as the constraints her family had imposed on her regarding the observance of a fundamentalist Islam.

She needed less a freedom to wear the veil and more an experience of limits. But the family could no longer impose those limits on her because the parents were desecrated, her father was more like an older brother and her mother an older sister, both lacking the sacred authority to impose standards beyond doubt on her. The veil was a self-imposed limit aiming at ending the confusing uncertainty of being a budding woman. She needed to have a defined social role, within a society finally endowed with a sense of limits. It is for this reason that the mythical neo-Ummah in the imaginations of these young people was above all characterized by restrictions and barriers between men and women, private and public, the status of the married and the single, Muslim and non-Muslim. The revolt in the name of the veil and, beyond that, the break with family and society were signs of a larger crisis in a secular world devoid of limits and barriers, in which the Sacred (synonymous with impassable limits and absolute prohibitions) had been shattered.

e-Jihadis with Mental Problems

If there is no strict causal relationship between jihadism and mental health issues; still, a sizeable minority of those involved in jihadism did have rather serious mental problems, ranging from depression to psychotic symptoms. As already mentioned, jihadism is a "total social fact" and, as such, involves a number of dimensions, of which mental problems are one.

Jihadism has opened up a new chapter on the studies of mental disease and terrorism. After the September 11, 2001, attacks in the US, many studies underlined the fact that jihadis were "normal" people, psychologically speaking (Sageman, 2004). Since then, several others have put this view into question. A research on a large sample of Dutch jihadis (319 people) who went to Syria showed that 72 percent had no reported mental health problems, 15 percent had some, and 13 percent had proven ones (Weenink, 2019).

Another research exploring the relationship between metal health, radicalization, and mass violence (for instance, terrorist attacks) showed that depressive symptoms might be associated with radicalization bias, although it remained unknown whether they were associated with resilience or vulnerability to radicalization (Misiak et al., 2019). Several personality traits, according to this study, might predispose people to develop extreme ideation (for instance, jihadi ideology). Lone actors ("lone wolves") could be characterized by high prevalence of psychotic and/or mood disorders.

The creation of IS meant new opportunities for individuals with psychological problems, who were recruited and given the opportunity to act cruelly toward the captives or the civilians in Syria. They put their misdeeds on display on social media and this, in turn, attracted other mentally disturbed people or those prone to violence, who would join them. The case of "Jihadi Jack" can provide an example. According to his parents, he suffered from obsessive-compulsive disorder (OCD) (Soni, 2016).

There is a soft consensus among psychiatrists as to the fact that in one-actor cases (the so-called lone-wolf terrorists) there is a strong link between mental illness and extremist action (Gill, Horgan, and Deckert, 2014; Corner and Gill, 2015; Gill, 2015; Pantucci, 2015; Royal College of Psychiatrists London, 2016).

Among those who suffered from mental problems and became jihadi, we can distinguish two types:

- The first is depressed people who found in violence a sanctuary against anxiety: action filled their minds and distracted them from anguish; with their adrenaline flowing, exalting violence broke with the monotony of everyday life (Knapton, 2014).

  Jihadism introduces a discontinuity into the existence, a vertiginous transition to the extreme violence in a sacred breach. It reminds us of the Kierkegaardian leap of faith over the abyss in a fateful decision (to die as a martyr in jihad), changing the meaning of time, and breathing life into the "instant" in which the jump happens, assuring in this way salvation (Kierkegaard, 1849. Jihadi credo overcomes the depressive time experienced as an aimless continuum. The anguish due to the meaningless time is overcome by a leap into the transcendence that fills life with a sacred purpose. Sanctified violence saves the soul of depressive jihadis by breaking with the times of peace in the name of an apocalyptic end of times that could only be violent. The monotonous peace in Western Europe is thus experienced not only as devoid of meaning and purpose, but also as sinful and anguishing. In the soul of depressed jihadis, anguish and sin are experienced as inseparable. Jihadi violence plays a cathartic role to escape not only from anguish, but also from sin.

- The other type are psychotic people who show signs of profound mental disturbance and discover in jihadi ruthlessness a catharsis in which cruel action and pathological gratification are tightly intertwined (not only violent, but cruel action fascinates these individuals by legitimizing their morbid will to destroy). For this type of jihadi, ruthlessness becomes the goal of life (torturing the prisoners while insulting and mocking them, breaking their heads with stones, or cutting off heads with an electric saw, for example).

For depressed people, violence and sacredness are intertwined. Psychotics are much more attached to violence than to the Sacred, releasing their sickly tension through an exacerbated violence on the victims, the Sacred being at best an outlet.

Al-Qaeda rejected Muslims with major mental problems, focusing only on adults who did not behave pathologically, who had a minimum knowledge of Islam, and were motivated to fight to the death against its enemies. Daesh, in contrast, made a deliberate choice to enlist all those who accepted its rule, including psychologically fragile people and mentally disturbed youth as well as teenagers.

For those who experienced mild forms of depression, some were aware of it and built a "theological" schema directly related to their discomfort: he who is depressed has committed sins. To recover mental health one must fight sin, the best way to achieve it being to perform jihad. Thus, the sinner breaks off his ties with *jahiliyah* (ignorance, an expression of Seyed Qotb and Mawdudi in reference to the societies who ignore Islam much in the same way as the pre-Islamic world ignored it), and recovers mental health in the holy war, without recourse to antidepressants. Depression and sin are closely linked, breaking with sin meaning overcoming depression.

The case of a twenty-four-year-old convert, Alexandre Dhaussy, from a middle-class background, is in point. He stabbed a soldier on May 25, 2013, in La Défense, northwest of Paris. He probably imitated an attack that had taken place three days earlier in London by two Blacks, Michael Adebolajo and Michael Adebowale, who killed a British soldier by the name of Lee Rigby. Dhaussy was diagnosed with schizophrenic psychosis, and according to an expert his mental disorder had abolished his judgment and control over his actions. According to psychiatric experts, he was subject to mental disorders and remained dangerous without proper medical treatment. He converted to Islam in 2009 and called himself "Abdelhak" or "Adelillah." He was homeless and lived like a vagrant. He had dropped out of school in the third grade (Seelow, 2015; Erlanger, 2013). He engaged in delinquent activities and committed robbery, which resulted in his name figuring in the National Automated DNA File (FNAEG), requiring "educational follow-up" in his case. Having reached adulthood, he joined Tabligh, which promotes a pietistic Islam, without calling for violence. He then dressed in a djellaba and grew a thick beard, living from time to time among the followers of Tabligh. His "radicalization" was rather the consequence of his psychotic crisis. In his case, conversion to Islam and identification with its radical version can be considered as a continuation of his delirium rather than a clear-sighted, ideologically motivated choice.

1-Examples of Jihadis with Mental Problems

The cases of Adebolajo and Adebowale show the combination of mental problems, social stigmas, the blurring lines between lower-middle-classes and the lower classes, and the identification with a radical version of Islam.[11]

The nineteen-year-old Adel Kermiche,[12] calling himself "Abou Jayyed al-Hanafi," was the killer of the Catholic priest Father Hamel in Saint-Etienne-de-Rouvray in Normandy on July 26, 2016. He showed signs of mental fragility at an early age. Between the ages of six and thirteen, he was under psychiatric care in a medico-psychological center. At the age of twelve he was hospitalized at the Rouen hospital, and a year later he was placed in a closed cell for fifteen days in a psychiatric unit before being sent to a therapeutic and educational institute. He was identified as unstable at school and was dismissed from it. At the age of fifteen, he returned to the school and then continued his schooling until high school, being physically and verbally abusive. He left school at the age of sixteen. A year later, unemployed, he met Adel Bouanoun, twenty-six, who literally bewitched him. He made him compare a so-called irenic situation in Syria with his pitiful unemployment in France and usurped his identity document to go to Syria (Cornevin, 2016).

On March 23, 2015, Kermiche made his first attempt at leaving for Syria. Arrested in Munich, then deported to France, he was placed under judicial control at his parents' home in Saint-Étienne-du-Rouvray. On May 11, 2015, he made a second attempt with fake identity papers. Arrested in Turkey, he was extradited on May 22 to France and incarcerated. He was released on remand on March 18, 2016, after ten months of detention. Like many psychopaths, Adel Kermiche had an acute sense of persuasion and manipulation, and he was able to deceive the judge whom he testified about his wish to renounce violence and start a peaceful life. He was freed on the condition that he wear an ankle monitor, which he threw away before he committed the murder of an old priest, with his accomplice Abdel Malik Petitjean. Not all those who suffer from mental problems become jihadis, but a sizeable minority of jihadis suffer from mental disorder.

Mohamed Lahouaiej Bouhlel was born in January 1985 in M'Saken, a suburb of Sousse, south of Tunis. According to his father, in the early 2000s Bouhlel had a depression and followed in 2004 the prescriptions of a psychiatrist in Sousse who diagnosed a beginning of psychosis ("Attentat de Nice," 2016). He prescribed Haldol, an antipsychotic medicine. Bouhlel was violent, and practiced bodybuilding to be able to fight. On different occasions, he locked up his parents. In 2004, Bouhlel moved to France, then obtained a yearly residence permit in 2008, followed by a ten-year residence permit. He settled in Nice on his own and committed various wrongful acts from 2010 to 2016, including theft and acts of violence, in particular against his concubine, without being incarcerated. Only once he was condemned to six months of suspended imprisonment for acts of violence with a weapon, following an argument with a motorist. He led a turbulent life, overconsuming alcohol and drugs. He had an unbridled sexuality: bisexual, he transgressed the basic laws of orthodox Islam, several of his male and female conquests being on his cell phone, including a seventy-three-year-old man who seemed to be his main lover. His wife with three children asked for divorce. He did not attend the local mosque and was considered by neighbors to be an unbalanced, violent, and alcoholic person. He did not fast during Ramadan, nor did he perform daily prayers ("Mohamed Lahouaiej Bouhlel," 2015); he ate pork and drank alcohol, according to his former wife. He was bipolar, and frequently doped with steroids. Hired as a delivery driver, customers were unhappy and accused him of aggressive behavior. He was fired in

2011 for serious misconduct. Psychologically unstable, impressionable, and separated from his wife and children, he was tempted by a large-scale attack in Nice, assuring him a posthumous glory that flattered his narcissism (a large number of selfies were found on his laptop) and punished society for his misery, in the name of radical Islam. He knew full well that it would draw worldwide attention, given Daesh's attacks in Europe since 2015. On July 14, 2016, he drove his truck into the crowd celebrating the French Revolution on the Promenade des Anglais, the major avenue in Nice, killing eighty-six people and maiming 458.

We can compare his case to the Germanwings pilot, Andreas Lubitz, who slammed his plane into the French Alps on March 24, 2016, killing the 144 passengers and five crew members, following psychotic troubles, with no ideological motive. He wanted to ensure fame even at the expense of the mainstream values. For him, the higher the number of victims, the more illustrious would be his fame. Bouhlel's reference to radical Islam was more of an aspiration to notoriety than an ideological affiliation to jihadism. It was at the same time a revenge against the humiliation of being regarded in a derogatory manner as an "Arab," carrying with him the complex of the ex-colonized individual, feeling inferior and deeply upset by it.

Up to then, he had expressed his revolt and indignation with great aggressiveness, particularly toward the clients of the company where he worked, who complained about his harshness.

Because his ancestors had suffered injustice through colonization, he felt free to act unjustly toward the citizens of the former colonial empire. As the victims' offspring, he claimed the moral right to crack down on the progenies of the former colonizers. It was legitimate in his view to mistreat the French in retaliation for the repression that France had carried out against his forefathers in the past. The moral contract was broken between him and the mainstream society, and the way was open to all excesses on his part. His mental problems amplified his feeling of persecution. He exclusively focused on his discomfort, accusing today's French of being the culprits of the acts committed by their predecessors more than a century ago. He could only rise up in his own eyes by persecuting the scions of the colonizers. The fact that he killed anonymous people (among them people like him, from the former colonies) and not a specific category such as policemen, journalists, Jews, or soldiers, reveals the blind side of his hatred, which he projected indiscriminately onto the whole society. In his mind, France was not only guilty of having colonized his ancestors, she was also guilty of continuing to humiliate their descendants, including him, even though it was he who had chosen to come to France to earn a living and no one had forced him to do so. In short, Bouhlel was the very embodiment of what we have called the complex of the ex-colonized man who feels intensely the weight of history that literally crushes him. What happened more than a century ago still held great acuity in his mind, as if those events had taken place a short while ago.[13]

Bouhlel's offensive attitude toward customers confirmed in their eyes the stereotype of "Arabs" as being aggressive and untrustworthy. His attack was premeditated. His case epitomizes that of a "fake jihadi" who cloaks his mental problems by legitimizing them under the label of radical Islam. Daesh exploited his attack by claiming its sponsorship (there is, however, no trace of Bouhlel's contacts with Daesh or its representatives on the web).

Born in Bangladesh, Ruhul Amin, aka "Abdul Rakib Amin," grew up in Aberdeen in Scotland. He played rugby and smoked and drank with his friends. After breaking up with his girlfriend, he was depressed, and his father sent him for a while to Bangladesh; he believed his son had become too Westernized. After returning to the United Kingdom, Amin became deeply religious and broke off ties with his old friends. Seeking to escape a depressive state, he discovered jihad via the internet. In 2014 he went to Syria and made a propaganda video for Daesh in English ("There is no life without jihad"), in which he encouraged young people to join him there to help launch the holy war. Ashamed of his attitude, his parents broke off their ties with him and returned to Bangladesh. We find here a difference from North African families in France where there is less sensitivity about the family's "honor" because of the breakdown of the patriarchal family, the father having often left home (or being sidelined or remarried), and the mother quite often raising her children alone within a single-parent family, particularly in poor districts. Among English Muslims, family traditions have been better preserved, notably because of the recognition of the community fact and a less-mixed marriage with the "White" people than in France. In the messages he sent to his family, Ruhul Amin expressed his love for them but he also declared that he loved Allah more, showing no sign of guilt for having left them. In an interview with a journalist, he said he was not afraid to die, faith in Allah giving him infinite confidence (McDonald, 2015), his death as a martyr literally meaning joining Allah and overcoming the anguish of facing his own fragility. He needed the test of sacred death to overcome depression and saw martyrdom as an opportunity to join Allah and live forever in paradise. He was killed in August 2015 at the age of twenty-six in Raqqa by British drones ("Aberdeen Jihadi Fighter Ruhul Amin," 2015).

The therapeutic use of jihad as a cure against depression obviously raises the question of the purpose of the holy war, which becomes a remedy, a prophylactic means much more than a sacred obligation to help other Muslims against the powers of evil.

Martyrdom is a catharsis against an anguish which is all the more pernicious as there is no cure for it in everyday life. One way to end anguish is to break away from life. Sacred death gives a sacrificial meaning to the will to commit suicide.

f-Desperate Jihadis

A specific idea of paradise is embedded in the psyche of a category of young Muslims (converts included) who seek to escape from a hopeless life in this world. This is particularly visible among those young Muslims who were often secularized and even de-Islamized. After joining IS, they sought to die as martyrs to ensure a happy afterlife in paradise. That seemed otherwise inaccessible to them, given their dissolute way of life prior to their espousal of authentic Islam, embodied in their eyes in jihadism. In early 2013, in prison (Fresnes), a Black Muslim of sub-Saharan origin, in his early twenties, became a born-again Muslim under the influence of a Frenchman of Italian origin who had converted to a Salafi version of Islam and had become a proselytizer. He expressed his deep guilt for his past and was convinced that salvation could only be achieved through martyrdom:

Mahmood: I was unaware of what God had commanded.
Question: What did you do that was sinful?
Mahmood: I sinned, I dated women without marrying them, I took alcohol, shit [drugs], *I did everything haram. Then, a few months ago in this prison I met an Italian convert with a beautiful voice who does the adhan* [the call to the prayer] *so well—you already talked to him in his cell and he advised me to talk to you. He said that you were not an informer. I had long discussions with him in the prison courtyard, and he made me aware of those mischievous things I had done: God is merciful* [*rahim*] *but He does not save me if I don't repent. One night I was desperate, prison made me miserable, I saw the story of my life run before my eyes. I was ashamed of what*

I had done, which had made me a sinful creature.. . . I cried, I sincerely asked for God's mercy and I fell asleep. The next morning, I went to my Italian preacher and asked him what I should do. He told me to repent sincerely and to promise to God not to sin again. I said that without stealing and trafficking I could not survive. He told me that in the land of kuffar [disbelievers], *the acts that are forbidden in an Islamic land are allowed, the more so as they weaken them. I asked how I could be redeemed for sure. He said through martyrdom.*

Question: Jihad?

Mahmood: He did not mention it, but he certainly meant it. I had to become a good Muslim and not indulge in daily sin. Since then, I fully respect it. I have even renounced non-halal meat.

Question: Did you believe in what he said?

Mahmood: I was quite desperate, and the idea of dying for Allah was quite attractive to me. I spend a great part of my life in prison. I know well that once I am out I would be caught and again find myself behind bars, even if I didn't do anything wrong. They always find a reason to lock you up. I grow tired and sometimes committing suicide becomes tempting. I think almost every repeat offender has a moment, in which he considers taking his own life. But suicide is a mortal sin and you go to hell if you do it. It is better to die as a martyr; in which case you directly go to heaven. Going to some of those countries like Afghanistan to fight against disbelievers can be rewarding.

Question: Some talk even of killing cops!

Mahmood: If they cannot go out of the country, some might choose that solution! But I prefer fighting a real jihad rather than attacking Americans in Afghanistan or Pakistan.

Jihad is put here at the service of sacred death, the major motive being to die and finish life in this vale of tears. This has become commonplace among some hardcore recidivists. When they grow tired of their life, which is largely divided into periods of incarceration and conditional freedom, they look for a way out that would not be sheer suicide but a meaningful death at the service of God. They cannot lead a normal life and they become fully aware of it when in midlife they physically begin to decline. That is why they are usually older (mid-thirties and forties) than average jihadis who are in their mid-twenties. Desperate, they aspire to have at least the promise of heaven and are ready to do whatever is necessary in order to enter paradise, after having endured hell in prison. To sum up, they have a threefold purpose: take revenge on a society that destroyed their life through prison and stigmatization; end on a high note (become famous in total contrast to their being "nobodies"), and reach heaven via martyrdom. The three aims can be achieved through martyrdom, a noble means to accomplish their goals in a "glorious" fashion.

A case in point is Chérif Chekatt, a French citizen of Algerian origin who had a difficult childhood. To punish him for his bad behavior, his parents forced him to go to school during the winter wearing light clothes. He had mental problems according to the people who knew him (in January 2019, a month after Chekatt's attacks in Strasbourg, I interviewed a psychiatrist who had dealt with his case). In short, he was a problem child and lived among religiously minded people who led an isolated social life, not even mixing with the Salafists. He joined with deviant youth and began stealing and drug trafficking at an early age. He was radicalized in prison in 2008 and sent his allegiance (*bay'ah*) to IS—the document was found on his computer. He was on the brink of being arrested for another criminal case, after the other members of the gang were put in custody. In December 2018, following the capture of some of his partners in a drug traffic affair, he took an old revolver, killed five people, and wounded a dozen more in Strasbourg. He had already been sentenced twenty-seven times and had received prison terms in France, Switzerland, and Germany (Khosrokhavar, *Le nouveau Jihad en Occident*, 2018, "La jeunesse féminine dijiadiste," 2018). In the name of jihad, he put an end to his life, sick and tired of being chased by the police for his misdeeds, seeing no end to his misery, and being unable to build a stable life. This type of desperate individual seeks salvation in jihad by putting an end to a distressful life, punishing society, and at the same time becoming a celebrity in the international jihadi star system.

The "desperate jihadi" usually has no project, no ties to any jihadi group, and his sole aim is to die like a martyr, rather than to accomplish any project, as was the case of those who committed the November 2015 attacks in Paris, aiming at reinforcing IS. Since 2015, Chekatt had frequently declared that he yearned for martyrdom.

One can also mention the case of Michael Chiolo, who wounded two guards on March 5, 2019, in a high-security French prison. He had been condemned to thirty years' imprisonment for the murder of a man. He had no future, and acting in that fashion gave him prominence in the jihadi star system through the world media, like Chérif Chekatt, whom he had known and whose death he intended to avenge.

This type of jihadi has no overall plan, contrary to those with a clear-cut project, like those who committed the March 2016 attack in Brussels. He also lacks any future prospect, having spent his life in jail for long periods and seeing no end to the vicious circle of felony and incarceration. He knows full well that by killing and maiming in the name of an Islamic holy war he will attain the "apotheosis" in terms of ill fame (but still fame in his eyes and in the eyes of his fellow jihadis), achieving his ultimate goal: to become a star for a while through the world media while dying as a martyr. In this way he has this world (becoming universally known, as the Greek hero in general longed for) and he will have the other world (becoming a martyr will secure him a privileged place in paradise with everlasting sexual pleasures close to the *huris* [beautiful maidens] and abundance in all respects).

Another desperate jihadi is Moussa Coulibaly, who attacked three soldiers in Nice in front of a Jewish Center on February 4, 2015. He was indicted for attempted murder along with a terrorist group. Originally from Val-Fourré, a poor neighborhood of Mantes-la-Jolie in the Yvelines in the suburbs of Paris where many people radicalized in the 1990s, he lived with his mother after the death of his father a few years earlier. Known to the police for theft, drug use, and contempt, he was sentenced to fines or suspended prison terms six times between 2003 and 2012. Unemployed, he went to Turkey to enter Syria, but was forced back by the Turkish police on the instructions of the French authorities. For a few months he became religious in an aggressive manner: in the gym he scolded a woman for not being veiled, and treated another man as a "dog" for not being decently covered ("Moussa Coulibaly, itinéraire d'un 'timide,'" 2015).

Zyed Ben Belgacem was another desperate jihadi. A French citizen of Tunisian origin, he was born in 1978 and was thirty-nine years old at the time of the attacks on March 18, 2017. On that day, at 6:55 am, during an inspection of his car by police officers in Stains in Seine-Saint-Denis, close to Paris, he opened fire on them, hitting one of them in the face. He fled, and at 7:40 in Vitry-sur-Seine, he entered a bar and fired shots, intimidating people without hurting anyone. Shortly after, he stole a car while aiming a gun at a woman and her daughter, driving to the Orly-Sud Airport where he entered at 8:50 am, assaulting a female member of Opération Sentinelle (the section of the French army specialized in combating terrorism), taking her hostage, and claiming martyrdom. He was shot. Belgacem was well known to the police for his criminal record: nine cases of armed robbery and drug trafficking. A multiple offender, he had served several prison terms, including five years for armed robbery and two sentences of three and five years' imprisonment for drug dealing. Between 2011 and 2012 he was identified in prison as being "radicalized," which often means adhering to a fundamentalist and ostentatious version of Islam. At the time of the attack, there was a warrant for his arrest. He had left prison a few months earlier, in November 2016. Toxicological tests revealed the presence of alcohol in his blood (0.93 g per liter) as well as cannabis and cocaine. He had shown no religious leaning in his life and did not pray or contact jihadis. He was what we call a desperate jihadi, made in most cases of individuals of migrant origin, their average age being higher than mainstream jihadis (who are between twenty-five and twenty-eight years), with a non-religious past and a life inextricably associated with prison, drugs (dealing but also consumption), and a willingness to fight and end their lives on a "high note." Death in the name of Allah embellishes a life that otherwise would have been notable only for its delinquency, immorality (according to the dominant standards as well as Islam), and violence. A desperate jihadi has in general no proven ties to any jihadi group, let alone Daesh.

More generally, there are many ambivalent cases, in which desperate or mentally disturbed individuals expressed their distress by choosing jihadi repertoire.

The model has become widespread. An individual, often armed with a knife or a machete or a bladed weapon, attacks people or preferably law enforcement officers, shouting "Allah o akbar" (God is the greatest), a rallying cry of jihadism (otherwise, "Allah o akbar" means public recognition of someone's Muslim faith). This was the case of a thirty-three-year-old Algerian, "K.B.," who took a machete out of his bag on August 6, 2016, in Charleroi, Belgium, and attacked two policewomen. He wounded one gravely in the face and slightly touched the other, while shouting "Allah o akbar." He was shot dead by a third police officer. He had been living in Belgium since 2012 and was not known for radicalization.

In 2019–2020 in Europe, many attacks by mentally disordered, desperate individuals with no religious background who indiscriminately assaulted others in the name of jihad occurred. In these cases, jihadism is a smokescreen to conceal mental disorder or despair through a violence that is often delusional.

g-Jihadi Recruiters and Preachers

In terrorist phenomena, potential candidates are encouraged in many ways to join the ranks of the group. This requires entrepreneurs who take risks to convince and seduce supporters to become active members of the group. The case of "self-radicalized" jihadis who would have been indoctrinated on the web is rather marginal in Europe, but if we add the case of mentally disturbed solo jihadis called "lone wolves," their number swells to a sizeable minority. Often in jihadi circles the functions of "recruiter" and "preacher" are interdependent. Sometimes one predominates over the other, but the goal, ultimately, is to commit individuals to the path of holy war. Thus, recruiters are often also preachers, which gives them an aura far beyond the neighborhood or the locality. The internet serves them to spread their message, mostly in linguistically homogeneous areas (e.g., Arabic, English, French).

As for the European jihadis, the majority of their sympathizers are among those who share the slum culture, as we have already depicted. Recruiters target them primarily in poor and ethnic neighborhoods, in prisons or on the web. Another category is that of middle-class Muslims and converts. The former suffer humiliation in many ways, and the latter need to prove to others the strength and authenticity of their faith and are sometimes in disarray over the lack of ties between individuals in fragmented societies, looking for a vibrant or even effervescent community that they discover in the imagined jihadi neo-Ummah.

In Europe, recruiters and preachers often present strong and charismatic personalities in front of weak individuals who have social problems and who have more or less abdicated their freedom or are looking for sacred mental support to discharge their responsibility. They reassure fragile individuals in search of mental support. They can manipulate them by taking advantage of their knowledge of Islam, especially in Europe where young Muslims are often lacking in Islamic culture and are marked by a deficient religious knowledge.

We can distinguish different types of recruiters/preachers. First is the preacher without direct involvement in action, whose aura is linked to his theological standing. This type of preacher writes or preaches sermons but does not engage directly in violent action. Contrary to traditional theologians, he proposes a radical synthesis of modern thoughts and feelings, related to the social, political, and urban environment, which he blends with theological considerations and ends with the call to sacred violence, without directly involving himself. He focuses on a synthesis of notions such as jihad and martyrdom that give meaning to the anger of young people and their frustration in a world where many people are destabilized as much by secularization as by the absence of utopia and social injustice. Among them are Abu Muhammad al Maqdisi, a Jordanian, one of the leading theologians of jihadism whose writings have been extensively translated into English (but also partly into French and other European languages), and Ahmad Musa Jibril (an American-Palestinian known as "Abu Khaled"), born in Dearborn, in the state of Michigan in the United States in 1972, who promotes a jihadi version of Salafism. He created the website AlSalafyoon.com in the late 1990s on which he downloaded videos of his sermons, promoting anti-Americanism, advocating a version of Islam that should be spread by the sword, and calling for jihad and the extermination of Unbelievers. His sermons in English influenced many young English speakers around the world. Anwar al-Awlaki, one of the leading figures of American jihadism (he also influenced some French people, like Saïd Kouachi whose journey to Yemen he financed in 2011) was the founder of the magazine *Inspire*, which had a significant impact on the radicalization of many American Muslims, including Omar Mateen (he killed forty-nine people on June 12, 2016, in Orlando, Florida), Nidal Hassan (he killed thirteen on November 5, 2009, in Fort Hood, Texas), the married couple Syed Rizwan Farook and Tashfeen Malik (they killed fourteen people on December 2, 2015, in San Bernardino, California), as well as the Tsarnaev brothers, bombers of the Boston Marathon (they killed three and wounded hundreds on April 15, 2013). Another internet preacher whose influence spread throughout the English-speaking world was Abu Haleema. Based in the United Kingdom, he mainly acted through social networks, including YouTube, Twitter, and Facebook. He was banned on them by the British government, but his videos could still be found in large numbers on the web. In his sermons he warned Muslims against the alliance with *kuffar* (disbelievers) and submitting to *Taqut* (anti-Islamic governments). Haleema notably influenced Khuram Shazad Butt, involved in the London Bridge attacks on June 3, 2017, which killed seven people and wounded forty-eight. After June 2017, YouTube removed Haleema's speeches from its platform in the UK but did not extend it to the rest of the world.

Often the recruiter acted as a symbolic father. He embodied an image of authority that operated in the name of the Islam and reconstituted an imagined patriarchal hierarchy that had been eroded in the modern family. God became the guarantor of the recruiter's legitimacy while the real father suffered the consequences of authority crisis.[14]

Among homegrown terrorist networks in the West, very few were made up of friends, without hierarchy or leadership. In most cases leaders played a key role, such as the so-called Buttes-Chaumont group dismantled in 2005 in which Farid Benyettou was the preacher and director of conscience. Similarly, the so-called Hofstad network in Holland, whose member Mohammed Bouyeri killed the filmmaker Theo van Gogh on November 2, 2004, was led by a spiritual leader, Redouan al-Issar. The Cannes-Torcy cell was led by Jérémy-Louis Sydney and, after Sydney's death during a clash with the police on October 6, 2012, by Jérémy Bailly. Overwhelmingly, groups had leaders. This model, based on charismatic leaders or intermediaries, has been the most recurrent in jihadism in Europe. With the gradual decline of IS since 2016, solo jihadis have acted without direct link with the IS, making allegiance to it in their last will or in their videos put on social networks. This was notably the case of Anis Amri, the Tunisian who attacked the Christmas market in Berlin on December 19, 2016, and was shot dead in Milan on the night of December 22 by the Italian security forces. This was also the case of the Tunisian Mohamed Laouaiej-Bouhlel, the author of the truck attack on the Promenade des Anglais in Nice on July 14, 2016 (a few people helped him get an old gun that was barely used by him, his main weapon being his truck). The case of Chérif Chekatt who killed five people in Strasbourg on December 11, 2018, was also of the same nature (some friends helped him buy a nineteenth-century weapon), and he made allegiance to IS on a USB key.

1-Examples of Jihadi Recruiters and Preachers

Charismatic leaders created fervor among their followers, encouraging them either to act locally or to go to Syria and join IS or al-Qaeda. They often focused on a major city and its satellites. like Fouad Belkacem who headed "Sharia4Belgium" especially in Antwerp (most of the thirty young Flemish people he sent to Syria were from that city). The case of Omar Diaby was also symptomatic: he operated in a poor district of the city of Nice but extended his influence through the web and reached young, French-speaking people far beyond that neighborhood. Still, a sizeable number of them were from Nice. Similarly, Anjem Choudhary wielded great influence in the UK (around one hundred radicals went to Syria under his sway), but also in Belgium ("Islam4Belgium") and Italy ("Islam4Italy") who followed in the footsteps of their English role model "Islam4UK."

A few cases can illustrate the role of the recruiters and preachers in enrolling young people into jihadism.

Khalid Zerkani was born in 1973 or 1974 in Zenata, northern Morocco, in a Berber region whose population has been repressed by the central government under the current monarchy. He stayed in Spain and Holland before moving to Belgium at the age of twenty-eight. According to the Belgian judicial authorities, he was the most important recruiter of jihadi candidates in Belgium. A resident in Belgium and a Moroccan citizen, he preached in a radical mosque in Molenbeek. He was called "Abu Riad." He worked in the maritime district of Molenbeek-Saint-Jean, a stronghold of the Abaaoud brothers, including Abdelhamid who played a key role in the deadly attacks of November 13, 2015, in Paris. He also headed another sector where lived Najim Laachraoui, an active member of the same Paris attacks, who blew himself up at Brussels Airport on March 22, 2016. He encouraged theft and fraudulent or even violent actions to finance the trip to Syria. The loot was used to cover travel expenses of the young people to whom he offered the plane ticket, hence his nickname "Santa Claus of Jihad" ("Papa Christmas"; "Khalid Zerkani, 'Papa Noël,'" 2015; Higgins and Freytas-Tamura, 2016). Zerkani extolled the merits of jihad to the young people he literally bewitched, without ever setting foot to the battlefield in Syria, endowed with an undeniable charisma. In his sermons he insisted on jihad not so much from an abstract theological viewpoint, but rather as something obvious, God-ordained, that had to be achieved through larceny or any violent means by the young people who surrounded him in the poor neighborhoods of Brussels. In a way, the less he developed the theological aspects of jihad, the more self-evident it became in regard to the estrangement of young Muslims, mired in the slum culture. His circle of influence was extensive in Molenbeek where some eighteen young people, influenced by him, left for Syria, including few entire families, among them a fifty-four-year-old mother with her two daughters, ages thirteen and fourteen. Zerkani was sentenced to fifteen years in prison for having sent young people to Syria. His strong personality captivated young people from ethnic and poor neighborhoods who had an unstable and fragile identity. What they were looking for was an unquestionable truth, and he instilled it in them without any doubt.

The Franco-Senegalese jihadi preacher Omar Diaby, known as "Omar Omsen," was one of the major recruiters for Syria in France. He was born in Dakar (capital of Senegal) around 1976 and arrived in Nice at the age of five with his parents, who were adepts of a traditional, mystical Tijani Islam, settling at the poor district of Ariane in Nice, which like most of these types of neighborhood has a bad reputation, in particular due to its coverage by the media. There he became a self-styled radical imam. Under his influence more than twenty people joined jihadi groups in Syria and Iraq.

Before becoming a recruiter, Omsen had rallied the organized crime in Nice as a small thug. He was incarcerated for attempted murder in the 1990s, spending several years behind bars. He moved close to the radical Islamic association Forsane Alizza, disbanded in 2012 by the public authorities. In Nice, he worked in a halal snack bar called "La Nusra" where he indoctrinated young people with the assistance of a trio made of Youssef E., Fares F., and a third man, whose name is unknown to the media. In December 2011, they decided to leave France to accomplish their *Hijra* (Islamic migration) to Syria but were stopped by the security forces. Fares F. stated that Omsen had indoctrinated him ("Nice, un terreau de radicalisation jihadie," 2016). The latter left France in July 2013 and formed his own battalion (*katiba*), affiliated with al-Nusra Front, a branch of al-Qaeda in Syria. He was massively present in the 19HH videos (about thirty), the number 19 symbolizing the nineteen attackers of September 11, 2001, in the United States, and HH representing New York's twin towers, destroyed that day ("Le jihadi français Omar Omsen est mort," 2015). He started producing the 19HH video series, very popular on YouTube and social networks, with the assistance of Mourad Farès, another popular French recruiter of Moroccan origin. By the end of 2012 Omsen's attention had turned toward Syria. In 2014, one of his video sequences, "Destination la Terre Sainte" (Destination the Holy Land), exceeded one hundred thousand viewers. Meticulously crafted, with alternating Arabic and Hollywood music, it mixed sermons and diverted cinematographic images, often from religious movies (*The Ten Commandments*), conspiracy (*The Matrix*), or messianic films (the American series *John Doe*), to support conspiracy theories, as well as anti-Semitism, millenarianism, Salafism, and takfirism (excommunication of fake or "bad Muslims" in an extremist manner) (Audureau, 2014). His videos fascinated many young people belonging to the slum culture.

Given the number of Muslims (mostly from poor districts) he sent to Syria, Omar Omsen was considered the most important recruiter in France.

His YouTube videos that often lasted two hours counted nearly eight hundred thousand viewers. In them he encouraged people to perform their *Hijra* by leaving for Syria. In the legends of his videos, he highlighted the importance of women in jihad, spurring families to go to Syria.

What singled out Omar Omsen was his "charisma" in the service of jihadism. As a delinquent Frenchman of Senegalese origin, he suffered racism as a Black man imbued with the slum culture. He went to prison where he radicalized, breaking the affective ties with the mainstream society, freeing himself from moral taboos on violence. All the taboos against the secular society in which he lived were over. Once out of prison, he proved able to federate young Muslims who suffered also from their inferior status as "Arabs" (Frenchmen of North African descent). He became a leader, attracting many candidates, mostly young French Muslims but also few converts. Daesh gave a nobility to the status of the recruiter for jihad, independently of their ethnic origin, the color of their skin, or their past deviant activities: membership to the group washed up the criminal record and allowed the recruit to begin a new life, former sins being absolved by God.

Omsen joined Syria in 2013 to head a group of young people from Nice, affiliated with al-Nusra Front, the Syrian branch of al-Qaeda. His group had up to 150 fighters at its apogee, including his brother Moussa (Thomson, 2016). From the end of 2013, his group suffered internal tensions after he refused to join IS, remaining loyal to al-Nusra Front (al-Qaeda). Within jihadism Omsen was able to become the leader of a group; Black and migrant, from inferior he became superior, his creativity in producing videos being put at the service of a cause that promoted him to the rank of an "Emir." Self-respect and pride replaced indignity and resentment. He gained self-esteem in his new status, which was inaccessible to people like him in Europe where the sons of Muslim migrants with a lower education had few opportunities to be proud of.

One can also mention the case of a French woman, Emilie König, who recruited women and young girls for IS. She was born in 1984 in Morbihan (in Bretagne, western France). She was placed in 2015 on the blacklist of terrorists by the US government. Her father, a rural police officer (*gendarme*), left the family when she was two years old, and her mother brought her up alone, with three other children. She was the youngest. She was an atheist of Catholic origin. As an adolescent, she had deeply hated her father for abandoning them. She went to school and converted to Islam at the age of seventeen. She obtained a professional diploma in Business (CAP) and went to Paris, in search of a job (Duplessy, 2018). She married her first husband from Algeria, who was later imprisoned for drug trafficking. She divorced him. She started learning Arabic and chose "Samra" as her name. She encountered an Islamist group, Forsane Alizza, that rejected her membership. She began to wear a full veil (*niqab*). In 2010 she distributed leaflets calling for holy war near the mosque of Lorient. Called to the court of Lorient in the spring of 2012, she appeared in full veil and refused to remove it (since 2010 it was illegal to wear the *niqab* in public in France), resulting in an altercation with a security guard. She filmed the scene and put it on YouTube. Following the banning of Forsane Alizza, she called for jihad on Facebook. She was looking for a romantic, grand love with a jihadi knight of faith but was shocked when one candidate she met on the web asked for her naked picture and put it afterward on display on social media. What mainly motivated her was hatred and revenge, especially since passers-by insulted her and the police fined her for her full veil. She married a French jihadi convert, Axel Baeza from the southern town of Nîmes, who had a son and had already left France for Syria, and in the spring of 2012 she left France and joined him, leaving her two children with her mother. Before Baeza died in the war, she begot a son. From 2013 she actively participated in IS propaganda on the internet under the nickname "Umm Tawwab," including videos to attract girls and women to Syria (De Féo, 2016). In one of them she carried a sawed-off gun; in another she spoke to her sons in France to remind them of their Muslim identity. She attacked the wives of French soldiers stationed in Mali and voiced her desire to commit a suicide attack in France. She bore a deep hatred toward the Western world, spreading the rejection of her father to the entire civilization he belonged to.

Targeted in France by an inquiry following the departure of a dozen young women from the Nîmes region to Syria, she became a popular figure in the French-speaking jihadi star system.

Emilie König matches the model of the rebellious woman who needed another path than feminism to distinguish herself from other women, and once joining jihadis, she refused to be a mere jihadi bride. She became a prominent recruiter of women for Daesh: dozens of girls and women were subjugated by her charismatic personality and her warrior identity, which she built by joining al-Khansaa Brigade in Syria under the aegis of Daesh. She devoted her stamina to her jihadi vocation, sacrificing her family and the education of her two children whom she entrusted to their grandmother in France. She was arrested by the Kurdish forces in Syria on December 2017 and awaits trial. In her case as in many others, family crisis due to the loss of the father was essential to her revolt and her desire for revenge. She intended to take the place of the hated father and to become a "man," radical enough to upset the secular society (the extension of the father figure) through radical Islam. Allah's religion in its extremist version did not attract her so much for ideological reasons as for the capacity it endowed her with to fight against the mainstream society whose standards she aspired to transgress. What became sacred was the urge to say no, to become a "negative heroine." She singled herself out in a transgressive manner, rather than joining the anonymous crowd of lower middle-class people to which she was destined to belong. Her commitment to the military brigade al-Khansaa and her aspiration to fight like men displayed her desire for a violent brand of feminism in the name of jihad.

Anjem Choudhary was able to become a transnational recruiter for jihad. Born in 1967, he is a British Muslim lawyer of Pakistani origin close to Omar Bakri Muhammad, with whom he founded the radical group "al-Muhajiroun." Son of a middle-class stockbroker, he resided at Welling in Kent. Having failed medical school, he turned to law. In his youth, he used to drink alcohol and take drugs. In 1996 he married Rubana Akhtar who had joined al-Muhajiroun. She became the head of its women's section. The couple have four children. In 2009 he called for the stoning of homosexuals. He founded "Islam4UK" (which was banned on January 14, 2010) to push the United Kingdom toward an Islamic state. He allegedly influenced Michael Adebolajo who beheaded the soldier Lee Rigby. He also justified the execution of the American journalist James Foley on August 18, 2014, by IS, in retaliation for the military intervention of the Western coalition in Syria. He strongly condemned the caricaturists of the Prophet Muhammad, especially following the attack against *Charlie Hebdo* magazine in January 2015, considering the new caricature of Mohamed published on January 14, 2015, in that journal as an act of war.

For nearly twenty years Choudhary preached radical Islam on the streets, in mosques, and on TV, building up websites in the UK and inspiring Muslims abroad (especially in Belgium, "Islam4Belgium"). He made public statements such as: "There will be no more pubs, casinos, national lottery. All women should be covered appropriately, put on the niqab or veil, and so there will be no more prostitution. Around 2050, Britain will be a predominantly Muslim country. It will be the end of the freedom of democracy and (the beginning) of submission to God. We do not believe in democracy; as soon as they take power, Muslims should apply Sharia law" (Kern, "Anjem Choudhary," 2014). Choudhary judges everything by the Sharia, portraying an apocalyptic picture of the world under the Islamic rule, which allowed him to say: "In the Qur'an you are not allowed to feel sorry for a non-Muslim. I do not have regret for him [the journalist beheaded by Daesh]" (Kern, "Anjem Choudhary," 2014).

According to a study published in September 2014 by the conservative London-based Henry Jackson Society, one in five terrorists among those sentenced in Britain in the previous decade was a member of al-Muhajiroun, founded by Choudhary and the exile preacher Omar Bakri Mohammed (Dodd et al., 2016). In September 2016, Choudhary was sentenced by a British court to five-and-a-half years in prison for publicly supporting IS.

Like many Pakistani-English citizens, Choudhary has been disgruntled at being a Muslim in the UK. His reaction to English multiculturalism has been to reverse the role: instead of accepting his place as a member of an ethnic and religious minority, he wants to impose his religion on the majority to reverse a subaltern ethnicity. Above all, he feels that multiculturalism is a version of secularism and that it dissolves Muslim identity under the pretext of recognizing its place in the plural culture of an England that professes a faith of tolerance.

Originally from Thonon-les-Bains in Haute-Savoie, Mourad Farès came from a Moroccan family of six children. After graduating with a degree in Sciences, he did piecemeal studies, and ended up in catering and food service, gradually becoming a follower of radical Islam. After the pilgrimage to Mecca he was called "Murad Hadji." He started producing jihadi videos. On Facebook he called himself alternately "Abu'l Hassan," "Abu Rachid," or "Mourad al-Faransi." He made a forty-five-minute video entitled "Al Mahdi and the second Khilafah [caliphate]" against the backdrop of an apocalyptic catastrophe. The film presented high-definition video tricks and totaled several hundred thousand views. In 2013 he left for Syria and marked on Facebook: "Yes, I'm a terrorist, and proud of it!!! It is the supreme commandment of Allah!" He became a star in jihadi social networks. His parents went to the Turkish-Syrian border to bring him back to France, but he refused to follow them.

His method consisted in seducing on social networks young people to whom he sent a private phone number they could call, once they reached the Syrian border. More than a dozen young people from Strasbourg, mostly from the Meinau district, between the ages of twenty-three and twenty-five, fell under his spell, including Foued Mohamed Aggad (one of the future kamikazes of the November 13, 2015, Paris attacks) and two teenagers, ages fifteen and sixteen: Leïla, a high school student from Avignon, and Imran, a seventeen-year-old from Nice.

One of his videos shows Messiah appearing in Syria, which inspired jihadi vocations among young people, fascinated by his end-of-time story. He also displayed on the web pictures of himself in Syria in a warlike posture, armed to the teeth, aboard his 4×4, or riding a black steed. The narcissistic and exhibitionist dimension attracted young boys in quest of glory and virility.

Mourad Farès was from a middle-class family and did not follow the model of the juvenile delinquent from the poor districts. Before leaving for Syria, he sold his flat in Lyon. He suffered the stigmas of his Arab origin, and jihadism offered him a golden opportunity to display his antagonism toward French society, putting his creativity (video sequences) at the service of a superior cause. He refused to be an isolated, insignificant, and despised "Arab." Instead, he sought to strike fear into mainstream society, giving free rein to his end-of-time fantasies through his videos, which were inspired in their visual effects by American movies, in this way fascinating young Muslims.

He became the leader of a band of young people in search of fame and a cohesive community on two levels: in miniature, the one they were building around his personality, and at the larger level, within the imagined neo-Ummah, to be built in Syria.

The case of Rachid Kassim as a recruiter shows the multicultural face of radical Islam's proponents. Born in 1987 to a Yemenite father and Algerian mother, he grew up in a poor district called La Bourgogne in Roanne (a city of about 35,000 inhabitants where the social housing HLM constitutes 34 percent of the housing stock). His parents were not practicing Muslims, and they divorced when he was young. They each remarried;. his father espoused a non-Muslim French woman, and his mother had three children with her second husband, whom she also divorced in the year 2000. The second divorce was a shock to the adolescent Rachid, who abandoned school (he had been a good pupil), practiced karate, dreamed of becoming a champion, and went so far as to wear the "kimono" in the street. He became a rapper (Peyrand, 2016). In 2009 he became an animator at the social center where he supervised children. He refused to shake hands with women and asked for a prayer room. For these reasons, his contract was not renewed. At twenty-four in 2011, he recorded his first rap album. The title L'Oranais including the song titles *First Weapon*, and "I am a Terrorist" announced radical views. It was a commercial fiasco. The premise of his radicalization was already laid in his rejecting secular France. He contrasted his fundamentalist Muslim identity to laïcité (French secularism), asserting provocatively the exclusive legitimacy of a counter-secular religiosity. He was proselytizing in his neighborhood, distributing the Koran in Arabic to passers-by, asking them to hand it to those who read Arabic, and criticizing them for not going to the mosque for their daily prayers. He married a middle-class woman who converted to Islam, wore an airtight hijab that entirely covered her face (forbidden in France since 2010), and gave up her nursing studies to look after their child in the social housing neighborhood (HLM) where they lived. Kassim made a trip to Algeria, and came back radicalized in 2011, worrying other Muslims in the mosque he attended with his extremist views. In 2012 (according to other versions, in 2015) he left for Syria with his wife and three children.

Kassim was influenced by a charismatic convert, Julien B., a thirty-nine-year-old who advocated a radical version of Islam and praised Osama bin Laden in his discussions with young people in Roanne (Phan-Lë and Garcia, 2016).

In Syria, he beheaded many prisoners and made a show of them on the internet. He was a charismatic recruiter who succeeded in attracting dozens of young men and women to Syria, encouraging those remaining in France to carry out attacks there. He influenced Larossi Abballa, the killer of a police couple in Magnanville in June 2016, Adel Kermiche, who was in touch with him on the encrypted Telegram network and who killed Father Hamel in Saint-Etienne-de-Rouvray in July 2016, and Ines Madani, one of the three young women who tried to blow up a car full of gas cylinders near Notre Dame Church in Paris in September 2016.

On his group chat site "Sabre de Lumiere" ("Saber of Light") in the Telegram messaging desk, he made propaganda about the use of violence in the name of the holy war: "Many of us are jealous of the brothers who directly attack the areas considered as non-Muslim (especially France).. . . We think that even a small attack in these areas is more valuable than a major attack in Syria." (Digiacomi, 2016). Al-Adnani, the propaganda minister of Daesh, advocated attacking the countries where jihadis lived, in case they could not reach Syria. Kassim went a step further: he reversed the order of priorities and credited more merit in the name of Islam to the attacks in Europe than to those committed in Syria against Daesh's enemies. He heavily insisted in his messages to the two hundred to three hundred Telegram subscribers on this issue. Under his influence, at least fifteen people, under-aged or grown-up, performed violent actions in Europe.

Kassim transformed his biography from an insignificant "Arab" into an influential Daesh personality, becoming a famous person in the jihadi star system, and beyond it, worldwide, throughout French media. He was a renowned negative hero, hated and notorious in Europe (and particularly in France), famous for his cruelty in the Western jihadi sphere. He was killed by an American drone in February 2017 in Mosul (Iraq). IS gave the opportunity to many "insignificant" young men, with no bright future prospect, to become stars and to lead a meaningful life in their own eyes, by fighting the Western countries where they felt stigmatized and victimized.

Kassim also settled accounts with his parents. They were secular and divorced. He became anti-secular and married a woman who converted to the fundamentalist version of Islam. She wore the *burqa* (total veil) and, unlike Kassim's mother, stayed home to bring up her children. Kassim's family was the reverse image of his parents' family.

His case fits well into the dominant model of European jihadis: a disunited family, life in a disaffected, poor, ethnic neighborhood, internalization of slum culture, deviance, an irresistible desire for revenge linked to the humiliation experienced in an "arrogant" society, the psychological complex of the "ex-colonized" individual who still bears the burden of his colonized ancestors, deviance, radicalization, and total commitment to violence as the only way to cope with the mainstream society in the name of radical Islam. One of the counter-values appreciated by Kassim and, more generally, by the born-again Muslims belonging to the slum culture, is proselytizing, regarded by the mainstream culture as an assault on a religiously neutral public space, particularly in France. The more European societies become secular in their mores and customs, the more these young people advocate proselytism in its most mystifying forms, not only to attract others but also to challenge secular societies they hate. The more these societies become tolerant toward diversity, the more the adepts of jihadism preach bigotry and reject compromise with the mainstream culture as a sign of weakness and surrender. They not only reject the mainstream culture, they want to display, even over-exhibit, their repudiating it by ostentatious attitudes of defiance: they resort to the media and the web and use harsh words, a body gesture that borrows many features from the mimetic forms used in hard music concerts, and an "arrogance" that is as much a sign of contempt for society as it is the expression of over-narcissism.

The case of Mohammad Fakhri al-Khabass is that of a middle-class—even upper-middle-class—individual who turned radical. He was a doctor, the director of the cultural Islamic Association of the prestigious Khartoum University of Medical Sciences and Technology. Twenty medical students of English or American nationality and Sudanese origin joined the IS at his behest.

Fakhri was not an Islamist or a practicing Muslim in his youth. Son of a Palestinian doctor living in North London, as a child he had no connection to Sudan. His Arabic was more than rudimentary, and he spoke English with a British accent. He was interested in girls, drinking beer, and playing football. Then, he joined the University of Medical Sciences in Khartoum to finish his studies, which was recognized by the English academic authorities and was significantly cheaper than its English counterparts. He became a member of its Islamic Cultural Association, which was not marked until then by radical Islam. In 2011, that association became more militant in its public announcements, threatening of the fire of hell for young women without a veil as well as those men who would watch them.

Fakhri identified with this version of Islam and became a recruiting agent for this association, of which he became later the president. He targeted students from English-speaking countries of Sudanese origin. He encouraged them to disobey their parents and join IS. From then on, the young female members of the association donned a total veil, a *niqab*, a practice that had no historical roots in Sudan. Fakhri's technique was based on young people's guilt feelings: "How can you sleep at night knowing that Muslims are dying in Syria?" About the West, he said, "The West and Americans in particular are killing Muslims, why is it not okay for us to do the same thing?" (Morrison, 2015).

Fakhri played a leading role among the Anglo-Sudanese youth who felt deeply uprooted, neither Sudanese nor English. He transformed this double "non-belonging" into an exclusive jihadi identity in the name of radical Islam. He used their bad conscience when he wrote on Facebook: "You are in comfort and the only legitimate Islamic state embodying the caliphate needs you." He praised Daesh as a "pure" Islamic government, denouncing Western secular democracies with "their legislative polytheism and Satanism," which aimed above all at breaking the Islamic bond of young Muslims.

About twenty medical students, including some doctors, joined the IS, which testifies to the extent of Fakhri's charisma. This type of radicalization within a specific institution did not exist in France where secular mono-culturalism was an obstacle to this kind of identity, more tolerated by multiculturalism. In Fakhri's case, Palestinian nationalism gave way to radical Islam. This was also the case for Palestinians in Lebanon who were more attracted by jihadism than by Palestinian nationalism, once uprooted (Rougier, 2004). Jihadism provides a more satisfying remedy for uprooting than classical nationalism, which focuses on a specific enemy. By pointing to a general enemy, the West or even the whole world, jihadism provides a more gratifying response to the crisis of an identity in distress.

Trevor William Forest was a Jamaican convert to Islam who became a radical Islamic cleric, known as "Abdullah el Faisal" but also by various other names, including "Imam al Jamaikee" and "Sheikh Faisal." Born in 1963 into an evangelical Christian family belonging to the Salvation Army Church, he grew up in a small farming village about 20 kilometers from the city of Montego Bay in Jamaica. At the age of sixteen he converted to Islam. In 1981 he attended a series of six-week courses on culture and Islamic religion funded by Saudi Arabia. In 1983 he moved to Guyana where he studied Arabic and moved to Saudi Arabia in 1984 where he studied at Muhammad Ibn Saud University in Riyadh for seven years, after receiving a scholarship from the Saudi Government.

On the initiative of Sheikh Raji of Saudi Arabia, he was sent to the United Kingdom and became an imam at the Salafi Brixton Mosque in London. In 1992, he chose a second wife, Zubeida Khan, an English woman of Pakistani origin, obtaining thus a residence permit in the United Kingdom. In 1993, he was removed from the Brixton Mosque because of his radical preaching. Breaking with Saudi Arabia, he organized a conference entitled "The Devil's Deception of the Salafi Saudis" in which he attacked the direction of the mosque because of its submission to Saudi Arabia. He opened a study center at Tower Hamlet in East London and lectured in Birmingham, Dewsbury, Manchester, Cardiff, Coventry, and other mosques. Some of these lectures were transcribed and sold in Islamic bookstores. He encouraged Muslim mothers to educate their children to become jihadi soldiers by the age of fifteen. He recommended them to buy toy guns so that they were gradually trained in the spirit of the holy war. He also tried to seduce male schoolchildren, promising them seventy-two virgins in paradise in case they died as martyrs, encouraging them to kill disbelievers, comparing the latter to roaches. He rejected democracy and advocated confrontation and violence: "Our ideology is the bullet, not the ballot" (Judgment in Appeal of Crown v. El-Faisal, 2004). In a tape titled "The Standards of Jihad" he stated: "You must learn to shoot. You must learn how to fly planes, drive tanks and you must learn how to load your weapons and how to use missiles. You can use nuclear weapons only in countries that are 100% [inhabited by] disbelievers." He encouraged the use of "everything, even chemical weapons" to "exterminate unbelievers." In a sermon he explained his approach: "You can go to India, and if you see a Hindu down the road, you can kill him and take his money, it is clear, because there is no treaty of peace between us." He also suggested that the body of Hindus be used as fuel for power plants. According to him, "Jews should be killed . . . as by Hitler. . .. People with British passports, if you fly to Israel, it's easy. Fly to Israel and do everything you can. If you die, you are in heaven. How do you fight a Jew? You kill a Jew. In the case of Hindus, bombing their companies" (Attewill, 2007; "Mother of J'can mullah," 2003).

El Faisal was arrested on February 18, 2002, and sentenced to nine years in prison and was extradited to Jamaica in 2007. He had a decisive influence on the radicalization of a whole generation of young English Muslims like Richard Reid (he had a British mother and Jamaican father), and Germaine Lindsay, an Englishman of Jamaican origin, and Sidique Khan, who participated in the London bombings of 2005. He seduced Umar Farouk Abdulmutallab, alias "Omar Farooq al-Nigeri," a Nigerian born in December 1986 and nicknamed the "Underwear Bomber" for attempting to blow up a bomb hidden in his underwear aboard Northwest Airlines Flight 253 from Amsterdam to Detroit on Christmas Day, 2009. This attack was claimed by al-Qaeda in the Arabian Peninsula (AQPA). He is the Black convert that is against both "White societies" (those Western societies that dominate the world) and "fake Islam" (meaning Saudi Arabia and the other Muslim countries). He was deported back to Jamaica after having spent four years in prison in the UK. Black Jamaicans, mostly Christian, convert to Islam and in some cases radical Islam, like "Abu Izzadeen" (Trevor Brooks). In their view, Christian faith does not let them fight against humiliation and subjection to racism, the more so as it was the religion of the conquerors and European colonialists.

"Mullah Krekar," whose birth name was Najmaddin Faraj Ahmad, was born in July 1956 in Sulaymaniyah in Iraq. In 1991 he arrived in Norway as a refugee from Iraqi Kurdistan. His wife and four children are Norwegian citizens, but he is not. He speaks Kurdish, Arabic, and Persian and knows bits of Norwegian and English. He became a Kurdish, Iraqi, Sunni, and jihadi cleric. He is the leader of the Islamist armed group Ansar al-Islam, which began to fight in northern Iraq while Krekar enjoyed political refugee status in Norway. Since 2003, an eviction order from Norway has been issued against him, but it cannot be implemented because of insufficient guarantees from the Iraqi government about torture or the death penalty against him. He was tried by the Norwegian Supreme Court as a "danger to national security."

In November 2009, in an interview with the Arab television channel al-Hiwar, Krekar stated that he wanted to establish a new Islamic caliphate in Iraq, the only legitimate Islamic state being from his viewpoint the Taliban-led Islamic Emirate of Afghanistan. For the new Islamic government he wanted Osama bin Laden, Ayman al-Zawahiri (the heads of al-Qaeda), or Gulbuddin Hekmatyar (the founder of Hizb-e Islami) as leaders (Akerhaug, 2009).

In 2012 he was sentenced to five years in prison for threatening Norwegian politicians and Kurds. Krekar issued a *fatwa* (a ruling on a point of Islamic law) against Mariwan Halabjee, a writer and human rights activist sometimes referred to as the Salman Rushdie of Iraqi Kurdistan. Halabjee wrote *Sex, Sharia and Women in the History of Islam,* published in 2005. In his book he denounced Islam and Sharia for oppressing Muslim women. He fled Iraqi Kurdistan to Norway because a fatwa was issued against him, ordering his killing if he did not repent and denounce his book. In particular, he wrote that the Prophet had had nineteen wives, including a nine-year-old girl, Ayesha, when he was fifty-four, and should be considered guilty of murder and rape. He was granted political asylum in August 2006 in Norway. Krekar compared Mariwan Halabjee to Salman Rushdie and Ayaan Hirsi Ali (each of whom had written works that criticized Islamic practices) and prompted his execution in February 2012, according to his statement in an Oslo District Court. On December 6, 2012, the Court of Appeal found him guilty of four counts of intimidation under aggravating circumstances. It ordered, among other things, Krekar to serve two years, ten months in prison.

Krekar does not belong to the category of disaffected youth who do not have a recognized identity and live in a double denial (neither French nor Arab, neither English nor Pakistani, etc.). He has a fundamentalist Muslim identity and it is by excess of its solidity that he inveighs against the West. Yet he has taken refuge in Norway and has benefited from many of its facilities. In his case, it is his intolerance of others that prevails, in regard to a fundamentalism that is rooted in the Islamic tradition. It is an incompatibility of values that is not rooted in a history of humiliation or symbolic abuse on the part of a European society. It is an incompatibility of values that is rooted in the opposition between tradition and modernity and not in the crisis within modernity itself.

Born in 1986, Mohyeldeen Mohammad is a Norwegian-Iraqi. He is closely related to the fundamentalist group "Profetens Ummah" and has become a controversial figure in Norway. Born in Manchester, England, in 1986 to Iraqi parents, his family emigrated to Norway in 1989 and settled in Larvik. In 2006 he legally changed his name to "Giovanni," an Italian name meaning "God is grace." In January 2007 he went back to his old name and in 2009 he began studying Islamic law at the University of Medina in Saudi Arabia until his expulsion in 2011 as a political activist. Back in Norway, during a demonstration in Oslo on February 12, 2010, he publicly denounced, in the face of some three thousand Muslims, the newspaper *Dagbladet*, which had published a caricature of the Prophet, portraying him in a disgraceful manner (https://upclosed.com/people/mohyeldeen-mohammad/). He denounced Norway's insensitivity, which could face an attack similar to those of September 11, 2001 in the US. His remarks were condemned by the Islamic Council of Norway. He had no job, at least since mid-2009. He married in 2011 but it ended in divorce after three months. In 2012 he left Norway for Syria. He was then photographed with jihadis, holding a machine gun in one of the photos. The following month he posted a video of himself on YouTube, armed with automatic weapons, warning Norwegian authorities against spreading lies. According to the authorities, he was one of at least thirty Norwegian Islamists volunteering in the war (Sandelson, 2012).

Returning the same year to Norway, he tried to raise funds for Islamist rebels, in conjunction with the "Profetens Ummah." His statements against homosexuals and their fully justified punishment in Syria as well as the legitimate beheading the American journalist James Foley, in his view, were the titles of his accusations in Norwegian courts.

First-Generation Radicalization

Mohyeldeen Mohammad's case as well as Mullah Krekar's point to the fact that some first-generation traditionalist Muslims become radical once they are in touch with Western secular societies. Their malaise is distinct from the second- or third-generation Muslims. In their case, Western society is sinful due to the large gap with their own traditional values. It is not an identity crisis that leads them to confront the West but a solid identity, firmly rooted in their psyche. They are not caught between two stools, torn between two equally inaccessible identities, as is the case of the second-or third-generation

Muslims in Europe. We are facing the incompatibility between a strongly rooted traditionalist Muslim identity that refuses to adapt, and the European secular way of life. It is not a fragile Self resorting to violence to overcome its weaknesses (the disaffected youth) but a strong traditionalist ego that rejects European standards (recognition of homosexuality, of religious "apostasy," of gender equality, and so forth) in the name of its own entrenched values. Radicalization is the consequence of the immersion of this identity within a non-religious culture where the individual is not inserted in a religious culture or in a traditional civilization where taboos linked to collective norms take precedence over freedom.

h-Jihadis and Prison

From country to country, different organizations can host radical people. For instance, Hizbu Tahrir had been able to marginally infiltrate some universities in the UK, but no such organization was active in France.

Likewise, the hospital and the faculty of medicine became a place of radicalization and refuge for some people in the UK, in France the hospital being mostly immune to it.

The mosque was for a long time directly (like the Finsbury Park mosque) or indirectly (like the Adda'wa mosque of the Stalingrad district in Paris) one of the locations of radicalization. It can also be a site of radical socialization for young people encouraged by the leadership of the mosque (this was the case of the Arrahmane mosque in Bienne in Switzerland) or without the knowledge of the latter (Adda'wa mosque in Paris).

Prison remains the major locus of radicalization throughout Europe.

According to official figures available in France, out of a population of around 70,000 detainees in 2019, 500 were imprisoned as terrorists (condemned or awaiting judgment) and 1,200 were considered as radicalized, although not condemned for terrorism ("Détenus radicalisés," 2019). Many violent jihadis who perpetrated attacks in France had spent long periods of time in prison, including Mohamed Merah, Fabien Clain, Mehdi Nemmouche, the Kouachi brothers, Amedy Coulibaly, and Chérif Chekatt.

Radicalization in prison is part of a trajectory through various stages for the people, mostly belonging to the poor ethnic districts in Europe. Radical socialization by the adoption of a counterculture (which I called the slum culture) grounded in the hatred of society becomes tenacious in prison, and the contact between different prisoners gives rise to informal networks, likely to be activated once they are freed.

The case of Mahmood, a recidivist in his early thirties in March 2013 when the interview took place in Fresnes (a prison close to Paris), gives an insight into radicalization there. Although in his case it did not end up with violent action, the influence of preachers and recruiters, family crisis, and misery in prison were undeniably important in his inclination toward radical Islam at that time:

Interviewer: Can you tell me the history of your family?

Mahmood (after a long negotiation): I didn't have a father worthy of the name. He was mute, he did not talk to us, and sometimes he beat us badly. Once my mother told me that he'd been bullied as a child. He didn't have a real childhood because he started working very early, at the age of nine or ten and then, in France, he had worked hard in the factory and when he was pensioned after more than three decades, his body was in bad shape and his mind was crushed. That made him insensitive to our pains. He did not provide us, three sons and two daughters, with what the French give to their children: love and education. He left us when I was fifteen, and went to Algeria where he married another woman, much younger. His pension was miserable in France, but in Algeria he was well-off and could take a young woman from a good family that could be his daughter. He left us alone, my mother took care of us. Among brothers, we fought a lot. My older brother tried to substitute for the father; he was brutal, and was almost four years older than me. He often beat me for peanuts, just to prove that he was the boss. I began stealing and had a gang leader [*caïd*] *who took what we got and paid me something in exchange. Then, I began selling shit* [drugs] *and I paid my mother. She was all too happy and did not ask me where the money came from, but she certainly knew that it was not legal. She acted like she didn't know.*

Question: you told me that in prison there was a man who tried to radicalize you.

Mahmood: I have been put in jail many times. Once, I was tired and sick. One day, in prison, a bearded man [*un barbu*, a Muslim fundamentalist, sometimes with a pejorative meaning] *told me that I was in* [a state of] *sin and would go to hell. If I wanted to be redeemed, I had to fight for the sake of Allah. We had discussions, he told me a lot about mischief against Muslims in the West, and particularly in France.*

Question: Why didn't you take his advice?

Mahmood: Because after a few weeks he was sent to another prison. The guards saw him proselytizing, and they changed his prison, to end his influence on other inmates. It's one of their strategies for keeping the peace in prison. For a while, I was impressed by what he said and to tell the truth, it was an escape from my life of misery: no real family, no father, no education, I had given up school at the age of fourteen, I was desperate for my life outside prison as well as inside it, and I didn't believe there was a way out at the end of my sentence. Dying for God was a reward and in the Next world I was sure I would find myself in heaven in spite of all the sins I'd committed in my life, if I died a martyr. I was close to act the way the bearded man had said, I could have killed a guard or two. But since he was sent away, I somehow lost the will to do so. If he was here, under his influence I would have taken the risk. But in his absence, I didn't have the push to go further. Even now, there are days when I feel like fighting with the guards and killing them in the name of Allah.

We see the importance of the preacher and recruiter, but the background is paramount: social misery and a deep sense of despair, as much in society as in the penitentiary, and beyond that, a moment of sickness: a mixture of revolt and fatigue is often decisive in making the transition to a violent action in the name of jihad in individual cases.

i-Jihadi Stardom

Jihadi stardom was based on the "deeds" of the agents (mostly male), on the spectacular actions they carried out in Iraq and Syria or in Europe. In the latter case, some jihadis became stars among the youth of the poor ethnic districts in Europe. For them, these people were a source of pride, they represented those who, while belonging to their social milieu, dared reject or even reverse humiliation and their sense of unworthiness, so deeply rooted in slum culture. Many admired them, although they did not follow them in their violent action. There were national and international jihadi stars. Mohamed Merah became a national star among the second- and third-generation North African youth of the poor districts in France, while Coulibaly brothers have attained international fame for having killed many journalists from the satirical magazine *Charlie Hebdo*. In France, Mohamed Merah has been at the apex of fame, in prisons (where there are a high proportion of poor suburbs' youth) and in the disadvantaged, ethnic districts all over the country. Born in 1988, he was killed in March 2012 by the police, refusing to surrender and seeking death through martyrdom. His violent acts in 2012 (he killed three Muslim military men and four Jews, among them three children) was not so much spectacular according to the number of people killed but through the staging and dramatization as well as his family's reaction: the mother said that her son had put France on its knees; his sister privately expressed pride about him. Beyond that, Merah opened a new cycle of jihadism in France. For seventeen years, French society did not experience jihadi attacks, the latest one being Khaled Kelkal's 1995 attacks in Paris subway. In contrast to Merah, Kelkal did not attain the same kind of fame; he had undertaken his actions for the sake of the Algerian jihadi group GIA, in order to punish France for its support to the Algerian military regime. Merah was acting in the name of Islam, not of another country, his aim was endogenous, namely to chastise those who acted against Islam: the Muslim soldiers he killed were part of the French army that made war in Afghanistan, against a Muslim country; as for the Jews, in his eyes their support for Israel and their privileged position in France were a splinter in the Muslims' bones. Merah is still regarded with pride by many young, disaffected youth in France. Jihadi stardom favors acts that highlight the humiliation of the former colonizer or the "White man," reversing the situation in a theatrical manner. Acts marked by unbearable cruelty, experienced as being sadistic and ruthless, find their ways in the pantheon of jihadi stardom. We can also mention the case of "Jihadi John" who beheaded, in front of the camera, prisoners of Daesh in 2014 and 2015. He was killed in a US drone attack in November 2015 and became notorious in the English world, although European jihadis credited him with virility and warrior's merits.

Jihadi stardom is based on the figure of the "negative hero" who embodies the counter-values of Western societies: they praise violence in ways regarded as excessive or even unbearable by the European public opinion (they cut off heads, take them by the hair, and parade them), and this violence is put on display on social networks. Exhibitionism of this type would not have existed without the new social media outlets that allow everyone to become a potential filmmaker. The web is a necessary condition for its thriving, the imitation effect being exponentially multiplied. The jihadi star system is mainly based on the spectacular transgression of the moral taboos in the modern world through violent action whose aim is to repel the majority and to attract a minority, namely those who resent the mainstream society and its values that exclude them. Because violence is illegitimate in its harsh forms even against the culprits in the mainstream European culture, jihadism encourages extreme forms of cruelty and displays them in a provocative manner, as much to frighten the onlookers as to seduce future candidates who would take pleasure in infringing moral canons (teenagers, belated adolescents, resentful people belonging to the slum culture, and the mentally disturbed).

Women took their place in the jihadi stardom system and reached celebrity by their messages on the web, their ability to lure other women to Syria or to make sensational statements drawing the attention of the world media. The negative heroines breached the image of female non-violence, making statements that declared Muslim values incompatible to those of the non-Muslims, denounced Western society characterized by vice and homosexuality, and often claimed their ability to directly exercise violence, if necessary, at the service of the caliphate. This was the case of the French female jihadi Emilie König, the English Samantha Louise Lewthwaite, and the Italian Maria Giulia Sergio, whose statements on the web were of unusual violence.

Jihadi stardom multiplies imitation effects, letting young people dream of fame through excessive deeds that are glorified in the European jihadi counter-culture.

V
The Jihadis and the Family

As regards Europeans jihadis, in many cases the analysis of their family background sheds light on their radicalization. Some configurations, such as the single-parent family or stepfamily, play a role in young people's radicalization, particularly broken families, especially among Muslims living in ghettoized neighborhoods.

Some people used family as the setting for their violent action, brothers, sisters, cousins, and, more exceptionally, fathers or mothers (Alexander, 2019). For others, coming from broken families, jihadi violence was a continuation of family violence. In some cases, members of crisis-stricken families (brothers, cousins) were reconciled through their joint participation in jihadi action.

The problem of jihadism in relation to the family is an essential theme that has been marginally developed so far from an anthropological perspective (Ferret, Khosrokhavar, and Domingo, forthcoming[1]).

Let's take the case of Adil, a French-Algerian in his twenties, a lower-middle-class man, with an undergraduate diploma from the university in computer sciences who had a job and was not among the disaffected Muslim youth. He had troubles with the Intelligence services for his radical writings on the web in 2014. His family ties had been broken, like those of many immigrants' sons, due to the diabolic design of France toward Muslims. According to him, the former colonial power intended to reign by dividing Muslims and destroying their identity via their families:

Question: How do you explain the crisis of the family among the migrants' sons and daughters, in particular the high number of single mothers?

Adil: Algerian families are in distress because the French did so much harm to them during the colonial times and after. They broke them. Islam scared them, it scares them now, in the past, and in the future! What bothers them so much is that Islam plays such an important role in our lives. We are Muslims before being Algerians, French, or anything else. The French don't like a Muslim family. They want a family in which the girls are unveiled

Jihadism in Europe. Farhad Khosrokhavar, Oxford University Press. © Oxford University Press 2021.
DOI: 10.1093/oso/9780197564967.003.0005

[sans voile], with short mini-skirts that show their legs, in brief, secular [laïque])and godless women. If our families are in such a bad shape, it's because the French wanted us to be inferior and always submissive. Muslim family is not what it used to be because the colonial power destroyed it from within.

Question: What happened to your family?

Adil: My father left my mother and went back to Algeria [au bled, literally "to the village"], *my mother had to provide for our shelter and everything, but the boys did not listen to her. She had no authority, and she was at times desperate. My eldest brother became a dealer to provide for the family. He ended up in prison. It is a miracle that I did not follow in his footsteps.*

Question: But you said that you were critical of your father, regarding religion as well.

Adil: Yes, he has been too submissive, and did not defend the rights of the Muslims. He accepted the French way of dealing with religion: "It is only private," as they say; but why? What God has commanded cannot be only private. I discussed with a Frenchman, a non-Muslim, he said that the French sought to break the Algerian family to smash any resistance against them in the colonial period. They succeeded only by half, and Algeria won its independence. But the family remains in bad shape. The sons challenge the authority of the father in the name of French modernism, that is French secularization [laïcité française].

Question: But after all, your father did not behave well towards you and your mother. The French had nothing to do with it!

Adil: Yes, but here too, France has broken the father's moral sense towards his family, she has filled his head with selfishness and lack of morals. My father went to Algeria and remarried twice, he trampled on his duty to his children and wife.

Adil finds two components in the crisis of the Algerian family (and, by extension, "Arab" family): on one hand, it is broken because of the French colonization; on the other hand, the authority of the father is contested by the sons under the impact of the French culture, the mother alone being unable to support the family, neither financially, nor in terms of moral authority. The sons become deviant to help her. The culture of laïcité is denounced as being godless and against Islam. Laïcité is, for many second- and third-generation sons of migrants, a neo-colonial way of acting against them; it combines the "arrogance" of the former colonizer with a deep disrespect for religion, and especially Islam, which is their culture. In so doing, it destroys the authority within Muslim families. At the same time, Adil is critical of his own father who was not confrontational toward the French in the defense of Allah's religion. He blames the French culture and society for the ills from which Muslim families suffer. For the sons and grandsons of the North African migrants, Islam has become a principle of identity because laïcité is experienced as another way of expressing colonial contempt toward them. In this respect, it is much more than a sheer religion, especially in confrontation with an aggressive version of secularism that seems to operate more and more as a civil religion in France. The latter acts, in turn, as a push factor toward radicalization, the defense of Islam becoming the defense of one's dignity against those who desecrated Allah's religion and colonized them in the past, showing now contempt for the culture of the ex-colonized people, adding insult to injury by treating them in a contemptuous manner.[2] Adil's attitude, attributing the crisis within North African families in France to the French colonial policy, is uncommon among those I interviewed. Still, it is in unison with the general view, largely spread among the sons of North African migrants, that all the ills are the fault of the former colonizer. In other European countries the mainstream culture is less confrontational, still multicultural policies are regarded as a means to exclude Muslims from the dominant culture by assigning them an inferior status in society, from the perspective of many disaffected young Muslims.

In the radicalization of young people of immigrant origin, the "complex of the ex-colonized" plays a significant role. It prevents them from taking responsibility for their own situation by constantly putting the blame on the ex-colonizer and thus, making themselves feel like total victims. The mainstream society's view of these young people is also imbued, in its own way, with the "complex of the ex-colonizer," who finds fault with them for many of the shortcomings due to the way society itself treated them, making them scapegoats for its inadequacies in their regard. A vicious circle sets in motion, which makes the problem insoluble unless both sides manage to increase their capacity for dialogue and self-criticism.

The traditional patriarchal family was based on the rigid distinction between the roles of the father, mother, and children. This model was put into question, especially under the impact of feminism, which sought to create an egalitarian family and challenged the subordinate role of women in the family and the public sphere. At the same time, the capitalist economy favored female labor and after the weakening of the Welfare State in the 1980s and 1990s, both women and men had to work to cover household expenses. Women have thus gained financial autonomy, which in turn enabled them to divorce more easily, and to have the subjective freedom to end life together in a family that did not meet their individual requirements. After several decades, a patriarchal family and its mindset based on the supremacy of the husband has become marginal and various configurations, more or less unstable, have emerged: single-parent, same-sex, stepfamilies, and non-legally married couples.

The non-authoritarian and sometimes even effusive relations within the modern family results in a new distribution of roles and power in it: the prominence of the father's authority is called into question, the culture of negotiation allows emotional closeness between parents and children, and practically nothing is taboo except physical violence, which causes revulsion, but also fascination, for example through imagined jihadi action.

The problem arises as to how, despite their culture of proximity, in so many cases parents were unaware of the radicalization and the departure to Syria of their adolescent progeny, girls and boys included. How did the latter manage to hide from them their feelings and inclinations toward Islamic radicalism? In a sense, one can argue that the concealment to parents came from the remnants of the old patriarchal culture that persists, despite major anthropological changes within the modern family. But more profoundly, modern culture introduces a growing distance between youth culture and the culture of their parents, the lack of formal authority liberating the former from the hold of the latter. The distance is accentuated on one hand by the attachment of their children to their peer groups, and on the other hand by communication technologies (internet and smartphones) that leave parents unaware of their children's exchanges with each other and with radicalized people who influence them through Facebook, Twitter, and the like, unbeknownst to them. The web creates areas that escape parental authority.

The aspiration to transgression has become all the more attractive as the authority has become more accessible, less frontal, more porous, less repressive, making its infringement the easier without any guilt feeling on the part of the teenagers who have not internalized the sanctification of authority, in contrast to the patriarchal culture. In the past, intangible boundaries between parents and children made transgression tantamount to desecration and resulted in severe punishment or even self-punishment through an intense guilt-feeling. The Oedipus complex meant that "killing" (disobeying) the father or rebelling against his authority would end up with chastising oneself (Oedipus blinded himself after having killed his father and married his mother). Teenage jihadis in general do not express guilt feelings, the sanctity of authority having been broken long before they joined IS. Among the girls, the mother has become the authority to demolish: young girls join Daesh in order to put into question the newly conquered authority of the mother by seeking early marriage, contrary to her (feminists married late in order to conquer their freedom as citizens), early motherhood (in contrast to their mothers who became pregnant in their thirties), a renewed creation of the private sphere devoted to the mother, and retreat from the public sphere (against the wishes of their mothers and grandmothers who had fought to conquer the public sphere through feminism). Due to the immanent and softened authority in the modern family, transgression has become all the easier, without the teenagers harboring a bad conscience. The success of jihadism in Europe is, among other things, the consequence of the lack of sacred standards embodied by the parents in the mainstream culture. The father who was the custodian of the sacred norms has become an old brother, transcendent authority changing into an immanent one. Authority can be challenged without a feeling of transgressing untouchable taboos. It has become lax and fragmented, with no sense of guilt surrounding its infringement, intellectuals even speaking of the end of authority, in particular at the political level (Renaut, 2004). In this new configuration, challenging the father has become easy, even mundane, contrary to the patriarchal authority whose questioning had an exorbitant price in psychological and institutional terms. The broken authority desecrates kinship, creating a vacuum in the minds of young people. Some of them who suffered from dismantled families dream of an idealized patriarchal family, in which universal harmony would be restored around the united parents (not separated or disunited, as it is nowadays). In that imagined neo-patriarchal family, an "authentic" authority, transcendent and even repressive, would replace the soft power of the father in the modern shaky family.

The shrewd IS propaganda machine used this crisis of authority to fit it into the video sequences that would make young wannabe jihadis dream about their future in Syria: a family made of a mother who would bear "lion cabs" and a father who would be a glorious knight of Islam, both united in their wish to build up an effusive community (the neo-Ummah) under the aegis of a super-father, the caliph. Through the dreamlike heroism of the father, and the outstanding dedication of the mother, coupled with romanticism, exoticism, and playfulness, these young people believed they could take part in a vibrant and organic community not only within their household but also in the imagined Islamic Umma at large (the neo-Ummah). IS also manipulated young people through recruiters (local or through the web) who played the role of dream merchants. Their maneuvering was based on the desire among young people to find a family of substitution (the neo-Ummah as an enlarged harmonious family), and a new idealized kinship that would end the desecration of authority. Restoring the authority, whose absence had caused young people to suffer, was one of Daesh's favorite themes, and it proposed an undisputed authority, that of the caliph, as a superlative father, in the face of the dislocated authority of the father within the European family.

In this context, the promises made by IS went hand in hand with the desire of empowerment by the young Europeans. There wasn't on the one side victims and on the other, manipulators. Each side tried to realize their aims by using the degree of freedom they acquired in their interaction. In the extreme cases of fragile adolescents or psychologically disturbed individuals, IS manipulation got the upper hand but in other cases, the dreams sold by the caliphate were partially realized during the years 2014–2016 in Syria, where young people did find the opportunity to become "heroes," benefit from a good standard of living among the European lower-class recruits, and change their status from "nobody" to "somebody" in a glorious manner, from their viewpoint as well as the thirty thousand Foreign Fighters who joined Daesh from all over the world.

Many adolescents expressed the desire to end the soft authority of their parents and establish themselves as poles of authority in the virtual world through playfulness, laughter, jokes, irony, and similar expressions on the web, like "PTDR" (short for *pété de rire*, literally "broken with laughter"), "MDR" (*mort de rire*, "dying of laughter") or "LOL" (laughing out loud) (McDonald, 2018). In this manner, the way out of adolescence through Jihadism borrowed many features from virtual games in which fun culture played a key role. Within it the frontiers between life and death became fuzzy, as in the games in which teenagers go to the extremes and sometimes die. Harassment in the internet games like "Momo Challenge" went hand in hand with games at school like hazing or initiation rituals.

Through new social technologies, teenagers bypassed parental authority. Young boys or girls who went to Syria had several Facebook accounts, hidden from their parents, by which they contacted Daesh recruiters or friends who were already in Syria. Their parents were "illiterate" compared to them, regarding the web. The internet enlarged adolescents' autonomy, making the already diluted parents' authority even shakier. The flaws were exploited by Daesh. The web was flooded with video sequences encouraging young people to leave, appealing to their cultural sensitivity (as when a young Daesh girl, imitating L'Oréal's advertising, claimed that she was leaving for Syria because she was "worth it").

The fragmentation of authority made the symbolic figure of the father accessible and instead of seeking to kill him, the young teenager intended to become his brother and be recognized as an adult on his side, so much that he had become harmless in middle class stepfamilies. The Oedipus complex did not seem to operate in that context. The adolescent sought at all costs to overcome minority and reach majority by achieving equality with his father who was not an obstacle to his self-assertion, society being the main culprit, with its norms and postponement of adulthood for teenagers. The desire to become adult seemed even more legitimate as in the handling of virtual technology the teenager was superior to his parents, feeling at ease on the keyboard of his computer, in contrast to them. Sometimes he was so deeply immersed in the new technologies that he almost lost touch with reality and lived through a "web-culture" that had its own rituals, its "family members," and its "enemies."

Until the last decades of the twentieth century, middle-class parents believed that their offspring would benefit from a higher standard of living than theirs. The ever-increasing social climb was part of the family's identity, and parents thought in brighter terms about the future of their children than theirs. In the last decades, this view has been shaken by the evolution of the Western world and its economy: parents are afraid for their children; they think social downsizing, or even proletarianization, lies ahead, and their progeny might have a lower standard of living than theirs. Social disorganization, especially the growing fragility of the family unit, haunts them as well. To the economic problems one can add up a sense of moral decay and cultural degeneracy: drugs, sexual permissiveness, fear of homosexuality—one can be open-minded about homosexuality in general but reject it when it comes to one's own children—and lack of social norms shake confidence in the future. This explains why sometimes members of the middle classes sold their goods and gave up the comfort of their present life to go to Syria and "participate in jihad," in part at least for fear of the future for their children, devoid of sexual and moral taboos. This was the case of a young middle-class family from the town of Orleans in north-center France, Antony and Sabrina, respectively twenty-eight and twenty-three years old, who left for

Syria. In their interview, the mother and the father talked about their three-year-old daughter for whose future, morally speaking, departure to Syria was the best solution in their eyes, to protect her from moral decay (Kefi, 2014).

In discussions with parents, I have been able to identify this anxiety about a future whose uncertainty, economic as much as moral, targeted their children, and sometimes made them slam the door and leave, although they were shielded from poverty in a foreseeable future. The imaginary that presided over this attitude was rooted in fear of the future and anxiety about the growing fragility of the family unit. In October 2014 a young Muslim Frenchman of North African origin, who was a computer science technician[3] with a good salary in Paris, was desperate, being caught between contradictory demands of his faith and the secular world he lived in:

Interviewer: How old are you and what is your project? You told me that you hesitate a lot.

Mohamed: I am twenty-six years old, I am an Information Technology specialist, married to a Muslim woman. We have a girl, a year and a half. I am a devout Muslim.

Question: What is your concern?

Mohamed: I am very much concerned about my girl's future in this country. She might turn lesbian, or have many sexual partners, without building up a pious family and living in a licit [halal] *manner, according to the laws of God. This society does not make life easy for me and my wife. We are afraid for the future of our daughter, morally speaking. Will she be a good Muslim in a country where Islam is disliked and everything is done to discourage her from following God's path? I am also obsessed with Syria. The new caliphate was declared a few months ago* [end of June 2014] *and it is my religious duty to go and help them, that overrides everything else.*

Interviewer: Do you intend to leave France for elsewhere, for instance Syria?

Mohamed: I am tempted. But on the other hand, I am also committed to life here. My wife teaches mathematics, she got a Capes [a state diploma to be a teacher, providing job security as a civil servant]. *With our incomes, we live well. Syria is a new country, IS is at war with its neighbors, and I very much doubt that Western countries will let it live, unless it gives up its principles. I also have a responsibility to my daughter: if she falls ill, who would care for her in Syria? I have family ties here: my brother and sister live here, my father is dead, but my mother is close to us. I am from a modest family. My father was a worker at Renault* [a French car maker] *and he was able to feed us all with his modest salary. He worked overtime and sold goods here and there. We have all good jobs, contrary to many young people from the poor suburbs. My father did everything he could to give us a decent life, and he kept a strict watch on us, so we wouldn't slip up like many young people from the poor districts. He wouldn't let us go out and mix with delinquent youth. We all owe him our good situation and an unending gratitude. . . .*

Question: What about Islam?

Mohamed: He gave us a real Islamic culture, we did our daily prayers, we never acted in a non-Islamic manner. But he never let politics mix with religion.

Question: Then, what is your problem?

Mohamed: I am caught between the hard and the rock: on the one hand, the imperative duty of joining the IS as an Islamic government, the fardh al ayn *as we call it, and on the other, family concerns, my mother and my siblings, and above all, my little girl and my wife. My way out is to say that Islam needs also to protect the family: taking care of my little girl is also an imperative duty. The choice between the two duties falls to the individual. I personally choose my girl.*

Like Mohamed, many young people hesitated and at the end, did not join IS for fear of losing their family ties and their jobs. They appreciated their middle-class status, being mostly of modest working-class origin. They owed to their parents their success stories, finding it hard to go to Syria against their parents' wishes. Between contradictory demands, some chose to go to Syria, many chose not to go, although they believed they should. Their habits of life and their sense of responsibility to their elders and their children averted their departure.

Part of the difference between them and those who went to Syria stemmed from ideology. Many like Mohamed thought that they had to join the Islamic state because it was the caliphate and they had to perform an imperative religious duty, in the traditional sense. They did not share Daesh's radical ideology; often their resentment against society was offset by their family loyalties and economic integration. It was an abstract religious duty that preoccupied them, as in the case of Mohamed we have just seen. When to this motivation was added another one, namely hatred of society and the will to fight against it, leaving for Syria became much more attractive. Add to this the quest for social ascension and revenge against a hostile world that had made life unhappy, especially in poor and excluded neighborhoods, and the attraction of Daesh became almost irresistible.

a-Major Types of Jihadi Families

A large number of jihadis come from four types of families.

The first is what we will call the headless patriarchal family, often found in the ethnic poor districts in Europe. It is mainly the case of many North African families transplanted in France since the 1960s. The French secular system contributed to the discredit of its religious dimension and the father lost much of his former authority. The disappearance of the latter (stretching from divorce to leaving France and joining Algeria or Morocco, or simply remaining idle within the family) left the traditional patriarchal family "headless," the vacuum of the father's authority not being filled by another member. Single parenthood (the mother assumes the role of the head of the family) became more and more frequent. The North African fatherless family kept alive the subliminal values of patriarchy, the family living in a crisis generated by the lack of legitimate authority within it. The big brother, or the one who was the most aggressive, often replaced the father, without yielding his moral authority, and, in the absence of this essential ingredient, he was forced to use sheer violence against other members of the family to establish himself as a de facto leader. Sometimes the uncle fulfilled that role for a while. The single-parent family is often more violent in the absence of the father than in his presence. The evanescent authority in these families causes many more clashes, each son trying to take the coveted place of the paternal authority. The young person who radicalizes often declares that he recognizes no other authority than God and denies his father's legitimacy, God's representative in the person of the caliph or the charismatic recruiter replacing the fallen father. The young man attributes to himself the privilege of designating the authority, assuming the role of the ultimate arbitrator, arrogating the right to cancel the father's authority in the name of his self-proclaimed legitimacy. The drama unfolds in three acts: the young son discovers the disappearance of the father and becomes an inconsolable "orphan" (the father is dead, or he is absent, at any rate dead in terms of his vanishing authority). Then he tries to take the place of the absent father by establishing himself through violence as the chief of the family. Then comes a moment when he discovers a godly authority, the "super-father," in the person of the caliph (or the guru, or the head of a jihadi group, the emir) who becomes the supreme authority. The vacant place of the father who was for a time filled by the son is eventually handed over to the caliph, the ultimate authority who finally restores the family to its integrity and puts an end to the discord within it. The caliph is the ultimate substitute for the father, his power extending to social relations, public and private. This is nothing less than totalitarianism in the name of the lost father.

The second type of Jihadi family is what we call neo-traditional. This is notably the case of many Pakistani or Bangladeshi families in the United Kingdom who have maintained a rigid structure because of their capacity to establish communities and to live within them in non-mixed neighborhoods. It is also the case of Turkish families in Germany. Their preserved or even stiffened structure is out of step with the English or German societies where the evolution is toward a patchwork family (stepfamily). However, one of the reasons for the survival of the neo-traditional family is precisely its stability, proposing a "haven of peace" within the modern, turbulent, unstable world. In the neo-traditional family, the gap is not as deep between the generations as in the headless patriarchal family, the authority of the father being preserved, arranged marriages being rather the norm, and the family being shielded from the external world by the patriarchal principle, which is respected by the younger generations. Unlike the single-parent model, this type of family within the Southeast Asian community preserves the paternal authority that remains forceful in everyday relations among the family members. Even though it shows signs of wear, it maintains its cohesion because it is the pole of stability in a multicultural system that fluctuates according to the communities and social values. But this type of family can generate a revolt and transgression, being too rigid and less and less adapted to the modern global setting. Young generations feel suffocated. Paradoxically, the urge to put it into question emerges among them by denouncing its lack of conformity to Islam rather than in terms of Western individualism. The younger generation's revolt against it voices its discontent through accentuating Islamic prohibitions. They criticize the father who drinks, the mother who is not tightly veiled, the sister who has a lax attitude to wearing the veil.

The third type of family within which jihadi attitudes emerge among the sons and daughters is modern and secular, and in particular is the stepfamily, particularly among converts or secularized Muslim middle classes. It is based on the egalitarian model in which the configuration and distribution of authority are constantly challenged and negotiated between husband and wife, as well as parents and children. This family is marked by a certain instability: children of the first marriage live generally with their mother (less frequently with their father), the authority being diluted between the father and the stepfather, the mother and the stepmother. Autonomous spaces appear because of the multiplication of the figures of "father" and "mother" and the authority split between them. The leitmotif of children to step-parents is often heard: "You are not my father (or my mother), don't give me orders!"

An intermediary case between the headless patriarchal family and the modern stepfamily in crisis is through a marriage between a person belonging to an ethnic minority and another one, of European cultural root: a North African and a French, a Pakistani and an English, man or woman. In these marriages, children become either non-religious or Muslim in many of the cases that I observed (mainly in prison and in the French poor districts), due to the fact that European identity is usually secular or softly religious. Muslim faith gives a status to the individual who suffers from a "diluted identity" and who seeks refuge in Islam. In prison I met with many people of this type (Khosrokhavar, 2016). What makes the progeny choose Islam over Christianity or agnosticism is the need to assume a strong identity: being French (or English) is usually too broad for those who suffer from an identity crisis. Being a Christian is not distinctive enough and does not provide an identity antagonistic to that of mainstream society. Islam makes it easy to define oneself in an assertive manner, and radical Islam, in an offensive manner. Within this type of family, father and mother live in two cultural worlds and their disagreement usually heightens the authority crisis. Children are caught between two cultural worlds whose bonds depend on the mutual understanding between their parents. The contradictions between the North African (Moroccan, Algerian, or Tunisian) and the French culture, or the Asian (Pakistani, Bangladeshi) and the English culture, surface vividly when parents part ways. For those descendants with social problems, their rupture can push them toward hyper-fundamentalism (Salafism) or even radical Islam. In both cases, Islam becomes a wholesale identity that pushes to the margins the secular or Christian part of their personality. In France, practically in every case I have encountered, people told me that the secular or Catholic parent did not provide them with any specific identity, in contrast to the Muslim father or mother who gave them some clues as to the meaning of Allah's religion. Even when they were not provided with any clues about Islam (as was the case among few of them), Islam became a means for them to take "revenge" against society and to claim a counter-identity, particularly if they had failed to become "normal" citizens by following the deviant path.

Generally, fundamentalist Islam provides the means to overcome a dichotomous identity and its radical version, a way of violently rejecting the other part of one's identity. We face here less a crisis of authority than a crisis of values, the progeny being caught between two cultures that present large differences in terms of rights and duties, right and wrong, gender relations, and so on. Usually this problem is smoothly solved by tacit attitudes between parents and children. Sometimes the contradiction heightens and turns into identity crisis, and one way to solve it is to choose one side and reject the other, radical Islam playing this role. Jihadism as a wholesale identity overtakes the person and provides him with a monolithic personality in contrast to his split identity before embracing radical Islam. This identity is the more appreciated as it opposes others, giving a sense of exclusive personality that reverses one's past broken identity.

Another subcategory of cultural crisis is when parents are both foreigners and children could not cope with them (for instance, both of them being Buddhist). Radical Islam marks the repudiation of both the culture of the parents and that of the mainstream society. This was for instance the case of Alix, a convert from a Buddhist family of Laotian origin in the so-called Cannes-Torcy jihadi cell in France. He could not endorse a French identity after many failures: he dropped out of school and tried to join the army but was refused admission because he was physically unfit for a military career. He only found menial jobs. He converted to Islam and after a while, he left for Egypt in order to learn Arabic. After six months, he came back to France and joined the Cannes-Torcy Jihadi group. Since he was neither a Buddhist nor a Frenchman (each of which is regarded as a positive or neutral identity in the mainstream society), he became a radical Muslim (which is a negative identity for the majority).

In his opinion, society had put him in the straightjacket of an inaccessible dual identity: the Buddhist-Laotian and the French. His sisters succeeded in their studies and became French women, but not Alix, who had taken another path. By opting for jihadism, he expressed a desire to reject the Buddhist and French identities that he could not assume, breaking at the same time the tacit contract that bound him to society, based on avoiding violence against others. Jihadi identity did the magic of frontally refusing what the individual could not in any way achieve, while giving him the feeling that he had ultimately refused the role bestowed upon him by the mainstream society. More generally, Jihadism restores a sense of individual initiative, fictitious in its excesses (one feels like a demigod through violence), accompanied by a vengeful feeling: he declines a subaltern identity that is partly due to his own deed and partly society's constraint. He refuses to acknowledge his part of the responsibility for his failure to become a successful citizen (Alix's sisters succeeded in becoming middle-class French citizens). He punishes society for having put him, in his eyes, in the unacceptable role of being "nothing," "nobody."

Jihadism turns a passively experienced situation by the individual into one in which he becomes active in a destructive way to himself and others. When he was passive, he was only hurting himself. Having become destructively active, he hurts himself as well as others.

1-The Headless Patriarchal Family: Violence as a Substitute for Authority

Those who belong to the headless patriarchal family are indelibly marked by patriarchy, even in the absence of the father. His vacant place haunts the family's psyche. The patriarchal model is in crisis and the family must face in anguish the father's vacuum. The mother is overwhelmed by outside work, often in menial underpaid tasks and child rearing, the family living in poor neighborhoods within a slum cultural setting. More generally, in France, single-parent families make up around two million households, or 40 percent of the families, and in 85 percent of them the mother assumes the responsibility to raise children, in most cases in precarious conditions (Cordier, 2019). Sometimes the father is physically present but the mother and the sons gang up against him to dethrone him, because he is useless or a burden to the family (he therefore prefers to leave or shut himself up in silence). A significant injury caused by the lack of paternal authority marks the sons' mental world and gives rise to violence. Life in a slum culture environment robs the family of a sense of decency, and the father is often taken by the sons as the target of their fury in the face of an unjust world where they are stigmatized and denied a sense of belonging to the mainstream society; he becomes a scapegoat.

More generally, four dimensions make this type of family a potential breeding ground for violence (jihadism being one among the others): indigence (living as a poor family); living in poor districts (mostly populated by Muslims from North Africa in France, from Morocco in Belgium, and from the former colonies in the United Kingdom); belonging to the slum culture within a mental universe marked by a strong sense of inferiority and humiliation (the "Arab" in France, the Jamaican, Pakistani, Bangladeshi in the UK, and the Moroccan in Belgium); and psychological injury (the trauma of a missing father within a symbolic family structure that gives prominence to him despite his having lost his authority, and more generally, the suffering due to the lack of authority related to the disappearance of the father figure-head). These dimensions are intertwined: the decay of the father whose departure, unemployment, or, more generally, demise, makes the family even more indigent and combines with cultural inferiority and locality stigma (the poor districts are regarded by the mainstream society as inhabited by "dangerous classes") to make the family members miserable.

These people do not master the dominant language—French, English or German—which degrades their image not only to others but also and mainly to themselves, creating an internalized negative image of their ego. In other words, they feel unworthy because they come from other horizons whose culture is devalued (one is "Arab" in France, "Asian" in the United Kingdom, "Turk" in Germany, "Moroccan" in Belgium, and so on), without a solid principle of identity (the father used to provide it traditionally to them). In a consumer society, poverty is a mark of lack of dignity. The disgrace, internal (internalized indignity) and external (the "dangerous class" as perceived by the public opinion) can lead to a revolt, and in few cases to jihadism. Through radical Islam, the individual not only recovers a sense of dignity, but he also finds a new "father" (the caliph or the divinely ordered Chief like Bin Laden, the head of al-Qaeda), overcomes the feeling of indignity (if he succeeds in joining Daesh, he ends the stigmas of being an "Arab" in France, a "Paki" in the United Kingdom, and so forth).

Young boys coming from headless patriarchal families often end up becoming delinquents in order to overcome poverty, help their family, and substitute for the failing father. But deviance can sometimes go further and turn into a holy war against society, jihadism being a total transgression where deviance is partial. One major cause of this possible transition is the hatred of society: the latter is desecrated due to the environment in which they live (poor districts, slum culture, high concentration of jobless migrants' offspring, daily humiliation). Added to it, the dream of joining Daesh.

Jihadism, and IS in particular, allowed these young people to go beyond individual transgression, declaring war on society by changing their core values: they no longer wanted to live in a fatherless society but in one in which they assumed the role of the father (get married and start a family) in the name of a super-father, the caliph. Toward the latter they played the role of subservient sons, but toward society they became inflexible and punishing fathers. They didn't challenge only partially, through deviant activities, social norms that were conducive to their stigmatization. This time they intend to establish a new system of values and standards that were antagonistic to those of the secularized European societies in which they lived. Under the new system they became a new, self-proclaimed elite and filled the role of father in their own family and, by extension, in the entire "heathen" society to which they denied the capacity to decide about their own fate. They were less than nothing, but after joining Daesh they pretended to lead the world in the name of the sacred values of radical Islam.

In summary, living in headless patriarchal families, these young people believed that society was fatherless and that there were no credible social standards. They breached the latter because they found them at the root of their stigmatization and poverty. Deviancy, they believed, ensured them access to the middle-class status, in the absence of other opportunities. However, the discovery of jihadism, especially in its IS version, provided their imagined community (the neo-Ummah) with a father, the caliph. Henceforth, in his name they intended to impose their rule on society through violence and played the father's role by proxy. The caliph became for these young people who had lost their fathers the absolute father in whose name they could impose their rule on others. The new father (the caliph) allowed them to elude insignificance, claim elite status in the name of Islam, and crush with contempt a society that had spurned them. Contempt changed sides; those who were humiliated sought to humiliate. They sought to humiliate, not in a manner equivalent to what they had suffered, but ten times, a hundred times more, going so far as to physically eliminate others whom they called Infidels by espousing Daesh's repressive ideology. Their attitude was a ruthless and dehumanizing counter-stigmatization that closed the door to any mutual understanding.

Many jihadis came from this type of family. Some examples can illustrate the link between the headless patriarchal family and the radicalization of its members, particularly the sons, and to a lesser degree the daughters.

Mohamed Merah, the killer of three Muslim military men and four Jews in 2012 in Toulouse and Montauban, was from a divorced family of Algerian origin. Merah's father was an unskilled worker at the foundry of Muret, close to the city of Toulouse in southern France. He divorced twice, had seven children from his two former wives, and married his third wife who was fifteen years younger than him. She begot five children, including Mohamed in 1988. Mohamed's father regularly beat his wife. In 1993, when Mohamed was five years old, they divorced. Early in 1992 his mother with her children took refuge for six months at a children's home in Aveyron, around 160 kilometers from Toulouse, to move away from his father. After the divorce of his parents, his mother moved with his brothers and sisters into a council flat in the poor ethnic neighborhood of Bellefontaine in the district of Le Mirail in Toulouse. Mohamed felt miserable about the dislocation of the family, and he asked in vain his father to return home. His mother, who made new encounters, left him for days alone in front of the TV. In a report in November 1995, social services expressed their worries about his violent and chaotic family environment, and at the age of six he was placed in a host family. In a 1997 report, the authorities proposed to separate him from his mother, due to her lack of care and supervision of him. He spent a year in this first foster home, and made five stays in the following years (Cazi, 2012). Family crisis was also reflected in the mutual violence among the brothers, and the radicalization of Souad, one of the sisters, as well as the mother. His brother Abdelkader benefited from social welfare and found small jobs for short periods. He stabbed his other brother, Abdelghani, in 2003 because he had married a woman of Jewish origin. He went to prison for violence against him, but also against his mother and sisters (Abdelkader, 2017). Mohammed Merah combined violent childhood, deviance, radicalization in prison, and travel to a foreign land of jihad (Pakistan). His case is almost a perfect model of a young man from a fatherless family with major problems, turning to violence and then, deviance, prison, and jihadism. In 2000 his father was sentenced to 5 years imprisonment for cannabis trafficking and nine months more for witness tampering. He was freed in 2004 and left France for Algeria, where he remarried twice. In 2011 Mohamed's mother married Mohamed Essid, a radical Tunisian Muslim, the father of the jihadi Sabri Essid. The marriage lasted only few months (he beat her quite often, according to witnesses). In the words of the elder brother, Abdelghani, family environment played a decisive role in the radicalization of his two brothers, Abdelkader and Mohamed, as well as their sister Souad (Sifaoui and Merah, 2012). Violence often occurred between the family members: their uncle who lived in the same district was frequently violent toward the brothers Merah, acting as a surrogate for their absent father (Domingo, 2020).

Merah was the first notable French jihadi to kill Jews for anti-Semitic reasons, but also because the Muslim military man that he was about to kill did not come to the appointment, the choice of Jews being made by him as a substitute. The youngest sibling among five children (two girls and three boys), he grew up in an atmosphere of domestic violence, religious intolerance, and anti-Semitism. According to the eldest brother, Abdelghani, the anti-Semitism of his brothers Abdelkader and Mohammed and his sister Souad was the result of the family culture under the aegis of a mother who taught them that "Arabs were born to hate Jews" (Pelletier and Pontaut, 2012). He killed three Muslim military men, a Jewish teacher, and three Jewish children in Toulouse and Montauban in March 2012.

The Merah family fits well into the model of the headless patriarchal family: crisis of authority, lack of father, break-up of the family, violence on the part of the elder brother extended to others, delinquency, prison terms, and so on.

It was also the case of Hayat Boumedienne, the wife of Amédy Coulibaly (she was only religiously married to him), of Algerian origin, from a family of seven children living in Villiers-sur-Marne in the eastern suburbs of Paris. Her mother died when she was six years old, and Boumedienne was placed in a children's home where her father rarely visited her. She then moved from one home to another because of her violent conduct, before being definitively expelled for attacking social workers. In her case, female behavior was not profoundly different from men's. Here too, the headless patriarchal family model fits well.

Mehdi Nemmouche was born on April 17, 1985, in Roubaix in an Algerian family. He was the son of a "Harki" (those Algerians who collaborated with the French army against the independence of Algeria and were abhorred by the Algerians, including those who later migrated to France in the 1960s). He was called a child of "sin" (*ouled haram*, a bastard) by the other "Arabs" in France. He never knew his father, and, his mother being impecunious, he was placed, when he was three months, in children's homes and foster families, like his two sisters. At the age of seventeen he was entrusted to his grandmother in Tourcoing, living in the poor ethnic district of La Bourgogne. In 1999 he participated in several burglaries and robberies, and in 2002 he abused a teacher under the threat of a weapon. In 2004 he was sentenced to two months in prison, and another suspended two-and-a-half months for violent robbery. He prepared a professional electrotechnical baccalaureate but did not show up for the exams in June 2006 ("Mehdi Nemmouche," 2014). Since then, he was convicted of many other violent acts and spent eighteen months in prison until November 2007. He recounted how in prison other "Arabs" called him a "son of a bitch": in their view, the mother had symbolically "prostituted "with the French because of the Harki father who collaborated with the French army against the Algerian independence fighters. Prison sentences followed one another at an accelerated rate for car theft, then robbery. From December 2007 to December 2012, he was incarcerated in four different prisons. He became an adept of fundamentalist Islam, proselytizing in prison, making calls to unauthorized collective prayers, and throwing projectiles at the prison guards.

In December 2012, he was freed from prison, left for Turkey, and joined IS. He became a jailer of Western hostages under the leadership of Salim Benghalem. He sometimes tortured them violently ("Mehdi Nemmouche," 2014).

Right from the beginning, through the family crisis (unknown father, a poor mother who could not take care of him) and his desperate situation, his path was mapped out to become a deviant. He became also a jihadi.

Among others, he committed anti-Semitic attacks. On May 24, 2014, he attacked the Jewish Museum in Brussels, killing four people and wounding one. The trajectory of Nemmouche matches the one we indicated earlier: birth into a broken family within a poor ethnic neighborhood, deviance, imprisonment, recidivism, and conversion to a jihadi version of Islam.

These young people belonged to what has been called a "fractured generation" (Devecchio, 2016), in the sense of disjointed families and a social environment that offers them little choice.

The Kouachi brothers who committed the attacks against *Charlie Hebdo* journalists in January 2015 also fit in this category. Chérif Kouachi was born in 1982, and his older brother Saïd in 1980, in Paris in a family of five children, of Algerian parents. Their father died early in their childhood, and their mother in 1995, Chérif being thirteen years old and Saïd, fifteen at that time. Their mother died during her pregnancy. She had prostituted herself to make ends meet. Her death was probably a suicide through overdose of medicines. The parking lot of their building in the 19th district of Paris had become a beacon for pedophiles, children becoming their victims, their parents being unable to watch over them. Saïd, his brother Chérif, their sister, and another brother were sent to a children's home in southern France from 1994 to 2006. The siblings spent a miserable existence with their family, and then, in different institutions. They were deprived of normal childhood and bereft of parental love and affection (Lebourg, 2015). Chérif obtained a diploma in electrotechnics, and Saïd, a professional qualification diploma in hotel trade. Both came to Paris, only to find small jobs. Being "Arabs," they were exposed to social prejudice, but they were not socialized for normal work either, as in many cases I encountered in prison (many were unable to work on a regular basis, they also rejected the authority of the "White man" as an employer, regarding it as a new kind of colonialism).

In Paris, Chérif met Farid Benyettou, the young spiritual leader of a jihadi group called "Buttes-Chaumont cell" in the 19th district of Paris who sent many people to Iraq to fight against the Americans after they occupied it in 2003. In January 2005, Chérif was arrested, attempting to leave for Damascus. Saïd had once been arrested for his relations to the Buttes-Chaumont cell. In 2011, Chérif went to Yemen for military training, his trip being financed by Anwar al Awlaki, the American-Yemeni jihadi leader.

The two brothers were killed on January 9, 2015, by the security forces after having put to death twelve people, among them eight journalists from *Charlie Hebdo*, on January 7, 2015.

The fact that they were born into a broken family, devoid of any authority regulating their lives, and were exposed to delinquent milieus within a slum culture was decisive in their deviant behavior. Radical Islam became a means to recover dignity and pride through violence, by punishing the journalists who had desecrated the Prophet of Islam.

The life stories of these fatherless individuals in families still dominated by a patriarchal worldview explains the appeal of jihadism, which offered a collective dream in the midst of an idyllic neo-Ummah, escaping from dissension, the believer submitting to the Caliph as a sacred super-Father (Bigo et al., 2014).

In France in the 1970s and 1980s, some North African families provided a "secular" identity to their offspring, changing their names (e.g., from Mohamed or Zeinab to Robert or Jacqueline) in order to facilitate their integration, following the spirit of the republican identity, in which reference to the ethnic origin is considered contrary to the French model of citizenship. Some North African families also ignored their Islamic roots and educated their progenies with no reference to Islam. This was the case of Zakaria Moussaoui's family in which no Islamic tenet was internalized, his mother leaving them unaware of Islamic mores. His discovery of radical Islam in Britain in the 1990s under the influence of extremist preachers created a shock in his family. He rejected his former French identity, opting for jihadism, brandishing his new Self against what he regarded as the domineering and arrogant Western culture. He achieved self-respect by casting off secular values and acting against *Taqut*, that is, the idolatrous Western governments whose most powerful representative was the United States. He tried to take part in the September 11, 2001, attacks but was rejected by al-Qaeda leadership, which found him unstable and untrustworthy. Moussaoui's case can be extended to many people of that generation, especially in France where French laïcité marginalized religion in the name of a secular modernity. The new spirit of laïcité that has become like a civil religion has led to increasingly strict prohibitions of the Islamic veil in the public space. This is interpreted by the sons and daughters of North African migrants as a neo-colonial means of humiliating them in the name of French-style modernity, even among many secular French North Africans. For them, France deprived them of their fathers and now tries to deny them their ancestral religion. During its heyday, Daesh provided them with a father and allowed them to retaliate against French "patricide [father killer] arrogance."

2-The Neo-Traditional Family

Family structure was transplanted in the West by Muslim families of various origins (Algerians, Moroccans, and Tunisians in France; Pakistanis, Bangladeshis, and Indians in the UK; Moroccans in Belgium; Turks in Germany; Somalis in Norway) since the 1960s, when they came to Europe, mostly as foreign workers who established themselves in the host countries.

Unlike the headless patriarchal family, the neo-traditional one has preserved its old traits. The fixed family structure can be in part explained by the preservation of a community structure in neighborhoods due to the high concentration of inhabitants of the same origin and lower-middle classes (for example, in the UK middle-class neighborhoods with a high concentration of Pakistanis and Bangladeshis, and in France the peripheric housing blocks that surround the poor suburbs and which are now inhabited in part by North Africans). Through an act of resistance to European modernizing trends, this family structure remains more or less frozen, in contrast to the country of origin (Pakistan, Bangladesh), where it remains more flexible and evolves more swiftly. Its subliminal aim is to preserve the group's identity in the face of a European society which, through secularization, but also the glamor of the dominant culture, imperceptibly pushes to dissolve ethnic specificities. Jihadism is an attempt at breaking ethnic identities and not preserving them. It is the swan song of Pakistani, Moroccan, Algerian, or Somali ethnicities in the name of a bellicose version of Islam that seeks to end the ambiguity of hyphenated identities (English-Pakistani, French-Algerian) and the nostalgia of a bygone past by imposing a single, bellicose identity. It rejects hyphenated identities in the name of radical Islam. It denies supremacy to the father within the neo-traditional family by worshipping a super-father in the figurehead of the caliph or the jihadi emir (military chief). It rejects the biological father, the keystone of the neo-traditional family, replacing him with the caliphal super-father.

The neo-traditional family is not affected by single parenthood to the same degree as the fatherless patriarchal family we described before: it has a father who watches over his children and a mother who takes care of their Islamic education, ensuring their conformity to the tradition, especially for girls, who often remain virgin until a much older age than their non-Muslim counterparts. Boys also have their first sexual intercourse later than their mainstream European counterparts.

The neo-traditional family can be fundamentalist, but it is opposed to radical Islam, perceived as a deviant form of religiosity. The parents from Pakistan are mostly Deobandi or Barelvi, and the patriarchal hierarchy is preserved in the UK. Jihadi socialization occurs most of the time outside the family, breaking with its standards. If radicalization can occur within the headless patriarchal family among the young boys and girls, it happens less often in the neo-traditional family, in which self-defense mechanisms are stronger. Unlike young people living in the French poor suburbs, where the family is often headed by a single parent, in a neo-traditional family the patriarchal structure remains intact, father and mother being present in the household, the hierarchy being well preserved. Its crisis develops due to its rigidity and its inability to change, rather than to its collapse as it occurs in the headless patriarchal family, mostly in France or Belgium. Too stiff to change, it is antiquated, and jihadism is an attempt at shifting it violently by denying the father figure his legitimacy. The smallest change can call the unyielding organization of the family into question. That was the case of Shamina Begum. She left her parental home for Syria in February 2015 after selling the family jewels to finance her plane ticket. Shamina was born into a family from Bangladesh, east of London, in 1999. In the fall of 2014, her father remarried after her mother's death, and on December 6 of the same year she left the United Kingdom for Turkey. The traditional family structure was shaken by the disappearance of the mother, the early remarriage of the father, the few years following her mother's disappearance deeply affecting her. The young girl had difficulties accepting the new wife of her father, affective ties to her dead mother being largely trampled on by his early remarriage, barely a few months after her death. Shamina thus found an escape in leaving her family for Syria, accompanied by two friends from the same school. The father had shaken the family, and in response she broke off her ties. Radicalization meant denial of legitimacy to him, as the head of the family, in addition to looking for a new life, far from a detested family, where the sacred memory of the mother had been desecrated by a careless father. In her case, her English identity was of little help: she could not use it to free herself from family guardianship, since she was part of a Bangladeshi community that was recognized by society, and she felt powerless and delegitimized outside of it.

Households of Pakistani, Bangladeshi, or even Palestinian origin in the UK are less disorganized than their counterparts of North African origin in France. This phenomenon can be illustrated in the case of Issam Abuanza. Born to Palestinian parents, Abuanza was a doctor working for the National Health Service (NHS). After he abandoned his wife and two children in Sheffield to join IS, his sister, Najla Abuanza, expressed her indignation—not in relation to the English society but to her parents, who would never forgive her brother for having broken the family ties: "My father's desire was to see him before he died. He spent all his money on him and his education, and that's what he did" ("Sister of NHS Doctor," 2016). Grievances are based on the family ethos of a subordinated son to the father. The son had broken the implicit pact between him and his parents, who had dedicated their lives to the prosperity of their children in order to have them on their deathbed. By leaving, he betrayed the sacred bonds that tied parents and sons. This feeling would not have occurred in the headless patriarchal family in France, in which sons compete to fill the void left by the demise of the father and have no guilt feelings toward him.

This family structure in which the father remains the pillar pushed Daesh to declare that jihad, as an imperative Islamic duty (*fardh ul ayn*), does not need parental approval for their taking part in it, as proclaimed the president of the Islamic Cultural Association of the University of Medical and Technological Sciences of Khartoum: *"It is important to understand according to Allah (Tribute to Him) that no one can prevent us from assuring the obligation to defend the Ummah and to make the word of God heard so that the Sharia returns to all the Muslim lands. Only then will the obligation of jihad be lifted. In this way, until that happens, we do not have to ask permission from anyone, whether parents, rulers, or anyone else. Authorization has already been granted* [by Allah]" (Spencer, 2016)

In a significant part of neo-traditional English immigrant families, because traditional ways of life are preserved (they are not fought against by the mainstream society, as is the case in France through laïcité), parental permission still has relevance and their offspring feel morally bound to seek their consent for major decisions, like marriage or leaving the parental home in order to become autonomous. In the same vein, in Germany, families of Turkish origin have preserved much more than in France the formal structure of parental authority and traditional Islam's frame. Thus, when the younger generations transgress religious prohibitions, they do it surreptitiously. It is this generation that Pierre Vogel, the converted German Muslim preacher, well-known in fundamentalist circles, calls the "Santa Claus Muslims": they transgress Islamic norms without changing the appearance of their adherence to Islam. They go to the mosque on Friday to reassure their parents and pretend to strictly follow Islamic standards, which they infringe occasionally while feeling subliminally guilty, unlike young French Muslims who barely have a bad conscience about it, let alone a guilt feeling.

In the neo-traditional Muslim family, where the authority of the father is seemingly intact, the internet indirectly challenges parental authority, siblings appearing to comply with the rules. In reality, though, they question the patriarchal order by substituting the caliph for their father. In this family, the son does not seek to take the place of the father who has left, in contrast to the headless patriarchal family in which he seeks to fill the vacuum. He embalms his father in a respect that apparently spares him. It is usually through fundamentalism that in the neo-traditional family the son desecrates the father, opposing "true Islam" to the latter's lukewarm religion. (In Holland, this aspect was underlined by Slootman et al., 2009.) Many English movies underline this attitude among the younger generation of Muslims, who criticize their parents for not being genuinely Muslim: the mother, for the lack of veil or her wearing it laxly; the father, for his hidden habit of drinking alcohol or not performing daily prayers, for example. One can quote the movie *My Son the Fanatic* by Hanif Kureishi, based on the novel by the same name, published in 1994, turned into a film in 1997 by Udayan Prasad, but also others, more or less in the same vein, like *The Reluctant Fundamentalist* in 2012, based on a 2007 novel by Mohsin Hamid, directed by Mira Nair. Through fundamentalism, the son dethrones his parents, without challenging patriarchal values.

As an illustration of the neo-traditional family crisis one can cite the case of Ali Almanasfi (Spencer, 2016). His father, a conservative religious man, came from Syria and became a bus driver. He had problems with his wife but did not divorce. Ali, in revolt against the family, joined a gang of young people in the district of Acton and was repeatedly arrested for various illegal acts. In desperation, his father sent him to his extended family in Damascus in 2008, to move him away from that delinquent community. The stay had no effect on him. One year after his return to Britain, he was sentenced to four years in prison in a minors' penitentiary for having beaten and stolen from a man. In prison he discovered Islam, let his beard grow and constantly quoted verses, which he insisted one should repeat continuously to benefit from their positive fallout. When he left prison in 2011, he decided to go to Syria, his parents' country, to fight the Assad regime, long before radical Islamists had taken root there. The discovery of Islam made him aware of his impure and illicit past actions. It was not so much the propaganda of IS (which only appeared in 2014) or that of other jihadi groups that touched him, but his personal experience. In January 2013 he left the flat he shared with his mother and went illegally to Syria. From there he sent a note to his half-brother, informing him of his departure and reporting his bad conscience and remorse for having beaten an old man in the past to rob him of his goods. For him, the fight in Syria was primordially an act of atonement, the redemption for his sins. He died five months later in Syria in a car attack targeted by the Syrian army. The case of Almanasfi is representative of young people from neo-traditional families in which having failed religious precepts and having broken them leads to intense guilt. The family was not the target of his attacks; he did not aim at his father to dethrone him, but he sought a new life to escape the malaise.

One can also mention the cases of the twin sisters Salma and Zahra Halane, the so-called Terror Twins (Tozer, 2014). They belonged to a Somali family. They went to Syria on July 2014 at the age of sixteen. The year before, their twenty-one-year-old brother had left the UK and joined IS in Syria. Their father was a devout traditional Muslim, a reciter of the Koran (he practiced *tajweed*, the art of cantillating Koranic verses), and he ran an Islamic school. The two girls were good students with high grades, and they aspired to study medicine. Once in Syria, Zahra took the *kunya* (Islamic name) of "Umm Ja'far" and did the propaganda for IS on the web, celebrating the anniversary of the 9/11attacks in the US, a few months after her arrival in Syria. Salma gave advice to prospective female migrants on marriage under IS. Both twins married in Syria, Zahra to a nineteen-years-old British man of Afghan origin who was killed few months later, and Salma to a young man who was also killed in an airstrike, in December 2014 (Saltman and Smith, 2015). On the whole, within the Halane family, a brother and two sisters joined IS, underlining the neo-traditional family's deep crisis.

The major difference between these and the modern middle-class families is that the latter have adapted to an egalitarian pattern and renounced patriarchy, whereas the former are hierarchic and the rigidity of the father, unable to adapt to a role more in line with modernity, induces a major crisis in the family. The "spiritual father" (be it the caliph or, at a more modest level, the charismatic recruiter or preacher) becomes a moral authority that imposes upon the "sons" his rules that are far more repressive than those of the biological father.

3-The Stepfamily and the Crisis of Authority

The stepfamily (or patchwork family) illustrates the growing fragility of family life in late modernity. We will focus on this type of family, given that remarks about it can be extended to many other forms of modern, diversified family models, where authority is being challenged, is subject to dispute, or is diluted.

In stepfamilies, in general, the son or the daughter has not been radicalized because of the destitution of the father as the pillar of the family (which is the case in the headless patriarchal family), nor in reaction to a stifling traditionalism (as in the case of the neo-traditional family). In these families, radicalization occurs in response to another type of malaise that undermines young people in search of meaning and identity. In traditional patriarchal families, the role of the father as the principle of legality and the ultimate norm-setting authority puts the child in a situation of subordination, forcing him or her to internalize the standards, engraving paternal authority in a permanent manner in his or her psyche. With the stepfamily, the father has lost his transcendent role, his authority being challenged in many ways (notably by his sharing it with the mother through endless negotiations, or by sharing it with the stepfather who has replaced him). The mother also does not replace the father but becomes a co-partner in the distribution of divided authority. It is from their mutual relationship and their agreement, always subject to dispute between the partners, that a fragmented, unstable authority emerges. Moreover, the biological father and mother contribute to further dividing authority, so that the child no longer has a pole of identification, navigating between a plurality of persons with partial, often fragmented authority, which no longer has a single locus; in addition, not only does it become desacralized, it actually loses credibility. In this context, the father is closer to a big brother than to the traditional *pater familias*, children assuming a status of "quasi-adult" in a family that has lost its former untouchable sacredness. Authority is no longer a given, it is subject to debate and manipulation between multiple polarities: husband and wife, children and parents, father and stepfather, mother and stepmother.

The length of studies (years of schooling) and the dependence on the family throughout childhood and adolescence into one's twenties turn a lot of young adults into "adulescents" or "kidults" (an uneasy mix of adolescence and adulthood), unable to empower themselves, financially dependent on the parents, with no stable employment. These tensions make the ego vulnerable. The eagerness for coming of age drove late teenagers to break with the past by embarking on the Syrian adventure, in order to end the long and unbearable predicament of "kidulthood." Daesh was able to bridge the gap between adolescence and adulthood and empower these young people to become grown-ups through violence, which took on a positive meaning in the minds of these adulescents. It provided them with a golden opportunity to break with mental and financial heteronomy and to join the circle of the would-be grown-ups, with pride, so to speak.

If in a headless patriarchal family, the vacant place of the father posed a major challenge to authority, in the stepfamily the emergence of the mother as a parallel authority, and children with new legal rights, set in motion another type of crisis. Some wannabe jihadi brides wanted to become mothers early and denied their own mothers the authority they had acquired within the family. Adolescents rejected gender-free family because it leveled the symbolic difference between men and women, fathers and mothers, and sons and daughters. In their perspective, feminism had devalued the role of the mother and marginalized childbirth in the name of women's rights. In their desire to be exclusively feminine, young girls questioned some of the fundamentals of feminism. By acting otherwise than their mothers, they intended to end the chronic instability of the stepfamily. Yet, stable in terms of gender roles (the wife clearly subordinated to the husband), the patriarchal family built in Syria was unstable due to the most probable early death of the husband in the battlefield. A superior kind of stability was supposed to govern the family, and beyond it, in the new society (the imagined neo-Ummah), the husband being only a deputy to the senior patriarch, the caliph.

4-Jihadi Fratriarchy

Besides recruiters and preachers on one hand, and the internet on the other, family ties—actual kinship as well as "imagined families" (friends who became like brothers)—were the main tools for the jihadi recruitment.

In many cases, family crisis was at the root of the young people's search for a solidarity that was lacking in their household: they found the solution in jihadism. Different groups used new types of organizations, some tied to the family, some creating bonds based on agnatic or cognatic relations, some teaming up with other groups that usually shun them: middle class "White" Frenchmen joining "Arabs" (the sons of North African immigrants), Black Englishmen joining "Pakis," or middle-class sons of migrants closing ranks with lower class migrants. Jihadism opened up new vistas for socialization among people who usually avoided each other. A new conception of an imagined enlarged family emerged among those who went to Syria, language being the cement: French binding together Frenchmen, French-speaking Belgians, and French-speaking Swiss, or German connecting Germans, Austrians, German-speaking Swiss, and so on. They built up what can be called "enlarged imagined jihadi families." Besides them, we find jihadi fraternities, that is brothers, cousins, and, more generally, blood relatives promoting jihad. In many cases the son took the initiative, sometimes the younger son (Chérif, the younger among the brothers Kouachi, was more active than Saïd, his elder brother); more often the elder one (Fabien Clain in the Clain family; in a few cases it was the father who indicated the way (Abdel-Majed Abdel Bary became an IS recruit and he was the son of Abdel Abdel Bary, an Egyptian who came to Britain in 1991 and was convicted in New York for his role in the attacks against the US embassies in East Africa in 1998).

Lack of father can induce the quest for a substitute, a charismatic figure that can replace the lost one. This was the case of Olivier Corel, the "White Emir" who accommodated in the village of Artigat many young men, born-again Muslims as well as converts, and became their spiritual father, many of them lacking real ones. That was in particular the case of the brothers Clain, who had come in their early childhood to Metropolitan France and had not been supervised by their father, who stayed in Réunion Island, several thousand miles away. This was also the case of Mohamed Merah, whose father divorced when Mohamed was five years old, his mother, who was fifteen years younger than her husband.

By "fratriarchy" I mean primarily the brothers, but also the cousins or the young members of the extended family, and often the elderly brother as a substitute to the defunct authority of the father who has been dethroned by the undermining influence of the Western societies after immigration to Europe, primordially within headless patriarchal families. Since the father has abdicated, usually the older brother (rarely, another brother) assumes his role. We are not facing an Oedipus complex revisited. The father is not put to death, he has renounced or quitted; he has not even been symbolically eliminated, the vacuum left by his demise being simply filled by the sons. The site of authority being vacant, the brothers occupy it: no need for evicting the father, he has died through exhaustion, not by their deed. That is why the sons do not entertain any guilt feelings in this regard, in contrast to the neo-traditional family within which the son who has left for Syria feels guilty toward his father.

Male brothers, in the headless patriarchal family, share some common traits: they mostly live without a horizon of hope, and suffer from their mental and social inferiority, dropping out of school being one of the most recurrent traits among them. They believe they cannot ascend through normal channels, therefore being condemned to be poor and insignificant if they do not enter the deviant world. Through departure to Syria at the service of God, the brothers make together the experience of a heightened life. Togetherness changes the meaning of sacrifice and martyrdom: the brothers take to heart having the male side of the family united, contrary to their life within their family at home, which was marked by dissension and violence (the Merah family is an exemplary case). Togetherness recovers its plenitude through departure and brotherly union on the frontline, and the mirage of a unified family is realized through holy death. For those who come from the poor districts, warlike action is an extension of suburban violence, but a grandiose one: if criminal and deviant violence is "insignificant" (a minor news item) with regard to the global society, violence in Syria or in Europe in the name of jihad yields a special meaning: it transcends individual stakes, its sacred value making it unique, the media worldwide covering it and turning them into supermen.

Finally, the relationship with other young men becomes "fratriarcal": they see in the chief (emir) who heads a brigade (*katiba*, plural *kata'eb*) the model to follow. For jihadi fratriarchy, death carries a new meaning: a recovered dignity that would have been otherwise impossible to achieve. On top of it, these young men aspire to fight to the death for a cause rather than live in the rarefied air of Europe where nothing happens and one dies of boredom, in the nightlife of poor districts on the street, or in the middle-class neighborhoods where only minor news items are worthwhile, and the young man remains nobody until the end of his life. Death as a martyr provides an absolute certainty to accede a bright eternal future (paradise), a fulfilled sexual life by the multitude of eternally virgin girls in heaven (the so-called seventy-two *houris* for each martyr) while the "hero" is filled with pride by the recognition of his deeds among his colleagues in this world and by being denounced by his foes worldwide (which he enjoys), in the Western media. By achieving this glorious destiny together, brothers open the road to eternal felicity within a reconstituted family in paradise, postmortem. What could not be achieved on earth is accomplished in heaven.

One major aim of fatriarchies is to overcome tension, even antagonism between brothers, especially between the "big brother" and the others. Their struggle is particularly heightened within the headless patriarchal family, torn by conflicts between brothers due to the demise of the father. Jihadi brotherhood puts an end to this antagonism by assigning to the members of the family a common violent vocation, establishing internal peace at the price of external war. It is also an attempt to prevent family break-up, otherwise brought about by internal strife. By taking on a religious form, the conflicts that shake the family for the appropriation of the father's place are occulted, put under the aegis of God, represented by the caliph or the emir, who takes the place of the father. The brothers submit to him in a consensual manner and restore cordial relations among them. But this "super-father" is far more tyrannical in his demands than the biological father. He subjects young persons to the ordeal of sacrificial death (martyrdom). Within jihadi fraternity, siblings try to restore lost harmonies through the unanimous fight of the brothers against the forces of evil.

Siblings of the first (the Tsarnaev brothers in Boston), second (most French siblings), or third generation (Abdelhamid Abaaoud and his younger brother, the thirteen-year-old Younès) can become involved in jihadism. They are particularly appreciated by jihadi organizations. First, because there is mutual trust between them through blood ties. They support and understand each other instinctively, which increases their efficiency.

In the context of radicalization, two models may arise: either the elder or the younger brother leads. There is no such thing as egalitarianism for the siblings, neo-patriarchal family logic implying hierarchy but also initiative through which it is restored (the older brother, and in some cases the younger one, becomes the head of the group). In the British cell that aimed to blow up the London Stock Exchange in 2010, the younger brother, Abdul Miah (twenty-five years old), led his older brother Gurukanth Desai (thirty years old), father of three children.

Sometimes the brothers entrust moral authority to a third member of the group. For example, in the Strasbourg group, Mourad Farès was the charismatic leader of the two pairs of brothers, Mourad and Yacine Boudjellal and Karim and Foued Mohamed-Aggad.

One can also mention the case of the two Moroccan brothers, Mohammed Oulad Akcha (born in 1976) and Rachid Oulad Akcha (born in 1971), who took part in the Madrid train bombings in March 2004.

As for the brothers Belhoucine, the youngest, Mehdi, twenty-four years old, holder of a Master of Science and Technology degree, had been hired in the leisure centers of Aulnay-Sous-Bois, a suburb of Paris. Mohamed, the eldest, age twenty-seven, was sentenced to two years in prison for his role in carrying Foreign Fighters to the Pakistan-Afghanistan zone, after turning to cyber-jihadism and translating jihadi films into French for as-Sabab, al-Qaeda's propaganda organism. The two brothers left France for Syria a few days before the January 2015 attacks in the company of Hayat Boumedienne, the Islamic wife of Amedy Coulibaly, the author of the attack against a kosher superstore in the Paris neighborhood in January 2015.

Others, like Karim and Fouad Mohamed-Aggad, illustrate the different destinies of two brothers: they entered Syria in December 2013, a few days apart, to distract the attention of the police. Foued blew himself up at the Bataclan in Paris after perpetrating a massacre in the concert hall in November 2015, his older brother Karim, twenty-five, having already returned to Alsace.

In some cases, one of the brothers assists the other one, the "combatant of the faith," without directly taking part in the attack. This was the case of the older brother of Mohamed Merah, Abdelkader, condemned to twenty years imprisonment for taking part in a terrorist group.

We also find a few cases in which one of the brothers, an adult, trains the other, a minor, and takes him under his protection: Abdelhamid Abaaoud brought his junior brother Younes to Syria.

More generally, a "jihadi meritocracy" has emerged in which the elder is not automatically at the helm.

Tension between siblings within oftentimes disjointed families are usually all the more vivid as they mostly have no material stake: no inheritance, no financial privilege, only the symbolic legacy of the patriarchal family, within which the older brother in the Muslim world has a superior status—in tribal or agricultural societies this means usually material privileges, but transplanted in Europe those prerogatives become purely symbolic. They are related to the exercise of patriarchal power, the big brother seeking to fill the father's vacant position, heavily insisting on the inferiority of the sister compared to the brothers in defiance of reality (the sister is often better at studying at school than the brothers and finds a job more easily).

The big brother especially wants to join the middle classes, even at the cost of legality, consuming and selling drugs, alcohol, and especially having access to sexuality out of wedlock, whereas the sister is denied the same rights by the family code of honor (she does not necessarily abide by it, acting furtively outside the neighborhood). Family peace is sometimes achieved by opting for fundamentalist Islam or jihadism ("sacrifice" overcomes dissension among brothers and sisters). Through the "neo-Ummah," jihadism proposes a "harmonious" solution against the antagonistic and sexually transgressive individualization among the family members. In deep crisis, without peaceful ties, conflicted families establish through jihadism (but also pietistic Salafism) quiet relations among their members, restrictions imposed on them coming this time from God, not human beings, and therefore being foolproof.

Notable Cases of Fratriarchy

The five Bekhaled brothers and their sister (who provided them with financial means, mostly for affective reasons) are a perfect example of jihadi fratriarchy within a counter-intuitive model of a family.

They grew up together, with parents who lived together, the father being a former foundry worker, and the mother, a house maid. They worked hard and were able to rise to the rank of the lower middle classes. They had the means to move from the poor district of Vaulx-en-Velin (suburb of Lyon) to a quiet, lower-middle class district in a pavilion. In that district, the first major French homegrown jihadi, Khaled Kelkal, was brought up, who had planned the 1995 attacks of Paris metro. Still, none of the Bekhaled siblings was involved in delinquent activities.

In this family of immigrant origin, the parents intended to "assimilate" into the French society by speaking, reading, and writing French inside and outside the family. They celebrated only the Islamic feasts of Eid and Ramadan.

Still, they did not succeed in giving a sense of Frenchness to their sons, who felt the difference between being a "native Frenchman" ("Français de souche") and a citizen of North African origin. That triggered a violent reaction on their part, as in the case of the Moussaoui family in which the siblings lived "à la Française." Their son Zacarias reacted violently to the humiliations and the denial of Frenchness by adhering to radical Islam during his stay in London in the 1990s (Khosrokhavar, 2009).The sons of migrants, called sometimes the "Greys" (neither White nor Black) are constantly reminded of their origin in everyday life, which creates a situation of total violence on their part, due to denial of citizenship by the mainstream society.

All the siblings of the Bekhaled family became involved in Jihadism. Three older brothers, Mohamed, Rafik, and Farid, left France for Syria in 2013. The two youngest, Karim and Réda, who remained in France, intended to stage a violent attack in Lyon in 2014 (Pilorget-Rezzouk, 2018). They also enrolled few others in their network (nine others were indicted in November 2018 by the tribunal).

Mohamed, the oldest (nom de guerre "Abu Abdillah"), left for Syria in 2013. He became a sniper of IS, and met major figures of the French jihad, such as those of the Bataclan attacks in Paris in November 2015 like Mohamed Bekhaled, or a convert, Maxime Hauchard, who cut off the head of a prisoner in order to show his loyalty to Daesh (he was until then suspected by them of being a spy).

Mohamed seemed to be at the root of the jihadi dynamic in the family. He was thirty years old when he left a first time in 2013 with his wife and children to Syria, then Egypt, supposedly to perfect his knowledge of Arabic. The two other brothers joined Mohamed and became policemen within IS. In his Skype conversations, Rafik, a trained electrician, expressed the desire to die as a martyr. Farid was reportedly seriously injured by grenade shrapnel in the summer of 2014 during an offensive against another jihadi group, Jabhat al-Nusra, a branch of Al-Qaeda. He is reportedly dead.

Réda, the junior member of the family who stayed in France, sent young people (and girls) to Syria for the sake of providing espouses for the Foreign Fighters.

From Syria, the Bekhaleds never cut the ties with their brothers who stayed in the Lyon region. In October 2013, they asked Réda to carry out research in France on a recruit named Maxime Hauchard. Daesh feared a possible infiltration by a Western spy and they asked their little brother to lead the inquiry.

As a minor, he had been indicted in connection with Forsane Alizza (disbanded in 2012 by the authorities), a radical Islamic association. Known under the pseudonym "Kalashnikov-Lyon" by the other members of the group, he was sentenced to two years in prison in 2015. He reportedly sought a letter of accreditation from the IS through his brothers that would have allowed him to claim his attack in France on Daesh's behalf (AFP, 2018). He was arrested mid-September 2014, a few days after Farida his sister, and Karim his brother who had spent two months in Syria from September to November 2013. As for the sister Farida, immature, she fulfilled in her eyes the role of a second mother by providing the brothers with financial means for their jihadi projects. Acting willfully in order to be fired from the company where she worked, she was able to collect €7,500 in compensation before taking out two loans, totaling €22,000. She was exploited by her brothers, who destroyed her professional and social life. She was less ideologically than affectively motivated toward her brothers in France, who wanted to commit attacks in the style of Mohamed Merah.

Family ties united almost all the actors indicted by the tribunal: twelve out of fifteen, which included the members of three fratriarchies: the Bekhaled siblings (Mohamed, Rafik, Farid, Karim, Réda, and Farida), the Fartas siblings (Habib and Fatima), and the Akaichi siblings (Kamel and Fatma). They loosely cooperated with each other.

Among fratriarchies, one can also mention the Bakraoui brothers, Ibrahim and Khalid. They were prominent, seasoned bandits whose main concern at the outset was not ideological. Moreover, they never went to Syria and their radicalization was modeled on the "homegrown terrorists" in touch with those who had made the journey to the lands of jihad. The fact that the two brothers chose to die the same day in two Daesh attacks shows the sharing of the same fate and the desire to recreate family ties eternally sealed through their martyrdom. Jihadism often falls back on the anthropological cell of siblings, because brothers are bound by blood ties and trust each other. Ibrahim, born in 1986, and Khalid, in 1989, both in Brussels, participated in the attacks of March 22,2016, in Zaventem and Brussels, in which they were killed. Their father, Jamal, was born in France where his Berber parents, native of the Moroccan Rif, came to work in the mines of the north. In the 1960s the family moved to Belgium, and Jamal grew up in the center of Brussels, in the so-called Chicago district. He married and became a butcher, his business flourishing as his three children grew up. Ibrahim and Khalid were thus part of the third generation of immigrants and belonged to the new middle classes of North African origin. They still suffered discrimination and humiliation. Their cousin Ali, speaking of Khalid, insisted on social injustice: "Khalid had a university education. But he never found a job in his sector, computers. Discrimination, when it spreads over three generations can weigh [heavily], it creates bitterness" (Vigoureux, 2016). Discrimination thus concerns not only-lower class, but also middle-class Muslims.

Before their engagement in Islamist extremism, the two brothers were known to the Belgian justice system for their involvement in organized crime. In 2009, Khalid was sentenced to five years in prison for carjacking. In 2010, Ibrahim fired at the Belgian police during a robbery, injuring a police officer. He was condemned to nine years in prison. In 2014, he received a conditional release and, in June 2015, tried to cross into Syria but was expelled to Holland by Turkey (he joined some of the wannabe jihadis who, after trying to leave for Syria without success (they were mostly prevented by the European authorities from going there, or were forcefully returned to their country by the Turkish authorities), turned their ire against their own country and committed attacks there). The young Khalid embarked on delinquency before enrolling in radical Islam, as in many other cases.

Like some other Jihadis, Khalid got married shortly before the attacks, and his wife was pregnant at that time. The will to die has been in many cases an eschatological vision, family considerations carrying little weight in that respect, salvation overriding family and, in particular, children's fate. Many jihadis die while leaving behind women and young children or even their pregnant wife.

As in Ibrahim's case, in his will he expressed his dismay at the possibility of being locked up for the rest of his life, along with "him" (presumably Salah Abdeslam, the jihadi attacker of November 13, 2015, in Paris). We can in his case evoke the "syndrome of Mesrine," the most famous bandit of France in the years 1960–1970: he was weary of long-term imprisonment, and wished to die as a star, proudly, head up, in full possession of his powers, instead of growing old in prison and dying, head down. In the case of jihadis, another factor comes also into play, and that is the desire for vengeance, killing and maiming as many "Whites" as they could, before succumbing to death. This is what I call the "desperate" or the "metaphoric" jihadi who yearns to die for lack of any hope to close the cycle of crime, indictment, long prison terms, and an endless misery and violence in and outside prison (Khosrokhavar, "Chérif Chekatt," 2018).

To summarize, we can distinguish five types of jihadi fratriarchies regarding the respective roles of the siblings:

- First case: the terrorist group is organized by two brothers. They are its architects and die together in the attack (the Kouachi brothers in the *Charlie Hebdo* bombing in January 2015 in Paris).
- Second case: the two brothers are members of a larger group (the Clains, the Bakraouis) in which each brother assumes a different role. They can die in different circumstances (Ibrahim Bakraoui blew himself up at the airport and Khalid at the Brussels metro station on March 22, 2016).
- Third case: one of the brothers executes the terrorist attacks and the other helps him without being directly involved in the violent action (the case of Merah brothers).
- Fourth case: the two brothers become jihadis but act each in their own way. This was the case of the Mohamed-Aggad brothers, who went to Syria: Karim chose to return to France and was arrested upon his arrival. Foued remained in Syria and returned to France within the terrorist project of November 13, 2015, blowing himself up at Bataclan Theater in Paris.
- Fifth case: the two brothers become Jihadis together because they are in a situation of exile or are first-generation diaspora and fail to integrate or identify with the host society. This was the case of the Chechen brothers Tamerlan and Dzhokhar Tsarnaev, who arrived in the United States in 2002 and who planted pressure-cooker bombs at the Boston Marathon on April 15, 2013. The others, the Bakraouis and the Kouachis, were second-generation Jihadis.

5-The "Jihadophile" Family

Jihadism, in particular during the Daesh period (mainly 2013–2016), was an era of experiencing new forms of ideologically motivated families. It unified the otherwise disunited and broken families, mostly of migrant origin, giving them an ideological cement that made them a setting for testing new forms of patriarchy.

In the vast majority of cases, the family did not support the son's jihadi vocation, let alone his leaving for Syria or Iraq. Parents and other family members were left in the dark and faced powerlessly the fait accompli. In a tiny minority of cases, though, not only the son but also the brothers, and even sisters, sometimes the father and the mother, embraced the jihadi creed.

This was notably the case of Boubaker el-Hakim: his brother Redouane and his mother reportedly had encouraging words for him. His sister was charged, and two other members of the family were suspected of complicity. One can also mention the case of Kevin Gonot, thirty-two, arrested in Syria with his mother, his wife, and his half-brother in December 2017 by the Kurdish forces, sent by them to Iraq, and condemned to death by an Iraqi tribunal in May 2019. The Clain and the Tahar Aouidate families (discussed in the following paragraph), illustrate what we call a jihadophile family, characterized by the fact that a large part of the household accepted, and even encouraged the others, to join IS or other jihadi organizations. The family aligned itself with the son who usually took the initiative of jihad and either moved with him to the holy land of jihad, or put at his disposal, as well as his brothers and sisters, the means to achieve their end. I already had observed this phenomenon in Iran in the 1980s when, sometimes, several members of the same family joined the organization of the Bassidj volunteers who fought against the Iraqi army of Saddam Hussein during the Iran–Iraq war (1980–1988), several of them being killed on the battlefield. I called this type of family "martyropath" (Khosrokhavar, 1997). While in most of the cases the family was against the martyrdom of their son, in this specific case, parents not only did not oppose their son's joining the battlefield, but approved it and sometimes, father and brothers joined him, risking death on the war front. We also find in a few cases parents, especially mothers, who aligned themselves with their sons, for the sake of supporting them or being united with them, jihadi utopia touching them because it was meaningful to their offspring but also because it touched a chord in their own psyche. This was the case of Christine Rivière, fifty-one, the admiring mother of a young Frenchman who had become an "emir" (battalion commander) in Syria. She visited Syria three times in 2013 and 2014, and she helped several other women to leave for Syria by supporting them financially. Her youngest son, Tyler, had converted her to Islam and she quickly embraced its radical version under his influence, wholeheartedly endorsing his jihadi commitment.

The Tahar Aouidate family is the epitome of the jihadophile family. Twenty-three family members left from the French city of Roubaix, close to Belgium, for Syria in 2014 to join IS. There was an undisputed leader within the family, Fodil Tahar Aouidate, born in 1986 in Roubaix, the only son among eight daughters, all the more cherished by the mother as he was the only male descendant, particularly appreciated in traditional Muslim families. He had two major characteristics: he was charismatic, and he was violent. He was seductive and intimidating. In a family where the women were supposed to follow the brother, he had managed to impose himself. The sisters often went to a music center near their home to play hip hop music and were passionate about it and dancing. Soon after becoming radicalized, he forbade them to go, dance and music being prohibited by Islam, in his view. He had become a truly "domestic tyrant" (Vincent and Kaval, 2020), and he imposed rigid standards on his sisters and, by extension, on their husbands and children. Yet Fodil was not a paragon of Islamic virtue. He led a more or less dissipated life, between banditry and international jihadism via Belgian channels close to Sharia4Belgium. He also linked up in Brussels with a known recruiter by the name of Khalid Zerkani.[4]

The family, partly under his influence, locked itself up, marked by the fear of defilement if it came into contact with *kuffars* (Infidels), isolating itself as the date of departure for Syria was nearing. Gradually the younger sisters, then their brother's wife (who seemed not to share, at least entirely, her husband's jihadi views), then the eldest of the siblings, then the sixty-three-year-old mother, then Fodil's nephews and nieces and the other sisters, as well as the husband of one of them and his daughter left France for Turkey and from there, reached Syria. After them, Fodil's uncle left, and in the end, his great-uncle and his father (who was totally withdrawn and resigned). His brother-in-law had a comfortable situation in Roubaix. He was the owner of a pastry shop and the manager of a snack bar. He left Roubaix to join his wife and daughter, who had already reached Syria. Still, Fodil wielded seduction and the promise of a better life in Syria, as well as the threat of violence against those family members who were reluctant to leave Roubaix and move to Syria. Only two of Fodil's sisters stayed in Roubaix to send him money. Every month, they had to collect pensions or family allowances and then send them to intermediaries in Turkey ("Jihad: Deux sœurs," 2019).

Fodil's sisters sometimes influenced their friends, like Nassima Elbahi, from a single-parent family, who was close to Selma, one of Fodil's sisters. Fodil had also developed a relationship with another jihadi family, the Bekhaleds, and Nassima married one of their sons in Syria.

In these cases, as in many others, we find the influence of charismatic personalities who are not the eldest members of the family, but individuals in their twenties or thirties (Fodil was twenty-six when he left for Syria in 2014, Fabien Clain, thirty-seven in 2015 when he joined IS).

Fodil accomplished a feat that was very rarely accomplished in Europe, by enlisting the entire family in order to send them to Syria. He deeply hated the French society "of Infidels" and, above all, had a hold on the family that could not be explained other than through the parents' resignation and the subjugation of his sisters. None of them rebelled, and they played the passive role of submissive sisters to the older brother. He was the de facto patriarch of the family. He was not impressed by the father (who followed him only reluctantly). As for his brother-in-law or uncles, they did not give any resistance to him. The family was in his grip, overpowered by him. He could sometimes prove to be dangerous: when he went out with his totally veiled wife, he demanded that the other tenants move away from their windows so that they could not look at her, threatening to cut their throats if they did not comply. He also intimidated the owner of his apartment so that she would not claim the arrears of the rent he owed her. Unlike the Clain clan where brothers, sisters, and friends were strong supporters of jihadism, in this family the passive character of the members is remarkable. This is a peculiar jihadophile family.

Jihadophile families can also be the nucleus of a clan, numerous members of the family, friends, and brothers-in-law as well as fathers-in-law accepting the leadership of one brother who builds up an informal cell, in which blood ties are paramount. This was particularly the case of the brothers Fabien and Jean-Michel Clain, under the leadership of the former. Their wives Mylène and Dorothée, their respective three and five children, their sister Amélie, her four offspring, and another nephew, made up around eighteen members who went to Syria. This was probably a clan that was unique in the history of European jihadism during the twenty-first century. The two Clain brothers were practicing Catholics before converting to Islam. Fabien was born in 1978 and Jean-Michel in 1980. Their mother taught Catholic religious classes (Catechism). Four siblings were born between 1975 and 1986 in a family in which the father, a military man, stayed in La Réunion, a French isle in the Indian Ocean, while the family went to Metropolitan France, first in Alençon in the department of Orne, then in Toulouse (Vincent, "En Syrie," 2019). The children were cut off early from their father and were raised by their mother. They converted to Islam in 1996. The mother followed suit.

The two brothers did not go to school for a long time. Fabien received a vocational diploma (BEP) in metalworking and Jean-Michel in accountancy, but did not find jobs and lived on social care, selling Islamic books on the market in the poor district of Toulouse, le Mirail. Their real "job," especially after joining the Artigat community, consisted in putting their talent at the service of radical Islam. A rapper, after his conversion to Islam Fabien called himself a *rappeleur* ("the caller," he who calls people to become Muslims by singing the Islamic religious songs, *anasheed*, without musical instruments). Neither of them had the profile of a common law offender when they switched with their mother to Salafist Islam, at the end of the 1990s, under the influence of the Tunisian husband of their older sister Anne-Diana.

Quickly, the older brother, Fabien, imposed himself as the new right arm of a charismatic Islamic figure named Olivier Corel, a Syrian born in 1946 who became a French citizen in 1983. Known as "The White Emir," he was the former president of the Toulouse section of the Islamic Students' Association, close to the Muslim Brotherhood through its ties to Union des Organisations Islamiques de France (UOIF). In the village of Artigat where Corel lived, Fabien Clain was nicknamed "Omar," his brother Jean-Michel "Abdelwali." Their respective wives, Mylène and Dorothée ("Fatima" and "Khadija") wore the burqa (total veil) and schooled their young children at home, to preserve them from the secular influence of the government school (*école publique*, where laïcité is the standard).

The Clain brothers were steadfast in their unwavering radical views of Islam and were in the Security Services' crosshairs since 2001. Not only were they steadfast in their ties with radical Islam, but also their wives followed suit. Fabien met Mylène at school and married her at the age of twenty-one, up to the end. She, for her part, converted to Islam after him and wore the "total veil." Fabien succeeded in converting his brother, mother, sisters, and some friends. Under the influence of Olivier Corel in the village of Artigat, in the middle of "nowhere," they built up a close-knit community, where they met with other radicalized young people—Mohamed Merah, Sabri Essid, and others like Thomas Barnouin and Mohamed Megherbi—all becoming active jihadis later on. The Clain brothers were looking for a father that would replace the absent one, finding him in Olivier Corel in Artigat. More than a decade later, Fabien himself fulfilled the role of the father to many young people whom he impressed by his knowledge of Islamic law (*fiqh*) and his charismatic personality (he was persuasive and physically awesome, weighing around 150 kilos [330 pounds] and tall, 1,90 meters [almost 6 feet, 3 inches]). Seductive and paternal at the same time, he succeeded in converting many young people, some of whom became entrenched zealous jihadis, like Adrien Guihal who went to Syria and triumphantly announced on the IS radio the killing of a policeman and his wife on June 13, 2016, in Magnanville by Larossi Abballa.

The Clain brothers were also forerunners of web-jihadism: they created one of the first radical forums on the web called Ansar al-Haqq before 2010 and they also steered the website of the radical association Sanabil (Vincent, "Fabien Clain," 2019).

Fabien contacted Belgian jihadi groups, and between January 2003 and May 2004 he stayed at the district of Anderlecht in Brussels. He established ties with them for the transfer of the European jihadis to Iraq, to attack Americans who had invaded it in 2003. The two brothers went to Egypt in order to improve their Arabic and their Islamic knowledge, Jean-Michel staying there from August 2005 until February 2008. On his return from Egypt, Fabien was condemned to a five-year prison term, remaining behind bars for three years before being released in 2012. He managed to join IS in March 2015 with his family.

Jean-Michel and Fabien Clain met Abdelkader Merah in Cairo, where he studied Arabic and the Koran in Salafist madrassas with his sister Souad, while his brother Mohamed, who perpetrated the Toulouse attacks in 2012, came to visit him twice (Seckel, 2019).

The Clain brothers, Thomas Barnouin, Mohamed Megherbi, Sabri Essid, Mohamed and Abdelkader Merah, and their sister Souad were all close friends. Some created family ties: Megherbi married a sister of Clain, Amélie Grondin; Jennifer Clain, the eldest daughter of Anne-Diane Clain, a sister of the brothers Clain, was the companion of Kevin Gonot ("Une figure de la filière djihadste d'Artigat," 2018). The father of Sabri Essid married the mother of the Clain brothers and then, Merah's mother while in Artigat in 2005–2006.

The Clain brothers proclaimed and celebrated the Paris attacks of November 13, 2015, in the name of IS on its social media. Their offspring became also involved in jihadi activities. According to Jonathan Geffroy, a French Jihadi close to the brothers Clain, arrested in Turkey, Daesh placed Othman, the son of Jean-Michel Clain, at the head of the "Children's External Operations." He chose children fighters who would be trained in order to carry out attacks in France, once they were sent back there (Seelow, "Enfants kamikazes," 2018).

In April 2015, intelligence identified an IS propaganda *nasheed* (Islamic song without a musical instrument) sung in French by Jean-Michel Clain:

> We have to hit France / it's time to humiliate / we want to see suffering / and deaths by thousands.

Most of the members of Artigat who went to Syria were petty employees or jobless: Sabri Essid was an occasional crane operator, Fabien Clain was an amateur rapper, writing down songs for his brother Jean-Michel, living on social welfare and occasionally selling Islamic books on the market in Le Mirail (the "poor district" of Toulouse). All of them stayed up to the very end in Syria as veterans of jihad, the holy war becoming their way of life, beyond every other goal. Thomas Barnouin was a son of teachers who belonged to a higher social milieu. He also remained a steadfast jihadi among a group of lower-class people. The brotherhood between them cemented their bond, which remained intact to the end, in spite of their different social origins.

Fabien and his elder daughter were killed in a drone attack in February 2019 in the last recess of IS in Syria, at Al-Baghouz Fouqani, his brother having been badly wounded.

The Clain Brothers (and particularly Fabien, the older brother) created in Syria a second, transplanted version of Artigat that we could call "Artigat II," many people from the "Artigat I" being among them. New people, seduced and converted by Fabien, also took part in it. Its members were in their thirties at the time of their arrest in December 2017 by the Kurdish forces in northern Syria: Mohamed Megherbi, thirty-six years old; Thomas Barnouin, also thirty-six; Thomas Collange, thirty-five; and Romain Garnier, thirty-four. The younger brother of Megherbi, Najib, was twenty-nine, and Kevin Gonot, the stepbrother of Thomas Collange, was thirty-one. Artigat I and II made jihad into a clan, their members being driven by the holy war but also by their multiple ties to each other: marriage, filiation, and strong group identity.

b-The Crisis of Authority as a Common Denominator among Jihadi Families

The major types of jihadi families described in this chapter have a common denominator: the crisis of authority within them. The few examples that follow show how this crisis can lead, in some cases, to jihadism. The latter, mainly through IS, substituted the figurehead of the superlative father (the caliph) for the failing father, and the neo-Ummah, the superlative mother, for the mother, and in particular as a role model for the girls.

In single-parent families, the absence of the father can be experienced in two distinct ways: through guilt ("I have lost my father due to my faults") or injustice ("my father is gone, he is unjust and bad"). In the first case, self-blame gives rise to a self-disesteem that is not necessarily projected onto others. Through sacred means, lack of respect for the Self can be translated into dismissal of others. That is what happened among the youth belonging to slum culture, once they embraced radical Islam. It allowed them to convert their sense of unworthiness into a sense of unworthiness of others. The more intense the ego's indignity, the more the others became the targets of their feeling of disgrace, extended to them. In the second case, the father is blamed and the feeling of injustice is projected onto the whole society: I have been unfairly treated, the society as a whole is the culprit, and therefore, she must be punished (stigmatization of society by the migrants' sons). Radical Islam opens up the door to incriminating others on the basis of hatred toward the lacking father. At the origin of this case we find the dismissal of others, without the depreciation of oneself, as among middle-class youth. In the second case, the father is incriminated without the Self being called into question. There is no disrespect for the Self, but only for the father. This is especially the dominant feeling among middle-class youth undergoing family crisis. In this case, disrespect for the father does not translate into self-blame. Jihadism allows, in this case, the extension of the accusation against the father to the whole society without self-hatred.

In both cases, when the teenager pledges allegiance to the caliph, he legitimizes his abomination of others in reference to a sacred principle, vindicated by the new symbolic super-father. Islam in its radical version shapes a new identity, the individual locating the source of evil in others, he himself being immune to any deficiency, all faults coming from others and their annihilation becoming fully legitimate in the name of a sacred principle.

1-Examples of Jihadis Marked by Family Crisis

One can illustrate family crisis among jihadis through few more examples.

The English jihadi woman Sally Jones grew up in a broken family: her parents divorced when she was very young, and her father committed suicide by taking an overdose when she was ten years old. She left school at sixteen and began working, selling cosmetics for the L'Oréal company (Humphries, 2017). Jones lived on welfare benefits in a council house in Chatham, Kent, and used a food bank before she left for Syria.[5]

Jason Walters or Jamal (his Islamic nickname) is a Dutch citizen born on March 6, 1985, as the son of an American Black soldier, Carl Walters, and a Dutch woman in Holland. He is part of a family of four children (two sons and two daughters). His father divorced Jason's mother when Jason was young, leaving his wife and children. She worked part-time at a center for asylum seekers. Jason converted to Islam around the age of sixteen and later adopted the name "Abu Mujahid Amriki." His divorced mother and her two daughters at home felt increasingly insecure due to the radicalization of the two sons, Jason and Jermaine, who in the name of Islam forbade them to watch TV or drink alcohol. For a while the mother ran away with her two daughters and lived in the north of Holland in a women's shelter.

Jason Walters was the only Black pupil in his school and was subjected to the sarcasm of White students who constantly humiliated him. Radical Islam became for him the means to take revenge against a society that rejected his Black skin, but also, against a father who had abandoned him and a mother who could not wield real authority over him and set limits he couldn't overstep. Islam, in its extremist version, was poised to fulfill this multiple role. It gave him the sense of a sacred vocation, made him share with an imagined Muslim community (the neo-Ummah) the indignation toward an oppressive West that made them suffer just as his school had made him miserable for the color of his skin, just as his father had ignored him by abandoning him to a mother who had not passed onto him a robust identity marked by a firm sense of values.

At school he tried in vain to prove that he was just like the others, but the color of his skin, his foreign father, and the trauma of living without paternal authority had made the common identity he longed for impossible. Islam became the operator of the reversal of values. It made him endorse the new values with a clear conscience. From then on, not only did he acknowledge his difference with others, but he over-emphasized it, made it ostentatiously visible, seeking to be provocatively different and proud of it in the name of Islamic values, higher than those of a secular West.

He proudly assumed the new Islamic identity in view of a punitive God, a substitute for an absent and unworthy father who had left him when he was a teenager. The new Father ordered him to chastise those who did not follow His rules. His Muslim identity became a principle of absolute superiority, in reference to which he forbade his mother and sisters to drink alcohol or watch TV. More generally, it allowed him to declare war against a society of

Infidels who had to be punished for having mistreated him and having been an accomplice of the West's domination of Muslims the world over.

His extremist views against the Infidels prompted el-Fath Mosque to exclude him from attendance and to warn the authorities about him and his brother Jermaine. Jason made at least one trip to Pakistan and eventually to Afghanistan, where he reportedly received military training at a jihadi camp. In 2003 he wrote a farewell letter to his mother; in case he became a martyr. In that long and rambling letter, he said: "I know, my dear mother, it will be difficult for you. Don't be sad. This life is temporary and short. I will have eternal life" (Richburg, 2004). A sense of the fragility of life is frequently found among young people whose lives have been shattered like the Walters brothers: a Black American father, divorce while they were children, a single mother with four children, harassment at school, and feelings of loneliness and stigmatization. Jason, nineteen years old at the time, was arrested with Ismail Akhnikh on November 10, 2004, after a siege of fourteen hours of his residence in the Hague by the police, during which he threw a grenade on them and injured three policemen. According to the police, he planned to kill Dutch political figures he considered anti-Muslim, his list including two members of the parliament, Ayaan Hirsi Ali, a Somali native and a radical denouncer of Islam, as well as Geert Wilders, a far-right politician and the founder of the Party for Freedom. On March 10, 2006, Jason was convicted with eight others for terrorist acts and sentenced to fifteen years' imprisonment. He was released in May 2013. Linked to the Hofstad group, his brother Jermaine was arrested in Amersfoor. He and his brother reportedly planned to attack Ayaan Hirsi-Ali. He was released in 2006. In September 2014 with his wife and three children, Jermaine left for Syria to join IS. He died in the air strikes in January 2015.

The two Walter brothers opted for a radical version of Islam in reaction to the Dutch multicultural society that was hypocritical in their view, since those who were different like them were stigmatized. They opposed their father, an American military whose country, the United States, had an anti-Muslim policy according to them. They also assailed their secular mother who did not share their extremist brand of religiosity.

The case of Denis Mamadou Gerhard Cuspert, aka "Deso Dogg" (or his nom de guerre, "Abu Malik" or "Abu Talha al-Almani") displays the explosive combination of family crisis and racism. He was a German rapper. His father was Ghanaian and his mother German. He was born in Berlin's Kreuzberg district and grew up in different districts of that city. His father was deported to Ghana early in Denis's childhood. His stepfather, with whom he came to constant quarrels, was a former US Army soldier with a rigid disciplinarian mindset. Denis was sent for five years to a home for difficult children. A mixed-race individual with brown skin, he was ill at ease in a German society with no historical experience of multiple races living together in the 1980s (he was born in 1975). According to his statements, he grew up with racism, despite his mother being a German. Some teachers called him, he recalled, "Negro" and treated Muslims with disdain (Mekhennet, 2011). He was sent by social workers to Namibia, to a special farm for the rehabilitation of juvenile delinquents. In reaction to the intolerable pressures imposed on him by his American stepfather, Denis became anti-American, and in 1990 he joined demonstrations in Berlin, burning the American flag in the wake of the first Persian Gulf war. The American invasion of Iraq in 2003 re-ignited conflict with his stepfather. He joined street gangs in Berlin with the sons of migrants. In 1995 he began a rapping career, but he became increasingly involved in street fights and eventually in crime. In 2002 he was under detention in an open prison for minor offenders. By mid-2004, he was repeatedly arrested for new offenses. His probation was revoked, and he was imprisoned in Tegel Prison in Berlin. He was a member of a gang called the "36 Boys," made up primarily of first-generation Turkish and Arab immigrants. The 36 Boys violently clashed with neo-Nazi gangs.

Cuspert collaborated with a gangsta rap label in 2002 through a friend who was a rapper and producer. He released a variety of rap songs, which were widely distributed on social media.

He released his first album, "The Black Eagle," in 2006. In his texts, Cuspert reproduced not only the typical aggressive-martial topics of the genre, but also personal experiences of discrimination and stigmatization, such as the following passage from the title "Who Is Afraid of a Black Man" (Wer hat Angst vorm schwarzen Mann):

> Seated in my skin like Tookie Williams in San Quentin
> [Williams was a co-founder of the "Crips," one of the largest US-American gangs, and was an icon of gangsta-rap." He was executed in 2005 for murder in San Quentin Prison],
> [with] No identity, how should that end?
> In a white world full of hatred and illusion
> The last option was only violence and emotion
> On the playground I was only the little Nigger boy

> with torn up jeans, evil eye and cheeky tongue . . .
> Who is afraid of the black boy? At that time not so many
> The fear they learned at the Federal Youth Games
> Watch how the black boy can run, fast!
> Watch how the black boy can jump, fast!
> Should have been ten times better, had to be ten times faster
> Must be ten times harder, ten little niggers! ("Lageanalyse," 2014)

Most of the topics developed in this book are summed up in that song: lack of recognized identity ("No identity"), imposition of a racialized, humiliating identity ("the little Nigger boy"), and contempt for the "black boy" that would change in the future into fear inspired to the mainstream society through radical Islam by the despised individual who would become violent.

From 2011 up to the end of his life in January 2018 in Syria Cuspert made Islamist propaganda on the web ("Syrie: Deso Dogg," 2018).He then converted to radical Islam and moved to Syria. He was injured in 2014 during an air attack. In a long interview, he called martyrdom the ultimate goal for Muslims and summoned believers to join him in Syria with their families, denouncing life in the countries of disbelief and urging them to settle in the "land of honor." In his mind, the center of gravity had gradually shifted from life to sacred death, martyrdom being not the disappearance but the rebirth of the believer, granting him and his relatives eternal salvation (Heinke and Raudszus, 2015). In Syria, he became an active IS propagandist, appearing in videos about the battle of Al-Chaer and the massacres of Ghraneidj and al-Keshkeyyi, where he brandished severed heads. He died in the town of Khara'ij in Syria on January 17, 2018, under the American air attacks.

Via jihadism, Denis Cuspert recovered pride through violence, in stark contrast to a Christian pastor, Martin Luther King, who countered racism with militant non-violence, in the name of his faith. It is true that he had no major family problem and had a legitimacy as a Christian in America, sharing the same faith as the White people, unlike Cuspert whose religion, Islam, is considered foreign by European public opinion. Racism and Islamophobia went hand in hand with ill treatment by his stepfather. His deviant trajectory, his prison terms, and his subsequent radicalization point to the dominant model of European jihadism: being rejected by others because of his non-White origin (being Black in this case, being an "Arab," or a "Paki"), suffering family breakdown, converting to Islam, a religion that is marked by suspicion, deviancy, imprisonment and, at the end, jihadi radicalization. The latter is anti-secular, violent, and anti-Western, its values being the opposite of those prevailing in Europe.

Radical Islam's essential function is to restore dignity to a humiliated person, not while preserving the honor of the former adversary (as Nelson Mandela did when he tried to integrate White South Africans into the new nation in reference to his conception of a "rainbow society") but by denying them the dignity they had stolen from him. Radical Islam does not reconcile the dominated with the dominators in a new deal, but it exacerbates their antagonism, going so far as to deny them humanity in an all-out war marked by the supremacy of a death-centered view (an extremist version of martyrdom and jihad).

The combination of being Black, mainly from the French overseas departments and territories (Dom-Tom) or from Black Africa in the UK (or, more rarely, from Germany in a mixed marriage of a Black American and a White German), with a family crisis and on top of it spending part of their childhood in children's homes, makes some people prone to violence, radicalization being a total revenge against stigmatization. This was the case of Jérémie Louis-Sidney, a Black Frenchman born in January 1979 in Melun (Seine-et-Marne, Ile-de-France). He was the only son of a Martinican family of six daughters. His schooling was grueling, and he committed small offenses that led him to a foster family, then to a children's home, from which he ran away at the age of seventeen, moving to the south of France (Rastello, 2012). He settled in Cannes where he met a woman who became the mother of his first child. In 2008, he was sentenced to two years in prison, one suspended. His conversion to Islam is generally dated from this period behind bars. He began rapping and released a video in May 2009 in which he violently attacked the West, denouncing child and organ trafficking, questioning the official version of the 9/11 US attacks by Bin Laden's group, and proposing a conspiracy-theory version of it. He became more radical during his stays in North Africa. In October 2011, he created a retail company in Torcy, close to Paris, that was only a cover for his terrorist projects. He was the leader of the so-called Cannes-Torcy cell. He shot at the police on October 6, 2012, and was killed by them. In his case, too, the dominant model of jihadism was replicated: family breakdown, humiliation through racism, identifying with slum culture, delinquency as a pathway out of poverty and as a means to retaliate against society, imprisonment, violence, and radicalization.

VI
The European Nations and Their Jihadis

The comparative analysis of jihadis in different European countries is an overdue task. Most studies focus on their common features, and their specific national, ethnic, and social backgrounds, but the political culture of each specific European society is not focused upon in a comprehensive manner. French laïcité has been analyzed by some scholars (Woodford, 2018; McCants and Meserole, 2016), but they mostly focus on French secularism (laïcité) to explain the higher number of jihadis in that country.[1]

The study of European jihadism in a comparative perspective is still in its early stages. Here we mainly focus on the French, English, and German cases, with emphasis on the ethnic backgrounds of the European jihadis. We examine, in particular, the specific causes of jihadism, shedding light on the differences among European nations.

Regarding the behavior and motivations of Western jihadis in comparative terms, three factors seem relevant: the ethnic and national origin of the migrants and their sons, the political culture of the host country, and the integration process within European countries.

a-The Ethnic and National Origin of the Migrants and Their Sons

The ethnic and national origins of jihadis must be considered in a study of the factors that lead young adults (and others) to choose such a path, because not all immigrant families' experiences are the same, and consequently, not all immigrant communities give rise to an equal proportion of jihadis. To take an example, in Germany, communities of Turkish origin did not send the same proportion of Foreign Fighters to Syria and Iraq as those of Moroccan origin.

The causes of this disparity were historical, anthropological, and social. To take an example, the Turkish community's cohesion is generally stronger than the Moroccan. The Turks work closely together, they marry among

Jihadism in Europe. Farhad Khosrokhavar, Oxford University Press. © Oxford University Press 2021.
DOI: 10.1093/oso/9780197564967.003.0006

themselves, the brides coming sometimes from the Turkish villages, they speak Turkish even in the second generation, and so forth. On the part of the Moroccans (many of Berber origin), the brutal and violent repression of the Rif revolt in 1958 by Hassan II in Morocco played a key role in their migration to Europe, the Moroccan government sending them in order to dispose of them. Moroccans who settled in Europe, largely from the Rif in the north of the country, spoke a specific language (Amazigh) and had a different political culture from the rest of the Moroccan kingdom. The Rif is characterized by a specific culture of dissent with respect to the Moroccan state (in the 1920s, an independent republic was created in the Rif region, but the Spanish and the French put an end to it in 1926). In addition, cannabis culture in the Rif rural areas (the production and export of which to Europe brings resources back to the local population and the underground economy) promotes a subculture of transgression that can more easily be put at the service of jihadism. Such a subculture does not exist among European Turks.

In recent decades in Europe, Moroccans have experienced a distinctive religious socialization, compared to the Turks: whereas the Turkish mosques are governed by a state structure, the *Diyanet*, which ensures the leadership of religious affairs and makes a rigorous selection of imams in Turkey before sending them to Europe, Moroccan imams have often been trained and socialized in the Persian Gulf countries, and in particular in Saudi Arabia, and many of them embrace the Salafist version of Islam, which is ideologically close to the religious radicals.

Among the Turks in France and Germany, family structure has also been much better preserved, and community ties are stronger than among North Africans.

Colonization in Algeria and an extremely violent decolonization (more than 250,000 deaths on the Algerian side) had a major impact on the subjectivity of the migrants and their children and grandchildren. Once in France after decolonization, Algerians did not build up strong community ties, as did the Turks, the bonds being to a large extent broken due to the colonial past. North African fathers did not ensure as strictly as their Turkish counterparts the religious socialization of their children, both in the mosque and in the family, these two institutions being much better maintained among the Turks because of the cohesion in their community, as my personal researches in Neuhof, a district close to Strasbourg where Turks and North Africans live, as well as in a poor district of Gien, have shown me. Ignorance of religious rituals is more widespread among North

Africans than among Turks. Jihadism prospered more easily among young people of North African origin than among those of Turkish origin, in part due to the fact that the former were more ignorant of religious precepts than the latter, and they were also less traditionalist. In a way, they had been too close to the French (a love–hate relationship), compared to the Turks, who were more distant.

The November 2015 attacks in Paris and the March 2016 attacks in Brussels illustrated the dominant role of Europeans of Moroccan origin. The specificity of Morocco and its significant presence in Belgium, Spain, France, and other European countries is due to various factors. France has around 1, 34 million Moroccans. (https://doi.org/10.4000/hommesmigrations.2543); in Holland they are one-third of the Muslim community, after those of Indonesian and Turkish origins. In Belgium, Moroccans constitute the largest Muslim community (around 430,000), about 4 percent of the total population, this country hosting the highest percentage of Moroccans in Europe (Statistics of the Research Center in Demography and Societies of the Leuven Catholic University, 2014). In Germany, they would be between 160,000 and 180,000 Moroccans, mainly from the Rif region (https://ma.boell.org/fr/2017/04/03/la-nouvelle-migration-des-jeunes-marocaines-vers-leurope-2015-2016-un-autre-regard/), whereas the number of Turks in Germany is estimated between 2.7 million and 3.5 million (https://www.dw.com/en/new-rules-for-muslims-in-german-state-blasted/a-1840793), their number in France being estimated at around 800,000 according to the French consulates in Turkey (https://www.diplomatie.gouv.fr/fr/dossiers-pays/turquie/presentation-de-la-turquie). Even though the years these statistics were gathered are not identical, and there is a large uncertainty over the exact numbers, it seems beyond doubt that the proportion of European Foreign Fighters of Moroccan origin was much higher than those of Turkish origin, be it in Germany or in France.

On the linguistic level, those of Moroccan origin in Europe express themselves in one of the idioms, mainly Rifian (from the Rif region) or in Moroccan Arabic; and in Belgium the youngest ones speak Dutch or French according to whether they belong to the Flemish or Walloon region of Belgium; in Brussels they speak the two dominant languages, namely French and Flemish.

Jihadi attacks in France (November 2015), Belgium (March 2016), and Spain (August 2017) were largely committed by people of Moroccan descent. We can mention the Liege bombing of December 13, 2011, which left seven dead and 125 injured, carried out by Nordine Amrani, of Moroccan origin, who committed suicide after the police assault. Similarly, Najim Laachraoui, Mohamed Abrini, and Ibrahim and Khalid El Bakraoui, who took part in three suicide bombings at Brussels Airport and the Maelbeek metro on March 22, 2016, were of Moroccan origin. Nearly 90 percent of Belgians who left for Syria were of Moroccan origin (Maroc: visite du quartier general de l'antiterrorisme, à Rabat, RTL INFO), which simply in this specific case is due to the fact that Moroccans are by far the largest minority among Muslims in Belgium: the Moroccan diaspora is demographically the first immigrant minority in Spain (around 792,000, or 16.4 percent of the 4,550,000 foreigners living in Spain; Urra, 2017).

In Spain, those of Moroccan origin played a significant role in the Madrid bombings on March 11, 2004, notably Hassan el-Haski, a Belgian of Moroccan descent, who was one of the major jihadis. As for the attacks of November 13, 2015, in France, they were mainly committed by Belgians or French jihadis of Moroccan origin: Bilal Hadfi, Brahim Abdeslam, Chakib Akrouh, Abdelhamid Abaaoud, Salah Abdeslam, Mohammed Amri, Hamza Attou, Al Ouikadi, and Mohamed Abrini.

The Dutch case unequivocally shows the overrepresentation of the people of Moroccan origin among the Foreign Fighters in Europe, compared to those of Turkish descent. A new database analyzes the profiles of 207 Foreign Fighters from the Netherlands who traveled to Syria or Iraq. Three-fourths of them were male and young, the average age being twenty-three years. The proportion of the Dutch of Moroccan origin was about 2 percent of the population (354,000 out of 17,000,000). In comparison, the percentage of Dutchmen of Turkish origin was slightly higher (378,330 people), while the proportion of Dutch Foreign Fighters of Turkish origin was 10 percent, less than one-fourth as many as those of Moroccan descent (46 percent; Bergema, 2017).

The question of the Rif, the northern region of Morocco, is at the heart of Belgian as well as Spanish jihadism. Salah Abdeslam belonged to the second generation of Rifians from Rif) in Belgium as did many other radicalized youth who took part in the attacks of March 2004 in Madrid as well as those in France by the gang of Roubaix in the 1990s. However, Abdelhamid Abaaoud was from Sousse, in southern Morocco, and the cell that committed the attacks of November 13, 2015, in Paris and March 22, 2016, in Brussels also had a few members of Algerian and Tunisian origin, although the majority were of Moroccan descent, largely from the Rif.

b-The Political Culture of the Host Country

The political culture of the host country, its history, and the perception of Self and others there is decisive in the socialization of the populations of immigrant descent. French universalism, secularism (laïcité), and republicanism are not of the same nature as English multiculturalism or German federalism, born after the Second World War. The same communities of origin (Moroccan, Turkish, Pakistani) do not behave similarly in one European country as another: men and women of Turkish origin present similarities but also differences in France, Germany, Belgium, or the UK.

Young Europeans who left for the "blessed land of Sham" (Great Syria) to accomplish jihad at the service of IS presented significant differences according to their nationalities. The goal pursued—the holy war—united them, but some of the motivations (for instance, regarding the veil, which is much more restricted in France than in other parts of Europe) and the groups that took part displayed marked differences in historical perspective (up to the year 2010, in France Algerians were the most numerous; during the years of the IS, 2013–2016, Moroccans became probably more numerous in that country). The political culture of the country of residence (laïcité distinguishes France, multiculturalism in the United Kingdom, federalism in Germany) plays a role in the radicalization of young people.

Beginning around 2010, a new generation of jihadis appeared in Europe. Data recorded by conservative organizations (European Jihad Watch, 2017) estimated the number of people involved in jihadi networks from January 2013 to March 2017 at 7,195.[2] Of the total, almost 70 percent came from three countries: France, the United Kingdom, and Germany. In detail, there were 2,299 people (32 percent) from France, 1,700 (24 percent) from the United Kingdom, 910 (13 percent) from Germany, 640 (9 percent) from Belgium, 355 (5 percent) from Sweden, 311 (4 percent) from Austria, and 285 (4 percent) from Holland.[3]

There are some specific features to French jihadis, principally a deeper "hatred" of society in reaction to the French political culture of laïcité. In the eyes of these young people the latter is neocolonialism disguised as secularism. For them laïcité is another way of secluding and belittling the sons and the daughters of the former colonial empire.

In Germany, the UK, or Sweden the political culture is more diffuse, less frontal, the Islamic veil and ritualism not being outright rejected in the name of secularism by force of law in the government bodies and institutions (government school, public servants being forbidden to wear the scarf, etc.). The successive headscarf issues in France and the promulgation of the laws banning it in government schools (law on ostentatious religious signs of March 15, 2004), then in the public sphere regarding the integral veil (law of October 11, 2010 on total veil, forbidding entirely covering the face in the public space), and the one that rejects veil in private day nurseries(law of May 13, 2015) impose numerous restrictions on wearing the veil in France, compared to other Western countries (in Belgium the total veil is also forbidden by law since July 2011; in Denmark, since August 2018; in Spain, at communal levels, the Islamic veil can be banned at school by municipal decree).

The frontality of the French political culture is based on two major principles: republicanism and laïcité. The former means that no community between the individual and the national community is publicly recognized: Muslim, Christian, Jewish, and other communities are treated as groups of people without public recognition, their bonds being restricted to the private sphere. An increasingly hardened version of secularism (laïcité) implies that religion should be strictly private, not public. Therefore, the veil (the scarf for most of the European Muslim women) is forbidden within the state apparatus (no public servant should wear it in office). On the other hand, most religious insignias like the scarf are meant to be worn in the public sphere (the scarf has its Islamic meaning outside the home, not inside it), and this creates a tension with those with traditional Muslim identity. Social and anthropological tension push some young Muslims toward radicalization in the country of Voltaire that embodies in their eyes the harshest expression of Western Islamophobia. In an interview in 2013, a young prisoner in Fleury-Mérogis did not conceal his dismissal of French Secularism:

Akbar: Look at France, there are so many laws that ban the hijab: in school, on the street [the total veil], *and elsewhere. A woman can be half-naked, nobody lifts a finger against her, but as soon as she wears the hijab the* [French] *Republic is in danger! Behind these taboos, hides the contempt for the Muslims. The French hate us, and they do everything they can to make our lives miserable. A Jew who wears the skull cap* [*kippa*], *no one dares to criticize him. It is republican at 150 percent, but if a girl wears the scarf, the republic is in danger! Add to this the contempt towards the young people from the poor suburbs, the war against Muslims in Afghanistan, Mali, Syria and many other countries by the French army and secret services. It is then understandable that Muslims in this country act like Merah* [who killed

> Muslim military and Jews in 2012]. *France hates Islam and Muslims. Before, they rejected the Arabs, now it's Muslims' turn, we are not citizens in this country, we are still colonized but they don't tell us outright. In short, we have two choices: either we exist as lice or as crocodiles! We'd better choose to be a crocodile to kill by the jaws and launch mortal blows by the tail and not a louse they can swat!*

French jihadis are in part influenced by the culture of frontality within the mainstream society, they are under the spell of a political culture that they denounce while accentuating its radicality.

c-The Integration Process within European Countries

Last, we should consider the integration process within European countries. The urban structure, the level of industrialization of the country, and the level of education of the community of origin—in brief, their social classes—play a role in their integration or marginalization in the host countries. In the United States, a sizeable part of the "White" Muslims (e.g., Turks, Moroccans, Algerians, Pakistanis) are middle-class, which makes them less likely to adhere to jihadism, compared to their European counterparts whose fathers and grandfathers were working-class people.[4] Compared to their European counterparts, American Muslims have a stronger attachment to the American society because of their status (
Ulloa, 2019), despite social prejudices against them, heightened by the September 11, 2001, terrorist attacks.

The comparison between European countries regarding the proportion of first- or second-generation women and converts, their educational level, and the proportion of teenagers among jihadis, shows disparities that are difficult to explain, considering the paucity of anthropological studies.

The question of generations also distinguishes different European nations. In France and the United Kingdom, second-generation youth of Muslim origin who left for Syria were the majority of the jihadis. In Spain, between June 2013 and May 2016, a study shows that the majority of those imprisoned for activities related to IS belonged to the first generation (51.7 percent), the second generation making up 42.2 percent of them, and 6.1 percent being made of Spanish citizens unrelated to migration (Reinares, and Garcia-Calvo, 2016). In Norway, 61 percent of jihadis were first-generation (*Report on Radicalization in Norway*, 2016). The question of generation is thus related to the host country (Bergema, 2017).

The proportion of converts among Foreign Fighters also varies from country to country: In France, a study on 137 jihadis published in April 2018 finds the proportion of converts to be 26 percent (Hecker, 2018); in Spain, 13.9 percent (Reinares and García-Calvo, 2016), and in Norway 18 percent (*Report on Radicalization*, 2016). In Holland, a study based on the profiles of 207 Foreign Fighters shows that 17 percent of them were converts, and this percentage was seven times higher than the proportion of people converted to Islam in Holland (Bergema, 2017). From Germany, 12 percent of those who went to Syria were converts (Van Ginkel and Entenmann, 2016).

Even though the data collection dates are not identical (some are from 2016, others from 2017), the results show nonetheless the high rate of radicalized converts in Europe and significant differences between different European countries in that respect. The historical context of each country, region, or city has to be considered in determining the commitment of jihadi converts.

Women made up a large minority of those who went to Syria during the IS period (2013–2016). In Spain, their proportion was 16.9 percent with a medium age of 22.6 years, compared to men, with a medium age of 31.6 years (nine years older; Reinares and Garcia-Calvo, 2016). The proportion of German women who went to Syria was higher than in Spain (21 percent; Datenreport, 2016).

The statistics on the French jihadis in terms of residence in disadvantaged districts and suburbs do not exist in an exhaustive way, but the data available point out the ethnic origins (mostly from North Africa) and social exclusion (living in poor suburbs): out of 137 jihadi cases analyzed, 40 percent of them (49) came from the "poor districts," 59 percent had North African parents, 9 percent had parents from sub-Saharan Africa, and 18 percent were of French parents (among them, naturalized Muslim citizens), with 7 percent being the descendants of mixed couples (French and non-French). All in all, at least 68 percent had parents from Muslim countries (Hecker, 2018).

France had the highest number of Foreign Fighters: 1,910 in comparison to 960 from Germany and 850 from the United Kingdom (Cook and Vale, 2018). In 2018, according to the available statistics, 38 percent of terrorist attacks or projects occurred in France, versus 15 percent in Germany and 19 percent in the United Kingdom (Chemel and Blanc, 2019).

Beyond this particular feature, there were many jihadi profiles in France and more generally in Europe, but the largest category, in number and proportion, was those of Muslim origin, who came from poor districts, belonging to a slum culture. Around two-thirds of the French jihadis among those arrested were of North African origin (mostly Algeria and Morocco), a few of them from sub-Saharan Africa (France, Saverot, Colomina," 2019).

Before 2013, young people in the poor suburbs overwhelmingly represented the dominant profile of jihadis in France, and middle-class youth were rather marginal. In the UK, in the same period, "disaffected youth" were predominant, even though young people from lower-middle classes appeared to be more numerous than in France (no valid statistics are available so far).

After 2013 and the influx to Syria and Iraq, and especially after 2014 and the creation of Daesh, young people, among them middle-class girls and women, but also converts, swelled the ranks of the wannabe jihadis. Despite that, those from poor districts remained the majority. Among those were a high rate of people with criminal records. In Europe, in a relatively large sample, 57 percent, had been incarcerated before their radicalization. In France, the partial data available suggest the same type of relationship: more than half of the jihadis had criminal records, or even came from criminal circles (Basra, Neumann, and Brunner, 2016). In this case, crime is related to social exclusion, stigmatized neighborhoods where the disaffected youth live, and ethnicity: young people of North African origin in France, and of Pakistani and Bangladeshi origin in the UK, moved toward delinquency as the major gateway out of social exclusion, identifying with a slum subculture prior to their "awakening" to jihadism and rejecting mainstream values. By joining IS, they went beyond the predicament of being humiliated in the eyes of others and in their own, moralizing their action as God's combatants. It was not primarily because they were criminals that they were attracted to Daesh but because through IS they earned self-respect and could repudiate their self-perception as deviants overburdened with indignity due to their ethnic origin, becoming thus noble fighters devoted to God. Those whom they fought were the very same people who, in their view, had prevented them from becoming "normal" citizens. The anthropological dimension is paramount: criminal behavior finds an explanation within it. A partial work on French jihadis, especially those who participated in the latest attacks in France, reveals a certain homogeneity. Of the twenty-two terrorists who hit France, from Mohamed Merah in 2012 to Adel Kermiche in 2016, there were fourteen Frenchmen (mostly of North African origin), three Belgians, one Algerian, one Moroccan, one unknown, one Tunisian, and one Turk (from Kurdistan). Among them, fourteen had criminal records or had been convicted (Laurent, 2016).

Jihadism in Germany has its own history. At the time of the war in Afghanistan, German jihadis were involved in guerrilla warfare against the Soviet Union, as well as in Bosnia and Chechnya. Multi-Kultur-Haus (MKH) in Neu-Ulm in southern Germany played an important role in the departure of young Germans to Bosnia and Chechnya. One of its members, Reda Seyam, born in 1959 in Egypt, later became the highest-ranking IS German fighter as the "Emir of Education in the Nineveh Region." In 1994 he fought in Bosnia, then moved to Riyadh in Saudi Arabia in 1998. He was deported to Germany after being interrogated by the CIA.

As already mentioned, the birth of IS led to a significant increase in the number of young Foreign Fighters leaving for Syria and Iraq all over Europe and, in particular, from Germany. From January 2012 to June 2016, 784 people left for Syria. Like everywhere else in Europe, the highest number of departures took place between the end of 2013 and the end of 2014. In the fourth quarter of 2014 the number of departures decreased significantly, this trend continuing thereafter: only seventy-four people left for Syria during the fourth quarter of 2014, twenty-eight in the first quarter of 2015, and only four in the last quarter of 2016 (Datenreport 2018: Social Report for the Federal Republic of Germany). This was largely due to Syria's increasingly difficult access via Europe through Turkey. The latter cooperated with Europe more closely since mid-2014 and stopped those who sought to cross the border and join IS. Regarding the profile of young people leaving Germany for Syria and Iraq, two-thirds of them were known to the police (26 percent for violent attacks, 24 percent for property offenses, 18 percent for political crimes, and 10 percent for narcotics). As for the causes of their radicalization, for 54 percent of them the influence of their friends was paramount, for 48 percent it was the mosques (which had a significant role at the beginning, even if it declined over time), for 44 percent it was the internet, and for 27 percent it was Islamic seminaries. Other reasons were the distribution of the Koran (in the "Lies!" Campaigns in Germany; 24 percent) and the influence of family members (21 percent). More than a quarter (27 percent) of those who left Germany had ties to jihadi Salafism. More than half of them (55 percent) began to radicalize at the beginning of the Syrian conflict in the spring of 2012. As for their motivation, more than half did so for jihadi reasons (54 percent), 27 percent wanted to migrate and join IS for their *Hijra* (migration to an Islamic land), and 18 percent acted for "humanitarian" reasons. A few had truly revolutionary motives (8 percent), and a minority wanted to marry (6 percent) or accompany a wife or a family member (5 percent). Half of the German people in Syria came from thirteen cities called "hotspots," in which there was a strong influence of Salafist-jihadi circles. In other cases, for the people from 149 other cities, radicalization occurred through the web or by propaganda (e.g., the distribution of the Koran). As for the age, of the 784 people who went to Syria, 56 were minors, which accounted for 7 percent of the departures. Forty-two percent of minors became radicalized in less than a year (80 percent of them had links with Salafist-jihadis). Seventeen percent of them were converts to Islam (compared to 21 percent for adults). Fifty-seven percent of those who joined IS were German citizens; 69 percent of them also had also another nationality (21 percent German-Turkish, 17 percent German-Moroccan, 13 percent German-Tunisian, 11 percent German-Afghan, 7 percent German-Syrian). The overall proportion of women was 21 percent; that of converts, 17 percent (39 percent for minors, 20 percent for adults).

What is peculiar to Germany in comparison to France is, first, the prominent role of recent immigrants, newcomers, or even asylum seekers in the jihadi attacks in Germany. Second, the Turkish community, the largest Muslim community, did not send a significant number of Foreign Fighters to Syria, compared to its sheer size as the largest Muslim community in Germany. In France, jihadis were mostly young people of North African origin (the majority Muslim ethnic group), in addition to converts. Another trait that distinguished Germany from France was the ethnically more diverse character of jihadis. An example illustrates this phenomenon: in early November 2016 German authorities arrested the members of a jihadi group claiming allegiance to IS. The alleged leader of the group, Ahmad Abdulaziz Abdullah, aka "Abu Walaa," thirty-two, was of Iraqi origin (he is a German Islamist preacher living in Hildesheim, Lower Saxony); among the other members was a Turkish citizen, Hasan Celenk, fifty (who seemingly had initiated the radicalization of the three German teenagers who blew up a bomb in a Sikh temple on April 16, 2016), a German-Serb named Boban Simeneovic, thirty-six, a German, twenty-seven, named Mahmoud Omeirat, of Arab descent, and Ahmed Fifes Youssouf, twenty-six, a Cameroonian. The group aimed to recruit candidates, to send them to Syria. Hasan Celenk and Boban Simeneovic had reportedly radicalized Anis Amri, who perpetrated the attacks of December 19, 2016, in Berlin (the so-called Cannes-Torcy group in France also had diverse origins). Still, German jihadis acting within a group were ethnically more diversified than their French counterparts, who were mainly made up of young people from the former colonies, mostly from North Africa, and especially Morocco since 2014.

Italy and Spain (but also Portugal with a small Muslim community) experienced much later Muslim migration than France, the UK, Germany, Holland, or Denmark (where immigration started in the late 1950s and early 1960s). Only in the 1990s did Muslims massively choose Italy and Spain as a migration target, reversing the customary flow of migrants from these two countries to the United States, France, or Latin America.

Italy's urban, social, and anthropological situation presents major differences with that of France or the United Kingdom. First, there is no major concentration of Muslims (with few exceptions; Conti, 2014) as is the case in the poor suburbs in France, where often a high proportion of the population is of North African origin. In Italy, Muslims are more or less scattered: they live in rural areas but also in small provincial towns where they work in small or medium-sized companies, some lawfully, others illegally. Muslims arrived in Italy in the 1990s and were more or less integrated into small economic units. Italian jihadis were not driven by the same intense animosity toward their host country as their French, Belgian or English counterparts. Giuliano (aka "Ebrahim") Delnevo, the Italian jihadi, attempted to "magnify" the Italian nation by pointing out the latter's convergence with jihadism, especially through anti-imperialist and leftist Italian traditions. This was not the case of French jihadis, even among converts, for whom France, particularly with regard to secularism and its foreign policy (bombing of Syria, fighting against jihadism in Mali), was the irreconcilable enemy.

In the UK, feelings of frustration, stigmatization, and the memory of past colonization opened up three different paths with regard to Islam:

- Some took the traditional Islamic course of action.
- Others defined their own identity in their personal capacity, as Englishmen, assuming an attitude that broke with the religious behavior of their parents and their community (this was the case of those like the novelist Salman Rushdie, who chose Britishness at odds with Muslim identity).

- Others sought to build up their identity either through fundamentalist Islam (a stiff version of Deobandi or neo-Wahhabi religiosity) or within jihadi movements.

The difference with France lies in the fact that in the UK the traditional Islamic way of life was better preserved, whereas laïcité and the republican French system of socialization pushed toward a more pronounced secularization, regarded as an emancipation by some migrants' sons and daughters, as an aggressive denial of identity in a neo-colonial manner by many others. The breakdown of the religious world has been more pronounced in France (where laïcité sometimes functions as a civil religion) than in Britain or Germany, where the government's and society's attitude toward religion is more neutral. Moreover, both countries have communities that historically were more integrated into the religious structures than Moroccans in France or Belgium—the Berbers (Amazigh) being more secularized, Turks building up more cohesive communities than Moroccans or Algerians, and Pakistanis having stronger religious ties (Deobandi/Barelvi) than North Africans, influenced by the cultural model of the former colonizer, France.

In the UK, most of the jihadis were recruited among the youth of Pakistani, Bangladeshi, Somali, Jamaican, or Nigerian (converts) origin.

As already mentioned, there are major differences between the religious landscapes in France and Great Britain. In the UK, along with Muslims (2,800,000), there are followers of the Hindu (835,000) and Sikh (43,200) religions who significantly diversify the religious landscape. The polarization between Muslims and Jews (there are 266,000 in the UK) is less pronounced than in France, where there are around half a million Jews. Although British jihadis are often anti-Semitic, they are less violent against Jews than in France (no major attacks on Jews were launched by jihadis in the UK, compared to France). In the country of Voltaire there is also a polarization between "Arabs" and Jews, the former blaming the latter not only for repressing the Palestinians in the Middle East but also for taking over public life and dominating the mainstream culture, turning it against them. In particular, they believe that the "Jews" have managed to get rid of the status of scapegoat by passing it to them, the "Arabs" (the same type of argument does not seem to be used by those of Pakistani or Bangladeshi origin in the UK). On the other hand, in the confrontational French culture, the "Arabs" reject the "Gaouris" (French people of European origin, in the language of the French poor suburbs). This bipolarity does not exist to the same extent and with the same intensity between the "White" Englishmen and the "Pakis" (a pejorative term designating young people of Pakistani origin and, by extension, Asians).

Although multiculturalism as the recognition of the dignity of minorities in their cultural differences is in crisis in Europe, the tolerance of the English society is greater than the French, marked by republicanism in what I have called "French mono-culturalism" (Khosrokhavar, L'universel abstrait, 1997): the Islamic veil is less decried, less repressed than in France, which possesses the most restrictive legislation in the Western world about it. Moreover, in the United Kingdom, relations with immigrants are less frontal than in France, where the gap between religious Muslims and the mainstream secularist society is greater. Nevertheless, the non-frontal nature of the cultural relationship in the United Kingdom does not prevent stigmatization: indeed, discriminations are significant in recruitment, and identity checks by the police are far more frequent than with "Whites" (Dobson, 2014; Dugan, 2014).

"Republican paternalism" as a version of republicanism implies a frontal relationship between government and citizens. The latter have demands vis-à-vis the government that are not found to the same degree in the English world. The demand to the governments to ensure social justice and provide means of subsistence to the poor are probably greater in Republican France than in the United Kingdom. In the years 2017–2020, France underwent three major social movements (La Nuit Debout (Night, Standing movement), Les Gilets Jaunes (Yellow Vest movement), and the trade unions strikes in December 2019–January 2020) to protest against social injustice, whereas in the United Kingdom there was none of the same magnitude. In poor districts in France, large sums have been invested in low-rent housing (HLM), in schools, and in public assistance to the poor; nevertheless, there is a deep feeling of social injustice. The slogan "France has let us go!" (Marlière, 2008) is widespread, and the feeling of a denial of dignity and insufficient public support is deeply rooted in those people's minds. Young people from the poor districts feel abandoned by the institutions, the relationship between the individual and the "paternalist" state being constitutive of the French Republican ideology. The requirement to be assisted, so deeply entrenched in French society, does not exist to the same extent in the UK or Italy. This does not mean that young people in the poor districts of those countries do not benefit from the Welfare State, but the legitimacy of this claim is deeply embedded in the French Republican ideology: a supposed failure of the French state to meet its obligations toward vulnerable groups results in a conflicting and frontal relationship. This is why these young people speak of the "country of misfortune" (Beaud and Amrani, 2005), a society that promises them, via the republican ideal, a life of equality and social justice, but in reality does not fulfill its commitment to the poor. In a sense, French Republicanism promises too much and accomplishes too little in regard to the extensive promises it makes, internalized by the poor classes. This dimension is less significant in English multiculturalism, which is also based on the partial withdrawal of the government from the welfare of the poor since Thatcherism: people rely less on the government and feel comparatively less revolted than their French counterparts, who denounce a republicanism that is out of step with the social ideals of equality and justice it conveys. In the UK, the culture of individual autonomy promoted in the Thatcher era pushes young people of immigrant origin into deviant or self-governing forms of sociability, the role of the government in their identity being less significant than in France.

Jihadis defend separation between Muslim and non-Muslim communities, and consequently are less antagonistic toward the English cultural model than the French. Secularism was denounced by French jihadis from the Cannes-Torcy and Buttes-Chaumont cells when they took part in the 2003 demonstrations against the law banning the headscarf in the government-sponsored schools (école publique). On the other hand, two jihadis who participated in the July 7, 2005, attacks in London, Mohamad Sidique Khan and Shahzad Tanweer, denounced in their videos the British involvement in the war against Iraq and its anti-Islamic policy, but they did not frontally criticize multicultural policies in the United Kingdom.

French Republicanism doubly destabilizes its Muslim youth: it is hypersecular, and is therefore opposed to certain Islamic norms in the public space, and, moreover, it is assimilationist in its mainstream ideology. English society, more tolerant of cultural differences, does not mix so much, members of English Muslim communities marrying more rarely with non-Muslims than in France, as already noted.

French society is more "intolerant" but more "integrative" than its English counterpart, which is more "tolerant" but also less "integrative." The second pattern is better suited to fundamentalists who are for separation. The French model further antagonizes Muslims who feel morally assaulted by the requirements of laïcité.

Despite the differences between France and Great Britain, a common denominator between them is the jihadis' social origin. In both cases, the vast majority of them are young, disaffected people of immigrant origin: in the UK, the majority are Bangladeshi and Pakistani (more than half) and, in France, of North African origin (presumably more than two-thirds; Stuart, 2017).[5]

Of the 264 people convicted of jihadi acts between 1998 and 2015 in Britain, the overwhelming majority (93 percent) were men. The average age at the time of arrest was twenty-two years. Even though 72 percent of those convicted were British nationals, slightly more than half of them were of South Asian descent (of Pakistani and Bangladeshi origin; Stuart, 2017).

In the UK, the link between social deprivation and jihadism is clear: among people who committed offenses, Muslims from poor districts were overrepresented. Nearly a quarter of the crimes were committed by individuals living in neighborhoods where the proportion of the Muslim population was over 60 percent. Thirty-eight percent were unemployed. Regarding the level of education, one fourth of the offenders had attended college. In the United Kingdom, most of the jihadis belong to poor Muslim communities (Stuart, 2017).

Another difference between France and the United Kingdom is the number of doctors and medical students who enrolled in jihadism, particularly Daesh. They went to Syria to save lives on IS's side (humanitarian care), but also to mark their allegiance to its ideology. They endorsed a vision that excluded equal rights for the patients and implied denying medical assistance to non-jihadis and even denouncing them to the repressive Daesh government.

Unlike France, where a very small number of doctors or medical students left to join IS, from Britain at least seventeen doctors or medical students left in 2015 for Syria, most of them of Sudanese origin. Former British colonies such as Sudan, some of whose elites live in the UK, studied medicine in the University of Medical Sciences and Technology of Khartoum, the capital of Sudan, an institution recognized by Britain, where many medical students were indoctrinated by its Islamic Cultural Association.[6]

In France, Amine L., twenty-nine, who called himself "Albistouri," is currently charged with the apology of terrorism and an attempt to leave for Syria. Ex-intern of the Timone Hospital in Marseille, he was expelled from Turkey on December 25, 2016, and sent to France, to be indicted four days later. He had been working for three years in the hospital services of Marseilles.

According to the police, he became radicalized through his contact with certain radicalized individuals, regularly consulting jihadi websites and threatening to commit attacks on his Twitter account. He was denounced in 2015 on the platform Pharos, set up to report illegal content on social networks.

The Scandinavian countries (Denmark, Sweden, and Norway) share a common characteristic: they did not have major colonies, unlike France, the UK, Spain, and Portugal (the former Danish colonies did not play any major role in jihadism).

What specifically made these countries the target of jihadi ire was the publication, on September 30, 2005, of twelve cartoons in the Danish daily *Jyllands-Posten* that were defamatory toward the Prophet Muhammad. The drawings were highly offensive to the believers.

Norwegian jihadis shared a number of traits with their French and English counterparts in their poor districts: low levels of education, deviant activities, high unemployment rates (only 4 percent of them had a stable job), family crisis, and so on. Similarly, the average age was 27.5 years (*Report on Radicalization in Norway*, 2016). In Europe the average age of the jihadis varied between twenty-six and twenty-eight years.

Other features deviated from the French poor suburban model. Thus, in Norway, jihadis who left for Syria were multi-ethnic. Some ethnicities were overrepresented (the Somalis) in proportion to their number. Another specific feature was that they did not primarily project their hatred on Norwegian society but on the Assad regime in Syria, contrary to the French or English jihadis who intensely hated their own societies as well as the Syrian regime.

The Dutch filmmaker Theo van Gogh was killed in November 2004 by Mohammed Bouyeri in Amsterdam for having defamed Islam and its Prophet. Bouyeri was part of a group of fourteen radical Islamists who planned to kill politicians and the police, called the "Hofstad group" by the security forces. Their members were sentenced in 2006 to up to fifteen years in prison.

Between April 2013 and June 2018, some 175 Dutch Foreign Fighters went to Syria, sixty of them returning to Holland (Cook and Vale, 2018). According to a global study (Van Ginkel and Entenmann, 2016), the majority of the Foreign Fighters from Holland belonged to the lower or lower-middle classes, had a low- or medium-level education, and their chances of entering the labor market were limited. They were generally raised in immigrant families (Moroccans, Somalis, West Indians, Turks) or in ethnically Dutch families (converts). They were often exposed to crime and drug addiction. Many, of immigrant origin, felt frustrated because of their disadvantaged social position and their ethnic group's stigmas, believing that they had no future. This type of feature is consistent with the dominant European model of jihadism.

One can also focus on those countries where jihadism remained marginal. Italy is a case in point. There, the lack of jihadi attacks in recent years shows, in contrast to the other Western European countries, that the absence of large ethnic ghettos has reduced the number of jihadi vocations. The relatively low number of jihadis (132 Italian Foreign Fighters went to Syria up to 2017) is due in part to the fact that the type of poor ethnic European districts in which a large number of migrants' sons and grandsons live is not widespread in Italy: most migrants either live in rural areas where small enterprises, partly legal and partly illegal, recruit them, or mostly in towns or cities where they do not concentrate in the same manner as in France or the United Kingdom in stigmatized, disadvantaged, ethnic districts. Muslim immigrants arrived in Italy in the 1990s, fathers working and sons not yet undergoing the same type of identity crisis as in France, the UK, or Denmark (unemployment, stigmatization, imprisonment, radicalization). The efficiency of Italian police is also due in part to its long experience with Mafia in the last half a century, and the extreme left movement, the Red Brigades, in the 1980s and 1990s.

The sense of non-belonging to the society was often extremely strong among the jihadis, in particular from the disadvantaged districts, that is to say those who were unemployed or in a precarious situation even if they had the level of education that would qualify them for white-collar jobs. Therefore, they did not have a feeling of emotional neutrality toward society: they responded to social prejudice by hatred or rebuff.

My own experience in the so-called poor suburbs in France showed me how aggressive they might be, over-reacting to the least remark that they wrongly felt was demeaning toward them, being unable to cope with the slightest frustration, particularly when caused by the "White" people. Their overall feeling of victimization made them prone to verbal and sometimes physical violence (Khosrokhavar, 2016). Racism and counter-racism in this type of predicament build up a vicious circle: the more they felt rejected, the more they developed an antisocial attitude whose culmination was jihadism among a tiny minority of them. In that case they went beyond their particular concerns, having been exposed to indoctrination or brainwashing. This feeling remained significant even after the individual had built a family and had children. Oftentimes jihadis left their pregnant women to make the attacks in the name of holy war. This was the case of Mohammad Sidique

Khan, the head of the cell that committed the attacks of July 7, 2005, in the London subway and bus. Several other cases existed, in which being the father of a family with young children did not prevent jihadi involvement and suicide attacks or departure to Syria without the family's knowledge. Data from a sample of 1,200 Western Foreign Fighters show that 52 percent of them were married, 46 percent single, and 2 percent divorced, and one-third of the married couples had children before leaving (Perliger and Milton, 2016). The religious dimension of their commitment was paramount to them, as a prisoner told me in March 2013 in the French prison of Fresnes, Ile-de-France, charged with "criminal conspiracy for a terrorist [jihadi] action": "If they die, God provides for the family. She will also be saved in the Last Judgment by the sacrifice of the martyr who guarantees divine benevolence for his relatives."

IS was quick to exploit the enduring malaise of young Muslims, middle-class or disaffected, into a massive fascination through its promises of reconquered dignity, economic promotion, and the status of hero in the war against the Infidels.

VII
The Jihadogenic Urban Structure

By "jihadogenic urban structure" I mean an urban setting that has been the stage for the departure of high numbers of jihadi agents to Syria in comparison with other districts.[1]

The urban dimension, be it in deprived poor districts or middle-class neighborhoods, underlines the fact that jihadism is a "total (or comprehensive) social phenomenon" in the Mauss sense, and the urban dimension is articulated with others, subjective as well as objective. In the case of the poor districts, the subjective side is humiliation and resentment, a strong feeling among the disaffected youth due to the denial of citizenship by the mainstream society—in part real, in part imagined—due to living in stigmatized towns or neighborhoods, coupled with a strong sense of "no future," being racialized, not only trapped in a ghettoized urban environment but also in a slum culture; the objective facet is high unemployment rate, poverty, low education, deviance among many young men, high prison rates, and a pervasive underground economy.

The transformation of many working-class districts into poor immigrant neighborhoods usually happens when "White" workers gradually leave the district and immigrants with a precarious economic status replace them. After a while, the concentration accelerates in such a way that the "Whites" become more and more invisible and often end up disappearing from the public space. The new residents suffer from social exclusion and economic marginality. Islam becomes a bulwark against stigmatization. It allows its adherents to be dignified despite marginalization; its Salafist version fosters a ghetto mentality and allows one to lock oneself in a sectarian identity, away from the mainstream society. It transforms the refusal of recognition *by* the society into the refusal *of* the very same society *by* those who suffer from it. In summary, Salafism builds up an identity that is proud of rejecting the mainstream society, instead of being ashamed of being secluded and stigmatized by it. In its jihadi version, Islam goes a step further, it reverses stigmatization and becomes stigmatizing, converting the Self's feeling of unworthiness into

Jihadism in Europe. Farhad Khosrokhavar, Oxford University Press. © Oxford University Press 2021.
DOI: 10.1093/oso/9780197564967.003.0007

the disgrace of others, changing internalized humiliation into arrogance toward those who become dehumanized disbelievers.

In the middle-class districts, among the Muslims prevails the impression that Muslims are under attack worldwide, the "evidence" being the UK participation in the Iraq war alongside the United States in 2003 and France's military action in Mali since 2013, unfair social inequality (with the same diploma, a "Mohamed" is not treated on a par with a "Robert" in the job market), anomie, and a meaningless life in a "cold society." The striving toward a cohesive, "warm," even effervescent commonwealth is at the root of the jihadi imagined community among middle-class youth.

a-The Jihadis and the Rural Areas

In Europe, the geographic location of jihadism has been overwhelmingly urban, with two major exceptions. The first is the Islamist community of Artigat in France. The second is the Balkans and rural Bosnia.

1-Artigat and Its Charismatic Leader, Olivier Corel

Artigat is a rural district of some six hundred residents in the rural region of Ariège in Southern France. In it, the hard core of a future jihadi community was built up around the personality of Olivier Corel, aka "Abdellah al-Dandachi," also called "The White Emir" (*l'Emir blanc*). As a Syrian he came to France in 1973 and became a French citizen in 1983. Three generations of Islamic radicals coming from different parts of France gathered in his hamlet in Les Lanes and some of them lived there for a while, enjoying his hospitality. With few exceptions, this generation of fathers, made of Algerians, Tunisians, and the Syrian Olivier Corel did not become jihadi, Corel having strong ties to the Syrian Muslim Brotherhood. The new generation of sons and daughters were either converts, like the brothers Fabien and Jean-Michel Clain and their wives, and Thomas Barnouin, or born-again Muslims, like Sabri Essid, Mohamed Merah, his sister Fouad, his brother Abdelkader, and Mohamed Megherbi (the husband of one of Fabien Clain's sisters), among others. Someone like Sid Ahmed Ghlam, who killed in August 2015 a woman in a failed attack on a church in Villejuif, close to Paris, had ties to this group as well. Some of them became affiliated with the Belgian group that committed the November 13, 2015, attacks in Paris.

There is probably no community equivalent to Artigat in Western Europe. More than a decade after its foundation, its influence was felt in the attacks of November 2015 in Paris by the Clain brothers, Sabri Essid, and Thomas Barnouin, among others, as well as the assaults in Brussels in March 2016.

Olivier Corel's role is subject to debate, but what is beyond doubt is that he was a charismatic patriarch in Artigat. His charisma, contrary to that of most of the jihadi leaders and recruiters, was a "mute" one, not that of an ideologist who would dispense an articulate jihadi vision of Islam. As a Muslim Brotherhood member, he contributed to the radicalization of the youth around him almost unwillingly, his role being that of a mentor, in particular for rituals (he performed marriage ceremonies for some of the future jihadis, he gave his views on what was licit and illicit in consumption, sexual relations, commercial activities, and so on). He was a mediator between the old and the new; he himself was not directly involved in jihadi acts, and he did not go to Afghanistan or Pakistan. His charisma was also based on his hospitality, his wife being a good cook.[2] He played the role of the father without the tensions besetting fatherhood, opening up an original chapter on charisma (neither based on eloquence nor on any specific function), his generosity and congeniality, his competence on matrimonial aspects of Islamic law, and his activist view of Islam being particularly appreciated by the young people who visited his abode.[3]

Artigat was not itself a jihadi cell but a melting pot, through the informal discussions with Olivier Corel, for future jihadi groups who would play a leading role in the attacks in France and Belgium. It became particularly significant in relation to the city of Toulouse, where the brothers Clain and Mohamed Merah resided. In the poor district of Toulouse, Le Mirail, the Clain brothers prayed at the el-Hussein mosque. They were from the French overseas department of Réunion and belonged to a practicing Catholic family. Both brothers converted to Islam in the 1990s. In 2001, Fabien Clain founded a Salafist group with his brother Jean-Michel in Le Mirail neighborhood. He held a stall at the Saint-Sernin market where the sale of Islamic books served as a pretext for his proselytizing.

Artigat served as a meeting place for the radical socialization of different individuals, some of whom later became notorious jihadis. It was the crucible where Fabien Clain met Mohamed Merah's older brother, Abdelkhader, and another Toulouse resident, Sabri Essid (whose father married the mother of the Clain brothers and then, the father of the Merah brothers). Corel assumed a "prophetic" charisma within the group and gave his vision of jihadi Islam, without entering concrete action. For his part, Fabien Clain had the charisma of an organizer, the man of action, and was admired for his acumen and his qualities as a combatant of Islam (*mujahid*).

More than a decade later, Clain rebuilt in Syria the Toulouse cluster with a dozen individuals, including Sabri Essid, who appeared in a video of the execution of an Arab hostage suspected of being a spy of the Israelis, in March 2015. Essid came from the district of Izards in Toulouse, like Merah. Activist Islam had attracted him since he was a teenager. At the age of sixteen he left his parental home to live with Fabien Clain for a few months in a poor district with a large majority of North African migrant sons and grandsons, Belle Fontaine, within Le Mirail. The indoctrination of these people by the "White Emir" in Artigat found in this way its jihadi setting in the poor districts of Toulouse and spread many years later, through jihadi attacks, to Europe via IS in Syria.

2-Bosnia and the Jihadi Movement

The other rural arena of radicalization is the Balkans and, in particular, Bosnia. Balkan jihadism is distinct from the dominant European one, in which the urban setting has been decisive. In Bosnia, rural areas were the major sites of jihadism. The war after the breakup of Yugoslavia played a significant role in it. Of the 875 fighters from the Balkans who went to Syria and Iraq between 2013 and 2016, at least 330 were from Bosnia. The war in Bosnia attracted many Foreign Fighters who sought to help Muslims, persecuted in the 1992 conflict. They spread the Salafist-jihadi ideology that took root there long before the creation of the caliphate in Syria in 2014 (Vervelli, 2016).

A large number of the jihadi-Salafists settled in rural areas, including the villages of Gornje Maoče and Ošve, located in northeastern Bosnia and Herzegovina, which became hotspots of Islamic extremism. In the past, those two villages had suffered from a massive exodus of their population during the conflict in 1992. Many of the displaced people did not return. Their absence facilitated the reception of Salafists who settled there and mixed with the local population.

The villages of Gornje Maoče and Ošve became Salafist, and they isolated themselves from other areas by practicing a rigorist Islam. They challenged the traditional authority of the Islamic Community of Bosnia and Herzegovina (BiH) and rejected their elected representatives. A charismatic preacher, Husein Bilal Bosnic, emerged as the jihadis' leader in Bosnia. He became the religious authority in many small remote villages where jihadis had taken refuge. Bosnia suffered an extremely high rate of unemployment among Muslim youth without any improvement in their lot in the foreseeable future. That created a favorable environment for jihadi propaganda that Bilal exploited skillfully. He offered them the means to make the trip to Syria. Until 2015, Daesh offered a monthly salary ranging from $400 to $600 and more, and living conditions regarded as "luxurious" for those disaffected young people. Bilal Bosnic turned Bosnia into a thoroughfare to Syria. He was arrested and sentenced in 2015 to seven years in prison.

On October 28, 2011, an attack targeted the US embassy in Sarajevo, Mevlid Sasarevic shooting at it and wounding a police officer. He had a criminal record and lived in the village of Gornje Maoče. A second attack occurred at the Rajlovac military airport, during which two members of the BiH armed forces died.

Gazibaba, a municipality in Skopje, the capital of Macedonia, attracted the Salafists, especially because of the Tutunzus mosque whose radical imam was able to mobilize a large number of sympathizers. He declared the elections illicit because they promulgated the law of the people instead of the law of God. Gazibaba sent dozens of Foreign Fighters to Syria and Iraq. All in all, 146 jihadis from Macedonia went to Syria (The Soufan Group, 2015).

Kaçanik is one of the poorest municipalities in Kosovo, in the southwestern region. From there twenty-three Foreign Fighters went to Syria out of the 232 Kosovar ones. It is also the region of Lavdrim Muhaxeri, leader of the Albanian jihadis, who appeared several times on social networks, while executing young civilians. From that city of thirty thousand inhabitants, almost two dozen fighters went to Syria. Kosovo, with a population of 1.8 million, sent some three hundred Foreign Fighters, making it the highest per capita jihadi country in Europe (Freeman, 2015). Kosovo's Muslims were saved by the NATO bombing of Serbian forces in 1999 and since then, its government has remained pro-Western. Most Kosovars followed a moderate version of Islam. But this system left elbow room for Islamist charities that flourished in the chaotic period after the civil war.

The radicalization of the people in Kaçanic could be understood in connection with the poverty in Kosovo where the gross domestic product was around £2,500 per year (less than €3,000) and youth unemployment was around 60 percent. Added to this was the proximity of Macedonia, where extremist preachers were able to express their views without any restraint.

Economic factors and the intervention of Saudi Arabia, which funded Wahhabi charitable foundations, played a key role in jihadism there.

As for Albania, there were three Salafist villages, Leshnicë, Zargoçan, and Rrëmenj, all in the region of Pogradec, that hosted radicals who subsequently left for Syria. Of the ninety Foreign Fighters of Albanian origin who traveled to Syria, 30 percent came from these villages.

b-The Jihadogenic Areas and the Poor Ethnic Districts

The overwhelming majority of jihadi areas in Europe have been urban. The cities' role has been paramount.[4] But these places had few salient features. They were of at least five types.

The first was the "poor suburb" or "the poor district" type, be it within the city or at its outskirts. In almost all Western European countries there are poor districts from which the proportion of young people leaving for Syria was significantly higher than the national average.[5] This was due to the high unemployment rate and a high concentration of people from the former colonies (in the cases of France and the United Kingdom) or from Muslim countries (people of Moroccan descent in Spain, Belgium, and Germany, from Turkish origin in Germany and France, or from Somali origin in Norway). They lived within ethnic ghettoes and were marked by deviancy among the disaffected male Muslims.

Another type of urban structure had not much to do with poverty or even relative deprivation. Within some specific middle-class areas there were high numbers of jihadis. The causes were formal or informal networks, friends, or members of the same extended family, recruiters and preachers or the establishment of radicalized agents there from the 1990s onward.

The third type was poor districts close to rich ones, usually within large cities, where jihadis could establish themselves and exploit the anger of the people.

A fourth type was cities in which Muslims were victims of racism, developing in turn a counter-racist attitude that turned, in few cases, into jihadism, IS agents manipulating the Muslims' resentment against the mainstream society.

A fifth type, meticulously identified and described by Jérôme Ferret (Ferret, 2021), is a type of city within a politico-ethnic division in society (for instance Catalans in Spain), like Ripoll in Spain, a city of Catalan culture in tension with Spanish nationalism, near Barcelona. Sons of migrants were welcomed there, supposedly without major problems, but they were deeply alienated due to the lack of understanding of their identity and culture. That city subordinated their existence to the major division between the Spanish majority and the cultural and ethnic Catalan minority to which it belonged. There, a group of young people of Moroccan origin were behind the jihadi attacks of August 17 and 18, 2017, although they seemed to be perfectly integrated into that small town of ten thousand residents. The division between Catalans and Spaniards left no room for self-assertion for this minority of Moroccan origin, which was suffocating there, while the city entertained the illusion of its hospitality toward migrants and their offspring.

1-The Poor Ethnic Districts in Europe

In Europe in the last few decades, a new urban entity has come into being, namely the poor ethnic districts, called by a wide variety of names in different countries: "banlieues," "cités," or "quartiers sensibles" in France; poor inner cities, poor suburbs, poor or disadvantaged districts in the United Kingdom; Elendsviertel (slums) in Germany. These neighborhoods have become "ethnicized" with the departure of the "Whites" (working-class natives who gradually moved off), attracting lower-class Muslims for their cheap rents or due to the construction of low-cost social housing units in their vicinity. The new generations who descend from Muslim migrants develop what we have called a slum subculture within this setting which becomes, over time, confrontational against the mainstream culture.[6]

Out of a sample of 1,200 Foreign Fighters from Western societies, 70 percent came from the same cities. Western cities from which the largest number of Foreign Fighters went to Syria were: London (thirty-eight recruits); Antwerp (Belgium), thirty-two; Brussels (Belgium), thirty; Ceuta (Spain), eighteen; Zenica (Bosnia and Herzegovina), fifteen; Nice (France), thirteen; Toulouse (France), thirteen; Lunel (France), twelve; Vilvoorde (Belgium), eleven; Sarajevo (Bosnia-Herzegovina), eleven; Molenbeek (Belgium), ten; Paris (France), ten; Dinslaken (Germany), nine; The Hague (Holland), nine;

Portsmouth (the UK), eight; Montreal, (Canada), seven; Delft (Holland), seven; Sydney (Australia), seven. (Perliger and Milton, 2016). Many of them came from disadvantaged poor neighborhoods (comprehensive European statistics are lacking in this respect).

In a study of 137 court sentences on French jihadis, around 40 percent of those sentenced came from the poor suburbs, and for 59 percent of them, their parents were from North Africa, 9 percent from Black Africa, and 18 percent from France. Among them 47 percent had no diploma, 24 percent had the baccalaureate (equivalent to A levels in the UK and the high school diploma in the US), 9 percent had the CAP (equivalent to the English NVQ, professional diploma), 9 percent BEP (vocational diploma), 4 percent BTS (UK equivalent HND, an advanced technician's certificate), 2 percent DUT (technology degree after 2 years of study in a technological college), 1 percent an engineering degree, 3 percent a bachelor's degree and 1 percent a PhD. Among them 36 percent were jobless, 22 percent had insecure jobs, 10 percent were low-level employees, 13 percent workers, 4 percent instructors (educators, teaching assistants), 4 percent military men, 2 percent middle managers, 3 percent students, 3 percent undeclared workers, and 3 percent shopkeepers (Hecker, 2018).

A general European model of jihadism based on the poor district environment can be found in many European countries. They can assume two configurations:

- First, the case of an enclaved district with most of the characteristics of the French "poor suburbs" (high rate of crime, school dropouts, unemployment, poverty, ethnic concentration, etc.).
- Second, the district or the city where historically jihadi veterans settled for several years, even decades, like some neighborhoods of Nice where members of the Armed Islamic Group (GIA) from Algeria settled in the 1990s and influenced new generations who subsequently joined Foreign Fighters in the twenty-first century. These neighborhoods are not necessarily marked by extreme poverty and social exclusion, in contrast to the poor districts.

As already mentioned, most of the European jihadis come from confined areas, mainly poor neighborhoods. These were "hotbeds," that is to say, jihadi recruiting crucibles (Vervelli, 2016).

We can take the Swedish case as a good example of jihadi urban setting. The majority of the Foreign Fighters (about 80 percent of them) came from four counties (from a total of twenty-one): Västra Götaland (one-third), Stockholm (one-fourth), Skåne (one-tenth), and Örebro (one-tenth). More than 70 percent lived in socially disadvantaged areas affected by high crime and low living standards (Gustafsson and Ranstorp, 2017). This confirms the dominant "European model" of jihadism, which mainly included candidates from poor neighborhoods with a high proportion of Muslim migrants' sons.

In France, besides the poor suburbs, one can also mention the case of some towns from whose poor districts a disproportionately high number of young people, mostly sons of North Africans, went to Syria. The southern town of Lunel is one of them. From it around twenty people went to Syria between 2013 and 2015, and at least six of them were killed there. The high rate of unemployment among the people of North African origin (40 percent, about twice the unemployment rate in that town, and four times the national level) and other "poor district" syndromes are found in this town: high unemployment rate, high rate of delinquency (one of the highest in France), a sense of confinement of the new generations in their districts with a feeling of "no future" among them. In the poor district of Abrivados, three young men lived close to each other: Ahmed, Houssem, and Sabri. They became friends. The three had dropped out of school and lived in single-parent families (Ahmad's mother had raised her children alone; the mothers of Houssem and Sabri had died). They suffered, according to the director of the district's Youth House, from the ordinary racism of others. One day, Ahmed and Houssem began to let their beards grow and started preaching to others in the name of Islam. Raphael was the only middle-class member of the group (his father was a computer scientist of Jewish descent and his mother, a psychologist). Feeling guilty of his class origins and being surrounded by poor Muslim friends, he converted to Islam. It resulted in a strong new sense of belonging. He joined Sabri, who had gone to Barcelona, unbeknownst to his parents, and on July 21, 2014, Raphael called his mother from his cell phone to announce that he was accomplishing his *Hijra* (religious migration) to Syria. Houssem and Raphael had been influenced by the Tablighi Jamaat, a fundamentalist non-political international Sunni missionary movement present in Lunel (Lambert, 2015). The evolution of these two young men shows that the transition from fundamentalist to jihadi Islam actually happens in few cases (in most cases the path to jihadism does not intersect with that of Muslim fundamentalism).

The urban setting where they grew up, and where they suffered humiliation and racism, played a significant role in their radicalization.

In order to understand the elective affinity between the ethnic poor districts and jihadism in spite of the lack of global data, we analyze documented cases of poor ethnicized districts in Europe, where jihadism touched many young people, mostly sons and grandsons of Muslim migrants.

Molenbeek, close to Brussels, is a case in point. The two major attacks on Paris (November 13, 2015) and Brussels (March 22, 2016) were perpetrated by the former residents of this district. A few kilometers from Brussels, it is the second poorest municipality in Belgium, with ghettoized neighborhoods. Around Brussels, with 25 percent unemployment rate, this district is, along with Sharbeek and Laeken, one of the three municipalities called the "poor crescent." It is an area extending along the west canal of Brussels, made up of seven of the nineteen municipalities in the Brussels region. It is the most densely populated, youngest, and poorest area where children and grandchildren of North African and Turkish migrants live (Lamant, 2016). In Molenbeek, Muslim neighborhoods include the town square and the Ghent Roadway, cut by the Canal which functions as a frontier that Muslims do not usually cross. The other side of the canal is in the process of "gentrification," whereas on the Muslim side one finds more or less the syndrome of the poor ethnic districts with a high unemployment rate, a high rate of delinquency, and a concentration of Muslim people. A recent study of the two most problematic districts of Molenbeek, namely the Maritime District and the Historic Center, shows that they are the poorest. A population of foreign origin which constitutes between 71 percent and 81 percent of the total population dwells there, the Muslim community being by far the most numerous, especially Moroccans among North Africans. Most of the jihadis of Brussels lived there. In the surveyed population, the major concerns of the inhabitants were unemployment (31 percent), education (15 percent), and incivility in the neighborhood (15 percent), and not jihadi radicalization. In addition, the low level of education (only 5 percent of the population had obtained a master's degree, compared to 33 percent of the Belgian average) was the hallmark of these districts. North Africans claim to be discriminated against (27 percent "very often," 32 percent "sometimes"; "Molenbeek and Violent Radicalization,", 2017). These data confirm the "poor district effect" in Molenbeek: feeling stigmatized, experiencing social and economic exclusion, self-perception of the residents as being rejected by others, low level of education. This goes hand in hand with the importance given to Islam (for 68 percent Islam played a very important role in their daily lives). Major ingredients of what we call "slum culture" are there.

There are twenty mosques and four churches in Molenbeek. The municipality covers 6 square kilometers (approximately 2.3 square miles) and has a population of some 100,000 residents, the majority being Belgo-Moroccans. It holds the record number of jihadis involved in terrorist attacks in Europe. It was the backbone of the GIA networks[7] in the Paris attacks in the 1990s and was the residence of Abdessatar Dahmane, one of the two assassins of Major Massoud on September 9, 2001, in Afghanistan, just before the attacks of September 11, 2001, in the United States. Hassan al-Haski, one of the masterminds of the 2004 Madrid bombing (191 dead), as well as Mehdi Nemmouche, the killer at the Jewish Museum in Brussels in 2014, lived there, as did Abbaoud, one of the brains of the November 13, 2015, attacks in Paris. In 2005, a journalist of Moroccan origin had sounded the alarm in a book on the "Little Morocco" that was Molenbeek (Fraihi, 2006). It had become the insular world of young Moroccan descendants who lived apart from the larger society, beset by social exclusion, deviancy, resentment, and indignity. This "Gangsteristan" was ready to become a "Jihadistan."

Historically, in the 1990s, Bassam Ayachi, a French-Syrian, set up the Belgian Islamic Center in Molenbeek, spreading a radical version of Islam. Residents and some city officials warned the authorities of his radical influence, but scant attention was paid to them. He prepared the ground for a more radical view of Islam under the aegis of Khalid Zerkani and others. The combination of segregation, stigmatization, unemployment, poverty, a parallel economy in conjunction with internalized rage and hate against others, as well as the feeling of double non-identity (neither Belgian nor Moroccan) and a history of radical Salafists established in the neighborhood for more than a decade, led to the radicalization of a minority.

Vilvorde, a town with forty-two thousand inhabitants bordering Brussels' region, is another case in point. Forty-three percent of the inhabitants are of foreign origin, and half of them are unemployed. Twenty-eight of its residents, including two girls and some underage boys, went to Syria and Iraq. Eight returned, at least five died there, and two were put in prison (Cendrowicz, 2015). The youth who left for jihad were mostly sons of Moroccans, unemployed, without a diploma, among them a large number of deviant recidivists ("De Vilvorde à la Syrie," 2014). We are looking at the classical jihadogenic urban structure of the poor ethnic districts.

The Belgian case presents peculiar features that exacerbate identity malaise: a culturally divided country between the Walloon (French speaking) and the Flemish (Dutch speaking), a split identity being already experienced through mutual rejections of the two major populations of the country. It is also a country where the government is divided along those linguistic lines, and through economics (the Flemish part being richer and unwilling to share its wealth with the poorer Walloons). Besides these peculiarities, the majority of Belgian Muslims are of Moroccan origin, concentrating around Brussels.

It is estimated that out of the 700,000 Muslims who live in Belgium, 500,000 belong to families from the Moroccan Rif, of non-Arabic origin (Amazigh). Problems related to the split identity are therefore reinforced among them, torn between Berber, Arab, and Belgian identities, denied to them by the Belgian mainstream society, as well as the Moroccan.

Antwerp is a Flemish city of a half -million dwellers, of which 20 percent are Muslims, mostly of Moroccan roots. In March 2010 in this city Fouad Belkacem, a radical Islamist of Moroccan descent, founded Sharia4Belgium, a group that sent many young people to Syria and Iraq. In February 2015, Belkacem was sentenced to twelve years imprisonment for having monitored dozens of young people to Syria.

Vilvoorde and Antwerp are about 30 kilometers (18.6 miles) apart. In September 2004, nine Foreign Fighters from Vilvoorde and Antwerp were killed in Syria, all of them of Moroccan roots. In May 2016, an assassination attempt by the sixteen-year-old Mohamed E.A, living in Borgerhout against Filip Dewinter, a member of a Flemish far-right group, was neutralized.

Antwerp is home to a Jewish community of some twenty thousand people, some of them involved in diamond trade. The development of jihadi pockets in the city worries them, given jihadis' anti-Semitism.

Borgerhout, a poor district of Antwerp, has more than forty thousand residents and is considered by some media as a second Molenbeek. It is home to individuals of ninety different nationalities, including a large Moroccan community. They share many features of the poor neighborhoods marked by slum culture: high rates of unemployment and delinquency, low levels of education, and stigmas affecting young Muslim people. Their attitude, regarded as anti-social, pushes the local population in their vicinity to vote for the far-right political parties.

A native of Morocco, Hicham Chaib was a son in a family of eleven children. He left school very young, wandered in the streets of Borgerhout, and embarked on crime. He displayed the characteristics of deviant young men from impoverished, stigmatized Muslim neighborhoods: leaving school at an early age, delinquency, membership in deviant gangs, violence, and finally, opting for radical Islam in an attitude of defiance, provocation, and revenge against society. He was for a time the "bodyguard" of Fouad Belkacem, the founder of "Sharia4Belgium." The arrest of a veiled woman in Molenbeek in 2012 sparked skirmishes (as in poor ethnic suburbs in France), which was an opportunity for Chaib to spur young Muslims to protest violently against the police in Borgerhout. Arrested, he was sentenced to one year in prison. In 2013, he moved to Syria with his wife. Among the protesters of 2012, seventy joined the ranks of Daesh. Hicham Chaib was responsible for many beheadings, crucifixions, and amputations in Syria. After the Brussels attacks on March 22, 2016, which resulted in the deaths of thirty-one people, he stated in a video that IS "will kill your people" in retaliation for the air strikes in Syria.

The Antwerp axis to the north, Brussels to the south via Vilvoorde, is one of the major jihadi recruitment areas in Belgium.

In Germany, Dinslaken, a town of around seventy thousand residents, is home to Lohberg, a district of some six thousand people, one-third of them Muslim, in which youth unemployment attained around 30 percent. Mining activity was the pillar of Dinslaken's economy, attracting foreign workers. With its decline, a large number of these workers lost their jobs. Lohberg became one of the focal points of jihadism in Germany. It is a Turkish district with three mosques, two Turkish supermarkets, an Arab restaurant, and very few women without a veil, gradually constituting a "monocultural zone," closed on itself, secluded, and at odds with the secular German society. The more the neighborhood became secluded, the more people felt stigmatized, due as much to its closure on itself as to its bad reputation of being a hotbed of fundamentalism, organized crime, and gangs. Lohberg was not originally part of the town of Dinslaken but a subdivision for foreign workers with three thousand residents on the sidelines of a neighborhood built to house workers of the mining industry. As "Gastarbeiters" (guest workers), they were supposed to return to Turkey at the end of their employment contract. Those who remained, and their children, have a deep sense of living in an inhospitable environment. Not considered as an organic part of Dinslaken but as a ghettoized quarter for the Turkish workers, this district is akin to the French poor suburbs, with the same social pathologies: enclaving, stigmas, high rates of imprisonment and unemployment: "the slum culture effect" plays an essential role both in the deviance and in the radicalization of Muslim youth in Lohberg, mentally separating it from the mainstream society. In addition to that, Lohberg was also geographically landlocked: it was connected to Dinslaken by an underserved bus line. A parallel society was established by jihadi-Salafists who set aside the "Infidels" in response to the ghettoization of their district, which was sealed off from the town by an invisible wall. Moreover, even before the grip of the Salafists, Turkish institutions that had spread there were marked by conservatism, be it those identifying with the party of Erdogan or those who followed Milli Görüs.

As a general rule, in Europe, in areas inhabited by working-class Muslim populations and their offspring, "slum culture effect" is recurrent and remains one of the causes of radicalization among marginalized youth.

At least thirteen young men left Lohberg to carry out jihad in Syria, where they gathered under the name of Lohberg Brigade. The number of radicalized youths in this neighborhood was estimated to be around twenty-five. Among them there were also converts, but the vast majority were of Turkish origin (Weisflog, 2016).

One can also quote the cases of East London and Birmingham, which hosted a large group of jihadis in the United Kingdom. East London was home to half of the London-based jihadis (22 percent overall), most of them from Tower Hamlets, Newham, and Waltham Forest.

In Birmingham, the constituencies of Hall Green and Hodge Hill accounted for three-quarters of jihadis based in that city. In addition, more than three-quarters of jihadi acts were committed by individuals living in disadvantaged neighborhoods, and nearly half of the jihadi actions were committed by people living in highly deprived neighborhoods (Monroe, 2017). The impact of the poor urban structure with a high concentration of migrant descendants on jihadism is difficult to question.[8]

Among the urban centers where jihadism thrived one can also cite Dewsbury, Bradford, Portsmouth, Cardiff, and Birmingham.

Dewsbury is a city where the proportion of the Asians has been on the increase in the last decade. It was the birthplace or residence of a dozen jihadis, including Mohammad Sidique Khan, the leader of the group that committed the London subway and bus bombings on July 7, 2005.

In Dewsbury there is a high concentration of Muslims in some neighborhoods, particularly in Savile Town. According to the 2011 census, only forty-eight "Whites" remained in this neighborhood, the other 4,033 residents being of Indo-Pakistani origin, the latter forming more than

97 percent of the local population. The scheme has become classic, as we have already seen: the settlement of Asian workers from the 1950s on, the gradual move of the "Whites" (mostly English workers) to other districts, the acquisition of properties by the Muslim lower-middle classes, which gradually have become the majority in the district, and the setting up of a cultural system where a fundamentalist version of Islam is adopted by a significant part of the new residents. Most of the Pakistanis in the UK belong to the Deobandi or Barelvi (the Tablighi pertaining to the Deobandi branch), 600 of the 1,350 mosques in Britain being affiliated to them ("Muslim Group Behind 'Mega-Mosque,'" 2007). The relationship between the neighborhood and other parts of the city deteriorated in the last decade, the "Whites" experiencing insecurity and refusing to venture out alone in the neighborhood, especially at night (Reid, 2015).

Dewsbury hosts the headquarters of the Tabligh movement whose mosque, Dar ul Ulum (House of Science) or Dewsbury Markaz, is one of the largest in Britain. Some jihadis passed through it; Mohammad Sidique Khan and Shehzad Tanweer, two of the four jihadis who perpetrated the London attacks in 2005 having probably been members of Tabligh in the past, though the latter rejects this allegation. Sidique Khan lived in a council house in Savile Town, as did Hammad Munshi, who was arrested in 2006 carrying bags containing materials for explosive belts.

Ravensthorpe is another part of Dewsbury where a large Muslim community, mostly Pakistani, resides. Muslims settled there since the 1960s. In recent years, people of Iraqi Kurdish origin have settled there, as well as Hungarians and Romas (Gypsies).

In neighborhoods like Savile Town, a new type of "mono-culturalism" emerges, mainly based on fundamentalist Islam that cements the relations between Muslims, principally by excluding "White society," the latter gradually vanishing by selling property. The situation is especially disadvantageous to the sons and daughters of migrants who do not encounter "White" people to socialize and internalize the basics of British culture, confined to a Muslim population that does not also reflect the culture of the countries of origin (it is cut off from the "Asian" culture evolving in the former countries of their parents). The phenomenon of migrant mono-culturalism based on the scarcity of day-to-day relations with the "native Europeans" (the "Whites") and leaning principally on fundamentalist Islam as a new common bond between people of different Muslim cultures is recurrent in many poor migrant districts in Europe where ethnic relations dominate social encounters and outside contact is rare, the neighborhood gradually closing in on itself. We call it "Islamistan."[9] The step can then be more easily taken toward the rejection of the outside world, jihadism being one of its violent forms.

Portsmouth as a port was one of the main destinations for migrant workers, especially from the former colonies. According to the 2011 census, 84 percent of its population is made up of White British, 1.8 percent of Bangladeshis, 1.4 percent of African Blacks, and 0.3 percent of Pakistanis.

In this city, the Charles Dickens district is one of the most deprived ones in the UK. In it, 57 percent of children live in poor families, with a weekly income around £430 , compared to the national average of £670. Bangladeshi and Pakistani communities are among the poorest. From the 7,100 people of the Muslim community, six young citizens of Bangladeshi origin were lured into jihadism. They went to Syria in 2013 to join Daesh, calling themselves "the Bad Boy Brigade al-Britani" or "the Pompey Lads" (Pompey being, for the local soccer fans, the name of Portsmouth).

The city of Bradford has a population of half a million, including a quarter of Muslims from India, Bangladesh, and especially Pakistan, according to the 2011 census. It was an industrial textile city in the 1970s. The decline of that industry and the gradual establishment of migrant Muslims changed its cultural environment. In 2001, a series of riots shook several cities in northern England—Oldham in May, Burley in June, and Bradford in July of the same year. The main cause of the uprisings in Bradford was the growing tension between immigrants of Pakistani, Bangladeshi, and Indian origin (the so-called Asian communities) and the "White" majority. Around one thousand young people were involved, and the riot quickly turned into an ethnic confrontation between "Whites" and "Asians." It was a wake-up call on the constitution of two "cities" of different cultures within the same city. It was a classic case of a predominantly working-class city converting into one where a surge of migrants and the economic and social decline of the "White" working-class population led to cultural and social tensions. The old working-class population felt more and more in exile at home, voting for the British National Party (extreme right). (In France they voted for the extreme-right party Le Front National, now renamed Le Rassemblement National.) Bradford is the second-largest English city in regard to the proportion of Pakistani descendants (around 68,000). Those of Indian origin are in smaller numbers (12,500); as for those of Bangladeshi descent, their number is even smaller (5,000). There is a growing segregation in the city center between Muslims and others, the former living their own lives according to a different value system than that of the mainstream society. In June 2015, Bradford witnessed the departure of three sisters—Khadija, Zohra, and Sugra Dawood, thirty, thirty-three, and thirty-four years old, respectively—to Syria after their pilgrimage to Mecca. Instead of returning home, with their nine children they went to Syria where they joined Ahmad, their twenty-one-year-old jihadi brother who had gone there in 2013.

In these segregated Asian neighborhoods, looking for wives or husbands from the parents' villages is standard practice, and the three sisters were married to men from Pakistan. One of the men returned to his country; the two others made emotional appeals on TV to their wives to return home.

The structure of the city center in Bradford has increasingly become "mono-cultural" (in fact inhabited mainly by "Asians," overwhelmingly Muslim), part of the population espousing fundamentalist Islam (Deobandi) and distancing themselves from non-Muslims. The "mono-cultural" phenomenon is on the rise in some neighborhoods such as Little Horton, southwest of Bradford, where Indo-Pakistanis ("Asians") constitute 57 percent of the population, compared to less than 20 percent in Bradford overall, according to the 2011 census. In this neighborhood, 35 percent of the population does not predominantly speak English, and 12 percent does not practice it at all. In the Moor district, east of the city, 80 percent of its ten thousand inhabitants are Indo-Pakistanis (British Asian; Pidd and Halliday, 2015). Of the fifty-four pubs that existed in the neighborhood, only three are left. There is also a class effect all over Europe: in Bradford, Molenbeek (Belgium), as in many districts within the poor suburbs in France and Germany (e.g., Lohberg), or in other European countries. Middle classes become scarce with the ethnicization of the neighborhood, and multiculturalism evolves into a mosaic of insular communities whose relations to the larger society can degenerate into violence as in the riots of 2001 in northern England. Segregation of the population of Muslim descendants, isolation, and withdrawal become a reality in everyday life of a large section of the population, reinforcing thus social exclusion, pushing toward a quiet or a provocative fundamentalism that calls into question secular values and norms (France) or multicultural dynamics (GB). This fundamentalism is often tinged with Salafism, a dominant form of Sunni Islam that has become the common denominator among Muslims of various origins who seek in it a common language and common roots, beyond their ethnicity.

Cardiff, the capital of Wales, with 8 percent Indo-Pakistanis ("Asians," including Bangladeshis), 1.4 percent Arabs, and 2.4 percent Blacks, is another case in point. Grangetown is its suburb, with a population of twenty thousand people. Grangetown and Butetown are marginalized suburbs and home to a Muslim population in which deviant gangs are rampant. They suffer from a high level of unemployment, and their residents are suspicious of outsiders (Kabir, 2012). From Grangetown, young members of local gangs went to Syria to fight under IS.

In France, the town of Sevran in the Parisian suburbs is a multicultural melting pot where more than seventy nationalities live side by side. In fact, the situation is that of a deficient identity among the youth of many different origins who live away from the people of mainstream French culture. They find themselves deprived of cultural integration within the mainstream society. As already mentioned, at school pupils of different cultures invent new types of socialization, but the "French ingredient" is missing there because of the absence of native French students who desert these schools, their parents sending them to better educational establishments outside the disadvantaged districts. In this context, Islam becomes the common denominator among those who have little in common (they come from more than seventy countries, different from each other), the religion of Allah being their only link. Fundamentalism is a version of Islam that becomes even more attractive to the enclaved population because it turns a passive exclusion into an active one: in the name of God they isolate themselves from others.

From Sevran about fifteen young Muslims left for Syria between 2014 and 2016. At least six of them died there.

In Sweden, among the cities and districts where the Foreign Fighters used to live, Malmö and Gothenburg were the most prominent. Rosengård (literally "Rose Manor") is a district in the center of Malmö municipality in southern Sweden. Built between 1967 and 1972 as part of the Million Programme (Miljonprogrammet) housing project, this district has a very high proportion of migrants and their descendants (around 88 percent of the population). The unemployment rate is beyond 60 percent (Hivert, 2016; Truc, 2016). The district evolved in a classical manner from a working-class neighborhood to a disaffected Muslim youth district: in 1972 the percentage of immigrants was around 18 percent, the majority being Swedish working-class people of rural origin. Their departure began around 1974 when Muslim migrants arrived, attaining 86 percent of the settlers in 2012 ("Another Side of Malmö's Infamous Rosengard," 2012). In Rosengård the slum culture is prominent. Located just over 4 kilometers (2.5 miles) from the city center, Rosengård is usually referred to as a "suburb." Close to central Malmö, it seems remote and is mentally divorced from the rest of Sweden's third-largest city: most people in Malmö avoid this notorious district, and those living there do not usually venture to Malmö. Despite cheaper rents, the derogatory image of a dangerous multi-ethnic community discourages people to settle there. Becoming a hotbed of social problems in conjunction with dangerous "non-Swedish" inhabitants, national media contribute to its bad reputation. The same process is visible in other multi-ethnic poor districts in Europe. In 2003, America's Fox News portrayed Rosengård as a virtual war zone, as it had done with other European poor neighborhoods inhabited by Muslims. This was, of course, a largely distorted portrayal of the district, but it resulted in reinforcing its gruesome image. This twisted picture is common to the mainstream media, but the derogatory view of the poor ethnic districts in Europe has become part of the social prejudices (partly true, partly false by exaggerating and skewing reality) that contribute to the stigmatization of their dwellers. Several jihadis lived in Rosengård. This was particularly the case of Osama Krayem, one of the terrorists of the Brussels metro. Born to Syrian parents, at the age of twenty-three he was arrested, on April 8, 2016, in Laeken, a Brussels suburb. In Rosengård, Osama Krayem had made the transition from delinquency to radicalization, the same path that we find among many jihadis of the poor segregated neighborhoods: social exclusion, integration into a criminal gang in the Malmö region, drug trafficking, and aggravated violence. Once indoctrinated by an extremist version of Islam, he put an end to his consumption of alcohol and drugs, broke off his ties with old friends, let his beard grow, and listened to the sermons of radical imams on his mobile phone, instead of rap music. In 2015 he left for Syria.

Another jihadi, Mohamed Belkaid, was killed on March 15, 2016, by the Belgian police in his attempt to protect Salah Abdeslam's escape during their raid on a flat in the Forest district. Of Algerian descent, he had married a Swede and lived in Rosengård since 2010. Unemployed, he lived off petty theft. The neighborhood had been subject of a report by the Swedish intelligence services, drawing attention to the radicalization within it, especially in semi-clandestine places of worship in the cellars. A dozen of the three hundred Swedish Foreign Fighters were from Rosengård.

Göteborg (or Gothenburg) is Sweden's second-largest city after Stockholm. A large number of Swedish jihadis (around 120) were from there, mostly from Bergsjön and Angered neighborhoods. A third of the population of Göteborg is of migrant origin with a Muslim majority, this proportion reaching 70 percent and even more in the suburbs of Angered (Hakim, 2016). Some of the

160,000 people who sought political asylum in Sweden found themselves in Angered, where rent was cheaper than in other parts of the city. School dropout was notable (two-thirds of fifteen-year-olds left school), and the unemployment rate was 11 percent, which is high by Swedish standards. Recruiters urged them to go to Syria instead of rotting in Angered. Insecurity due to the gangs' dominance in the neighborhood was also high. During the 2014 election, gangs of men threatened the locals at polling stations. In December 2015 Police in Sweden placed the district in the most dangerous category of urban areas regarding its high crime rates (Lowe, 2017). A study showed that in 2017, Angered was the district of Göteborg with the least educated adult population. About 30 percent of pupils had not completed primary education; about half of the population was jobless. The residents of Angered had no real trust in the police and the judiciary. They refused to denounce the gangs, for fear of reprisal. Criminal gangs sold narcotics in schools, and their violence occurred openly in the public space ("Särskilt utsatta omraden," 2017). These are the major characteristics one finds also in the poor ethnic districts in France, the UK, and other parts of Western Europe. In this type of neighborhood, jihadis prospered during the rule of IS, which gave them the opportunity to look for a better future (at least in their imaginary world).

In Sweden, a significant part of the second-generation Muslim youth who attend school feel ostracized by the Swedes who do not offer them, in their eyes, a chance to become normal citizens. According to a recent survey, one in ten students in schools in the northeastern suburbs of Göteborg sympathized with jihadis and rejected the democratic vision of society ("Sweden: One in Ten," 2016). The study underlined the split in Göteborg between those who shared the mainstream Swedish values and those who rejected it. These students felt alienated and, in turn, rejected the mainstream values of society, which humiliated them and subjected them to segregation. We find this feeling of double denial, the neither/nor (neither Swedish nor belonging to the parents' country) widespread among marginalized Muslim youth in Europe. Fascination for jihadism among them was as an attempt at overcoming an undignified identity, substituting it with a dignified one through violence. By joining jihadi groups, they became proud of being part of a neo-Ummah that was feared rather than despised by the global society.

According to the Swedish authorities, jihadis from Göteborg were recruited from the criminal gangs of its suburbs. In December 2015, two Swedes who joined IS from that town, al-Amin Sultan and Hassan al-Mandlawi, were sentenced by the Göteborg court to life imprisonment for having slaughtered two prisoners in Syria in 2013.

In Norway, the Grønland district in the eastern inner city of Oslo is two metro stations from the Parliament and only one from the Central Station. Along with the suburb Tøyen to its north, Grønland hosts a multiethnic population of first- and second-generation migrants. The neighborhood became impoverished by the settlement of deprived migrants and their offspring. It suffers from a bad reputation through the media. It progressively espoused a fundamentalist-Salafist subculture, its inhabitants dissociating themselves from the Norwegian secular mainstream culture. The Salafist environment accentuated their mental split with the larger society. A vicious circle was set in motion: those who felt marginalized isolated themselves further by adhering to a fundamentalist version of Islam. The difference was in the transition from passivity to activity, from inferiority to superiority. Marginality was imposed on them. By becoming Salafists, they were the ones who rejected an integration that was otherwise inaccessible to them. Also, being in a ghetto that insulated them from other people, they felt inferior. By opting for Islamic fundamentalism, it was they who rejected the mainstream society, the initiative giving them a sense of superiority, reversing their inferiority relationship to the mainstream society. The consequences were intolerance vis-à-vis those who were not religiously minded. Mafia groups controlled the neighborhood, their puritanical lifestyle legitimizing their illegal economic activities in an underground economy. Violence, theft, and intimidation went hand in hand with Salafism.

The neighborhood was exposed to the cultural closure onto itself ("it is more Morocco than Norway," said one inhabitant), and the insecurity related to the bands and the local mafia chiefs was exacerbated by slum subculture, at variance with the mainstream culture ("Norway," 2016). As a rule, the move to radical Islam is not automatic; the neighborhood may drift into it if the local mafia is not strong enough to prevent it. The latter's main concern is to continue its "business"; Islamic extremism draws the attention of the police and the media, thereby endangering the mafia's illegal activities. Marseille is a good case in point, where local mafias have successfully opposed jihadism in order to pursue their lucrative business, away from the inquisitor eye of the police.

In Denmark, Mjølnerparken is one of Copenhagen's "ghetto" neighborhoods. It was built in 1987 in a housing project with some six hundred apartments ranging from studios to spacious three bedrooms, close to the Nørrebro train station. It quickly became a haven for migrants from Turkey, Pakistan, Morocco, and many others. Some 2,340 residents live in four buildings and their courtyard, stigmatized and marginalized, the neighborhood suffering from a bad reputation. People of migrant background make up 92 percent of their population, the highest percentage in Denmark's social housing. There are 34 percent Palestinian refugees from Lebanon, 13 percent from Iraq, and 9 percent from Somalia. A third of the population is under the age of eighteen, compared to 17 percent in the municipality of Copenhagen. Arabic speakers outnumber the others. The daily experience of the youth there is that they do not belong to Danish society, being confined in this district which is, *de facto*, a ghetto. Their school is deserted by native Danes, and socialization within it occurs in the absence of young Danes who could show them the basics of Danish culture. Interviewed in a report on Mjølnerparken, one young man expressed the overall feeling: "We were not born here and can never become 100 percent Danish. Our society is different, we feel safe and comfortable by dealing with people from our own culture" (Lau and Mathiesen, "Straight Outta Mjølnerparken?").

In this neighborhood a slum culture had developed as in many other poor districts of Europe where citizens from the mainstream culture are rare: many cultures mixed there with the exception of the national Danish culture, absent due to the lack of Danish youth at school and in the area, native Danes refusing to live in this district. Slum culture is marked by its members' awareness of not being legitimate, lacking also the means of adequate communication with the outside society. In reaction to its disparagement, this subculture can evolve into a stiff fundamentalism, putting into question the secular tendencies of the modern European culture: it becomes "exclusively religious" through Salafism, rejecting those who exclude them, internalizing social and cultural relegation by loudly claiming it as their identity, at variance with the mainstream secular culture.

Developing a sense of unbridgeable difference and inferiority as well as a cultural rift with society, a large part of this youth finds no job: they live in these districts, aware of their exclusion in the present and in the future. By their aggressiveness and lack of empathy, they contribute to their exclusion, their attitude being regarded as anti-social and threatening by others. Although in Denmark the Welfare State is more developed than in the larger European countries, even there the social question remains at the root of jihadism. The latter instilled pride and an intense sense of belonging within an imaginary, would-be fraternal community (the neo-Ummah) under the aegis of the caliph, in contrast to the hostile society that left them with a chilly sense of non-belonging. On February 14, 2015, the Palestinian-born Dane Omar El-Hussein, twenty-two, attempted to kill as many people as possible at the Krudttønden Cultural Center, where the debate on blasphemy and freedom of expression was taking place. Journalists like Lars Viks, the Swedish cartoonist who made the caricatures of the Prophet of Islam, were present at the ceremony. El-Hussein killed a filmmaker and then headed to the synagogue, where he shot and killed a thirty-seven-year-old Jew. El-Hussein pledged allegiance to Daesh on social networks on February 14, only nine minutes before the attack. He was born and raised in Mjølnerparken (Chrisafis, 2015). He was a member of the Brothers and Soldiers gang, known as "the Brothas" in Mjølnerparken. Brothas was involved in gang warfare between Hells Angels and various migrant groups in 2008–2012 period ("Brothas-banden fra Nørrebro," 2016). It played a crucial role in the gang war in Nørrebro in 2017. The neighborhood covers an area of 3.82 square kilometers (about 1.5 square miles) with 72,000 residents. Of them, 28.3 percent are of migrant origin, particularly from the Middle East. Often in Denmark this type of neighborhood is the birthplace of small mafias, which take into their hands the control of the cannabis circuits. Apart from delinquency, they resent the police for being racist and Islamophobic. Denmark, like France, has a hypersecular mainstream culture in which the desecration of religion is legitimate and, of course, legal. The cartoons were part of this secular conception for which ridiculing religion is regarded as a jocular exercise of freedom. In dire contrast to them, second- or third-generation Muslims not only display their creed much more ostentatiously than their parents, but they even do it provocatively to assert their views, contrary to the dominant trends in society, in an inflexible manner. They find in the public over-assertion of their faith a retaliation against society and a way of ostentatiously displaying their antagonistic identity, in reaction to its denial by mainstream culture. The caricatures by Lars Vilks in *Jyllands-Posten* disparagingly portrayed the Prophet of Islam. The Danish history of the conflicted relationship with Christianity is not understood by the second- or third-generation Danish Muslims. They regard Islam as a bulwark against the malaise of exile and an expression of their dignity in a situation of marginalization within an unfriendly social and cultural setting. El-Hussein attempted to kill Lars Vilks.

Schilderswijk is a district of 31,715 inhabitants (in 2014) located in the south-central part of The Hague in Holland.

The planning for the construction of social housings in Schilderswijk dates back to the 1960s. New buildings started in 1973 with the first construction plan around the Oranjeplein with 444 homes. It was the prelude to a radical urban renewal that would last for more than thirty years and have its peak in the 1980s. In a few years, many old buildings were demolished and replaced by new ones, consisting mainly of social rental homes. With the buildings, the composition of the Schilderswijk population also changed. From the 1970s, more and more immigrants settled in the neighborhood. It changed from a working-class into a poor, multi-ethnic neighborhood (called "multicultural neighborhood" in the official language): in 2008 more than 90 percent of the registered residents was made up of migrants and their descendants, especially of Turkish, Surinamese, and Moroccan origin. Because of migration, the neighborhood changed not only physically but also socially. The number of unemployed people heightened, the neighborhood physically deteriorated, crime increased as well as nuisance from drug addicts; vandalism and uncivil acts multiplied in the first decade of the twenty-first century. Mobility within it remained high; every year around 30 percent of the houses in the district swap between residents, undermining solidarity among them. Many left the area, which had a negative impact on social cohesion in the neighborhood, impairing contact with the municipality and other local institutions. In 2006, 70 percent of its residents had a low income, 25 percent average, and 5 percent high income. In 2007, 42 percent of its households lived close to the poverty line, compared to around 16 percent in The Hague. In 2015 there were 31,639 inhabitants in Schilderswijk, 90.5 percent of whom were of migrant origin. According to official data, 27.4 percent of the population were of Turkish origin, 22.9 percent of Moroccan, 17.3 percent of Surinamese, 14.3 percent of other non-Western, and 6.8 percent of Western origin ("Den Haag in Cijfers," 2015).

The transformation of a district like Schilderswijk from a native Dutch working-class district into an immigrant locality following the departure of "Whites" and the establishment of an ethnically segregated poor Muslim population is recurrent in many neighborhoods in contemporary Western Europe. New residents suffer from social exclusion, non-recognition, and indignity, Islam becoming a mental bulwark against stigmas, allowing them to be dignified in their eyes, despite marginalization. Its Salafist version allows the individuals to lock themselves into a group identity, away from society, as a self-proclaimed religious elite. As we have seen, it transforms the refusal to recognize them as genuine citizens *by* the mainstream society into refusing the legitimacy *of* the very same society *by* the excluded Muslims. They build up a new identity, and take pride in being rejected by a society of "Infidels," a sign of their own election by God. In this way they "proudly" reject the mainstream society instead of being ashamed of their being rejected by it. In its jihadi version, Islam goes a step further; it reverses stigmatization and becomes stigmatizing, converting indignity of the Self into disgrace of society, the internalized contempt into arrogance toward those who become dehumanized disbelievers. Dutch jihadis came largely from the district of Schilderswijk, called "Sharia Triangle" by the media. In 2014 about twenty men belonging to a jihadi group from Schilderswijk manifested in a video on social media, waving the black flag of IS. They sang slogans such as "Down with America" and "Death to the Jews." Several of them were arrested, among them two converts and a woman. She played a marginal role, sending only inflammatory tweets (Holligan, 2014).

In Amsterdam migrants live mainly in the west and the southeast of the city. Those of Turkish or Moroccan origin choose Nieuw-West while those of Surinamese descent opt for Zuidoost (Shaw, 2012). Formerly a suburb populated by young Dutch families, Overtoomse Veld is now almost entirely inhabited by immigrants and their descendants, mainly of Moroccan or Turkish roots. Areas like the west, east, and north of Amsterdam are often referred to as "parabolic towns" because of the numerous satellite dishes pointed at North Africa and the Middle East. The pattern is classic in Europe. Men first came as migrant workers in the 1970s to take on jobs that the Dutch no longer wanted to carry out like menial, hard, and low-paid work in industry and services. Women followed them about a decade later as spouses, often illiterate, arriving directly from their villages. A few decades later, most of the former workers were retired or unemployed, living on family allowances or meager pensions. Their wives lived in a host country whose language and customs were alien to them. The streets of the old quarter of Overstoomse Veld were empty of passers-by, some veiled women and old men in djellaba visiting *halal* butchers who offered cheap telephone connections for North Africa in the first decade of the twenty-first century (Buruma, 2005). Young men called *hangjongeren* ("those who are crane feet") lingered around the Square August Allebe where delinquency was high, their equivalent in Algeria being the "hittistes" (literally, "those who lean against walls") or the "trabendistes" (smugglers, jobless youth awaiting an opportunity to make ends meet through the underground economy). This type of neighborhood offers favorable conditions for the development of radical

Islam through isolation, poverty, stigmatization, and a sense of "no future." Daesh provided them the opportunity to overcome their desperation by offering them the prospect of bright future at the service of God.

Ceuta, an autonomous Spanish enclave bordering Morocco, has witnessed notable changes in recent decades. In Melilla, another autonomous Spanish town in the Moroccan territory, Christian majority (65 percent of the population) shrank due to Muslim immigration (45 percent or more). As for the Jews who made up 20 percent of the population before the Second World War, they now constitute less than 5 percent, having migrated mainly to Israel or Venezuela. Spaniards and Berbers from Rif in northern Morocco have become the main population. The same holds true for Ceuta, where next to the Berbers there is a significant Arab population, half of the inhabitants being Spanish and Christian, the other half Muslim, Arab, and Berber. This town holds the highest unemployment rate in Spain. Príncipe, a poor neighborhood in Ceuta, counted between twelve thousand and twenty thousand immigrants in 2007, the unemployment rate exceeding 70 percent. Between June 2013 and May 2016, 60.6 percent of prisoners convicted of terrorist activities related to IS in Spain were born in Ceuta, 27.3 percent in Melilla. In 2014, out of twenty Foreign Fighters who had joined Syria between 2012 and 2013, eleven were Spanish citizens, most of them from Ceuta (Reinares and Garcia-Calvo, 2016).

Many perpetrators of the attacks in Paris in November 2015, in Brussels in March 2016, and in Catalonia in August of the same year had ties to these territories.

Spanish and Moroccan police working together arrested in December 2014 the members of an organization recruiting women to send them to Syria as future brides for the Foreign Fighters there. Seven suspects were arrested, including four women in Ceuta and Melilla, in the neighboring town of Finideq in Morocco, and in Barcelona.

In early 2012, the thirty-three-year-old Rachid Wahbi, a taxi driver from Príncipe district in Ceuta, left for Syria with two other friends, ages thirty and twenty-four. Married with two children, he left his family unattended. Before he died, he was videotaped by the al-Qaeda affiliate al-Nusra Front. On June 1, 2012, he took a truck full of explosives and rushed into the al-Nairab military base in Idlib in northern Syria, killing 130 people, including himself (Musseau, 2015; Rotella, 2013).

Again, in Príncipe, on January 24, 2015, four young people, two pairs of brothers of Moroccan origin, were arrested as members of a local cell whose mentor was Rachid Wahdi. They were physically and militarily well trained, ready to commit an attack in Ceuta. On March 10, two members of the cell were arrested in the same neighborhood. The majority of the fifty Spanish Foreign Fighters who went to Syria belonged to the Príncipe district in Ceuta. This is a Muslim ghetto where people speak mostly Darija (Moroccan dialectal Arabic stuffed with Spanish words), the Spanish people (called Cristianos) being rare. There live the poorest of the poor: lack of deed of property, faulty sewage system, absence of pharmacy on duty, and so on. The unemployment rate exceeds 70 percent, and school failure is close to 80 percent, young people entertaining no hope for integration into the formal economy. Smuggling of hashish from Morocco and counterfeit products are the main resources of the district. Príncipe presents the eminent features of the "ethnic poor districts" described at length in this book: a neighborhood with a high unemployment rate and a high level of school dropouts, a large immigrant population, a high rate of delinquency, social exclusion, and lack of perspective for the future on their part. Jihadism is often experienced by those young people as a salvific action against a world in which they have no place. Through jihad they fulfill the promise for a better future, possibly in this world but surely in the hereafter, death as a martyr opening up new vistas for felicity in heaven. They punish a world that denied them decent life and a sense of dignity.

Geography plays a role in the radicalization of young people in Príncipe. The towns of Tetouan and Fnideq in Morocco (the latter being 8 kilometers, or 5 miles, from Ceuta) are home to families split between Morocco and Spain. Asia Ahmed, from Príncipe, was able to visit Syria after her brother's suicide bombing there. In Syria, she married "Kikito," a twenty-eight-year-old Moroccan from Finideq, who earned notoriety by posing in a video sequence next to five severed heads of victims, offering to his young bride an explosive belt as a wedding present.

A few months earlier, in March 2014, Moroccan and Spanish police had dismantled in Melila a cell of seven jihadis including two Frenchmen. They sent fighters to Syria but also to Mali and Libya.

Faced with Muslim neighborhoods that increasingly escape their control, Spanish authorities have called in the Moroccan police to fight jihadism, networks often straddling between the two countries in the towns close to the border.

On September 16, 2013, Yassine Ahmed Laarbi (alias "Pistu") was arrested in Ceuta. He was the leader of a network recruiting and sending Foreign

Fighters to Syria: at least eight people were sent there, three of them having died in suicide bombings.

Jihadis take advantage of the proximity of the towns and relations within the family. This was the case of a cell composed of nine people, straddling Melilla and the neighboring Moroccan town of Nador, whose members were arrested in May 2014. They had Spanish citizenship.

The areas La Meinau, Cronenbourg, and Schiltigheim, close to Strasbourg in northeastern France, have a poor reputation. They host large social housing blocks in which lived many young people who became radicalized and joined IS.

A group of ten young people who went to Syria, came mostly from La Meinau, a poor district in Strasbourg that was classified in 2013 as a "priority security zone" for its high number of delinquent people. It was also the case of the members of the Strasbourg cell who were from that poor ethnic neighborhood, where unemployment exceeded 20 percent according to the French statistical organization INSEE in 2013 (twice the national average). Social housing blocks accommodate young people who are caught between the boredom of everyday life and a life they think has no future. The Neuhoff district next to Meinau, where violence and delinquency are high, suffers from the same ills. From there departed an individual in 2013 to Syria who was married but abandoned his family.

Cronenbourg is another district classified by the authorities as a priority security zone, where delinquency is high. It belongs to the same category of poor ethnic districts as Meinau. There resided jihadis including Muhammad al-Ashram, a Palestinian imam, and Mourad Fares.

2-Middle-Class Jihadi Districts

Jihadism is not confined to poor districts, although the latter are the major jihadogenic urban settings in Europe. Some middle-class neighborhoods have also been the stage for jihadism. They have few characteristics. We proceed through concrete examples to identify them.[10]

Waltham Forest was set up in 1965 by the merger of three constituencies and is located in the northeast part of Greater London, with some 270,000 inhabitants. It is the third area to host Muslims in London after the districts of Newham and Tower Hamlets, with 48 percent of its inhabitants belonging to ethnic minorities. The largest consists of Pakistanis (12,700), followed by

Poles (8,200) and Romanians (4,300). Twenty-two percent of the population is Muslim (compared to 5 percent at the national level). Waltham Forest stands out for the high number of Foreign Fighters who left for Syria, mostly of Southeast Asian descent: up to fifty young people from this district became radicalized, and about twenty of them joined Daesh. Eight of them died there and two of them, on their return, were put under an arrest warrant by the courts. At the origin of this phenomenon was the establishment of a group of Islamists who supported al-Muhajiroun, a Muslim association founded by Anjem Choudhary and Omar Bakri. Once it was banned by law, it was renamed Islam4UK, and once that was outlawed, Muslims against the Crusades, then Sharia4UK, then United Ummah, each time after its being outlawed. The permanence of this group under different denominations had a great influence on radicalization in Waltham.

In July 2011, about fifty members of the Muslims Against Crusades (MAC) and Waltham Forest Muslims (WFM), two clusters linked to radical Islamist groups, demonstrated for two hours, shouting the slogans "democracy—hypocrisy," "Sharia for Britain," and "Secularism go to hell!" Against them, leftist organizations, unions, and anti-fascist groups demonstrated on July 30. MAC had tried to promote "Sharia zones" in Waltham Forest by posting notices banning alcohol, games, music, prostitution, and cigarettes. The municipality removed them and threatened to sue MAC. MAC was led by the radical cleric Anjem Choudhary, sentenced in 2016 to five-and-a-half years in prison for hate speech. WFM was led by Abu Izzadeen, who was sentenced to four-and-a-half years in prison for fundraising for terrorists in 2008. That activist group, ready to use legal mechanisms to fight against being outlawed and dedicated to the cause of fundamentalist Islam, had a deep influence on Muslims in Waldham Forest.

The tourist city of Brighton in the southeast of the UK is another case of middle-class district with a high number of Foreign Fighters. It has the largest proportion of gay residents in Britain (more than 10 percent) and a small Muslim minority of "Asians" (Indian, Pakistani, Bangladeshi, etc.) at 1.85 percent of the population. In Brighton, four high school students became jihadis, not because they lived in deprived or isolated neighborhoods but due to the fact that three of them went to Syria via their father who brought humanitarian aid there. Amer, twenty, left Brighton in 2013 to join Al-Nusra Front, the al-Qaeda affiliate. Two months later, two of his three younger brothers, Abdullah and Jaffar, joined him with their friend Ibrahim, of Sierra Leonean origin. They were influenced by their elder brother, Amer.

Another Brighton resident, Mohammad Raja Khan, of Bangladeshi origin, had a meteoric rise as an emir within al-Nusra in Syria (Townsend, 2016).

In this district, family ties between the sons and the unintended role of the father in bringing these young people into contact with Syria were decisive in their departure to that country.

In Portsmouth, racism furthered radicalization. The rejection of Muslims had racist undertones among far-right fraternities like the English Defense League (EDL). In their manifestations they sang "You are not English." Yet in Portsmouth, unlike Bradford, there was no district populated by poor Muslims.

While in Bradford and Dewsbury, it was mainly young people of Pakistani descent that were involved in jihadism, in Portsmouth those of Bangladeshi origin were its main agents. The al-Britani Brigade Bangladeshi Bad Boys, also called "The Pompey Bad Boys," made of six young men, departed from Britain on October 8, 2013, and joined IS. Except for one who returned home and was sent to prison, the others died on the battlefield. They had been in touch with one of the family members of the group who had joined IS earlier, Iftikhar Jaman, who encouraged them to join the caliphate. They used to meet in a café after Friday prayers, and Hassan, one of the bright members of the group who had studied in a Catholic school with good grades, joined Dawah, a proselytizing group with some others. Members of the group had jobs like being a supervisor in a supermarket (Primark store), but the future did not seem bright to them, the more so as the daily routine, according to the tweets of a member of the group, was boring and aimless (Saner, 2015; Townsend, 2014).

The city of Wolfsburg in Germany (where Volkswagen was founded in 1938) is home to a population of some 125,000 residents with a middle-class standard of living and a low rate of unemployment. The hallmarks of "poor districts" are absent there. Yet up to fifty jihadis were tallied there, twenty of them having joined the neo-caliphate in Syria. In Wolfsburg a large working class of Turkish origin lives next to the former working-class people of Italian descent.

The root cause of the departures was a charismatic Tunisian, "Sheikh" Yassin O., who came from Tunisia to Wolfsburg in 2011 (the year of the Tunisian Revolution) to take care of young "Arab" Muslims. At first, he moved to the mosque of the Islamic Association of Wolfsburg. Becoming aware of his extremism after a few weeks, the official imam forbade him to enter the mosque. Accompanied by his flock, he moved to the Turkish Ditib mosque near the city's central station. Speaking dialectal Arabic with them, his language was beyond the reach of the Turkish imam. A few weeks later, the sheikh and five of his young acolytes left Wolfsburg for Syria. According to some of his associates, he had an answer for every question and managed to make young people feel guilty, particularly about their lives of comfort in Germany, pointing to the fact that their bellies were full while their hungry Muslim brothers in Syria were killed by the idolatrous Assad regime. He reminded them of their imperative religious duty (*fardh ul ayn*): as Muslims they had a religious obligation to come to the aid of other Muslims attacked by Infidels (and Bashar Assad, as an Alawi, was a disbeliever), or face punishment of hell. Yassin succeeded in convincing several young Arabs to leave for Syria.

One of the members of the group who returned to Germany, a twenty-six-year-old man with dual nationality (Tunisian and German), believed that their desire for cohesion was the decisive factor for their enrollment in jihad, religion playing a less significant role in his eyes than group dynamics (Neumann, 2016).

More generally, we find the dual role of the urban imaginary in the jihadi phenomenon, according to the social classes: among excluded youth in the poor ethnic districts, jihadism takes advantage of the internalized indignity of the sons of Muslim migrants who feel ostracized and, in turn, reject society, recourse to violence toward it in the name of radical Islam seducing them greatly. In the second case, within the Muslim middle classes, it is their guilt feelings that are instrumentalized: they live in relative comfort and ease, compared to their brothers in religion in Syria, their empathy toward them mixed with a diffuse sense of culpability, pushing them to become Foreign Fighters in the name of Islam. "Sympathy by distance" toward the Syrian Sunnis repressed by the deviant Shiite Assad regime (belonging to the Alawite group) is set in motion (Boltanski, 1993). At the same time, the mechanism of "humiliation by proxy" (Khosrokhavar, 2009) was activated: Syrian "brothers" being humiliated by the heretical Alawite regime in turn humiliated those Tunisian-German Muslims.

Sometimes, middle-class converts become protagonists of jihadism, as in Solingen, a German town of about 160,000 inhabitants, in which a Salafist mosque close to the Islamist group Millatu-Ibrahim raised a movement of panic and popular protest against it.

In July 2011 two German converts, Robert Baum and Christian Emde, were arrested in Dover in the UK for carrying texts of radical Islamic propaganda as well as texts by al-Qaeda on how to make homemade bombs. They attended the Solingen mosque. Robert Baum was not only one of the participants in its activities but also the one who resided in that mosque for a while. In 2014 he appeared under the nickname of "Abu Sara al-Almani" in social networks. He was one of the three activists who launched a bomb attack in Syria on behalf of Daesh. He was twenty-six and had converted to radical Islam at the Milatu-Ibrahim mosque in Solingen. Another resident accompanied Robert Baum and was arrested in Britain for the same reasons, Christian David Emde, a convert from Solingen who had also lived for a while in the Milatu-Ibrahim mosque. The two converts befriended on the basis of their radical vision of Islam. Robert Baum blew himself up with explosives in 2014 in Syria. Emde, thirty years old, was in Mosul in 2015 at the service of IS. In an interview with a German journalist, he said: "We do not just want to conquer Europe; we will conquer it!" Further on: "We will continue to behead men, whether Shiites, Christians or Jews" (Asche, 2015).

The founder of the Milatu-Ibrahim mosque in Solingen, Mohamed Mahmoud (aka "Abu Usama al-Gharib") was an Austrian citizen of Egyptian origin who took up residence in Solingen by crossing the border in 2011. He was sentenced in 2007 by an Austrian court to four years in prison because of his support for al-Qaeda within the Global Islamic Media Front (GIMF), which carried the Islamist propaganda. He was released in 2011 and stayed first in Berlin and then in Solingen. He became the preacher of the local Salafist community who lacked an imam. He transformed the al-Rahman mosque into another, called Milatu Ibrahim, a meeting place of Islamists in the region. Milatu Ibrahim in Solingen espoused an uncompromising fundamentalist attitude (total veil, forbidding men and women to mix, and so forth), a political vision of Islam that the group spread on social networks, and particularly, the absolute obligation to participate in jihad (*fardh ul ayn*). The sermons were made with the standard of al-Qaeda often pinned on the wall, while radical statements were made: "It is not the problem of al-Qaeda, Taliban, Sheikh Osama (Bin Laden), but that of Islam! Either we live in honor or in humiliation! I speak while I am still standing (proud), I will die while I remain still standing. By Allah, I will never humble myself before a disbeliever (*kafir*)!" (Flade and Frigelj, 2012).

Other radical imams preached in the mosque, including the German convert Abu Dawud and the Turkish-German Hassan K., nicknamed "Abu Ibrahim." The mosque encouraged heading for Muslim countries where jihad was taking place. In February 2012 a German of Turkish origin was stopped from joining the al-Shabab jihadi organization in Somalia. He had attended the Solingen mosque sermons.

On June 14, 2012, the police invaded the Milatu-Ibrahim mosque after its ban by the justice. Seventy establishments of this association, including places of worship in Berlin, Hessen, Nordrhein-Westfalen, Hamburg, and Niedersachen, were closed.

Solingen's reputation as a "jihadi city" was founded on the allegiance of the two already-mentioned converts to a radical version of Islam and their departure to Syria under the influence of the Milatu-Ibrahim mosque, which had become the rallying point for Muslim extremists in the region.

Through radical Islamism in Solingen we see the involvement of three countries: Germany, Austria where the radical imam came from, and the UK where the two jihadi converts were caught and convicted. In Solingen people did not become jihadi out of economic exclusion or social stigma. A mosque was at the forefront of the radicalization process.

In Norway, two cities have been the hotspots of jihadism, Fredrikstad and the Grønland district in Oslo.

Of Catholic parents, Torleif Sanchez Hammer converted to Islam with some friends. He lived in the small district of Lisleby of six thousand residents, in the town of Fredrikstad, with some eighty thousand inhabitants. He and his friends were in constant trouble with the police. They smoked marijuana and celebrated loudly at Hammer's mother's house. One day they stopped smoking and partying, and soon after, Hammer and his seven friends, all living around the same street in the Lisleby district, left for Syria. It is less the urban environment, which was non-Muslim middle class, that was the source of their radicalization than the influence of friends, some imitating each other, all attending the same school, their spatial proximity within the same quarter reinforcing their radicalization. The central charismatic figure was the soccer player Abdullah Chaib, of Algerian origin, according to a former member of the radical group "Ummah Mohamad" who has since broken with extremism and works to prevent youth radicalization. In 2012, the twenty-three-year-old Chaib left for Syria for humanitarian work and died there a month later. His friends dedicated a Facebook page tribute to him, and six of them prepared to go to Syria. Members of the "Ummah of the Prophet" focused on these psychologically fragile youth to radicalize them and send them to Syria, the mother of one of them lodging a complaint against them for harassing her psychologically disturbed son. According to the police officer in charge of the case, the group was united in its alienation from society. Some converted to Islam, like Hammer (who became "Abdul"), whose mother was from the Philippines and who was feeling lost after many sexual relations and drug use; or Samiulla Khan, son of Pakistani migrants, who lived on the same street as Hammer and attended the same school as the soccer star Chaib, suffered from a split identity marked by a double denial (neither Pakistani nor Norwegian). This dialectic operates mainly on young people of immigrant origin, especially from Muslim countries, Samiulla Khan's case being replicated by many young men, mainly from the poor districts in France ("neither French nor Arab") and in the UK ("neither Pakistani nor Bangladeshi, nor English"). Being from a single-parent family (often found in the French poor suburbs) aggravated the case of Samiulla, his father having been convicted of murder. On his release from prison, being drunk, he killed a person behind the wheel (Higgins, 2015).

Another member of the group was Abu Aluevitsj Edelbijev, an athlete and a bodybuilder, a high-level kickboxer of Chechen origin. He sought to join the Norwegian army but failed, due to eye problems, and like many European jihadis who tried to embrace a military or police career were rejected (Mohamed Merah tried to join the French Foreign Legion in July 2010), he embraced jihadism as much out of spite as out of need for strong framing. The family moved to Norway in 2002 as Russian war refugees from Chechnya. Edelbijev became radicalized in 2012 in Norway and traveled by car to Turkey in 2013, along with other radicalized Fredrikstad friends. Thanks to his acquaintances, he contacted the young Diana Ramazanov from the Russian region of Daghestan and married her religiously. In July 2013 the couple crossed the Syrian border and joined Daesh. He chose the name of "Idris," and his wife chose "Sumeyra." Edelbijev was killed in December 2013 on the war front. As for his wife, she clandestinely crossed Turkey in December 2013 and made a suicide attack at the Istanbul police station on January 6, 2014, detonating two grenades. The first did not go off. While pressing the trigger of the second, a policeman shot her. She was killed with another policeman and a second was injured. She was eighteen years old and four months pregnant (Stewart and Tomlinson, 2015). She was called a "black widow" by Russian media, as she was seeking revenge for her husband's death (Turkey, as a Western ally, was an appropriate target in her view).

The story of Edelbijev is that of the first generation (he was born outside Norway but was socialized there); he had ties to Norwegians in his neighborhood. He was influenced by the charismatic personality of Abdullah Chaib, in association with a radical association, Ummah of Mohamad in Oslo, his death on the frontline triggering the activism of the other members of the group who sought to join Syria. That project originated in a district of the Norwegian city of Fredrickstat, Lisleby. It highlights the combination of several factors: belonging to the same high school in the city; the quest for cohesive ties among friends through a charismatic figure, Abdullah Chaib, who galvanized them while he was alive but even more so after his death in Syria. His memory on Facebook became an iconic exhilaration of death as a martyr, prompting the other members to follow in his footsteps. The project aiming at their holy death did not seem incompatible with founding a family, the wife and husband deciding to die as martyrs in the path of the holy war, the former being pregnant.

3-The Proximity of Poor and Rich Districts

Sometimes, the proximity of a poor and a rich neighborhood gives rise to frustration and indignation, leading to extreme action,—among others, jihadism—when some people find the means to achieve that goal. This is the case of North Kensington. This poor district adjoins affluent districts with absentee landlords and luxury hotels. A few minutes' walk from the opulent-looking buildings of Set Notting Hill lies a poor stretch to the west. Children living in the North Kensington estates and blocks were among the poorest in the capital, and a number of them were killed in jihad. The district belongs to the poorest 10 percent of the neighborhoods in the UK.

This is also the case of the 19th district in Paris, becoming gradually gentrified. Part of it is social housing in which lived some members of the so-called Buttes-Chaumont cell (the name of a public garden in that neighborhood). This was also the case of the young people of Molenbeek in Belgium: in it, the poor neighborhood is separated by a bridge from the part that undergoes gentrification.

Spatial proximity of rich and very poor creates an outrageous sense of social injustice among the poor. A minority was influenced by IS utopia and found violence to be legitimate against others in the name of jihad.

Aarhus is the second largest city in Denmark. In 2013, thirty-one Muslims from there went to Syria, intent on joining IS. Twenty-nine among them were second-generation Muslims. A clear majority came from African families, mainly Somalis. Others were of Turkish, Palestinian, and Iraqi origin: they were a sample of immigrant communities in the city. Migrants and their offspring represented almost 15 percent of the population of Aarhus, although in some neighborhoods—including Brabrand, which housed the radical mosque Grimhojsvej—the figure was two-thirds.

Brabrand district, from which most of the young people from Aarhus left for Syria, is divided into two sectors by a crossroad, Silkeborgvej. The middle-class Danish neighborhood is separated by it from a district where marginalized Muslims live. The Grimhojsvej mosque is located in the ghettoized Muslim part of Brabrand, made up of twenty-three concrete blocks built in a field. The few thousand people who live there represent eighty different nationalities, including Palestinians, Lebanese, Syrians, Sudanese, Yemenis, Somalis, Algerians, and Nigerians. Danes are a rarity among them. Those who grow up there and who are called "Mohamed" or "Hassan" suffer from discrimination and a sense of disparaged existence. What we called a slum subculture is in full swing: all the nations except Danes (they are a tiny minority) are present in the ghetto, and a few young Danes among them become socialized in the same way as the youth from that district, their culture being closer to the slum subculture than to the Danish mainstream culture. About 80 percent of the young Muslims who traveled to Syria attended the Grimhojvej mosque in the ghetto. A significant number of them were of Somali origin, those with dark complexions regarded more or less as "Niggers," on top of their being "Muslims." They were lured by the propaganda of the radical Somali group al-Shabaab. Since 2013 they were, like the Somalis in the United States, coaxed by jihadi groups in Syria.

Bispehaven is located to the west of Aarhus, one of the most implacable ghettoes in Denmark. The city also hosts another ghetto, Gellerupparken. It was the largest housing project in Denmark, with approximately eight thousand residents, and was originally planned to accommodate more than twice as many people in six thousand apartments.

The Grimhøj mosque is located in this district. The imams at the mosque repeatedly preached radical views of Islam. According to them, being unfaithful to a husband should be punished with stoning or whipping according to the Sharia law. One of them preached during a Friday prayer that Muslims should kill all Jews ("Aarhusiansk Imam," 2015). The imams and the former chairman of the mosque, Oussama El-Saadi, also expressed sympathies for IS in several Danish media. In 2014, police authorities found that of the twenty-seven individuals who had traveled from the Gellerup area to Syria, twenty-two had been visitors to the Grimhøj mosque. In 2015, politicians called for its closure. After public criticism, the mosque changed its policies, advising worshippers against taking part in a war where Muslims fight other Muslims. Still, in 2016 journalists visited the mosque with a hidden camera and imam Abu Bilal preached that women unfaithful to their husbands should be stoned or whipped and Infidels (who did not take part in Ramadan fasting) should be executed. The combination of poor ethnic districts and radical Islamic preaching awakened vocations among disparaged people who felt dignified to brandish the standard of jihad against the mainstream society.

c-The Fundamentalist District: "Islamistan"

Birmingham is the second-most populous city in Britain after London, with more than one million residents, and more than three million if we include its adjacent urban areas. One-fifth of the population is Muslim, and five out of forty constituencies in the city were the locus for the activity of twenty-six convicted jihadis out of 269 in Britain, between 1998 and 2015 (Benhold and Freytas-Tamura, 2017). Sparkbrook is among the five constituencies that had the highest number of jihadis and was called by the British media the English Molenbeek (Christys and O'Brien, 2017). As for the city, the number of its sentenced jihadis was thirty-nine. Historically, these districts were inhabited by Kashmiris, for whom the war with India to achieve Kashmir's independence was paramount. Identification with this ideal ultimately pushed them toward al-Qaeda in the first decade of the twenty-first century. The neighborhoods in question are marked by a high rate of unemployment, crime, and school failure. These constituencies are characterized by several features, one being what we might call "Islamistan," namely a population that withdraws into itself partly to avoid contact with the mainstream society that might stigmatize it because of its ethnic origins, partly out of a desire to maintain its Muslim identity that risks being swept away by the mores and customs of a secularized society. The latter does not respect Islamic norms on sexuality, alcohol consumption, and gender division. By behaving in this way, residents of Islamistan accentuate those traits that are at odds with the mainstream society and thus contribute to their marginalization. Among Muslims, fundamentalism is one major way of sustaining Islamic identity in regard to a non-Islamic environment, which makes cultural integration into the mainstream society difficult. Up to 30 percent of the population in Parkbrook were not born in Britain, and a significant number of them were ill at ease with English or did not speak it at all (Bracchi, 2017). The dialectic between unemployment, delinquency, and stigmatization on one hand, and a fundamentalist religiosity and closing onto oneself on the other, as well as the development of a jihadi religiosity among a small minority of them, make up the canvas of social and cultural life within Islamistan. Instead of creating cultural links between the migrants' sons and daughters and the English society, the cultural setting in Islamistan creates a puzzle of different identities devoid of any significant ties with the mainstream society, giving birth in the UK to a paradoxical subculture marked by the diluted presence of the British culture. Through fundamentalist (and exceptionally, jihadi) Islam, young people of Bangladeshi, Pakistani, Caribbean, Somali, and Nigerian origin constitute thus a kind of lingua franca among them in the quasi-absence of British White culture that should have played a vital role in their socialization. In Sparkbrook, as in some other towns in Britain (and poor suburbs in France), we find this type of population that becomes "introverted" for lack of contact with the mainstream culture and society. In Sparkbrook around Ladypool Road, at the center of the Balti Triangle, shops are mostly Islamic. Due to the settlement of a large Muslim majority, non-ethnic businesses have almost disappeared. The predominantly Muslim ward is riddled with problems related to poverty, underground economy, deviancy, and drug trafficking.

In many European countries we witness this type of urban structure that we call Islamistan. It can be of two types. The first has as principal feature the combination of poverty, ghettoization, cultural withdrawal, deschooling of children, unemployment of grown-ups, delinquency, hatred of the others and the self through the internalization of indignity, and lack of hope. Social exclusion and the adoption of a more and more intolerant and inflexible religiosity (for instance, the expansion of the "total veil" among other signs of introversion) lead to a lack of communication between the neighborhood and the mainstream society. A slum subculture, marked by the refusal of a shared culture with the global society, is set in motion. We already have seen that this refusal is in part a reaction to the stigmatization and denial of recognition by the mainstream society of the sons and grandsons of migrants.

The second type of Islamistan is an urban quarter in which cultural introversion prevails, partly imposed, partly promoted with the complicity of the inhabitants who foster an inward-looking Islamic culture to the exclusion of the secular or non-Islamic mores. This occurs with the connivance and consent of a large part of the population. Middle- or lower-middle-class Muslims build up a district in which only Muslims live, the others leaving gradually, non-Islamic businesses disappearing, exclusive *halal* food replacing the more diversified ones, and women without veils almost vanishing from the public space within the neighborhood.

In France the first type of Islamistan has been developing in deprived ethnic areas, especially in the so-called poor suburbs. In the United Kingdom, the second type seems paramount. One example of English Islamistan can be found in Birmingham, in the vicinity of Sparkbrook, in Washwood Heath and Alum Rock, home to many Birmingham Muslims, where a dozen mosques mark the cityscape, some offering Shariah tips for family affairs. Koranic schools meet a growing demand from parents, intent on socializing their children in Islam by protecting them against a Western world they perceive as immoral and licentious.

The case of Small Heath Park, where young girls play soccer in headscarves and men picnic in Islamic garb, leaves little room for the "other Britain" that is non-Islamic or even non-religious.

In this type of neighborhood, withdrawal into the district, mistrust of the police, and the exacerbation of social ills such as unemployment, crime and incarceration create proclivities toward radical Islam, as a kind of escapism. While official mosques reject radical Islam and their imams denounce jihadism, they are often powerless in the face of the surge of religious extremism. Belonging to an Islamist cell partly replicates the neighborhood gang model, where unemployed youth feel at home. They often combine Islamic fundamentalism and delinquency. Eloquent preachers provoke public opinion by making outrageous remarks, as did Anjem Choudhary. He gave sermons in Birmingham and was surrounded by a band of acolytes who proposed to the young Muslims the status of jihadi gangsters, similar to "Salafist-robbers" (*salafistes braqueurs*) or "Salafi-traffickers" (*salafo-trafiquants*) in the French poor suburbs, as they are called by the media.

In some cases, particularly in France but also in Britain, Islamistan combines "poor district effect" (social exclusion, delinquency, lack of mainstream culture representatives in the neighborhood) and the cultural-religious closure (slum subculture) of the quarter as an Islamic unit, deepening mutual distrust between the mainstream secular society and an introverted, gradually fundamentalist culture imposed by pressure groups to the residents. Their legitimacy is based on the alienation of excluded sons of Muslim migrants from the mainstream society.

In France, one finds poor districts that become introverted by adopting Salafist Islam, a hyper-fundamentalist religious tenet that mentally separates the district from the rest of the society, introducing a way of life that is far away from the secular French culture (Khosrokhavar, Le nouveau Jihad en Occident, 2018).

In the two types of Islamistan (the poor versus middle-class district) we find an imagined identity that is more or less at variance with the mainstream society. It can use, for instance, the colonial past in a mythological manner. For example, Belgium colonized Congo (the former Congo Belge) but did not colonize Morocco (which was colonized by France and Spain). Still, young people of Moroccan origin call themselves the "new Congolese" of Belgium, transposing in their imagination the former colonial domination of Belgium on "Congo Belge" over themselves.[11] The distortion between the imaginary and the real is obvious, but a wounded identity twists reality. It compounds, by this very misrepresentation, the aggressiveness of the sons of Muslim migrants and, in return, amplifies stereotyping by mainstream society against them. A vicious circle sets in: the more "White men" are regarded as colonialists, the more the attitude toward them will be tainted with distrust and suspicion, the more aggressiveness is developed toward them, and the more social prejudice will be reinforced against those who imagine life in this way. Social stereotypes about the "Arabs," "Pakis," Blacks, and so forth become the more persistent.

d-Districts with Historical Jihadi Agents

Sometimes, the local history of the city becomes a breeding ground for jihadism. Algerian jihadi influence in France was felt in some cities, like Nice, where the neighborhoods with a high proportion of jihadis in the years 2010 would correspond, according to some researchers, to the locations where GIA members established themselves in the 1990s (Amoyel, 2016).

The town of Trappes, close to Paris, is not an urban ghetto or a poor district; the unemployment rate is lower there than the national average in France. The history of jihadism in Trappes dates back in the 1990s at the time of the Algerian Islamic armed group (the GIA) when some radical Islamists settled in Trappes (Guéguen, 2016). This type of radicalization is similar to that of the city of Nice, where the same phenomenon gave rise to a significant number of jihadi candidates two decades later. More than sixty young people left Trappes to enact jihad in Syria. Six of them had proven links with the

Verviers cell in Belgium, which was behind the attacks of November 2015 in Paris and March 2016 in Brussels.

Maaseik, a Dutch-speaking Belgian city in the Flemish region of northeastern Belgium, a few kilometers from Holland and Germany, has a population of twenty-three thousand inhabitants. Less than a thousand people of Moroccan origin live there. The city was one of the loci of jihadism not so much because of its urban structure and poor migrant neighborhoods, but on account of the history of the influx of North African jihadis there. At first, it was a gathering place for the members of the Algerian group Islamic Armed Group (GIA), several of them, like Farid Mellouk, having escaped the anti-terrorist investigations in France after the terrorist attacks in the metro station Saint-Michel in Paris in 1995. In the late 1990s, GIA members joined al-Qaeda. A second phase began with the arrival of the members of the Moroccan jihadi group Groupe Islamique Combattant Marocain (GICM), the al-Qaeda branch that took part in the train attacks in Spain on March 11, 2004. GICM partly operated from Maaseik. A third period began in the late 2000s with a new generation of jihadis in Europe, including the Islam4Shariah movement which created a branch in Belgium (Sharia4Belgium) under the leadership of Fouad Belkacem. The cooperation was launched between him and the followers of Omar Bakri and Anjem Choudhary in London (Nesser, 2016). Maaseik put in touch old and new jihadis, owing to the existing networks there (van Vlierden, 2016).

e-Conclusion on the Jihadogenic Urban Structure

On the whole, observing those urban dwellings where jihadism prospered, one can mention local history, youth networks, and charismatic leaders who played a key role in the radicalization of the settlers. The intrinsic peculiarity of the urban setting seems not to exist in middle-class districts, in contrast to the poor ethnic districts where structural factors led to the radicalization of disaffected youth. In middle-class districts, the urban dimension was relevant only in combination with social and anthropological problems within the group and its dynamics or the individual and his solitary radicalization. In middle-class quarters, contrary to the poor districts, there was no cement like the slum subculture that would provide a strong polarization against society, and the urban dimension served as a crucible in which various ingredients pushing toward radicalization mixed together. In poor, ethnic districts, the environment is predisposed to violent action against society and, by extension, against others globally. Radicalization in this context is appealing through humiliation, resentment, and an undignified identity. In brief, the ingredients of the slum subculture are there that make life unbearable to the individual. Jihadism, in this case, is the quest for dignity through absolute violence. That is possible when a strong utopia and practical means to achieve it are present. IS provided them momentarily.

VIII
European Jihadi Cells and the motivations behind them

Cells have a life of their own. Group dynamics and the origin of the leaders, the interaction between their members, and their cultural and economic homogeneity or heterogeneity all play a significant role in their radicalization but also, in their effectiveness to implement their goals. They are more or less loosely structured, and it is very rare to find "egalitarian cells" or "leaderless" groups of friends or buddies, contrary to the claims of some researchers (Sageman, 2008). Sometimes, they have more than one leader, a division of tasks occurring between them (for instance the ideological and the military), as we shall see in some cases.

Jihadi actors choose to belong to a group for many reasons: friendship, spatial proximity (they live in the same neighborhood), and/or attendance at the same university, high school, sports association, or mosque. These facets have been frequently studied, some researchers focusing on the horizontal relationships (a group of friends without formal hierarchy) or vertical (the presence of a leader and his lieutenants), their actual link with a larger network (al-Qaeda, IS) or imaginary (laying claim or making allegiance without any effective ties), the degree of their dependence on the web, or the greater or lesser scope of the group (from a solo Jihadi to large groups of more than ten or fifteen people). Cells can be more or less diversified (they can be diversified according to the origin, age, socio-economic status, or gender of their members); they can be circumscribed to a neighborhood or a city or be national or even transnational, and they can be made of specialized and effective individuals or incompetent amateurs who miss their targets.

Jihadism in Europe. Farhad Khosrokhavar, Oxford University Press. © Oxford University Press 2021.
DOI: 10.1093/oso/9780197564967.003.0008

a-The attack of a Muslim country

Five countries in Europe have been the major loci for the development of cells of a certain size (more than two individuals): France, the UK, Belgium, Spain, and Holland. Germany did not have any significant cell up to 2019.[1]

We can distinguish three types of cells according to their leadership:

- Those which have no leader, in which there is an implicit hierarchy among the members, and the division of labor between them is made by a more or less consensual agreement between them. Some "homegrown terrorists" from the period 2002 to 2012 fall into this category; still, jihadi groups are not egalitarian, and even in this case, some members are more prominent than others.
- Those with a leader are the most common. The leader serves as an ideologue as well as a recruiter and coach. This was the case of the Cannes-Torcy cell whose leader was Jérémie-Louis Sydney, who boasted of his religious knowledge as well as his warlike skills. After his death in a clash with the police, the leadership of the group switched to his deputy, Jérémy Bailly.
- Those with a dual leadership, along the dividing line of ideology on one hand and military function on the other: in the Buttes-Chaumont group, the charismatic religious chief was Farid Benyettou and the function of the hero warrior devolved on Boubaker el Hakim.

The invasion of Iraq by the United States and the United Kingdom in 2003 outraged Sunni Muslims in the world, and particularly in the West. Three major cells were built against its backdrop that were successful in their terrorist actions: the al-Qaeda cell in Spain, the London cell, and the Buttes-Chaumont cell in Paris. The first initiated attacks against the Madrid trains in March 2004 in Spain (they were successful not only in their terrorist action but also politically, because the newly elected government withdrew its troops from Iraq after the attacks). The London cell committed attacks in July 2005, to punish Britain for its involvement in the 2003 war in Iraq. The third sent, between 2004 and 2005, Foreign Fighters to Iraq to combat the United States and the United Kingdom who had invaded and occupied Iraq.

The Spanish jihadi group that attacked the commuter trains in Madrid was created between March 2002 and November 2003. On March 11, 2004, explosions in the Madrid trains killed 191 people and wounded more than 1,800, making that the deadliest attack in Europe since the 1990s. Four small groups were involved. Two of them were tied to each other and were established from a hardcore al-Qaeda cell in Spain, led by Imad Eddin Barakat Yarkas, alias "Abu Dahdah." The cell was partially neutralized after the attacks on September 11, 2001, in the United States. The third was linked to the Moroccan Group of Islamic Fighters (GMCI, Groupe Marocain de Combattants Islamiques), which launched its offshoots in Western Europe in the 1990s, mainly in France and Belgium. The fourth consisted of a criminal gang, active in Spain and specialized in drug trafficking and the sale of stolen cars. At least nine individuals made up this group. It was led by Jamal Ahmidan, born in 1970 in Sidi Moumen, Morocco, in a poor district east of Casablanca. It consisted of outlaws, and the leader's radicalization pushed the other members in that direction.

Around twenty-seven individuals were involved in carrying out attacks on March 11, 2004, in Madrid trains. Seven of them later blew themselves up in a flat in the Spanish city of Leganés on April 3, 2004, while they were encircled by the police.

The large group consisted exclusively of men, among them twenty-one Moroccans, three Algerians, one Egyptian, one Lebanese, and one Tunisian, none of them being of Spanish descent. Most of them were economic migrants with a low level of education and menial jobs. Twenty-four were residents in Spain, two of them lived in Brussels, and one in Milan. Most of them had arrived in Spain as first-generation economic migrants and among them, only Rachid Aglif could be considered a "homegrown terrorist." He settled in Spain at the age of ten, followed the Spanish school curriculum, and started working in his father's shop at the age of sixteen. Of the twenty-seven members of the group, eleven were born in Tetouan and Tangiers in Morocco. They were mostly Berbers of the Rif. Jamal Zougam and Said Berraj lived in the same neighborhood in Tangier. Jamal, Hicham, and Hamid Ahmidan were all from Tetouan, and they also had family ties.

Mohamed and Rachif Oulad Akcha, born in Tetouan, were brothers. In fact, one-quarter of the twenty-seven individuals in the network had at least one other family member involved in the attack. Recent research has shown that they were connected to al-Qaeda (Reinares, 2017).

The group was also made of a small mafia. Its leader was Jamal Ahmidan, nicknamed "The Chinese." Born in 1970 in Morocco, he led a drug trafficking network in Madrid and a life of dissipation and conspicuous spending, using luxury cars and an entourage of pretty women as a sign of social and economic success. He was of modest origin, from a poor district, Jamaâ Mezouak, northwest of the Moroccan city of Tetouan. Through his mob ties with Rafa Zouhier in the province of Asturias, north of Madrid, Ahmidan was able to procure explosives that he used in the attacks in Madrid. He had rented a farm east of Madrid at Morata de Tajuna, where the bombs were manufactured. Those engaged in criminal activities headed by Jamal Ahmidan showed great loyalty to him, religion not playing a decisive role. On the evening of April 3, 2004, when Spanish police surrounded his flat in the suburbs of Madrid in Leganes, Jamal Ahmidan and four accomplices blew themselves up. His brother, Hamid Ahmidan, was later accused of helping him blow up the Madrid trains and was sentenced to twelve years in prison. Several other members of the group received sentences ranging from life imprisonment to a few years.

The comparison of this cell with that of Ripoll thirteen years later in the Barcelona attack on August 17, 2017, shows major differences. In Ripoll, young people of the second generation (apart from the imam) were the protagonists of the attacks, whereas in the 2004 cell, all except Rachid Aglif were migrants of the first generation.

In both attacks, people of Moroccan origin were overwhelmingly present (especially from the Rif in northern Morocco). This phenomenon is linked to the massive presence of Moroccans in Spain, by far the most numerous Muslim ethnic group. The origin of several of them from Tetouan in the 2004 jihadi cell was due to family ties, friendship, and bonds to a mafia group led by a Moroccan (Jamal Ahmidan) from a working-class district of Tetouan.

This cell and the overwhelming majority of others operated without a woman. The proportion of women, whether before 2013 (where it was marginal) or between 2013 and 2016 (where it was around 17 percent of the young people who departed to Syria and Iraq) was not similar in jihadi cells, almost all of them in Europe operating without women. Only two cells were made of women, one French, the other English, but these failed to achieve their terrorist aims.[2]

On July 7, 2005, four coordinated explosions, killing fifty-six people and injuring seven hundred, hit London's subway and bus, targeting the Circle Line near Aldgate, Edgware Road, and Piccadilly Line near Russell Square. Four British jihadis had carried out the attacks: Mohammad Sidique Khan, thirty, living in Dewsbury with his wife and young child and working as a student mentor in a primary school; Shehzad Tanweer, twenty-two, living in Leeds with his parents and working in a fish-and-chips shop; Germaine Lindsay, nineteen, living in Aylesbury in Buckinghamshire with his pregnant wife, and the eighteen-year-old Hasib Hussain, residing in Leeds with his brother and sister-in-law. Two of the bombers made videotapes explaining the reasons for their involvement in the attacks. In a videotape broadcast by Al Jazeera on September 1, 2005, Mohammad Sidique Khan claimed his membership to al-Qaeda and listed the motives for the attacks:

> I and thousands like me are forsaking everything for what we believe. Our drive and motivation do not come from tangible commodities that this world has to offer. Our religion is Islam, obedience to the one true God and following the footsteps of the final prophet messenger. Your democratically elected governments continuously perpetuate atrocities against my people all over the world. And your support of them makes you directly responsible, just as I am directly responsible for protecting and avenging my Muslim brothers and sisters. Until we feel security you will be our targets and until you stop the bombing, gassing, imprisonment and torture of my people we will not stop this fight. We are at war and I am a soldier. Now you too will taste the reality of this situation. . . . I myself, I myself, I make dua [prayer] to Allah . . . to raise me amongst those whom I love like the prophets, the messengers, the martyrs and today's heroes like our beloved Sheikh Osama Bin Laden, Dr Ayman al-Zawahri and Abu Musab al-Zarqawi and all the other brothers and sisters that are fighting in the . . . of this cause. ("London Bomber: Text in full," 2005)

On July 6, 2006, a videotaped statement by Shehzad Tanweer was broadcast by Al Jazeera:

> What you have witnessed now is only the beginning of a string of attacks that will continue and become stronger until you pull your forces out of Afghanistan and Iraq. And until you stop your financial and military support to America and Israel. ("Video of London Suicide Bomber," 2006)

According to Tanweer, non-Muslims of Britain deserved those attacks because they voted for a government which "continues to oppress our mothers, children, brothers and sisters in Palestine, Afghanistan, Iraq and Chechnya."

As for the Buttes-Chaumont cell, it sent young people to Iraq to fight the American occupation after 2003. Its members, a dozen, were between nineteen and twenty-four years of age at the time of their arrest and were mostly from the 19th district in Paris. Some dwelt in a social Housing (HLM) conglomerate, La Cité Moderne, inhabited by the charismatic leader of the group, Farid Benyettou, and his disciple Thamer Bouchnak, twenty-two years old. Under the former's influence, the other members embraced a radical version of Islam; they attended the Adda'wa mosque of Tanger Street in Paris. Its Imam Larbi Kechat stated that he was unaware of their endorsement of the radical version of Islam. They joined the large crowd of believers (three thousand to five thousand) who rushed to the mosque every Friday.

This cell had a major characteristic: it wasn't looking to fight in France but to wage war against the American army in Iraq. It mainly consisted of Farid Benyettou (the spiritual leader), Boubaker el-Hakim (the military leader), Mohamed el-Ayouni, Thamer Bouchnak, Cherif and Said Kouachi, Peter Cherif, Youssef Zemmouri (mentor and brother-in-law of Farid Benyettou), and Amedy Coulibaly.

Between 2003 and 2005, around ten young people from this cell left France to carry out the holy war in Iraq, under the pretext of learning Arabic and perfecting their knowledge of Islam in Syria. They were hosted in Syrian Salafist schools, then went to Iraq by crossing the border between the two countries. Three of them died there. The cell was dismantled in 2005. Cherif Kouachi and Thamer Bouchnak were arrested before their departure to Syria, as was Farid Benyettou, and were sentenced to prison terms.

Later on, some of its members turned from Foreign Fighters into homegrown terrorists. This was particularly the case of the Kouachi brothers and Amédy Coulibaly, who launched the attacks against *Charlie Hebdo* and a kosher supermarket in January 2015.

Jihadi cells and attacks existed long before IS. But the creation of the Islamic State made them better organized, more motivated, more "patriotic" (they could claim belonging to the caliphate, the only legitimate state), and far better trained. The two major attacks, one in Paris on November 13, 2015, and the other on March 22 of the same year in Brussels, both bearing the hallmark of IS, were the most spectacular ones.

The attacks of November 13, 2015, were the deadliest organized by IS in Europe, with 130 dead and 351 wounded, and the worst attack in France since the Second World War. They also were the deadliest after those of Madrid on March 11, 2004, with 191 dead, carried out in the name of al-Qaeda. They took place in several locations east of Paris and Saint-Denis according to a complex plan that required a rigorous organization.

Three separate commandos were involved. The first attacked in Saint-Denis, near the Stade de France where a friendly soccer match between France and Germany was taking place. It ended in a half-failure: three jihadis blew themselves up, killed one person, and injured a dozen. Their aim was to enter the stadium to kill as many people as possible, but they fell short of the goal. One of them was an Iraqi, Mansour Mohamad al Sabaawi. Of rural origin, about twenty years old, he had moved to the city of Mosul in Iraq, conquered by IS in June 2014. He was sent under a false name and a Syrian passport to Europe to commit the attacks. He mixed with migrants who arrived by boat on the island of Leros in Greece, on October 3, 2015. Another was also probably an Iraqi under a false name with a Syrian passport, and the third, a Frenchman, Bilal Hadfi, twenty, was from a district in Brussels.

The second attack took place in the 10th and 11th districts of Paris where three jihadis, Brahim Abdeslam, thirty-one, Chakib Akrouh, twenty-five, and Abdelhamid Abaaoud, twenty-eight, targeted the terraces of cafes and restaurants, leaving thirty-nine dead and thirty-two wounded. Brahim Abdeslam triggered his explosive belt in a cafe on Boulevard Voltaire and caused two serious injuries.

The third, and the deadliest, took place in the theater of Bataclan in the 11th district of Paris where 1,500 people attended a rock concert. Three French jihadis—Foued Mohamed-Aggad, twenty-three, Ismael Omar Mostefaï, twenty-nine, and Samy Amimour, twenty-eight—opened fire, killing ninety people and injuring dozens.

The attacks of March 22, 2016, in Brussels were, like those of November 13, 2015, in Paris, well organized. Its members were part of the same cell that had committed the assaults in Paris four months earlier. It was, like in Paris, a series of three suicide bombings: two at Brussels Airport in Zaventem and a third one in a Brussels subway train near the Maelbeek station, causing thirty-two deaths and 340 wounded, making them the deadliest in Belgium.

The attackers were the brothers Ibrahim and Khalid el Bakraoui, from Schaerbeek, a district in Brussels. They were linked to Salah Abdeslam. The first bomb was detonated at the airport and the second in the metro station. Najim Laachraoui, from Schaerbeek, was the kamikaze who blew himself up in the registration hall of Brussels Airport. Mohamed Abrini was the third terrorist at the airport; he fled and was arrested on April 8. They were also involved in the attacks of November 13, 2015, in Paris. Its members, as well as those of the Paris attacks, were friends, working together during their stay in Syria.

The two attacks were directly sponsored by IS. They were organized with defined targets and a rather meticulous execution that contrasts with the amateurism of a group like Cannes-Torcy whose bombing at McDonald's failed because one of its members did not wake up on time.

The majority of their agents were Belgian-Moroccan or French-Moroccan, but two Iraqis were also involved, as well as a Swede of Syrian parents, the twenty-three-year-old Ossama Krayem, a thirty-five-year-old Algerian staying illegally in Belgium. He was killed on March 15, 2016, in Brussels by the police who, four days after the Paris attacks, had wired under a false name €750 to Hasna Ait Boulahcen, a cousin of Abdelhamid Abaaoud, one of the main instigators of the attacks, to pay for their accommodation in Paris.

Allegiance to IS and the stay of most of them in Syria brought together, in the same group, those individuals of diverse origins. Some of them previously knew each other in the Brussels districts where they lived. Military training in Syria made them capable of deadly action on a large scale. Salah Abdeslam was reportedly not trained in Syria, but he frequently traveled to different parts of Europe and met with many Syrians willing to cross swords with the West. In 2015 he traveled successively to the Netherlands, Germany, Greece, Turkey, Austria, and France, to collect men and equipment and prepare for the attacks of November 13 of the same year in Paris.

The same cell launched the attacks in Belgium, IS exploiting the weakness of a divided state: the Belgian state and its Flemish/Walloon duality as well as the role of Molenbeek's mayor who had an extensive power in the context of decentralization in Belgium and underestimated the danger of jihadis.

b-The Blasphemy against the Prophet

A major topic of anger among Muslims was the desecration of the Prophet and blasphemy against Islam. It pushed jihadis to act against those who had drawn the caricatures and the media that published them. These caricatures were the climax of a deep estrangement between part of Europe (mainstream media in the United Kingdom and in the US did not replicate them) and much of the Muslim world. They amounted to a double transgression: the representation of the Prophet of Islam in images on one hand, his profanation in denying him respect and picturing him in disgraceful ways, on the other. An important part of the Muslim diaspora shared the indignation of radical Muslims even though it refused to legitimize violence. In France, following the attacks against *Charlie Hebdo*'s journalists (their cartoons of the Prophet of Islam being deeply insulting to many Muslims), in many schools in the French poor districts where Muslim youth are in the majority, a significant proportion of students refused to observe a moment of silence in homage to the victims. From their perspective, those journalists deserved punishment for their desecration of the Prophet who represented not only Islam, but Muslims' dignity that was often trampled on by French secularism (laïcité). In contrast, after the attacks of November 13, 2015, many of those same young people shared the indignation of the mainstream society because the attacks were carried out indiscriminately against the civilian population, Muslims included.

The indignation caused by the cartoons was the cause of several attacks, organized or advocated by jihadi groups including al-Qaeda and IS. The most important was that of *Charlie Hebdo*, January 7, 2015, but there were also others in Europe. In Sweden, on December 11, 2010, two explosions occurred in the center of Stockholm, killing the bomber Taymour Abdel Wahab and causing two light injuries among people. About ten minutes before the attacks, a claim by e-mail was sent to the press agency and the Säpo (Swedish security police). It contained audio files on which a man speaking in Arabic and Swedish to "Sweden and the Swedish people" referred to one of the major drawers of the cartoons of Muhammad, the Swede Lars Vilks, pinpointing as well to Sweden's involvement in the war in Afghanistan, claiming that revenge would fall on children, girls, and women: sisters of Swedes should perish like family members of Muslims in Afghanistan. Another series of attacks occurred in Copenhagen on February 14 and 15, 2015, during a public conference in support of the victims of the *Charlie Hebdo* attack on January 7, 2015. Lars Vilks, the cartoonist who represented the Prophet in a very disrespectful manner in 2007 in the Swedish newspaper *Nerikes Allehanda*, was the main target of the shooting.

c-European Jews as culprits and scapegoats

Jews have also become the targets of jihadi attacks, due to the influence of the modern anti-Semitic ideologies propagated by Western extreme-right movements, the Judeophobic traditions in Islam, and Israel's policies toward the Palestinians.

A jihadi group that aimed at executing Jews was the Cannes-Torcy cell. It was officially created in July 2012 in the city of Cannes, in southern France: the members of the group of Torcy arrived in a motorhome which they parked in front of the mosque al-Madina of Cannes where they socialized with those of the Cannes group. Many members of the two groups already knew each other, but this meeting solidified the links between them in a solemn way, unifying them under the aegis of Jérémie Louis-Sidney, a Black man from the Dom Tom (French overseas territory), born in Melun (in the department of Seine-et-Marnes, near Paris). On September 19, 2012, two hooded men, Jérémie Louis-Sidney and Jérémy Bailly, broke the window of a kosher supermarket in Sarcelles (a Paris suburb) and threw inside it a hand grenade that made only one light injury, having gotten stuck under a cart. A third accomplice, Kevin Phan, drove the car they ran away in. This failed attack resulted in the police dismantling the so-called Cannes-Torcy cell. They were preparing to leave for Syria. Apart from the kosher supermarket in Sarcelles, the group planned three more attacks between 2012 and 2014, one of them targeting a McDonald's restaurant in Lognes (Seine-et-Marne, close to Paris), which failed because the person who had to carry gasoline to set it on fire did not wake up on time in the morning. A third attempt targeted in June 2013 the military camp of Canjuers (Var, a department in southeastern France). The female companion of Meher Oujani, an undocumented Tunisian who was supposed to attack the barracks with three other partners, filed a complaint against him for domestic violence and revealed to the police the planned attack. Finally, a project of attack against the carnival of Nice in February 2014 did not succeed, following the arrest of the group's members prior to it. The cell was built around two converted leaders, Sidney and Bailly, but it also had another prominent member, Ibrahim Boudina of Algerian origin who was closely linked with Abdelkader Tliba and Rached Riahi, members of the group. The cell was made up of young men in their twenties and thirties, with a history of delinquency for some, most of them being unemployed, belonging to different faiths (Catholic, evangelical, Buddhist, Jewish). A significant number of these young people had recently converted to Islam and quickly radicalized. Of the twenty-two members, there was one cook who had lost his job, two temporary workers, a facilitator, a safety officer, a warehouseman, an employee, a formwork assistant, a gardener, a store man-driver, and a sailor: in all, that was twelve unemployed and ten others with poorly paid jobs. Ten of them were of North African origin, eleven were converts. One of them, Alix Seng, twenty-nine, was the son of Laotian Buddhist refugees whose father had fled the Khmer Rouge dictatorship in Cambodia. He expressed his apologies to the victims. As for the two brothers Elvin and Joan-Mich Bokamba, they are the sons of a senior Congolese politician of evangelical faith; another convert, Victor Guevara, twenty-eight, came from an upper-middle-class family, living in the affluent 8th district of Paris. The two leaders, Jérémie-Louis Sydney and Jérémy Bailly, were converts of modest origin.

The January 2015 attacks had an anti-Semitic slant. On January 9, 2015, Amedy Coulibaly killed four Jews in an attack against a kosher supermarket at the door of Vincennes (close to Paris). The day before the attack he had killed a young intern municipal policewoman in Montrouge (close to Paris).

In the years 2002–2003, the three perpetrators of the January 2015 attacks came from a group of young jihadis within the so-called Buttes-Chaumont cell. In 2015 Cherif was thirty-two and Said, thirty-four. As for Amedy Coulibaly, he was the same age as Chérif. These men in their thirties had begun their jihadi activities when they were in their twenties. All three were of migrant families, lived in poor, ethnic neighborhoods, had major family problems, and had gone through prison; their commitment to radical Islam was the endpoint of a trajectory in which the choice of total violence was regarded by them as legitimate, almost unavoidable.

d-Examples of Jihadi Cells

One can mention a group of four Asian jihadis from Stoke-on-Trent, a town in the north of the UK, three of them calling themselves "The Three Musketeers," the name originating from a novel by the nineteenth-century French author Alexandre Dumas—although they were probably unaware of its origin, knowing only of Walt Disney's cartoons of the same name. Through the denomination of The Three Musketeers they communicated with each other, using encrypted messages on the Telegram network.

Two of them—Naweed Ali, age twenty-nine, and Khubaib Hussain, age twenty-five, had previously joined an al-Qaeda training camp in Pakistan in 2011, but found the discipline too hard and returned to the UK. On their return, they were arrested and sentenced to prison terms for terrorism.

Mohibur Rahman, age thirty-three, who was sentenced to five years in prison for membership in a terrorist group, joined them. He was a delivery driver for home cooking. The father of two children, he had recently broken up with his wife and had become a born-again radical Muslim. The members of the group were arrested on August 26, 2016, and were sentenced to long prison terms.

Ali and Hussain were neighbors living with their families in semi-detached houses in Sparkhill, Birmingham. Hussain had completed a bachelor's degree. Ali had failed at school and worked in a canteen.

The four were Asians (from the Indian sub-continent), pointing to the postcolonial dimension of this group, three of them having already tried to embark on a jihadi action. Prison was their meeting ground with a fourth member, all denoting the characteristics of many European jihadis: stigmatization, delinquency, repeat offense, radicalization, and travel in countries at war in the name of jihad. They belonged to the lower-middle classes, not disaffected youth. Still, their feeling of humiliation as Asians was strong; in particular, the sense that Islam was in jeopardy pushed them toward armed struggle in the name of holy war.

One of the largest English jihadi cells set its sights on blowing up the London Stock Exchange. It was made up of nine men from Stoke-on-Trent, Cardiff, and London. Seven of them were British nationals of Pakistani and Bangladeshi descent. Among them, Mohammed Chowdhury and Shah Rahman were born in Bangladesh. They were arrested in December 2010. Their group was established in October of the same year. Its members came from three different cities: Mohammed Shahjahan, age twenty-seven, Usman Khan, twenty, and Nazam Hussain, twenty-six, were from Stoke-on-Trent; they planned to set up a military training camp in Kashmir, where Usman Khan's family had a property that could be used for this purpose. They were also looking for sources of funding in Britain. Gurukanth Desai, thirty, Abdul Miah, twenty-five, and Omar Latif, twenty-eight, were from Cardiff; Mohammed Chowdhury, twenty-two, Shah Rahman, twenty-eight, and Mohibur Rahman, twenty-eight, were from London. The jihadi apprentices were of Asian origin. They were in their twenties and thirties, the average age being twenty-three. The ethnic homogeneity of the group (Asians, from Pakistani and Bangladeshi descent) was its distinguishing feature compared to others that included converts and people of other origins.

Moreover, jihadis of Stoke-on-Trent were the initiators, the court identifying them as the most dangerous, their aim being to place bombs in the toilets of the pubs of their city as well as in the London Stock Exchange. The leader of the Cardiff subgroup was Abdul Miah, sentenced to sixteen years, ten months in prison because of his criminal background, maturity, and strong personality that captivated others. The London subgroup was headed by Mohammed Chowdhury, twenty-two, sentenced to thirteen years, eight months in prison. In these three cells, the oldest did not necessarily take the lead, the two members of the London group being twenty-eight years old and their leader, twenty-two; in the same vein, in Cardiff's cell, the leader Abdul Miah was twenty-five, the other two being, respectively, thirty and twenty-eight years old.

The cells have often been sites of "jihadi meritocracy," with more motivated young people leading sometimes older members. They have enabled the youngest to assert themselves in their new authority by challenging the traditional Islamic hierarchy. In a way, they replicated the role of IS in Syria, which fascinated young people because it allowed them to rise above a delayed adolescence, a youth without purpose or ideals, to thrive in the heat of battle in a new military hierarchy.

The North London Boys cell aimed at sending English people as well as equipment and financial resources to Somalia's jihadi groups. They set up a network of radicalized activists in 2012, composed of one group based in the United Kingdom and another in Somalia. Mohamed Emwazi was one of them, and he left Somalia in 2009. After the return of the cell's leadership to the UK, the focus shifted to Syria. Emwazi left for Syria and was later identified as the infamous "Jihadi John," the hostage killer, decapitating his victims in video scenes in the name of IS.

The originality of this cell lies in its dual character: on one hand the London pole, on the other Somalia. Like the Buttes-Chaumont cell in France, the North London Boys aimed at sending candidates for the holy war outside the country (Foreign Fighters) and not to perpetrate attacks in the United Kingdom (homegrown terrorists). The first sent young recruits to Iraq to serve al-Qaeda, the second under the banner of al-Shabaab, to Somalia, and later on, Syria.

In France, the Buttes-Chaumont cell was dismantled and did not have the opportunity to evolve. But some of its former members became IS recruits and perpetrated the November 2015 attacks in Paris.

A major French jihadi group is the so-called Strasbourg cell. It was made of ten friends who went to Syria, under the spell of Mourad Fares, a charismatic figure who brought them together. They were from Meinau, a neighborhood located southwest of Strasbourg where, next to the industrial sector and the residential area, the social housing sector (HLM) is situated. In these areas the sons of migrants live in large pockets. They develop a specific malaise as non-citizens, as those who bear a negative identity filled with a sense of outrage, which can result in the extreme violence of jihadism as a revenge. According to the accounts of the defendants, they had contacted each other on Facebook, had meetings in La Courneuve (close to Paris), Strasbourg, and Lyon, and were convinced by Mourad Fares, a Daesh recruiter, to help Syrians against the Assad regime. Fares, from Savoy, fascinated these Alsatian youth by his eloquence and a veneer of Islamic knowledge.

Originally from Strasbourg's poor neighborhoods (Meinau and Neuhoff), they left before Christmas 2013, keeping their parents and sometimes their wives in the dark about their departure. Between the ages of twenty-one and twenty-seven in 2013, they took four different flights to Turkey, so as not to draw the attention of the authorities. Two brothers among them, the Boudjllals, died two weeks after their arrival in Syria in the clash between two jihadi groups, Jabhat al-Nusra (branch of al-Qaeda) and EIIL, which later became Daesh, Mourad Farès having left the second to join the first. Seven returned to France a few months after their departure, totally disappointed. Karim Mohamed-Aggad was among them. Foued, his brother, died on November 13, 2015, in the Paris attacks, after committing a massacre at Bataclan.

The band of friends had met in a bar in Kehl, a German town on the other side of the French border where they gave free rein to their passion to leave, creating an internal group dynamic, permeating them with an esprit de corps that undermined their individuality: all of them blindly followed the "guru" Mourad Farès. But he behaved casually on the Syrian front by not greeting them upon their arrival and later on, by leaving IS and joining al-Nusra, the al-Qaeda group, without consulting them. They were almost all of North African origin. What distinguished them was that none had a criminal record, besides Mokhlès Dahbi who was three times convicted for theft, violence, and drug trafficking. Among them were an animator, a trader, a service station employee, and a jobless person. They suffered from the slum culture syndrome, based on a feeling of social and cultural exclusion and a deep sense of not being recognized as rightful citizens by the mainstream society.

The mix of young people from different social backgrounds, among them a young "thug" and a majority with low socioeconomic status, underlined the essential role of the guru, Mourad Farès. His strong personality literally mesmerized these young people, debilitated by an identity caught between two stools (neither French nor Arab), who discovered in him a super-father. Farès enabled them to distinguish the true from the false in a fictitious transparency. His role as a cement between the members of the poor and middle classes was similar to that of Daesh which managed, within the combat groups in Syria, to bring together the poor and the less poor, the middle classes and the working classes, driven by the same goal and the same ideal, that of extending the caliphate to the entire region, if not the world.

The jihadi group of Orléans (a town in central France) was made up of at least nineteen individuals. It was set up in 2012, well before the advent of IS in Syria. Around twenty young people between the ages of twenty-two and thirty-three of various origins (French converts, French-Algerians, French-Moroccans [binationals], and Black Africans) were its members, their essential link being the attendance at the mosque of the Carmes in Orleans, whose moderate director from the Paris Mosque (Mosquée de Paris) was unaware of their radicalization (Barbereau, 2016). The individual who indoctrinated and radicalized them was a North African preacher who was expelled, and whose name was withheld from the public. They left for Syria in 2012, being among the first Frenchmen to take the plunge. They enlisted under the banner of Katiba Jaish Muhammad (Muhammad's Brigade), made up of around four hundred fighters at its peak, close to Jabhat al-Nusra, affiliated with al-Qaeda. One of the them eventually became an emir (military leader) within the organization. Of those young people who left, some died, nine were put on trial by a Paris Criminal Court in 2017, and some were judged in absentia. The members of the group were of diverse social origins; one of them, the father of a child, was an employee at the primary fund of Medicare. Some members of the Orléans group lived in social housing (HLM), some were converts. Three members of the group purportedly went on a pilgrimage to Mecca in January 2012 in Saudi Arabia, but they were found five months later in Pakistan. They were sent back to France along with a Franco-Algerian, Naamen Meziche, a recruiter for al-Qaeda. The three individuals, Mohamed el-H., a twenty-nine-year-old father of three children and a former delivery driver; Mehdi H., twenty-six, a bus driver in Orléans; and Grégory B., twenty-eight and jobless, were put on trial in France for their involvement in a terrorist group. They were in a semi-precarious situation and attended a mosque in the poor district of Argonne in Orleans.

Two others, respectively twenty-one and twenty-two, were also tried for membership in a terrorist group. The first held a diploma of vocational qualification in painting (CAP), was married and the father of a toddler; the second was married and owned a small transport company. They were two childhood friends and had converted to Islam. Both were described as "immature and infantile" by experts. One of them admitted that he wanted to go to Syria, but his wife had dissuaded him. The other denied the charge outright.

The psychological trait that united them was a deprecatory reference to *dunya* (this material world with its noxious attractions as opposed to the blissful afterlife, the *akhira*, for the martyr). The growing fragility of the family, and Islamophobia, played a role in their repudiation of the "material world" as well as an economy that progressively removes the social warrants of the Welfare State in the name of competitiveness. More generally, this complex social situation contributes to discredit this world in the name of another where these constraints would not exist. Jihad is experienced as a glorious way out of a situation that is experienced as devoid of a horizon of hope for those who are at the bottom or are stuck in dead-end jobs or stagnate at subaltern ones and who believe there is no future for them. There is, of course, no strict causality, but elective affinities do exist between the fragile social status of most jihadis and their worldview.

One major case of homegrown terrorists of middle-class origin was the jihadi doctors' cell that organized the attack on Glasgow International Airport on June 30, 2007, in Great Britain. A car bomb loaded with propane canisters crashed into the main gate of Terminal 1 at Glasgow International Airport in Scotland. The driver was seriously burned, and five people were slightly injured. The two passengers in the car were arrested. One of them was Dr. Bilal Abdullah, a twenty-seven-year-old Iraqi-raised Muslim doctor originally from the UK who worked at Alexandra Hospital in Paisely, about 10 kilometers from Glasgow, and Kafeel Ahmed, age twenty-seven, who had worked at Alexandra Royal Hospital for three months. He died of his injuries two days later. Bilal Abdullah was sentenced to life imprisonment.

Dr. Bilal Talal Abdullah was born in Aylesbury about sixty miles from London, but he grew up in Baghdad. He earned his medical degree in 2004, the American and British invasion of Iraq inspiring him with hatred toward the West. Abdullah began his medical career in the UK in 2006 without his radical past being checked. His family was Wahhabi of strict obedience. He had many extended family members in Cambridge where he completed his training at the prestigious Addenbrooke Hospital. During his stay in that city, he made contacts with Hizb ut-Tahrir. He did not conceal his approval of the killing of Americans and English in Iraq. He became closer to Kafeel Ahmed, a driver. Both worked at the Royal Alexandra Hospital near Glasgow and shared the same flat. He was born and raised in Bangalore, India, and studied medicine at Rajiv Gandhi University in the city. The driving force behind this duo was Bilal Abdullah, who was deeply traumatized by the 2003 American and British attack and occupation of Iraq.

The "Hofstad network" was originally the code name given to a jihadi group made up of young Dutch people, mostly of North African origin (mostly Moroccans), by the Dutch secret service. The hard core of the network was set up between 2002 and 2003. The name of the group became public after Mohamed Bouyeri murdered the Dutch film director Theo van Gogh on November 2, 2004, for having made the movie *Submission* in collaboration with Ayaan Hirsi Ali, in which the treatment of women in Islam was criticized in a controversial manner. Islam and its desecration were the focus of the attack rather than the American invasion of Iraq in 2003.

The spiritual leader of the group was Redouan al-Issar, called "The Syrian." During the year 2005 a new network emerged which could be considered as its follow-up. Some of the original group members who were no longer in detention played a central role in shaping the new network. Other people joined, from the same social background, whether neighbors, relatives, or friends. The new Hofstad network operated along the lines of Mohamed Bouyeri and the Syrian Abu Khaled. Samir A., who had been very active since 2003, played a prominent role in the network. In October 2005, some of its members were arrested on suspicion of preparing attacks on political figures and the headquarters of the Foreign Intelligence Service of Holland, the AIVD (Algemene Inlichtingen- en Veiligheidsdienst).

The Hofstad network had a considerable impact on the radicalization and networking of Dutch jihadis, as a model to follow, due to its "success" in killing the Dutch filmmaker Theo van Gogh. For their attacks, they tried to select local politicians and opinion leaders. Their pattern of action was in unison with the jihadis of the neighboring countries, who targeted either journalists guilty of desecrating Islam or its Prophet (those of *Charlie Hebdo*), Jews, the military, or the police (Muslim or not). Bouyeri targeted Van Gogh, a person that the killer—but also his jihadi friends—considered an enemy of Islam.

The group was estimated to consist of fourteen members, among them two converted brothers, the Walters brothers, and the spiritual leader, Mohamed al-Issar, a Syrian. The others were of Moroccan origin. In December 2010 the Amsterdam Court of Appeal declared the Hofstad group a terrorist one. Seven of its members were sentenced for terrorism, five of them were condemned to fifteen months' imprisonment.

The spiritual leader of the Hofstad group, Mohamed Bassem al-Issar (aka "Redouan al-Issar" or "Abu Khaled"), was born in Hama in Syria between 1955 and 1965. He is a geologist by profession. In 1995, he arrived in Germany as an asylum seeker, declaring that he had been detained for fourteen years in Syria where he allegedly had been tortured. In October 2003 Issar was arrested in Holland and sent back to Germany. He had made radical sermons in several Dutch cities, including Schiedam and The Hague. His ideology was influenced by the Egyptian jihadi group Takfir Wal Hijra. The organization has been banned in the European Union since December 12, 2002. On November 2, 2004, the day of Theo van Gogh's murder, al-Issar left Holland with the assistance of Rachid Belkacem and via Belgium he went to Greece, then to Turkey, ending up in his native Syria. On April 29, 2005, al-Issar was arrested and incarcerated in the Palestinian prison of Fereh in Damascus. He was involved in developing a plan for the attack on Ramstein Airport in Germany. The members of the Hofstad group were arrested in 2007.

Samir Azzouz was born in 1986 in a Moroccan family in a poor district of Amsterdam, Nieuw-West. He completed his primary school, but he dropped out of high school and began to radicalize. In January 2003, at the age of seventeen, he was arrested in Ukraine with a friend, seeking to move to Chechnya, to promote jihad against Russia. Back in Holland, Azouz and four of his friends were arrested, suspected of building up a terrorist cell, but they were released for lack of evidence. In 2004 he was arrested for armed robbery in a supermarket. Police detected evidence of imminent jihadi attacks in Holland, but he was only sentenced to three months in prison for illegal possession of weapons. On December 1 of the same year, he was sentenced to eight years in prison for attempting to carry out terrorist attacks against politicians and public buildings. The judges considered that the twenty-year-old Dutch Islamist played a central role in a terrorist group, some of whose members had in the past been linked to the Hofstad network. Nourridin El-Fatmi, who was already sentenced to five years in prison in another terrorist case, was sentenced to four additional years, as was Mohamed Chentouf. Soumaya Sahla, El-Fatmi's wife, was sentenced to three years in prison for assisting the group. A fifth accused, Brahim Harhour, was sentenced to three months in prison for providing false identity papers. As for the last defendant, Mohamed Hamdi, he was acquitted. The six accused formed a terrorist group in the wake of the Hofstad group. However, the judges found that the group around Samir Azzouz was too loose to qualify as terrorist under the law. Samir Azzouz had several characteristics of disaffected youth: he lived in a poor neighborhood called Niew-West, with a high concentration of people of immigrant origin, where he dropped out of school and became involved in armed robbery and became radicalized under the influence of a Syrian by the name of Mohamed al-Issar.

In Paris, on January 7, 2015, a group made of two brothers, Saïd and Chérif Kouachi, committed a major attack against the weekly newspaper *Charlie Hebdo* in order to kill its journalists who had posted satirical cartoons of the Prophet Mohammad. They also killed an agent responsible for the maintenance of the building and a policeman, Ahmed Merabet, during their flight. The final toll was twelve dead and eleven wounded, four seriously. These murders were committed on behalf of al-Qaeda in the Arabian Peninsula (AQPA). They were loosely associated with Amedy Coulibaly, who killed a young policewoman and five people in a Kosher store near Paris.

On September 30, 2005, the Danish newspaper *Jyllands-Posten* published twelve caricatures of the Prophet of Islam, which in 2006 triggered numerous demonstrations and boycott movements of Danish products in Muslim countries, putting Denmark in a situation that its first minister, Anders Fogh Rasmussen, declared as the worst international crisis in the country since the Second World War. On February 1, 2006, the daily *France-Soir* published the cartoons out of solidarity, and on February 8, 2006, *Charlie Hebdo* published them in turn, adding a drawing of the cartoonist Cabu in which Muhammad took his head in his hands and exclaimed, "It's hard to be loved by idiots." On September 19, 2012, the newspaper published new caricatures of Muhammad that triggered a heated controversy, in a news marked by the broadcast of the American video "The Innocence of Muslims" attributed to Nakoula Basseley Najoula, an Egyptian Copt residing in California, who virulently denounced the Prophet of Islam. The film was at the origin of the attacks of September 11, 2012, against the American diplomatic missions in Egypt, the consulate of the United States in Benghazi in Libya and Sudan, and the embassies of Germany and the United Kingdom.

In Paris, the attacks against *Charlie Hebdo* pursued the same goal as elsewhere: to kill those who desecrated the Prophet of Islam by their cartoons. Its perpetrators in France, the brothers Kouachi, were affiliated with the Buttes-Chaumont cell jihadis, described previously.

e-Conclusion on Jihadi Groups and Cells

A first conclusion is the specific nature of large jihadi cells (those with four or more members) whose general composition does not follow the global statistics of radicalized individuals. One example among others illustrates this phenomenon: big cells, whether before or after 2013, are devoid of women (attacks of Barcelona, August 17, 2017, attacks of November 13, 2015, in Paris, and March 22, 2016, in Brussels) even though the proportion of women who left for Syria after 2013 is about 17 percent (the cell that attempted the failed attack of September 3 and 4, 2016, was made of three women, like another English cell made of the female members of the same family). We can also take the case of converts. In Spain, statistics account for

13 percent of converts among jihadis. In the Barcelona-Ripoll cell, their rate is zero. Similarly, in France, the estimate for converts is around 23 percent. But if we consider the Cannes-Torcy cell, this rate is much higher: eleven converted from some twenty-three members, almost 50 percent. This is partly due to the fact that the leader of the group, Jérémie-Louis Sydney, and his right-hand man, Jérémy Bailly, were both converts and attracted others. Similarly, the average age of European jihadis is twenty-six to twenty-eight years. However, the three jihadis who made the attack of *Charlie Hebdo* and the Kosher supermarket in January 2015, were between thirty-two and thirty-four, which largely exceeds the average age.

The second conclusion is the active influence of the community of origin on the jihadi cells: in London the attack of July 7, 2005, was committed by four individuals, three of them of Pakistani origin (Mohammad Sidique Khan, Shehzad Tanweer, and Husaib Hussein). Those of November 13, 2015, in Paris were mainly committed by individuals of Moroccan origin, of French or Belgian nationality (few were of Algerian and Syrian origin).

The third observation is that cells are evolutive: in 1995 the attacks of the intercity train (RER) of Paris by the Algerian Armed Islamic Group (GIA) members aimed at punishing France, and the problem was confined to that country, which had supported the military coup in Algeria. We witness the preponderance of the so-called homegrown terrorists generation, which was partly the case of the 1995 jihadi group in France: Khaled Kelkal, its emblematic figure, had lived and grown up in France since his early childhood. Seventeen years later, Mohamed Merah committed in 2012 attacks against the military and the Jews in Toulouse and Montauban.

Besides them, homegrown jihadis in Europe were generally incompetent, and their damage to society was more psychological than real (few people were killed, explosives did not usually detonate, the militants' action was inefficient). With the creation of IS a sea change occurred in the terrorist attacks: its cells were of a formidable efficiency (attacks of November 13, 2015, in Paris and March 22, 2016, in Brussels with respectively 130 and 32 deaths).

With the exception of the September 11, 2001, cell (nineteen hijackers), what differentiates Europe from the United States is the existence of "large cells" (more than three individuals), whether in the UK (cells up to eleven individuals), France (cells up to more than twenty individuals, like Cannes-Torcy), Spain (twenty-seven individuals were indicted for the attacks of the Madrid train on March 11, 2004), Belgium (the cell that committed the attacks of November 13, 2015 in Paris and March 22, 2016, in Brussels were made up respectively of nine and four members, the two groups making up the same cell), or Holland (the so-called Hofstadt cell in which at least thirteen people were involved, several others playing a role in the organization of the attacks). In Europe, large cells (more than three people) or very large (more than nine people) were found only in Spain, France, the UK, Holland, and Belgium. Denmark, Norway, Sweden, Italy, Portugal, Germany, and Switzerland were spared.

European large cells were often concentrated in a city (the Buttes-Chaumont cell in the 19th district of Paris, the Barcelona cell in the town of Ripoll, the cell of English doctors in Glasgow); less often, a cell was split between two or three cities or towns, through their inhabitants (the Cannes-Torcy cell in France between the town of Torcy close to Paris and the city of Cannes in southern France, the cell that intended to blow up the London Stock Exchange and was made of nine men from Stoke-on-Trent, Cardiff, and London), or between a city and a country (the North London Boys cell between London and Somalia). Small cells were different in nature and could be made of two individuals living thousands of kilometers away (the case of the fifteen-year-old Englishman who manipulated an eighteen-year-old Australian to commit an attack on Anzac's day in April 2015).

General Conclusion

The sociology of jihadism in Europe is manifold:

- It is a sociology of humiliation, stigmatization, hatred, and resentment, particularly within impoverished, ethnic neighborhoods where poverty, relative frustration, and internalized indignity are rampant, amplified by a victimized imaginary.
- It is also a sociology of revolt against an unjust world, first of all by lower classes, mostly of migrant origin, left behind in late capitalist societies, but also by fragile middle classes threatened by social decline and uncertainty about their future. Their imagination attributed to IS a capacity to promote their social status and restore justice that was more a matter of fantasy than reality.
- It is also a political sociology of state-building: Daesh attracted so many young people due to its territorial extension, awakening the dreams of a renewed Islamic community in which Muslims could rebuild their lives with dignity, buoyed by a utopia of a reinvigorated caliphate, rising from the ashes of the past glorious Islamic empires, restored in their past greatness imagined as a Golden Age during the reign of the first four well-guided caliphs, after the death of the Prophet.
- It is an anthropology of utopia. Before Daesh, the number of young Europeans attracted to jihadism was marginal. After its creation, their numbers greatly increased. The utopia of a new community (neo-Ummah) under the umbrella of a new state (the caliphate) brought meaning (projected into the future) to the often aimless lives of underprivileged youth or the middle classes, the first suffering from humiliation, the second mainly from lack of purpose in life and threat of social decay. They wanted to combine the quest for purpose and meaning with social advancement in a new society, organically uniting Muslims into a close-knit community.
- It is a sociology of false hope and "false consciousness" through identification with a radical ideology (jihadi Islam) as a panacea to the ills of

Jihadism in Europe. Farhad Khosrokhavar, Oxford University Press. © Oxford University Press 2021.
DOI: 10.1093/oso/9780197564967.003.0009

> modernity. Belief in radical Islam as a solution to the plight of modern life denotes the crisis of togetherness. The tragedy is that a system of thought and representation, which is as simplistic as it is repressive, could attract and convince so many young people (and many more if they had been able to join Daesh). The failure of modernity is especially in the environment created by the new economy and globalized politics in which self-assumption and self-construction are primarily achieved through a self-centered individualism, consumerism, and their adjunct narcissism of boundless wealth, the Welfare State being more and more marginalized and collective solidarities of the past being in decline, without utopias instilling a meaning to social life. Up to now, globalized modernity is devoid of credible utopias that would inspire a noble sense to collective life. A major crisis of a global nature is at the heart of this soulless modernity that promises nothing but material and selfish well-being and robs people of social justice and spirituality.

Understanding jihadism within a sociology of a limited group of radicalized and dangerous individuals is legitimate, but at best partial. Besides the crisis of Muslim societies in the Middle East and North Africa, many Muslims find themselves in a humiliating predicament in Europe, jihadism being embedded in an urban setting that needs deep reforms, being pushed by family crises, denoting major gender issues and reflecting significant problems of adolescence and crisis of authority, encompassing lower as well as middle classes. In a word, jihadism denotes a global crisis of social bonds within advanced, modern, capitalist societies, particularly in the old Europe.

At the same time, though a major crisis, jihadism cannot be compared in extension as well as intensity, to those that shook the world in the 1920s and ended up in fascism and Nazism. European political systems are beset by populism, but not by totalitarianism. The jihadi crisis is manageable, due to its incapacity to propose anything constructive, sheer blind violence convincing less the new generations. In Europe jihadism is not over, but it is on a decline. The end of IS as a territorial state, and the emergence of new social movements like those on climate change or against social inequality might weaken it by occupying the public space, polarizing the youth around new utopias that are less violent and more constructive than jihadism.

Notes

Preface

1. These were published in 2004 (*Islam en prison*), 2005 (*Challenge and Change: Muslims in French and British Prisons* with James Beckford and Danièle Joly), and 2006 (*Quand al-Qaeda Parle*).
2. *Les prisons de France*, published in 2016.

I

1. Data recorded from European Jihad Watch (March 2017) estimated the number of people involved in jihadi networks from January 2013 to March 2017 to be 7,195, significantly higher.
2. The ideological dimension has been largely covered by me (Khosrokhavar, 2009, 2011) and by many other scholars (Esposito, 1998; Euben and Zaman, 2009; Lohlker, 2013; Mura, 2015; Winter, 2015; McCants, 2015). IS did not make any major ideological innovation, only its action was more violent, combining the utopia of the caliphate and the end-of-time mythology to this end. This book does not focus on this aspect other than referring to some of the jihadis' tenets.
3. See Cacciari and Prodi, *Occidente senza utopie* (A West without Utopias), il Mulino, Bologna, 2016. In this book, quite independently of my stance on this matter that I discussed in 2014 and before, the two authors analyze the loss of utopia in the West philosophically and historically.
4. The first time I drew attention to the death, inflicted or suffered, in the 1979 Revolution in Iran and in the 1980–1988 was in regard to the war between Iran and Iraq, in which martyrdom was at the core of the Islamic revolutionary ideology (Khosrokhavar, 1995, 1998).

II

1. Even his successor, Abu Ibrahim al-Hashimi al-Quraishi, who became caliph after al Baghdadi's death in October 2019 under American Bombings, spent many months in the US prison in Bucca in 2004 where he met al Baghdadi (Filiu, 2020).
2. See Chapter 5, "The European Nations and Their Jihadis."
3. See the interviews that follow.

4. We deal with the subject of humiliation exhaustively in the section "Humiliation and Radical Islam" in Chapter 2.
5. This type of martyrdom is not sufficiently covered by scholarly studies that deal with martyrdom from a global historical perspective (see, for instance, the otherwise well-documented books of Meir Hatina, 2014, or David Cook, 2005) and lose sight of the subjectivity of those who mobilize religion in the service of their aspirations or desires or even frustrations within disparate settings. Religious history plays a marginal role in those cases and modern affects play the major part in mobilizing for the sake of sacred death. This phenomenon is pertinent not only in the West but also in Muslim countries (see Khosrokhavar, 1995, 2018).
6. One can mention the cases of Foued Mohamed-Aggad, who failed the entrance exam for the French police around 2009, and Jahangir Alom, twenty-six, who had tried to join the British army in 2006 but had to give up for medical reasons. The latter became a police assistant in 2007 but renounced it in 2009, as the tasks were not as demanding as in the army.

III

1. See chapter 3, "Jihadi Actors."
2. We do not have aggregate statistical data on this problem but national data, partial as they are, tend to confirm this view. See chapter 6, "The Jihadogenic Urban Structure."
3. See the subsection "Humiliation at School," later in this chapter.
4. We will deal with aggressiveness in the later subsection, "Aggressiveness and Humiliation: The Easy Transition to Jihadism."
5. This was underlined in my interviews with young women of North African origin in the university, who denounced once again the "neo-colonial" attitude of the French society toward them, considering them not as equals with French women but as pitiful victims of male Muslims.
6. This sheds light on why there are significant numbers of Black converts to Islam who became radicalized, like Germaine Lindsay (London bombings of July 7, 2005) and Michael Adebolajo and Michael Adebowale (killing of the soldier Lee Rigby in London on May 22, 2013), among others.
7. The language is full of "verlan" (inverted syllables in words) and expressions, peculiar to the slang of the banlieues, that are difficult to translate, and I unconsciously eliminated many in my notes and replaced them with "normal" words (I did not have the right to record in prison and had to rely on my transcriptions).
8. For concrete cases, see the subsection "From Negotiated Recognition in Life to Forced Recognition in Death."
9. The concrete cases studied (and some of them presented in this book) show that empirically, few jihadis had joined quietist, pietistic Salafists prior to their allegiance to radical Islam. See in particular the biographies of jihadis in this book.
10. In Great Britain, the equivalent to the Salafists in continental Europe are the neo-Deobandis.

11. This was confirmed to me by Jérôme Ferret, a French anthropologist, about some other jihadis, in our discussion on these matters in February 2019. Merah is discussed later in this section.
12. In French the verbal form *tutoyer (old English Thou)*, the familiar form instead of the respectful verbal form, addressing "you," *vouvoyer*.
13. Dhimmis were Christians and Jews under the Islamic law, particularly in the Ottoman Empire, with a recognized but inferior status.
14. This was the case of Karim Cheurfi. He was obsessed with the policemen he hated for their humiliating attitude toward him and, more generally, the sons of Muslim migrants. He tried to kill them several times. He was born on December 31, 1977, in Livry-Gargan, a commune of Seine-Saint-Denis, where there is a high concentration of North Africans and their sons and grandsons. As a young adult, he was jobless and had already clashed with the police several times. In February 2005, he was sentenced on appeal to fifteen years in prison for attempting to kill a policeman and his brother. His obsession with the police dated back to 2001: Cheurfi, driving a stolen car in Roissy-en-Brie (Seine-et-Marne, a southern suburb of Paris), fled after hitting another vehicle. Armed with a revolver, he seriously injured the two policemen who were trying to arrest him. Two days later, he attempted to kill another policeman, whose weapon he had seized while in police custody. His desire to kill police officers found religious justification in Daesh's call to kill people on the spot in Europe rather than come to Syria, to which travel had become increasingly difficult since 2015. On April 20, 2017, the thirty-nine-year-old Cheurfi fired on policemen on the Champs-Elysées Avenue in Paris and killed one of them, wounding two others and a passer-by. He was shot dead. He had had significant mental problems related to extreme violence and a criminal record, with fifteen years in prison for attempts to kill police officers in 2001 (during which he assaulted supervisors and a fellow prison inmate). A year after having left prison, in 2012, he had committed a robbery in Ferrières-en-Brie (Seine-et-Marne, a southern suburb of Paris) and was sentenced to four years of additional prison. At the end of his term, he had left prison with the obligation of periodically consulting a psychiatrist. During this period, he was attracted by IS propaganda and sought to procure weapons, which resulted in his registration on the "S" file (Security file) of the French police.
15. See Khosrokhavar, December 14, 2018.
16. Since Edmond Goblot's major study on French school in 1925 (Goblot, 2010), studies on school show its role in reproducing social classes rather than assuring social mobility (Duru-Bellat, Farges, and Van Zanten, 2018; for Europe, see Heath and Cheung, 2007).
17. Rebellion against God by the West is one of the classical themes of jihadi theology. It is found, for example, in Mohammad Qutb, the brother of Seyed Qutb, for whom Western civilization's essence is in the revolt of Prometheus against God (Zeus) and his eternal punishment by him. Islam, according to Qutb, is marked by the relationship of submission to Allah, which is in accordance with human nature (Khosrokhavar, 2009, 2011).
18. Kevin McDonald (2018) develops the Sublime among the jihadis in a sense distinct from this one, by stressing its aesthetic side.

19. Even though the year of the census does not exactly cover the same period, the respective rates are significantly different, and on the whole the result can be extended to the same year.

IV

1. This topic in comparative European studies on jihadism needs further research.
2. This analysis has been inspired to me by the case of some enriched North Africans in the city of Roubaix (February 2020) who complained about this type of racism. Some of their sons had become involved in illegal activities due to their crisis in the wake of this type of racism.
3. I propose this interpretation by drawing inspiration from the case of Djamel Beghal, a charismatic jihadi with a strong personality who has strongly shaped the personalities of people like Chérif Kouachi and Amedy Coulibaly, whom he met in 2005 at the Fleury-Mérogis prison. Both played a key role in the January 2015 attacks against the weekly *Charlie Hebdo*. Djamel Beghal was their mentor. All the inmates I met in prison, including guards, who knew Beghal, told me about his attractive and strong personality. He managed to bewitch those prisoners he frequented in prison, often easily influenced individuals in rebellion against society whose shaky personalities he bolstered into monolithic Jihadis.
4. One can quote the story of a young woman and her setbacks in a book *In the Night of Daesh*, an autobiography written by Sophie Kasiki (pseudonym), in collaboration with Pauline Guena (a journalist). The woman, a nurse, Cameroonian by birth, recounts her conversion to Islam and, following her recruitment by young men who went to Syria to join the ranks of Daesh, the abandonment of her husband and her flight to Raqqa, in Syria, in September 2014, accompanied by her four-year-old son, in order to work in a hospital and bring humanitarian assistance to the caliphate. After spending two months in that city and expressing her disapproval of the way the patients were treated by the Islamic State, she was finally locked up in a building for foreign women, where mothers and children were shown decapitation videos throughout the day. She escaped and took refuge in a family who risked their lives to help her cross the Turkish border and return to France (Kasiki and Guéna, 2016). Many other cases pinpoint the disillusionment of young women who encountered nightmare rather than the dream world they imagined before joining Daesh.
5. At least in France and Italy, the Communist Party and its trade unions played a major socializing role among working-class people, providing them with a utopia and galvanizing them through their ideology and festivities (Lavau, 1981; Lazar, 2002).
6. My analysis of his case is based on my encounter with a radicalized young man in Saint-Maur Prison in 2013 who suffered from paranoia and had found a respite by meeting a recruiter who attempted, rather successfully, at radicalizing him, radicalization operating like a cathartic cure in his case. The recruiter was sent to another

prison to prevent him from radicalizing further the young man. The illness of the latter, which had marked an improvement through relying on his mentor, worsened, his psychological situation becoming critical after his departure.

7. "Five-star" jihad" was first popularized by at least seventeen British jihadis boasting of fighting at the service of al-Qaeda in 2013 (Wright and Bains, 2013). Later on, jihadis used it to show how comfortable life was under IS rule in the 2014–2015 period.
8. One can consult Behr et al., 2013, for a criticism of the self-radicalization thesis.
9. See the section "Jihadi Recruiters and Preachers" later in this chapter for a more comprehensive description of Diaby's case.
10. The Durkheimian notion of collective effervescence is mythologized by the young Europeans coming from "cold" societies in which social cohesion has slackened by the lack of collective utopia. It is the nostalgia of collective effervescence, and the longing for it that motivates young Europeans to join jihadi movements in general.
11. For an analysis of their cases see the subsection "Examples of Jihadi Converts."
12. His case has already been dealt with under the heading of Jihadi converts. Here we focus on his psychological disorders.
13. This part has been inspired to me by the narrative of some prisoners and in particular, of a Tunisian prisoner who explained to me that colonization of Tunisia by France meant that he could act immorally towards the French because they had done so in the past towards his forefathers. This feeling is even more intense among the French-Algerians, and more generally, among many sons of the formerly colonized people, particularly those living in the country that had colonized their ancestors.
14. See chapter IV, "Jihadis and the Family."

V

1. A group of sociologists in Toulouse, headed by Jérôme Ferret and including Bruno Domingo, David Vavassori, Sonia Harrati, Bartolomeo Conti, Ferret's PhD student Mamadou Daffé, and this author have been working on the anthropology of the family among the jihadis in the Toulouse area and Spain, by focusing on the categories developed in my book, *Le nouveau jihad en Occident* (Khosrokhavar, 2018).
2. This is what the political movement "Indigènes de la République" in France gives as its motto, criticizing the right- and left-wing political parties as being colonial at their core, the only way to fight against racism being a "de-colonial" action, which rejects laïcité as much as universalist ideologies as the remnants of colonial views.
3. Many middle-class North Africans told me that they chose digital fields because they would have jobs that made them free from French bosses who reminded them of colonial times or of their parents' exploitation.
4. See his short biography in the subsection "Examples of Jihadi Recruiters and Preachers" in Chapter 3.
5. See also the subsection "Examples of Radicalized Young Women" in Chapter 3.

VI

1. If we take the case of the jihadist attacks that caused the death of men or women in Europe—those that were prevented or made no casualties were not always covered by the media and were difficult to account for—according to my count, from 2001 to 2017, there were twenty-three jihadist attacks in France, compared to ten in Great Britain, five in Germany, two in Spain, and seven in Belgium. Similarly, there were 247 deaths in France, compared to 93 in England, 15 in Germany, 36 in Belgium, and 208 in Spain. In other words, France is the country in Western Europe with the highest number of deadly Jihadi attacks and deaths. The aggravating cause, next to those described in this book, is French secularism (laïcité) and its radicalized version, if one assumes that the French police are no less effective than those of other European countries. The number of Muslims is not lower in Germany.
2. They were estimated at 5,904 Europeans by Cook and Vale (2018).
3. These data refer to the commitment in jihadi networks, not only in jihadi attacks.
4. Around 200 Foreign Fighters left the United States between 2012 and 2015 for Syria and Iraq, compared to 1,550 from France, 700 from the UK, and 700 from Germany (Perliger and Milton, 2016). Even considering the number of Muslims in the US, which is estimated at around 3.45 million by the Pew Research Center (65 percent of them Sunnis), their proportion is much lower in the US than in the three European countries mentioned (in France, Pew estimated the Muslim population at around 4,704 million, in Germany 4,119 million, and in the UK 3,106 million in 2011).
5. Some of the analyses of this Think Tank have been contested.
6. See, for more details, the subsection "Examples of Jihadi Recruiters and Preachers" in Chapter 3.

VII

1. The study of the urban structures in which more jihadi recruits have been enrolled than the other parts of the city or other urban areas, needs further development. Some characteristics of the "hotspots" have been studied so far, but they have to be examined in depth in the future.
2. This information was given to me by Jérôme Ferret.
3. See Ferret, Khosrokhavar, and Domingo, 2021.
4. The study of the urban setting in relation to jihadism is still underdeveloped.
5. There is no exhaustive quantitative data on this subject, but the concrete cases analyzed in this chapter show the importance of the urban ghettos in European jihadism.
6. See the section "European Slum Subculture Proper" in Chapter 2.
7. Groupe Islamique Armée (GIA) is an offshoot of Front Islamique du Salut (FIS), an Algerian Islamist political party that radicalized after the military coup in Alger in 1992, in the wake of its electoral victory in December 1991.
8. It is also difficult to prove beyond doubt due to the scarcity of statistics and urban studies.

9. See the subsection "The Fundamentalist District: 'Islamistan'" toward the end of this chapter.
10. Research in this area is poorly developed.
11. As already mentioned, this type of imaginary is also found among the young "Pakis" in the UK who blame forces of law and order to be as harsh toward them as the Indian military toward Muslims in Kashmir. In the same vein in France, according to young Muslims, French police acts toward them as brutally as the Israeli army vis-à-vis the Palestinians.

VIII

1. Al-Qaeda, which committed the attacks of September 11, 2001, in the United States was in "transit" in Germany, its members being from Saudi Arabia, the Emirates, and Egypt, not from Germany.
2. See the section on "Women and the new Jihad" in Chapter 3.

Bibliography

Books and Articles

Adida, Claire L., David D. Laitin, and Marie-Anne Valfort, "Women, Muslim Immigrants, and Economic Integration in France", *Economics & Politics*,Volume 0, John Wiley & Sons Ltd, 2013.

Agoz, Pérez-Alfonso, The Social Roots of Basque Nationalism, Reno, University of Nevada Press, 2011.

Alexander, Dean C., *Family Terror Networks*, Portland, OR, Book Baby, 2019.

Almond, Gabriel A., R. Scott Appleby, and Emmanuel Sivan, *Strong Religion: The Rise of Fundamentalisms around the World*, Chicago, University of Chicago Press, 2003.

Al Subaie, Mohammad, *L'idéologie de l'islamisme radical*, Paris, L'Harmattan, 2012.

Amjad, Naumana, Alex M. Wood, "Identifying and Changing the Normative Beliefs about Aggression which Lead Young Muslim Adults to Join Extremist Anti-Semitic Groups in Pakistan," *Aggressive Behavior* 35, 29 September 2009. https://www.onlinelibrary.wiley.com/doi/abs/10.1002/ab.20325

Anatrella, Tony, *Interminables Adolescences*, Paris, Cerf, 1988.

Anderson, Elijah, *The Code of the Street: Decency, Violence and the Moral Life of the Inner City*, New York, Norton & Company, 1999.

Aqiqi, Seyyed, *Theoretical Foundations of Daesh in the Shiite Islamic Law*, 2014, www.Letoarafu.blog.ir. (Originally *Mabani nazari Daesh dar fiqh sonnati shieh*, by Mohammad Mousavi [in Persian], 1393.)

Arena, Maria do Céu Pinto, "The Portuguese Foreign Fighters Phenomenon: A Preliminary Assessment," *Journal of Policing, Intelligence and Counter Terrorism*, 13 (1), 7 March 2018.

Atran, Scott, *Talking to the Enemy: Sacred Values, Violent Extremism, and What It Means to Be Human*, London, Penguin, 2011.

Atran, Scott, *L'État islamique est une révolution*, Paris, Les Liens qui Libèrent, 2016.

Bagguley, Paul, and Yasmin Hussain, *Riotous Citizens: Ethnic Conflict in Multicultural Britain*, Aldershot, Ashgate, 2008.

Baker, Edwin, *Jihadi Terrorist in Europe: Their Characteristics and the Circumstances in which They Joined the Jihad: An Exploratory Study*, The Hague, Netherlands Institute of International Relations, Clingendael, 2006.

Bakker, Edwin, and Seran de Leede, "European Female Jihadists in Syria: Exploring an Under-Researched Topic," *ICCT Background Note*, April 2015.

Basra, Rajan, Peter Neumann, and Claudia Brunner, *Criminal Pasts, Terrorist Futures: European Jihadis and the New Crime-Terror Nexus*, London, ICSR, 2016.

Bataille, Philippe, *Le racisme au travail*, Paris, La Découverte, 1997.

Bauman, Zygmunt, *Liquid Love : On the Frailty of Human Bonds*, Cambridge, Polity Press, 2003.

Bauman, Zygmunt, and Jean-Yves Mensat, "Qui sont les jihadies français? Analyse de 12 cas pour contribuer à l'élaboration de profils et à l'évaluation du risque de passage à l'acte," *Annales médico-psychologiques, revue psychiatrique*, March 10, 2016.

Beaud, Stéphane, and Younes Amrani, *Pays de malheur! Un jeune de cité écrit à un sociologue*, Paris, La Découverte, 2005.

Beckford, James A., Daniele Joly, and Farhad Khosrokhavar, *Muslims in Prison: Challenge and Change in Britain and France*, London, Pluto Press, 2006.

Behr, Ines von, Anais Reding, Charlie Edward, and Luke Gribbon, *Radicalization in the Digital Era: The Use of the Internet in Fifteen Cases of Terrorism and Extremism*, Cambridge, RAND, 2013.

Benslama, Fethi (sous la direction de), *L'idéal et la cruauté*, Paris, Lignes, 2015.

Benslama, Fethi, *Un furieux désir de sacrifice, le surmusulman*, Paris, Seuil, 2016.

Benslama, Fethi, and Farhad Khosrokhavar, *Le jihadisme des femmes*, Paris, Seuil, 2017.

Benson, David, "Why the Internet Is Not Increasing Terrorism," *Security Studies* 23 (2), 2014.

Bergema, Reinier, *Jihadgangers zijn relatief vaak bekeerlingen; 45 procent is van Marokkaanse komaf*, The Hague Center for Strategic Studies, May 7, 2017.

Bertho, Alain, *Les enfants du chaos, Essai sur le temps des martyrs*, Paris, La Découverte, 2016.

Bertlett, Jamie, Jonathan Birdwell, and Jonathan King, *The Edge of Violence*, London, Demos, 2010.

Bertossi, Christophe, and Catherine Wihtol de Wenden, *Les couleurs du drapeau: l'Armée française face aux discriminations*, Paris, Robert Laffont, 2007.

Bhui, Kamaldeep, Warfa Nasir, and Edgar Jones, "Is Violent Radicalisation Associated with Poverty, Migration, Poor Self-Reported Health and Common Mental Disorders?," *Plos One*, 9 (3), March 2014.

Bigo Didier, Laurent Bonelli, Emmanuel-Pierre Guittet, and Francesco Raazi, *Preventing and Countering Youth Radicalisation in the EU* (Briefing paper), Parlement Européen, 2014.

Birnbaum, Jean, *Un silence religieux, la gauche face au jihadisme*, Paris, Seuil, 2016.

Blin, Louis, *Le monde arabe dans les albums de Tintin*, Paris, L'Harmattan, 2016.

Boltanski, Luc, *La Souffrance à distance: Morale humanitaire, médias et politique*, Paris, Metailié, 1993.

Bonhoeffer, Dietrich, *Résistance et soumission*, Geneva, Labor et Fides, 2006.

Borum, Randy, "Rethinking Radicalization," *Journal of Strategic Security* 4, 2012.

Bourdier, Maxime, "Mohamed Lahouaiej Bouhlel, un homme décrit comme violent, buvant et 'se foutant de la religion,'" *Huffington Post*, July 15, 2015.

Bouzar, Dounia, *Comment sortir de l'emprise jihadie?*, Ivry-sur-Seine, Les Editions de l'Atelier, 2015.

Bouzar, Dounia, and Farid Benyettou, *Mon djihad: Itinéraire d'un repenti*, Paris, Editions Autrement, 2017.

Brace, Charles Loring, *The Dangerous Classes of New York, and Twenty Years' Work among Them*, New York, Elibron Classics, 1872

Brachman, Jarret, and Alix Levine, "The World of Holy Warcraft: How al-Qaeda Is Using Online Game Theory to Recruit the Masses," *Foreign Policy*, April 13, 2010.

Breen, Richard, Ruud Luijkx, Walter Müller, and Reinhard Pollak, Long-Term Trends in Educational Inequality in Europe: Class Inequalities and Gender Differences, *European Sociological Review* 26 (1), February 2010.

Breton, David Le, *Rites de virilité à l'adolescence*, yapaka.be, 2015.

Breton, David Le, "Jeunesse et jihadisme," *Le débat* 188, 2016.

Bronner, Gérald, *La Pensée extrême: Comment des hommes ordinaires deviennent des fanatiques*, Paris, Presses Universitaires de France, 2015.

Burgat, François, *Comprendre l'islam politique: une trajectoire de recherche sur l'altérité islamiste, 1973–2016*, Paris, La Découverte, 2016.

Buruma, Ian, *Murder in Amsterdam: The Death of Theo van Gogh and the Limits of Tolerance*, New York, Penguin Press HC, 2006.
Cacciari, Massimo, and Paolo Prodi, *Occidente senza utopie*, Bologna, Mulino, 2016.
Castels, Robert, *Les métamorphoses de la question sociale*, Paris, Fayard, 1995.
Castel, Robert, *La discrimination négative, Citoyens ou indigènes?* Paris, Seuil Publishers, 2007
Caillé, Alain, *Don, Intérêt et Désintéressement*, la collection Recherches/MAUSS, Paris, La Découverte, 2005.
Caillé, Alain, and Jean-Edouard Grésy, *La Révolution du don*, Paris, Seuil, 2014.
Cantillon, D., W. S. Davidson, and J. H. Schweitzer, "Measuring Community Social Organization: Sense of Community as a Mediator in Social Disorganization Theory," *Journal of Criminal Justice*, 31(4), 2003, 321–339.
"CBS StatLine—Bevolking; generatie, geslacht, leeftjid en herkomstgroepering, 1 januari". Statline.cbs.nl. Retrieved December 1, 2017. https://www.cbs.nl/nl-nl/cijfers/detail/37713
Celso, Anthony, *Al-Qaeda's Post-9/11 Devolution: The Failed Jihadi Struggle against the Near and Far Enemy*, New York, Bloomsbury, 2014.
Cendrowicz, Leo, "Vilvoorde: The Brussels District Fighting Radicalisation with Kindness," *The Independent Online*, December 30, 2015.
Chaarani, Ahmed, *La mouvance islamiste au Maroc*, Paris, Karthala, 2004.
Chapoutot, Johann, "Virilité fasciste," in Jean-Jacques Courtine (sous la direction de), *Histoire de la virilité, Tome 3: La virilité en crise?* Paris, Seuil, 2011.
Chauvel, Louis, *La spirale de déclassement*, Paris, Seuil, 2016.
Chemel, Manon, "Blanc Méalisse," CAT. http://cat-int.org/index.php/2018/01/23/terrorisme-dans-lunion-europeenne-bilan-2017/?lang=en
Colombo, Valentina, "Multiple Layers of Marginalization as a Paradigm of Tunisian Hotbeds of Jihadism," in Arturo Vervelli (editor), *Jihadist Hotbeds: Understanding Local Radicalization Processes*, Milan, ISPI, Epoké, 2016.
Conti, Bartolomeo, *L'islam en Italie. Les leaders musulmans entre intégration et séparation*, Paris, L'Harmattan, 2014.
Cook, Bernard A., *Women and War: A Historical Encyclopedia from Antiquity to the Present, Volume* 2, Santa Barbara, California, ABC-CLIO, 2006.
Cook, David, *Understanding Jihad*, 2nd edition, Berkeley, University of California Press, 2015.
Cook, David, "Women Fighting in Jihad," *Studies in Conflict & Terrorism* 28, February 2005.
Cook, Joanna, and Gina Vale, *From Daesh to "Diaspora": Tracing the Women and Minors of Islamic State* (Report), London, ICSR, 2018.
Coolsaet, Rik, "Radicalisation, entre contexte et responsabilité individuelle," *L'Observatoire* 86, March 2016.
Coolsaet, Rik, *Facing the Fourth Foreign Fighters Wave: What Drives Europeans to Syria, and to Islamic State? Insights from the Belgian Case*, Egmont Paper 81, Brussels: Egmont, March 2016.
Corner, E., and P. Gill, "A False Dichotomy? Mental Illness and Lone-Actor Terrorism." *Law and Human Behavior* 39 (1): 23–34, 2015.
Couldry, Nick, *Media, Society, World: Social Theory and Digital Media Practice*, Cambridge, Polity Press, 2012.
Crettiez, Xavier, "Penser la radicalisation," *Revue Française de Science Politique* 66 (5), October 2016.
Crone, Manni, "Radicalisation revisited," *International Affairs* 92 (3), 587–604, May 2016.
Dawson, Lorne L., Amarnath Amarasingam, and Alexandra Bain, *Talking to Foreign Fighters: Socio-Economic Push versus Existential Pull Factors*, Canadian Network

for Research on Terrorism, Security and Society (TSAS Working Paper No. 16-14), July 2016.

Datenreport 2016 : Social Report for the Federal Republic of Germany

Datenreport 2018: Social Report for the Federal Republic of Germany

Dawson, Omar, and Karim Bellazaar, *Reality Taule, au-delà des barreaux*, Grignywood / icetream editions, 2009.

Debord, Guy, *La société du spectacle*, Paris, Buchet et Chastel, 1967.

De Féo, Agnès, *Émilie König vs Ummu Tawwab* (documentary, 26 min.), Sasana Productions, 2016.

De Féo, Agnès, *Le voile intégral en perspective, France, 2008–2019*, Thèse (PhD), Ecole des Hautes Etudes en Scicences Sociale, Paris, 2019.

Derrida, Jacques, and Jürgen Habermas, *Philosophy in a Time of Terror*, Chicago, Illinois, University of Chicago Press, 2003.

Détienne, Marcel, *Les maîtres de vérité dans la Grèce archaïque*, Paris, Librairie générale française, 2006.

Devecchio, Alexandre, *Les nouveaux enfants du siècle—Jihadies, identitaires, réacs: Enquête sur une génération fracturée*, Paris, Cerf, 2016.

Dodd, Vikram, Jamie Grierson, "Revealed: how Anjem Choudary influenced at least 100 British jihadis", The Guardian, 16/08/2016

Domingo, Bruno, *Le clan "Merah": Trajectoire familiales et transformation de l'économie des violences*, November 2021.

Dubet, François, *La galère: Les jeunes en survie*, Paris, Fayard, 1987.

Dubet, François, *Le Déclin de l'Institution*, Paris, Seuil, 2002.

Duru-Bellat, Marie, Géraldine Farges, and Agnès Van Zanten, *Sociologie de l'école*, Paris, Armand Collin, 2018.

Duffy, Brendan O, Radical Atmosphere: Explaining Jihadi Radicalization in the UK, *Political Science and Politics* 41 (1), January 2008.

Ehrenberg, Alain, *La fatigue d'être soi*, Paris, Odile Jacob, 1998.

Erelle, Anna, *Dans la peau d'une djih@diste: Enquête au cœur des filières de recrutement de l'Etat islamique*, Paris, Robert Laffont, 2015

Esposito, Johan, *Islam and Politics*, Syracuse, New York, Syracuse University Press, 1998.

Esposito, John, *Unholy War: Terror in the Name of Islam*, New York: Oxford University Press, 2002.

Eubank, William Lee, and Leonard Weinberg, "Does Democracy Encourage Terrorism?," *Terrorism and Political Violence*, 6 (4), 1994.

Eubank, William Lee, and Leonard Weinberg, "Terrorism and Democracy: What Recent Events Disclose," *Terrorism and Political Violence* 10 (1), 1998.

Euben, Roxanne L, and Muhammad Qasim Zaman, *Princeton Readings in Islamist Thought*, Princeton, New Jersey, Princeton University Press, 2009.

Felouzis, G., F. Liot, and J. Perroton, *L'apartheid scolaire: Enquête sur la ségrégation ethnique dans les colléges*, Paris, Seuil, 2005.

Ferret, Jérôme, "New Fraternal Scenes and Jihadi Violence. (Ripoll, Catalonia, Northern Spain)," in F. Khosrokhavar and J. Ferret (editors), *Family and Jihadism: The French Experience*, London, Routledge, Book Series, Social Movements in the 21st Century: New Paradigms, November 2021.

Ferret, Jérôme, and Farhad Khosrokhavar (editors), *Family and Jihadism. The French Experience*, London, Routledge,November 2021.

Ferret, Jérôme, Farhad Khosrokhavar, and Bruno Domingo, "Conclusion: Jihadism and the family: A heuristic model questioned, dynamized and augmented," in F. Khosrokhavar and J. Ferret (editors), *Family and Jihadism: The French Experience*, London, Routledge, Book Series, Social Movements in the 21st Century: New Paradigms (ed. Kevin McDonald), November 2021.

Filiu, Jean-Pierre, *L'Apocalypse dans l'Islam*, Paris, Fayard, 2008.

Filiu, Jean-Pierre, *Les neuf vies d'al-Qaeda*, Paris, Fayard, 2009.

Fraihi, Hind, *Infiltré parmi les islamistes radicaux*, Paris, La Renaissance du Livre, 2006.

Frazer, Egeton, *Jihad in the West: The Rise of Militant Salafism*, New York, Cambridge University Press, 2011.

"From Criminals to Terrorists and Back?", Quarterly Report: France, GLOBSEC, 07/01/2019

Gambetta, Diego, and Steffen Hertog, *Engineers of Jihad: The Curious Connection between Violent Extremism and Education*, Princeton, New Jersey, Princeton University Press, 2016.

Gamson, William, *Talking Politics*, New York, Cambridge University Press, 1992.

Gauchet, Marcel, *L'avènement de la démocratie* (Vol. 4), Paris, Gallimard, 2017.

Geiselberger, Heinrich (Sous la direction de), *L'Âge de la Régression: Pourquoi nous vivons un tournant historique*, Paris, Première Parallèle, 2017.

Gill, Paul, John Horgan, and Paige Deckert, "*Bombing Alone: Tracing the Motivations and Antecedent Behaviors of Lone-Actor Terrorists*," *Journal of Forensic Sciences*, 59 (2), 2014.

Gill, Paul, *Lone-Actor Terrorists: A Behavioural Analysis*. London, Routledge, 2015.

Goblot, Edmond, *La barrière et le niveau: Étude sociologique sur la bourgeoisie française moderne*, Paris, Presses Universitaires de France, 2010.

Goffman, Erving, *Stigma: Notes on the Management of Spoiled Identity*, New York, Simon & Schuster, 1963.

Göle, Nilüfer, *Musulmans au quotidien: Une Enquête européenne sur les controverses autour de l'Islam*, Paris, Editions La Découverte, 2015.

González Casanova, Pablo 1963, "'Sociedad plural, colonialismo interno y desarrollo' en América Latina." *Revista del Centro Latinoamericano de Ciencias Sociales* (México DF) 6 (3), July–September.

Goodwin Jeff, James Jasper, and Francesca Polletta, "The Return of the Repressed: The Fall and Rise of Emotions in Social Movement Theory" in Mobilization: An International Journal, 2000, 5(1): 65-83

Gordon, Diana R., *The Return of the Dangerous Classes: Drug Prohibition and Policy Politics*, New York, W. W. Norton, 1994.

Gori, Roland, *Un monde sans esprit: La fabrique des terrorismes*, Paris, Les Liens Qui Libèrent, 2017.

Goris, Indira, Jobard Fabien, and Lévy René, *Police et minorités visibles: Les contrôles d'identité à Paris*, New York, Open Society Institute, 2009.

Guidère Mathieu, *Le retour du califat*, Le débat Gallimard, 2016.

Guilluy, Christophe, *La France périphérique*, Flammarion, 2014.

Gustafsson, Linus, and Magnus Ranstorp, *Swedish Foreign Fighters in Syria and Iraq: An Analysis of Open-Source Intelligence and Statistical Data*, Swedish Defence University, 2017.

Hafez, Mohammed, and Creiphton Mullins, "The Radicalization Puzzle: A Theoretical Synthesis of Empirical Approaches to Homegrown Extremism," *Studies in Conflict and Terrorism* 38, 2015.

Hartog, François, *Régimes d'historicité: Présentisme et expérience du temps*, Paris, Seuil, 2003.

Hatina, Meir, *Martyrom in Modern Islam: Piety, Power, and Politics*, New York, Cambridge University Press, 2014.

Heath, Anthony, and Sin-Yi Cheung, *Unequal Chances: Ethnic Minoroties in Western Labour Markets*, Oxford, Oxford University Press.

Hecker, Marc, *137 Nuances de terrorisme: Les djihadies de France face à la justice*, Etudes de l'Ifri, *Focus Stratégique* 79, Avril 2018.

Hecker, Marc, and Élie Tenenbaum, "Quel avenir pour le djihadisme? al-Qaeda et Daech après le califat," *Focus Stratégique* 87, Ifri, January 2019.

Heinke, Daniel, and Jan Raudszus, "German Foreign Fighters in Syria and Iraq," *CTC Sentinel* 8 (1), January 2015.

Herf, Jeffrey, "Killing in the Name," *New Republic*, April 8, 2010.

Hoffman, Adam, and Yoram Schweitzer, "Cyber Jihad in the Service of the Islamic State," *Strategic Assessment*,18 (1), April 2015.

Hoffman, Bruce, "IS Is Here: Return of the Jihadi," *The National Interest*, January-February 2016.

Hoffman, Bruce, "The Myth of Grass-Roots Terrorism," *Foreign Affairs* 87 (3), 2008.

Hong, Sun-ha, "When Life Mattered: The Politics of the Real in Video-Games: Reappropriation of History, Myth, and Ritual," *Games and Culture*, 10 (1), 2015.

Honneth, Axel, *The Struggle for Recognition: The Moral Grammar of Social Conflicts*, Cambridge, Polity Press, 1995 [1992, German].

Honneth, Axel, *Reification: A Recognition-Theoretical View*, Oxford University Press, 2007.

Honneth, Axel, *Disrespect: The Normative Foundations of Critical Theory*, Cambridge, Polity Press, 2007 [2000, German].

Horgan, John, *Walking Away from Terrorism: Accounts of Disengagement from Radical and Extremist Movements*, New York, Routledge, 2009.

Hoyle, Carolyn, Alexandra Bradford, and Ross Frenett, *Becoming Mulan? Female Western Migrants to IS*, London, Institute for Strategic Dialogue, 2015.

Igielnik, Ruth, and Rakesh Kochhar, *GOP Gained Ground in Middle-Class Communities in 2016*, Pew Research Center, August 12, 2016.

Joscelyn, Thomas "US Counterterrorism Efforts in Syria: A Winning Strategy?" *Long War Journal*, September 29, 2015.

Johnson, Toni, "Muslims in the United States," *Council on Foreign Relations*, September 19, 2011.

Kabir, Nahid Afrose, *Young British Muslims: Identity, Culture, Politics and the Media*, Edinburgh, Edinburgh University Press, 2012.

Karoui, Hakim El, *Un Islam Français est possible*, Paris, Institut Montaigne, September 2016.

Kasiki, Sophie, and Pauline Guéna, *Dans la nuit de Daech*, Paris, Robert Laffont, 2016.

Kepel, Gilles, and Jean-Pierre Milell, *Al-Qaeda dans le texte*, Paris, Presses Universitaires de France, 2005.

Kepel, Gilles, and Antoine Jardin, *Terreur dans l'Hexagone*, Paris, Gallimard, 2015.

Kern, Soeren, "Anjem Choudhary, in His Own Words," *Gatestone Institute*, September 30, 2014.

Kern, Soeren, "Britain's Female Jihadists," SOEREN KERN.COM, September 21, 2014.

Khosrokhavar, Farhad, *L'Utopie sacrifiée: sociologie de la révolution iranienne*, Paris, Presses de Sciences Po., 1993.

Khosrokhavar, Farhad, *L'islamisme et la mort, le martyre révolutionnaire en Iran*, Paris, L'Harmattan, 1995.

Khosrokhavar, Farhad, "L'universel abstrait, le politique et la construction de l'islamisme comme forme d'altérité," in Michel Wieviorka (editor), *Une société fragmentée?* Paris, La Découverte, 1997.

Khosrokhavar, Farhad, *L'islam des jeunes*, Paris, Flammarion, 1997.

Khosrokhavar, Farhad, *L'anthropologie de la révolution iranienne*, Paris, L'Harmattan, 1998.

Khosrokhavar, Farhad, *Islam en prison*, Paris, Balland, 2004.

Khosrokhavar, Farhad, *Quand al-Qaïda parle, témoignage derrière les barreaux*, Paris, Grasset, 2006.

Khosrokhavar, Farhad, *Inside jihadism*, Boulder, Paradigm, 2009.

Khosrokhavar, Farhad, *Jihadi Ideology, The Anthropological Perspective*, CIR, Aarhus, Denmark: Aarhus University, 2011.

Khosrokhavar, Farhad, "Le Héros Négatif," in Fethi Benslama (editor), *L'idéal et la cruauté*, Paris, Editions Lignes, 2015.

Khosrokhavar, Farhad, *Prisons de France*, Paris, Robert Laffont, 2016.

Khosrokhavar, Farhad, *Radicalization: Why Some People Choose the Path of Violence*, New York, The New Press, 2017. (2014 in French)

Khosrokhavar, Farhad, *Le nouveau Jihad en Occident*, Paris, Robert Laffont, 2018.

Khosrokhavar, Farhad, "La jeunesse féminine dijiadiste et le désir du don. Le don et sa polysémie," *Revue du Mauss*, 201852, 89–107.

Khosrokhavar, Farhad, Cherif Chekatt ou le faux djihadiste, Le Monde, December 14, 2018

Khosrokhavar, Farhad, "Récit d'un ressenti musulman," in Charles-Yves Zarka (editor), *La France en Récits*, Paris, Presses Universitaires de France, 2020.

Kierkegaard, Soren, *The Lilies of the Field &the Birds of the Air, The Instant*, Oxford University Press, 1961 (1849).

Knapton, Sarah, "British Jihadis Are Depressed, Lonely and Need Help, Says Prof Kamaldeep Bhui," *Science Editor*, October 15, 2014.

Lacey, Colin, *Hightown Grammar: School as a Social System*, Manchester University Press, 1970.

Lachance, Jocelyne, *Les images terroristes*, Toulouse, Editions érès, 2017.

Lagrange, Hugues, *Les adolescents, le sexe, l'amour*, Paris, Syros Publishers, 1999.

Lahoud, Nelly, "The Neglected Sex: The Jihadis' Exclusion of Women From Jihad," *Terrorism and Political Violence* 26, May 2014.

Lapeyronnie, Didier, *Ghetto urbain*, Paris, Robert Laffont, 2008.

Lasen, Amparo, and Edgar Gomez-Cruz, Digital Photography and Picture Sharing: Redefining the Public/Private Divide. *Knowledge, Technology, Policy* 22 (3), 2009.

Lau, David, and Mads Mathiesen, "Straight Outta Mjølnerparken?" http://www.humanityinaction.org/knowledgebase/258-straight-outta-mjolnerparken

Lavau, Georges, *A quoi sert le parti communiste français ?*, Paris, Fayard, 1981.

Lazar, Marc, *Le communism, une passion française*, Paris, Editions Perrin, 2005.

Leiken, Robert, and Steven Brooke, "The Quantitative Analysis of Terrorism and Immigration: An Initial Exploration," *Terrorism and Political Violence* 18 (4), 503–521, 2006.

Lenz, Ryan, *Age of the Wolf: A Study of the Rise of Lone Wolf and Leaderless Resistance Terrorism*, Montgomery, Alabama, Southern Poverty Law Center, 2015.

Lepoutre David, *Cœur de banlieue: Codes, rites et langages*, Paris, Odile Jacob Publisher, 1997.

Lewis, Oscar, *Five Families: Mexican Case Studies in the Culture of Poverty*, New York, Basic Books, 1959.

L'Heuillet, Hélène, *Tu haïras ton prochain comme toi-même*, Paris, Albin Michel, 2017.

Liogier, Raphaël, *La Guerre des civilisations n'aura pas lieu: Coexistence et violence au XXI e siècle*, Paris, CNRS Éditions, 2016.

Li, Quan, and Drew Schaub, "Economic Globalization and Transnational Terrorist Incidents: a Pooled Time Series Analysis," *Journal of Conflict Resolution* 48 (2), April 2004.

Lohlker, Rüdiger (editor). *Jihadism: Online Discourses and Representations.* Vienna University Press, 2013.

"London Bomber: Text in full" http://news.bbc.co.uk/2/hi/uk_news/4206800.stm

Lyotard, Jean-François, *La condition postmoderne*, Paris, Les éditions de minuit, 1979.

Malet, David, "Foreign Fighter Mobilization and Persistence in a Global Context, Terrorism and Political Violence," *Journal of Terrorism and Political Violence*, 27, 2015. www.davidmalet.com/uploads/Malet_Foreign_Fighters_Global.pdf

Manchester University, Centre on Dynamics of Ethnicity, *Britain's Ethnic Minorities Are Facing Barriers to Social Mobility and Job Opportunities*, 2014. https://www.cmi.manchester.ac.uk/search/?q=Britain%E2%80%99s+Ethnic+Minorities+Are+Facing+Barriers+to+Social+Mobility+and+Job+Opportunities%2C+2014&btnG=Search#stq=Britain%E2%80%99s%20Ethnic%20Minorities%20Are%20Facing%20Barriers%20to%20Social%20Mobility%20and%20Job%20Opportunities,%202014

Mantzikos, Ioannis, "The Greek Gateway to Jihad," *CTC Sentinel* 9 (6), June, 2016.

Marcuse, Herbert, *One-Dimensional Man: Studies in the Ideology of Advanced Industrial Society*, Boston, Beacon Press, 1964.

Margalit, Avishai, *La société décente*, Paris, Flammarion, 2007.

Margalit, Avishai, and Ian Burma, *Occidentalism: The West in the Eyes of Its Enemies*, New York, The Penguin Press, 2004.

Margel, Serge, *Critique de la cruauté*, Paris, Belin, 2010.

Markit IHS, "Islamic State Territory Down 60 Percent and Revenue Down 80 Percent on Caliphate's Third Anniversary," June 29, 2017.

Marlière, Eric, *La France nous a lâchés!*, Paris, Fayard, 2008.

Maroc: visite du quartier général de l'antiterrorisme, à Rabat http://www.rtl.be/info/video/569141.aspx

Marone, Francesco, "Italian Jihadis in Syria and Iraq," *Journal of Terrorism Research* 7, (1), January 2016.

Martin, Jean-Pierre, and Christophe Lamfalussy, *Molenbeek-sur-Jihad*, Paris, Grasset, 2017.

Mauss, Marcel. *Essai sur le don: Forme et raison de l'échange dans les sociétés archaïques.* Paris: Presses Universitaires de France, "Quadrige" collection, 2012, 1ère éd. 1925; *The Gift: Forms and Functions of Exchange in Archaic Societies.* London: Cohen & West, 1966.

McCants, William, *The IS Apocalypse: The History, Strategy, and Doomsday Vision of the Islamic State*, New York, St. Martin's Press, 2015.

McCants, William, and Christopher Meserole, "The French Connection: Explaining Sunni Militancy around the World," *Foreign Affairs*, March 24, 2016.

McDonald, Kevin, *Radicalization*, Cambridge, Polity Press, 2018.

Meijer, Roel (editor), *Global Salafism: Islam's New Religious Movement*, London, Hurst & Co. Publishers, 2009.

"Mes 150 films Banlieue, jeunesse, délinquance préférés" (My 150 Favorite Suburb, Youth, Delinquency Movies), *Sens Critique*, accessed 19 December 2019 https://www.senscritique.com/liste/Mes_150_films_Banlieue_jeunesse_delinquance_preferes/497148

Misiak B., J. Samochowiec, K. Bhui, M. Schouler-Ocak, H. Demunter, L. Kuey, A. Raballo, P. Gorwood, D. Frydecka, and G. Dom, "A Systematic Review on the Relationship between Mental Health, Radicalization and Mass Violence," *European Psychiatry* 56: 51–59, February 2019.

"Molenbeek and Violent Radicalization: A Social Mapping," *European Institute of Peace*, Belgium, June 2017 (Foreword by Rik Voolsaet, Preface by Martin Griffits, director—no name of the author(s) is provided). https://view.publitas.com/eip/eip-molenbeek-report-16-06/page/1

Monroe, James, "Islamist Terrorism: Analysis of Offences and Attacks in the UK," Event Summary: HJS Report Launch, London, The Henry Jackson Society, August 3, 2017.

Moos, Olivier, "Le jihad s'habille en Prada," *Religioscopie*, Numéro 14, Août 2016. https://www.religion.info/pdf/2016_08_Moos.pdf

Mullins, Sam, *Australian Jihad: Radicalisation and Counter-Terrorism*, Real Istituto Elcano, October 18, 2011.

Mura, Andrea, *The Symbolic Scenarios of Islamism: A Study in Islamic Political Thought*, London, Routledge, 2015.

Nair, Mira, The Reluctant Fundamentalist (film), 2012.

Neiwert, David, Darren Ankrom, Esther Kaplan, and Scott Pham, *Homegrown Terror*, New York, The Investigative Fund at the Nation Institute, 2017.

Nesser, Peter, *Islamic Terrorism in Europe: A History*, London, Hurst, 2016.

Neumann, Peter R., *Victims, Perpetrators, Assets: The Narratives of Islamic State Defectors*, London, ICSR, 2015.

Neumann, Peter R., *Der Terror ist unter uns*, Berlin, Ullstein Verlag, 2016.

"Norway: Extremism & Counter-Extremism" (report), The Counter Extremism Project http://www.counterextremism.com/sites/default/files/country_pdf/NO-04142016.pdf

O'Duffy, Brendan, "Radical Atmosphere: Explaining Jihadi Radicalization in the UK," *Political Science and Politics* 41 (1), January 2008.

Otreppe, Bosco d', Fouad Belkacem, le gourou de plus en plus abandonné

https://www.lalibre.be/belgique/fouad-belkacem-le-gourou-de-plus-en-plus-abandonne-54d8fd3f35701001a1a29c41

Panini, *Islam and the Clash of Civilizations*, Amazon Printed Book, 2015.

Pankhurst, Reza, *The Inevitable Caliphate? A History of the Struggle for Global Islamic Union, 1924 to the Present*, London, Hurst, 2013.

Pantucci, Raffaello, "We love death as you love life." Britain's suburban terrorists, December 2015, International Studies Interdisciplinary Political and Cultural Journal 17(1)

Pape, Robert, *Dying to Win: The Strategic Logic of Suicide Terrorism*, New York, Random House, 2005.

Passoni, Laura, and Lorsignol Catherine, *Au cœur de Daesh avec mon fils*, Paris, Éditions La Boîte à Pandore, 2016.

Pelletier, Eric, and Jean-Marie Pontaut, *Affaire Merah: l'enquête*, Paris, Michel Lafon, 2012.

Pérez-Agoz, Alfonso, *The Social Roots of Basque Nationalism*, Reno, University of Nevada Press, 2006.

Perliger, Arie, and Daniel Milton, *From Cradle to Grave: The Lifecycle of Foreign Fighters in Iraq and Syria*, West Point, NY: U.S. Military Academy, Combating Terrorism Center at West Point, 2016.

Peyrat, Sébastien, *Justice et cités. Le droit des cités à l'épreuve de la République*, Paris, Anthropos, 2003.

Philips, Mélanie, *Londonistan: How Britain Is Creating a Terror State Within*, London, Encounter Books, 2006.

Piazza, James A., "Poverty, Minority Economic Discrimination, and Domestic Terrorism," *Journal of Peace Research* 48 (3), 2011.

Piketty, Thomas, *Le Capital au XXI$_e$ siècle*, Paris, Seuil 2013.

Pollack, Detlef, Olaf Müller, Gregely Rosta, and Anna Dieler, *Integration und Religion aus der Sicht von Türkeistämmigen in Deutschland*, Münster, Religion and Politics Cluster of Excellence, WWU Münster, 2016.

Prasad, Udayan, My Son the Fanatic (film), 1997.

Pujol, Philippe, *La Fabrique du monstre: 10 ans d'immersion dans les quartiers nord de Marseille*, Paris, Les Arènes, 2015.

Qehaja, Florian, "Beyond Gornje Maoče and Ošve, Radicalization in the Western Balkans," in Arturo Varvelli (editor), *Jihadi Hotbeds: Understanding Local Radicalization Processes* (Report), Italian Institute for International Political Studies, 2016.

Raflik, Jenny, *Terrorisme et mondialisation*, Paris, Gallimard, 2016.

Rastello, Céline, Jérémie Louis-Sidney, itinéraire d'un délinquant tenté par le jihad (archive), nouvelobs.com, 11 October 2012.

Ranstorp, Magnus, *Mellan salafism och salafistisk jihadism - Påverkan mot och utmaningar för det svenska samhället* (PDF). Swedish Defence University, 2018.

Rekik, Fethi, "Les jeunes Salafistes en Tunisie: le retour du sujet par le portail des liens 'souterrains,'" (à paraître) in *Revue Bouhouth Jamiiya*, Tunisia, Faculté des lettres et sciences humaines de Sfax.

Reinares, Fernando, "Who Are the Terrorists? Analyzing Changes in Sociological Profiles among Members of ETA," *Studies in Conflict and Terrorism* 27 (6): 465–488, 2004.

Reinares, Fernando, "Jihadist Radicalization and the 2004 Madrid Bombing Network," *CTC Sentinel* 2 (11), November 2009.

Reinares, Fernando, *Al-Qaeda's Revenge: The 2004 Madrid Train Bombings*, New York, Columbia University, 2017.

Reinares, Fernando, and Carola Garcia-Calvo, *Terroristas, redes y organizaciones: Facetas de la actual movilización yihadista en España*, Documento de trabajon [working paper] 17/2015, November 16, 2015.

Reinares, Fernando, and Carola Garcia-Calvo, *Estado Islámico en españa*, Madrid, Real Instituto Elcano, 2016.

Renaut, Alain, *La fin de l'autorité*, Flammarion, 2004.

Report on radicalization in Norway, PST, Politiets Sikkerhetstheneste, 14 September 2016, https://pst.no/alle-artikler/utgivelser/report-on-radicalisation-in-norway/

Reynolds, Sean C., and Mohammed M. Hafez, "Social Network Analysis of German Foreign Fighters in Syria and Iraq," *Terrorism and Political Violence*, Routledge, 2017. https://goo.gl/j5vogj

Rigg, Bryan Mark, *Lives of Hitler's Jewish Soldiers: Untold Tales of Men of Jewish Descent Who Fought for the Third Reich*, Lawrence, University Press of Kansas, 2009.

Rougier, Bernard, *Le Jihad au Quotidien*, Paris, Presses Universitaires de France, 2004.

Roy, Olivier, *Le Jihad et la mort*, Paris, Seuil, 2016; *Jihad and Death*, Oxford, Oxford University Press, 2017.

Roy, Olivier, *L'Europe est-elle chrétienne?*, Paris, Seuil, 2019.

Roy, Véronique, *Quentin, qu'ont-ils fit de toi?*, Paris, Robert Laffont, 2017.

Royal College of Psychiatrists London, *Counter-Terrorism and Psychiatry*, Position Statement PS04/16, September 2016.

Sageman, Mark, *Understanding Terror Networks*, Philadelphia: University of Pennsylvania Press, 2004.

Sageman, Mark, *Leaderless Jihad: Terror Networks in the Twenty-First Century* Philadelphia: University of Pennsylvania Press, 2008.

Said, Benham T., *Islamischer Staat, IS-Miliz, al-Qaeda und die deutschen Brigaden*, München, C. H. Beck, 2015.

Saltman, Erin Marie, and Melanie Smith, *"Till Martyrdom Do Us Part": Gender and the ISIS Phenomenon* (report), London, ICSR, Institute for Strategic Dialogue, May 28,2015. https://erinmariesaltman.com/2015/05/28/till-martyrdom-do-us-part-gender-and-the-isis-phenomenon/

Sandler, Todd, "On the Relationship between Democracy and Terrorism," *Terrorism and Political Violence* 7 (4), 1995.

Schmid, Alex P. (editor), *The Routledge Handbook of Terrorism Research*, London, Routledge, 2011.

Schuurman, Bart, Shandon Harris-Hogan, Andrew Zammit, and Pete Lentini, "Operation Pendennis: A Case Study of an Australian Terrorist Plot," *Perspectives on Terrorism* 8 (4), 2014.

Scott, James, *La domination et les arts de la résistance: Fragments d'un discours subalterne*, Paris, Amsterdam Éditions, 2009.

Sedgwick, Marc, "The Concept of Radicalization as a Source of Confusion," *Terrorism and Political Violence* 22 (4), 2010.

Seib, Philip, and Dana Janbeck, *Global Terrorism and New Media: The Post al-Qaeda Generation*, New York, Routledge, 2010.

Sennels, Nicolai, *Psychology: Why Islam Creates Monsters*, September 27, 2013. https://www.jihadwatch.org/2013/09/nicolai-sennels-psychology-why-islam-creates-monsters

Shabestari, Mohamad Modjtahed (in Persian), *Les écrits* (majmou'eh Asâr, 1395 (2016), "Les fondements théoriques de Daesh" (mabna haye teorike daesh); "Si Daesh demande aux juristes islamiques" (faqih), (agar Daesh az faqihan beporsad). www.book-house.blogsky.com

Shaw Clifford, R., and Henry D. McKay, *The Social Disorganization Theory, Juvenile Delinquency and Urban Areas*, Chicago, University of Chicago Press, 1969.

Sieckelinck, Stijn, and Micha de Winter, *Formers and Families. Transitional Journeys In and Out of Extremisms in the United Kingdom, Denmark and the Netherlands*, Technical Report, National Coordinator for Security and Counterterrorism, Ministry of Security and Justice, Government of the Netherlands, November 2015.

Sifaoui, Mohamed, and Abdelghani Merah, *Mon frère, ce terroriste*, Paris, Calmann-Levy, 2012.

Shmitz, Sina, Hanna Grande, and Kai Hirschmann, *Dschihadismus: Prozesse des Radikalisierung in Deutschland*, Berlin, BWV, 2016.

Shtuni, Adrian, "Ethnic Albanian Foreign Fighters in Iraq and Syria," *CTC Sentinel 8 (4)*, April 2015. https://www.ctc.usma.edu/posts/ethnic-albanian-foreign-fighters-in-iraq-and-syria

Simcox, Robin, *We Will Conquer Your Rome: A Study of Islamic State Terror Plots in the West*, London, The Henry Jackson Society, 2015.

Slootman, Marieke, Jean Tillie, Amin Majdy, and Frank Buijs, *Salafi-jihadi's in Amsterdam: Portretten*, Amsterdam, Aksant, 2009.

Snow, David, and Robert Benford, "Ideology, Frame Resonance, and Participant Mobilization," *International Social Movement Research*, 1 (1), 1988.

Sofsky, Wolfgang, *Traité de la violence*, Paris, Gallimard, 1998.
Sonia, with Claire Andrieux, *Témoin*, Paris, Robert Laffont, 2016.
Soufan Group, The, *Foreign Fighters* (report), December 2015.
Spencer, Robert, "UK: Muslim Medical Student was Recruiter for the Islamic State," jihadwatch.org, April 7, 2016.
Stern, Jessica, *Terror in the Name of God: Why Religious Militants Kill*, New York, Harper Collins, 2003.
Storm, Mortem, Paul Cruickshank, and Tim Lister, *My Life Inside al-Qaeda and the CIA*, London, The Penguin Group, 2014.
Stuart, Hannah, *Islamist Terrorism: Analysis of Offences and Attacks in the UK* (1998–2015) London, The Henry Jackson Society. https://smartthinking.org.uk/islamist-terrorism-analysis-offences-attacks-uk-1998-2015/
Stuster, J. Dana, "9 Disturbingly Good Jihadi Raps," *Foreign Policy*, April 29, 2013.
Thomas, Dominique, *Générations Djihadies, Al-Qaïda, État islamique, histoire d'une lutte fratricide*, Paris, Michalon, 2016.
Thomas, Dominique, *Le Londonistan—Le jihad au cœur de l'Europe*, Paris, Michalon, 2005.
Thomson, David, *Les Français djihadies*, Paris, Les Arènes, 2014.
Thomson, David, *Les Revenants*, Paris, Seuil, 2016.
Torrekens, Corinne, and Adam Ike, *Belgo-Marocains, Belgo-Turcs: (Auto)portrait de nos concitoyens*, Brussels, Fondation Roi Baudoin, 2015.
Touraine, Alain, *Pourrons-nous vivre ensemble?* Paris, Fayard 1997.
Touraine, Alain, *La fin des sociétés*, Paris, Seuil, 2013.
Trévidic, Marc, *Terroristes: Les 7 piliers de la déraison*, Paris, Éditions JC Lattès, 2013.
Truc, Gérôme, and Fabien Truong, Cinq femmes fortes: Faire face à "l'insécurité" dans une "cité de la peur," *Mouvements* 92, *Mouvements : des idées et des luttes*, Paris, Publishers La découverte, 2017.
Truong, Fabien, *Jeunesses françaises, Bac+5 made in banlieue*, Paris, La Découverte, 2015.
Truong, Fabien, *Loyautés radicales*, Paris, Editions La Découverte, 2018.
Ulloa, Marie-Pierre, *Le nouveau rêve américain, du Maghreb à la Californie*, Paris, CNRS Editions, 2019.
Ungerleider, Neal. "Welcome to JihadVille," *Fast Company*, April 22, 2011.
Van Ginkel, B., and E. Entenmann (editors), "The Foreign Fighters Phenomenon in the European Union: Profiles, Threats & Policies," *The International Centre for Counter-Terrorism – The Hague* 7 (2), 2016.
Venhaus, John M., *Why Youth Join al-Qaeda*, Washington, DC, United States Institute of Peace, 2010.
Vergani, Matteo, "Neo-Jihadi Prosumers and al-Qaeda Single Narrative: The Case Study of Giuliano Delnevo," *Studies in Conflict & Terrorism* 37 (7), 2014.
Vermeren, Pierre, *La France en terre d'islam: Empire colonial et religions XIX–XX e siècles*, Paris, Belin, 2016.
Vervelli Arturo (editor), *Jihadist Hotbeds Understanding local Radicalization Processes*, ISPI, 2016
Victoroff, Jeff, "The Mind of the Terrorist: A Review and Critique of Psychological Approaches," *Journal of Conflict Resolution* 49, 2005.
Victoroff, Jeff, Janice Achelman, and Miriam Matthews, "Psychological Factors Associated with Support for Suicide Bombing in the Muslim Diaspora," *Political Psychology* 33 (6), 2012.
"Video of London Suicide Bomber", The Times, 06/07/2006.

Vidino, Lorenzo, and Seamus Hughes, *IS in America: From Retweets to Raqqa*, Washington, DC, The George Washington University, December 2015.
Vidino, Lorenzo, Seth Harrison, and Clarissa Spada, "IS and al-Shabaab in Minnesota's Twin Cities: the American Hotbed," in Arturo Varvelli (editor), *Jihadi Hotbeds: Understanding Local Radicalization Processes*, Milan, ISPI, Epoké, 2016.
Vlierden, Guy van, "Profile: Paris Attack Ringleader Abdelhamid Abaaoud," *CTC Sentinel*, December 15, 2015.
Voortman, Aude, "Terrorism in Europe: Explaining the Disparity in the Number of Jihadi Foreign Fighters between European Countries," Institut Barcelona Estudis Internacionals, September 2015.
Warner, Jason, and Hilary Matfess, "Exploding Stereotypes: The Unexpected Operational and Demographic Characteristics of Boko Haram's Suicide Bombers," Combating Terrorism Center at West Point, August 9, 2017.
Weeks, Douglas, "Hotbeds of Extremism: The UK Experience," in Arturo Varvelli (editor), *Jihadi Hotbeds: Understanding Local Radicalization Processes*, Milan, ISPI, Epoké, 2016.
Weenink, Anton W., Adversity, Criminality, and Mental Health Problems in Jihadis in Dutch Police Files, *Perspectives on Terrorism* 13 (5), 2019.
Weirt, Xavier De, and Xavier Rousseaux (editors), *Violences juvéniles urbaines en Europe: Histoire d'une construction sociale*, Louvain, Presses Universitaires de Louvain, 2011.
Weisflog, Christian, "Von der Gartenstadt zum 'terrornest'" (From the Garden City to the "Terror Nest"), *Neue Zürcher Zeitung*, February 18, 2016. http://www.nzz.ch/international/deutschland-und-oesterreich/von-der-gartenstadt-zum-terrornest-1.18696902
White, Robert, "Structural Identity Theory and the Post Recruitment Activism of Irish Republicans: Persistence, Disengagement, Splits and Dissidents in Social Movement Organizations," *Social Problems* 57, 2002.
Wieviorka, Michel, *Sociétés et terrorisme*, Paris, Fayard,1988.
Wieviorka, Michel, *La Violence*, Paris, Pluriel, 2012.
Willis, Paul, *Learning to Labour: How Working Class Kids Get Working Class Jobs*, Saxon House (UK), Columbia University Press (US), 1977.
Winter, Charlie, *Documenting the Virtual Caliphate*, London, Quilliam Foundation, 2015.
Wolfgang, Marvin E., and Franco Ferracuti, *Subculture of Violence: Towards An Integrated Theory in Criminology*, London and New York, Tabistock Publications, Barnes & Noble, 1967.
Woodford, G. E., *Secular Fundamentalism and Islamist Radicalisation in the West: An Investigation into Processes of Homegrown Islamist Radicalization in France*, Thesis, Faculty of Humanities, Universiteit Leiden, August 2018.
Yaman, Neriman, *Mein Sohn, der Salafist: Wie sich mein Kind radikalisierte und Ich es nicht verhindern konnte*, Munich, mvg Verlag, 2016.
Zammit, Andrew, "Explaining Australia-Lebanon Jihadi Connections," Global Terrorism Research Centre, Victoria, Australia, Monash University, 2010.

The Media

https://sn.dk/Danmark/Aarhusiansk-imam-idoemt-boede-for-opfordring-til-joededrab/artikel/476340
AFP, "Le jihad en famille: Ouverture du procès de la fratrie Bekhaled aux assises à Paris," November 12, 2018.

Abdelkader, Merah, Le frère qui se faisait appeler Ben Laden, *Le Figaro*, October 2, 2017.
"Aberdeen jihadi fighter Ruhul Amin 'had no fear of death,'" BBC, September 8, 2015.
Akerhaug, Lars, "Krekar vil ha islamsk stat ledet av Osama bin Laden," *VG Norway*, November 24, 2009.
Amoyel, Patrick, "Il faut travailler sur le terreau de la radicalization," *L'Humanité*, July 18, 2016.
"Another Side of Malmö's infamous Rosengard," *The Local*, March 2, 2012.
Asche, Christoph, "Interview mit deutschem IS-Kämpfer Christian Emde: 'Wir werden weiterhin Menschen köpfen,'" *Huffington Post*, January 14, 2015.
"Attentat de Nice: Le père du tueur parle de ses 'troubles psychiatriques,'" *metronews.fr*, July 15, 2016.
"Attentats: Najim Laachraoui s'était radicalisé à 17 ans," *Le Parisien*, May 7, 2016.
Attewill, Fred, "Race hate preacher Faisal deported," *The Guardian*, May 25, 2007.
Audureau, William, "Plongée dans la folie de '19HH,' principal canal français d'embrigadement djihadie," *Le Monde,* December 8, 2014.
Balboni, Julien, "Najim Laachraoui se racontait sur Twitter et Facebook," DH.be, May 7, 2016.
Barbereau, Stéphane, "Orléans: des djihadis présumés ont fréquenté la mosquée des Carmes," *France Bleu Orléans*, March 18, 2016.
"Belges en Syrie: Jean-Louis Denis et Mickaël Devredt libérés sous conditions," *BELGA, LA LIBRE.BE*, September 12, 2014.
Bendavid, Rose-Laure, and Delphine Byrka, "Les enfants perdus de la famille Bons," *Paris Match*, January 20, 2014.
Benhold, Katrin, and Kimiko de Freytas-Tamura, "Why Do All the Jihadis Come to Birmingham?," *New York Times*, March 26, 2017.
Bracchi, Paul, "Inside the jihadi capital of Britain," *Daily Mail*, March 19, 2017.
Bronner, Luc, "Amédy Coulibaly: 'La prison, c'est la putain de meilleure école de la criminalité,'" *Le Monde*, January 13, 2015.
"Brothas-banden fra Nørrebro smider hættetrøjen og får rygmærker," Retrieved from https://www.tv2lorry.dk, February 29, 2016
Bui, Doan, "Filière jihadie Cannes-Torcy: le calvaire du père de Jérémy Bailly," L'Obs, June 23, 2017.
Buruma, Ian, "Final Cut," *New Yorker*, January 3, 2005.
Callimachi, Rukmini, "The IS Files," *New York Times*, April 5, 2018.
Casciani, *Dominic*, "Who Is Siddhartha Dhar?," BBC, January 4, 2016.
Casciani, Dominic, "The radicalization of Safaa Boular: A teenager's journey to terror," BBC, June 4, 2018.
Cazi, Emeline, "Merah, l'enfance d'un terroriste," *Le Monde*, June 12, 2012.
Chrisafis, Angelique, "Copenhagen Shooting Suspect Omar el-Hussein—A Past Full of Contradictions," *The Guardian*, February 16, 2015.
Christys, Patrick, and Zoie O'Brien, "Inside Britain's Molenbeek: Is Birmingham's Sparkbrook the Beating Heart of British Jihad?," *Express*, April 13, 2017.
Cordier, Solène, "Le quotidien difficile des familles monoparentales," *Le Monde*, July 3, 2019.
Cornevin, Christophe, "Adel Kermiche, un ado perturbé devenu terroriste," *Le Figaro*, July 27, 2016.
Cour des comptes, "Rapport public annuel, 2019," February 6, 2019, www.ccomptes.fr

"De Vilvorde à la Syrie, comment de jeunes Belges rejoignent le jihad," *AFP*, October 22, 2014.

"Den Haag in Cijfers" (The Hague in Figures), 2015, https://denhaag.incijfers.nl/homedh.aspx

"Détenus radicalisés: Belloubet (minister of Justice) admet 'des failles' dans leur prise en charge", RTL and AFP, March 6, 2019.

Digiacomi, Claire, "Rachid Kassim, l'un des plus influents jihadies français de Daesh, témoigne pour la première fois," *Huffington Post*, November 19, 2016.

Dobson, Roger, "British Muslims Face Worst Job Discrimination of Any Minority Group, According to Research," *The Independent*, November 30, 2014.

Dubois, Christophe, and François Labrouillère, "Itinéraire d'un petit Français saisi par le djihad," *Paris Match*, March 13, 2008.

Dugan, Emily, "Britain's Hidden Racism: Workplace Inequality Has Grown in the Last Decade," *The Independent Online*, December 3, 2014.

Duplessy, Jacques, "Emilie König, portrait d'une djihadie française arrêtée en Syrie," *Paris Match*, January 3, 2018.

Eaton, Joshua, "U.S. Military Now Says IS Leader Was Held in Notorious Abu Ghraib Prison," *The Intercept*, August 25, 2016.

En direct—Attentat à Magnanville: Abballa a diffusé la vidéo des meurtres sur Facebook, la police recherche des complices, *France Soir*, June 14, 2016.

Erlanger, Steven, "Man Held in France in Attack on Soldier," *New York Times*, July 19, 2013.

European Jihad Watch, Issue 3, Center for the Analysis of Terrorism, March 2017 http://cat-int.org/wp-content/uploads/2017/03/European-jihad-watch-mars-2017_eng.pdf

Féo, Agnès de, Vidéo in Marie Lemonnier, "Exclusif: Les confessions d'Emilie König, la jihadiste bretonne de Daesh" (Vidéo), *L'Obs*, May 12, 2016.

Flade, Florian, and Kristian Frigelj, "Wie der Staat Salafisten aus Solingen verjagt," *Die Welt*, June 14, 2012.

Fontaine, Guillaume, "Combien l'État islamique compte-t-il réellement des combattants?" *Slate*, May 12, 2015.

Freeman, Colin, "Inside Kacanik, Kosovo's Jihadi Capital," *The Telegraph*, August 23, 2015.

Froelig, Caroline, "Lunel: Alerte aux cambriolages sur le quartier des Abrivados," *Midi Libre*, April 1, 2014.

Filiu, Jean-Pierre, "Le nouveau chef du groupe Etat islamique (EI) n'est pas arabe, mais turc," *Le Monde*, June 28, 2020.

France, Olivier de, Damien Saverot, Pierre Colomina "From Criminals to Terrorists and Back?" Quarterly Report: France, GLOBSEC, January 7, 2019.

Gabizon, Cécilia, "Pourquoi la France compte 27% de mariages mixtes," *Le Figaro*, June 21, 2010.

Garcia, Victor, and Jérémie Pham-Lê, "Tu vas dans une église, tu fais un carnage: l'enregistrement glaçant de Kermiche," *L'Express*, July 28, 2016.

"German female IS recruit 'let slave child die of thirst' in Iraq," BBC, December 28, 2018.

Gezer, Özlem, "Islamist Mind Games: How Young German Men Are Lured into Jihad," Spiegel Online, August 23, 2012.

Girard, René, "Ce qui se joue aujourd'hui est une rivalité mimétique à l'échelle planétaire," *Le Monde*, November 5, 2001.

Greene, Richard Allen, "Britain's Big Race Divide," *CNN*, June 22, 2020.

Guéguen, Elodie, "Les femmes dans le jihad," *France Inter*, January 8, 2016.

Guéguen, Elodie, "Trappes, bastion du jihadisme français," Radio France, April 29, 2016.

Hackett, Conrad, "5 facts about the Muslim population in Europe," Pew Research Center, November 29, 2017.

Hakim, Yalda, "How Sweden Became an Exporter of Jihad," BBC, October 7, 2016.

Hall, Allan, and Nick Fagge, "German Schoolgirl, 16, Found in Mosul Was Married to a Chechen IS Fighter and Was Captured with a Gun in Her Hand before Admitting to Killing Iraqi Soldiers," *Mail Online*, July 20, 2017. http://www.latribune.fr/opinions/tribunes/musulmans-la-realite-des-discriminations-au-travail-467384.html.

Higgins, Andrew, "A Norway Town and Its Pipeline to Jihad in Syria," *New York Times*, April 4, 2015.

Higgins, Andrew, and Kimilo de Freytas-Tamura, "A Brussels Mentor Who Taught 'Gangster Islam' to the Young and Angry," *New York Times*, April 11, 2016.

Hivert, Anne-Françoise, "A Malmö, le jihad à la suédoise," *Libération*, April 21, 2016.

Holligan, Anna, "Dutch Grapple with Jihadi Threat," BBC, August 22, 2014.

Hughes, Trevor, "Teenage Jihad Suspect Sentenced to 4 Years," *USA TODAY*, January 23, 2015.

Humphries, Will, "Sally Jones Profile: How Online Love Affair Turned Single Mother into a Fanatic," *The Times*, October 13, 2017.

Jaffer, Nabeelah, "The Secret World of Isis Brides: 'U dnt hav 2 pay 4 ANYTHING if u r wife of a martyr,'" *The Guardian*, June 24, 2015.

Jaffer, Nabeelah, IS Bride Reveals an Unprecedented Look Inside the Terrorist Organization, *The Guardian*, June 25, 2015.

"Jihad: Deux sœurs roubaisiennes envoyaient des allocations familiales à leur frère djihadie," *La Voix du Nord* and AFP, January 17, 2019.

Jones, Sam, "More Than Half World's Countries Now Producing Jihadis," *Financial Times*, May 27, 2015

Judgment in Appeal of Crown v. El-Faisal, Supreme Court of Judicature, Court of Appeal, March 4, 2004.

Archived from the original (PDF) on 19 May 2012. Retrieved 25 September 2015.

Kefi, Ramses, "Le reportage surréaliste de M6 sur un couple paumé parti faire le djihad en Syrie," *L'Obs*, September 29, 2014.

"Khalid, Zerkani, 'Papa Noël' du jihad en Syrie," site de Libre.be, May 8, 2015.

Khosrokhavar, Farhad, "Le jihadisme européen reflet de la crise du politique," *Orient XXI*, July 20, 2015.

Khosrokhavar, Farhad, "Attentats de Strasbourg: Chérif Chekatt, le faux 'chevalier de la foi,'" *The Conversation*, December 21, 2018.

Khosrokhavar, Farhad, "Chérif Chekatt ou le faux djihadie," *Le Monde*, December 14, 2018.

"Lageanalyse: Denis Cuspert eine jihadiische Karriere," Berliner Landesamt für Verfassungsschutz, September 2014.

Lamant, Ludovic, "Pourquoi Bruxelles n'a jamais résorbé son «croissant pauvre," *Mediapart*, March 24, 2016.

Lambert, Elise, "A Lunel, la mosquée cristallise de nouvelles tensions entre les fidèles," francetvinfo.fr, November 3, 2015.

Lanigan, Michael, "The Jihadi Khalid Kelly Was Not a Clown, but a Warning for Ireland," *The Guardian*, November 11, 2016.

Larossi, Abballa, "Itinéraire d'un djihadie ordinaire," https://www.lindependant.fr/2016/06/14/larossi-abballa-itineraire-d-un-djihadie-ordinaire,2214155.php, June 14, 2016

Lau, David, and Mads Mathiesen, "Straight Outta Mjølnerparken?" http://www.humanityinaction.org/knowledgebase/258-straight-outta-mjolnerparken

Laurent, Samuel, "Français, fichés, anciens prisonniers: Portrait des jihadies ayant frappé en France," *Le Monde*, July 29, 2016.

Lazard, Violette, Michel Caroline, Monnier Vincent, Rastello Céline, and Toscer Olivier, "Amedy Coulibaly et Hayat Boumedienne: Du braquage au carnage," *L'Obs*, January 13, 2015.

Lebourg, Eloïse, "L'enfance misérable des frères Kouachi," *Reporterre*, January 15, 2015.

Le Devin, Willy, "De Lunel à la Syrie, le jihad entre amis," *Libération*, July 2, 2015.

Leech, Robb, "My Brother the Islamist," BBC3, April 4, 2011.

Leech Robb, "My Brother the Terrorist," BBC3, April 28, 2014.

"Le jihadi français Omar Omsen est mort," *Le Monde*, August 8, 2015.

Leroux, Luc, "Villes face au jihad: Marseille sourde aux sirènes," *Le Monde*, January 29, 2016.

"Les discothèques perdent du terrain en France," RTL, May 27, 2014

"Leytonstone Tube Attacker Muhiddin Mire Jailed for Life," BBC, August 1, 2016.

"London Bomber: Text in Full," BBC, September 1, 2005

Lowe, Josh, "Are There No-Go Zones in Sweden?," *Newsweek*, June 21, 2017.

McDonald, Kevin, "Vie et mort de trois cyber-jihadies," *The Conversation*, September 25, 2015.

"Mehdi Nemmouche: Un enfant des quartiers de Roubaix et Tourcoing 'parti en vrille,'" Agence France-Presse, *La Voix du Nord*, June 2, 2014.

"Mehdi Nemmouche: Un enfant des quartiers de Roubaix et Tourcoing 'parti en vrille,'" *La Voix du Nord*, June 2, 2014.

Mekhennet, Souad, "German Officials Alarmed by Ex-Rapper's New Message: Jihad," *New York Times*, September 1, 2011.

"Mes 150 films Banlieue, jeunesse, délinquance, préférés," www.senscritique.com/liste/Mes_150_films_Banlieue_jeunesse_delinquance_preferes/497148

Morrison, Dan, "The Sudanese Medical School That's a Pipeline to the Islamic State," https://medium.com/@dmsouthasia/the-sudanese-medical-school-that-s-a-pipeline-to-the-islamic-state-6e7009e816d#.pxkl4axiw, July 22, 2015.

"Mother Feared to Have Taken Children to Syria Linked with High Ranking IS Man," *Guardian*, September 1, 2015.

"Mother of J'can Mullah Says He Is Welcome Home," *Jamaica Observer*, March 8, 2003.

"Moussa Coulibaly, itinéraire d'un 'timid' repéré pour 'prosélytisme,'" AFP, *Le Point.fr*, February 4, 2015.

"Muslim Group Behind 'Mega-Mosque' Seeks to Convert All Britain," *Times of London*, September 10, 2007, http://www.timesonline.co.uk/tol/comment/faith/article2419524.ece.

Musseau, François, "Ceuta, l'extrémisme enclavé," *Libération*, April 26, 2015.

"Nice, un terreau de radicalisation jihadie," *Les Echos*, July 15, 2016.

Office fédéral de police criminelle, Office fédéral de protection constitutionnelle et centre d'information et de compétences contre l'extrémisme, *Analyse du contexte et des processus de radicalisation des gens qui sont partis de l'Allemagne vers la Syrie ou l'Irak à partir d'une motivation islamique*, 2018.

"Paris Attacks: Was Salim Benghalem the Real Ringleader?" BBC, January 26, 2016.

Peachey, Paul, Jonathan Brown, and Sengupta Kim, "Lee Rigby Murder: How Killers Michael Adebolajo and Michael Adebowale Became Ultra-Violent Radicals," *The Independent*, December 19, 2013.

Pew Center, *The American Middle Class Is Losing Ground*, December 2015.

Peyrand Michel, "Rachid Kassim: Enquête sur le donneur d'ordre de Daech," *Paris Match*, September 23, 2016.

Phan-Lë, Jérémie, and Victor Garcia, "Julien B, converti 'charismatique' et gourou du djihadie Rachid Kassim," *L'Express*, September 26, 2016.

Pidd, Helen, and Josh Halliday, "One City, Two Cultures: Bradford's Communities Lead Parallel Lives," *The Guardian*, June 19, 2015.

Pilorget-Rezzouk, Chloé, "Les six frères d'armes du jihad," *Libération*, November 11, 2018.

Pleasance, Chris, "British Jihadi Medical Student, 21, is Pictured Holding Severed Head While Wearing Her White Doctor's Jacket," *Mail Online*, September 14, 2014.

Plummer, William, "En 2009, Coulibaly dénonçait les conditions de détention à Fleury-Mérogis sur France 2," *Le Figaro*, January 13, 2015.

Rapport sur l'évaluation et l'orientation des politiques publiques mises en œuvre à Grigny (Essonne), July 2016.

Rasheed, Ahmed, "IS Suffers Near Collapse in Oil Revenue as It Loses Territory in Iraq," *Reuters*, July 28, 2016.

Rastello, Celine, and Jérémie Louis-Sidney, "Itinéraire d'un délinquant tenté par le jihad," *L'Obs*, October 11, 2012.

Reid, Sue, "The Breeding Ground for Jihadis," *Daily Mail*, June 15, 2015.

Reitman, Janet, "The Children of IS," *Rolling Stone*, March 25, 2015.

Report on Radicalization in Norway, PST, Politiets Sikkerhetsthenest, 2016.

Rey-Lefebvre, Isabelle, Piel Simon, Bastuck Nicolas, and Aubenas Florence, "Hasna Boulahcen, entre vodka et niqab," *Le Monde*, November 22, 2015.

Richburg, Keith B., "From Quiet Teen to Terrorist Suspect," *Washington Post*, December 5, 2004.

Ritzou, Af, "Aarhusiansk imam idømt bøde for opfordring til jødedrab" (Aarhusian Imam Sentenced Fine for Encouraging Jew Killings), *Fyens Stiftstidende*, March 20, 2015.

Robinson, Martin, "Kit Kat, Snickers and the best cappuccinos around!," *Daily Mail*, January 5, 2016.

Rogers, Thomas, "Heil Hipster: The Young Neo-Nazis Trying to Put a Stylish Face on Hate," *Rolling Stone*, June 23, 2014.

Rose, Steve, The Isis Propaganda War: A Hi-Tech Media Jihad, *The Guardian*, October 7, 2014.

Rotella, Sebastian, "Syria's Jihadi Migration Emerges as Top Terror Threat in Europe, Beyond," *PROPUBLICA*, July 24, 2013.

Rougier, Bernard, "Le jihadisme est devenu un instrument de revanche sociale," *Le Monde*, February 15, 2016.

Royen, Marie-Cecile, "Jean-Louis Denis, dit 'Le Soumis,' croit à la fin des temps en Irak-Syrie," *Le Vif*, January 15, 2015.www.levif.be

Saint-Jullian, Elise, "Femmes de jihadies ou jihadies femmes? Un rôle ambigu," TV5monde, March 5, 2016.

"Sa mère raconte sa descente aux enfers. Bilal Hadfi, une 'cocotte-minute prête à exploser,'" *Paris Match*, November 18, 2015.

Samson, Thomas, "Radicalisation à l'école: 857 cas signalés," AFP, December 5, 2015.

"Saint-Étienne-du-Rouvray: La messagerie d'Adel Kermiche réactivée," *Le Point*, August 3, 2016.

Särskilt utsatta omraden I Göteborg (report), Gothenburg, Municipality of Gothenburg, January 2017.

Sandelson, Michael, "Norway Radical Islamists in Syria, UK Imam Helps," *The Foreigner*, October 19, 2012.
Saner, Emine, "How the 'Pompey Lads' fell into the hands of Isis," *The Guardian*, July 27, 2015.
Schmuck, Pascal, "Ya-t-il une filièr jihadie à Winterthour?" *Le Matin*, March 27, 2015.
Seckel, Henri, "Au procès d'Abdelkader Merah, l'itinéraire d'un délinquant devenu un islamiste radicalisé," *Le Monde*, March 30, 2019.
Seelow, Soren, "A 14 ans, des jeunes Françaises qui rêvent de "tuer pour Allah," *Le Monde*, March 4, 2016.
Seelow, Soren, "Alexandre Dhaussy n'est pas un fou de Dieu, il est fou," *Le Monde*, September 25, 2015.
Seelow, Soren, "Enfants kamikazes: Le projet secret des frères Clain," *Le Monde*, June 26, 2018.
Seelow, Soren, "Je n'étais pas musulman, j'étais Daech," *Le Monde*, April 9, 2018.
Seelow, Soren, "Attaque de Nice: Le suspect connu depuis plus de dix ans par la police," *Le Monde*, April 2, 2015.
Sengupta, Somini, and Hwaida Saadjuly, "New Dangers Stalk Syrian Children Still Haunted by Horrors Under IS," *New York Times*, July 31, 2017.
"Sharia4Belgium trial: Belgian court jails members," BBC, February 11, 2015
Shaw, James, "Amsterdam: A City Divided?" *Expat Info*, April 16, 2012.
Sheikh, Jacob, "Denmark's Children of Holy War," *Danish Literary Magazine*, April 12, 2016.
Sherlock, Ruth, "Inside the leadership of Islamic State: How the New "Caliphate" is Run," *telegraph.co.uk*, July 9, 2014.
Siddhartha, Dhar, "'New Jihadi John' Rails against Western Media and Shia Islam in YouTube Rant," *International Business Times*, May 1, 2015.
Siddique, Haroon, "Minority Ethnic Britons Face 'Shocking' Job Discrimination," *The Guardian*, January 17, 2019.
"Sister of NHS doctor who joined Isis says parents will 'never forgive him,'" *The Guardian*, May 24, 2016.
Smit, Peter Hotse, "Van onthoofdingen verdachte jihadi Marouane B. rapt voor zijn moeder: 'Ik kom ooit terug,'" *de Volkskrant*, July 12, 2017.
Soni, Darshna, "'Jihadi Jack' has mental health condition, say parents," Channel 4 News, February 4, 2016.
Statistics of the Research Center in Demography and Societies of the Leuven Catholic University, 2014. https://uclouvain.be/fr/instituts-recherche/iacchos/demo
Stewart, Will, and Simon Tomlinson, "Pregnant teen suicide bomber . . .," *Malonline*, January 17, 2015.
"Sweden: One in Ten Muslim School Students in Gothenburg 'Sympathize' with Jihadis; Gothenburg 'One of Europe's Most Segregated Cities,'" *The Local*, October 28, 2016.
"Syrie: Deso Dogg, ancient rappeur allemande devenu djihadie, tué par une frappe aérienne?," *Le Parisien* and AFP, January 19, 2018.
The Foreign Fighters Phenomenon in the EU-Profiles, Threats & Policies, 1 april 2016, International Centre for Counter-Terrorism – The Hague
"The Jihadi Cure for Depression? More Jihad!," *Midnight Watcher's Blogspot*, June 24, 2014.
Tomlinson, Simon, "Only Allah Can Judge Me: Muslim Convert Richard Dart Refuses to Stand in Dock," *Daily Mail*, April 26, 2013.

Toscer, Olivier, "Djihadies français: Comment Jérémy Bailly est devenu Abderrahmane," *L'Obs*, December 7, 2012.
Townsend, Mark, "The Pompey Jihadis: How Did One English City Produce Six Young Fighters for Isis?," *The Guardian*, October 26, 2014.
Townsend, Mark, "From Brighton to the Battlefield: How Four Young Britons Were Drawn to Jihad," *The Guardian*, March 31, 2016.
Tozer, James, "The Jihad Sisters: Bubbly and Exceptionally Bright, These Twins with 28 GCSEs Were Set to Train as Doctors. Now They're in Syria 'Training to Be Killers'", *Daily Mail UK*, 2014.
Truc, Olivier, "Le deuxième terroriste du métro de Bruxelles serait un Suédois de 23 ans, Osama K.," *Le Monde*, April 11, 2016.
"Two London Girls in Syria Have Married, Families Say," BBC, July 4, 2015.
Understanding Muslim Ethnic Communities, Communities and Local Government, London: Department for Communities and Local Government www.communities.gov.uk, April 2009.
"Une figure de la filière djihadste d'Artigat interpellée en Syrie," *Le Point*, January 5, 2018.
United Nations Security Council, Letter dated May 19, 2015 . . . concerning Al-Qaeda and associated individuals and entities.
University of Manchester, Centre on Dynamics of Ethnicity, *Britain's Ethnic Minorities Are Facing Barriers to Social Mobility and Job Opportunities*, 2014.
Urra, Susana, "Spain's Population Declines for Fifth Year in a Row," *El País*, April 27, 2017.
Vermeren, Pierre, "Au cœur des réseaux jihadies européens, le passé douloureux du Rif marocain," *Le Monde*, 23/03/2016.
Vidalle, Anne, "Quentin Roy, vie et mort d'un converti au jihad," *L'Express*, April 1, 2016.
"Video of London Suicide Bomber Released," *The Times*, July 6, 2006.
Vigoureux, Elsa, "Attentats de Bruxelles: Plongée dans l'enfance des El Bakraoui, les frères kamikazes," *L'Obs*, March 27, 2016.
Vincent, Elise, "En Syrie, la mort du djihadie Fabien Clain confirmée par la coalition internationale," *Le Monde*, March 1, 2019.
Vincent, Elise, "Fabien Clain, du prosélytisme au djihad," *Le Monde*, March 2, 2019.
Vincent, Elise, "Magnanville: Larossi Abballa, histoire d'une haine 'anti-police,'" *Le Monde*, July 30, 2016.
Vincent, Elise, "Le procès de la cellule 'Cannes-Torcy,' matrice du djihadisme hexagonal," *Le Monde*, April 20, 2017.
Vincent, Elise, and Allan Kaval, "Mourad? On l'avait tous noté mort . . .": A Roubaix, dans les pas d'une famille dont 23 membres sont partis faire le djihad," *Le Monde*, January 20, 2020.
Vlierden, Guy van, "IS Fighters from the Belgian Town of Maaseik: A Rare Connection between Actual Networks and Old School Terrorists," *emmejihad* (blog), January 4, 2016
What Does the 2011 Census Tell Us about Inter-ethnic Relationships?, Office for National Statistics, July 3, 2014.
"Who Are Spain's Jihadis?" *The Local*, November 16, 2015.
Wright, Stephen, and Inderdeep Bains, "The British Muslims Waging 'Five-Star Jihad' for Al-Qaeda: At Least 17 Extremists Post Messages about Experiences in War-Torn Syria," *Daily Mail*, November 21, 2013.

Index

For the benefit of digital users, indexed terms that span two pages (e.g., 52–53) may, on occasion, appear on only one of those pages.

Printed in the USA/Agawam, MA
May 3, 2024

865425.018